READING THE EPISTLE OF JAMES

RESOURCES FOR BIBLICAL STUDY

Editor
Davina C. Lopez, New Testament

Number 94

SBL PRESS

READING THE EPISTLE OF JAMES

A Resource for Students

Edited by

Eric F. Mason and Darian R. Lockett

SBL PRESS

Atlanta

Copyright © 2019 by SBL Press

Library of Congress Cataloging-in-Publication Data

Names: Mason, Eric Farrel, editor. | Lockett, Darian R., editor.
Title: Reading the Epistle of James / edited by Eric F. Mason and Darian R. Lockett.
Description: Atlanta, Georgia : SBL Press, 2019. | Includes bibliographical references and index.
Identifiers: LCCN 2019032627 (print) | LCCN 2019032628 (ebook) | ISBN 9781628372502 (paperback) | ISBN 9780884143932 (hardcover) | ISBN 9780884143949 (ebook)
Subjects: Bible. James—Criticism, interpretation, etc.
Classification: LCC BS2785.52 .R435 2019 (print) | LCC BS2785.52 (ebook) | DDC 227/.9106—dc23
LC record available at https://lccn.loc.gov/2019032627
LC ebook record available at https://lccn.loc.gov/2019032628

Contents

Acknowledgments

The editors wish to thank a number of people who have played vital roles in this project. Tom Thatcher served as the New Testament editor for the Resources for Biblical Study series when this project was approved, and it has reached its fulfillment under the series leadership of Davina C. Lopez. We thank both Tom and Davina for their confidence in and support of this volume. Likewise, we are indebted to Bob Buller and Nicole Tilford at SBL Press for their advice and insights at various points along the way. In the late stages of the process we received valuable assistance from several people at Judson University: Thomas Atamian, Kim Johnson, and undergraduate students Gene Crume III and Carista Ritchie. Special thanks go to Wes Lynd, an MA student at Talbot School of Theology, for his assistance in compiling the indices. Finally, we are most indebted to the friends and colleagues who contributed the various chapters to this collection, thus making it possible, and to Kevin Johnson for his lucid translation from Spanish of the chapter by Elsa Tamez.

The publisher and editors gratefully acknowledge permission to reprint portions of the following material: Richard Bauckham, "The Wisdom of James and the Wisdom of Jesus," in *The Catholic Epistles and the Tradition*, ed. Jacques Schlosser, BETL 176 (Leuven: Leuven University Press; Leuven: Peeters, 2004), 75–92; and Richard Bauckham, "James and Jesus," in *The Brother of Jesus: James the Just and His Mission*, ed. Bruce Chilton and Jacob Neusner (Louisville: Westminster John Knox, 2001), 100–137.

Abbreviations

Primary Sources

1 Apol.	Justin Martyr, *First Apology*
1 Clem.	1 Clement
1 En.	1 Enoch
1Q26	Instruction
1Q27	Book of Mysteries
1QH	Thanksgiving Hymns
1QM	War Scroll
1QS	Rule of the Community
2 Apol.	Justin Martyr, *Second Apology*
2 En.	2 Enoch
4Q149–155	Mezuzah Scrolls
4Q184	Wiles of the Wicked Woman
4Q185	Sapiential Work
4Q299	Mysteries
4Q370	AdmonFlood
4Q414	Ritual Purity A
4Q415–418	Instruction
4Q422	Paraphrase of Genesis and Exodus
4Q423	Instruction
4Q424	Instruction-like Work
4Q426	Sapiential-Hymnic Work A
4Q436	Barkhi Nafshi
4Q473	The Two Ways
4Q474	Text Concerning Rachel and Joseph
4Q476	Liturgical Work B
4Q498	papSap/Hymn
4Q510	Songs of the Maskil
4Q524	Temple Scroll

4Q525	Beatitudes
4Q560	Exorcism
4QShirShab	Songs of the Sabbath Sacrifice (4Q400–407)
11Q11	Apocryphal Psalms
11Q19	Temple Scroll
11Q5	Psalm Scroll
Abr.	Philo, *On the Life of Abraham*
A.J.	Josephus, *Jewish Antiquities*
Apoc. Ab.	Apocalypse of Abraham
Apos. Con.	Apostolic Constitutions and Canons
ʾAvot R. Nat.	Avot of Rabbi Nathan
b.	Babylonian Talmud
B. Qam.	Bava Qamma
CD	Damascus Document (versions A and B from the Cairo Genizah)
Cher.	Philo, *On the Cherubim*
Comm. Jo.	Origen, *Commentarii in evangelium Joannis*
Comm. Ps.	Eusebius, *Commentary on the Psalms*
Conf.	Philo, *On the Confusion of Tongues*
Deus	Philo, *That God Is Unchangeable*
Dysk.	Menander, *Dyskolos*
Ebr.	Philo, *On Drunkenness*
Ep. fest.	Athanasius, *Festal Letters*
Epist.	Jerome, *Epistulae*
Fam.	Cicero, *Epistulae ad familiars*
Fr. Jo.	Origen, *Fragementa in evangelium Joannis*
Garr.	Plutarch, *De garrulitate*
Haer.	Augustine, *Heresies*; Irenaeus, *Against Heresies*
Her.	Philo, *Who Is the Heir?*
Herm.	Shepherd of Hermas
Hist. eccl.	Eusebius, *Ecclesiastical History*
Hom. Exod.	Origen, *Homiliae in Exodum*
Hom. Lev.	Origen, *Homiliae in Leviticum*
Inst.	Quintilian, *Institutio oratoria*
Invid.	Dio Crysostom, *Envy*
Jub.	Jubilees
Leg.	Cicero, *De Legibus*; Philo, *Allegorical Interpretation*; Plato, *Laws*
m.	Mishnah

Magn.	Ignatius, *To the Magnesians*
Mand.	Shepherd of Hermas, Mandate(s)
Migr.	Philo, *On the Migration of Abraham*
Mos.	Philo, *On the Life of Moses*
Mut.	Philo, *On the Change of Names*
Nat.	Seneca, *Naturales quaestiones*
Off.	Cicero, *De officiis*
Opif.	Philo, *On the Creation of the World*
Pan.	Epiphanius, *Refutation of All Heresies*
Phil.	Polycarp, *To the Philippians*
Phld.	Ignatius, *To the Philadelphians*
Plant.	Philo, *On Planting*
Pol.	Aristotle, *Politics*
Post.	Philo, *On the Posterity of Cain*
Prog.	Theon, *Progymnasmata*
Ps.-Phoc.	Pseudo-Phocylides
QG	Philo, *Questions and Answers on Genesis*
Resp.	Plato, *Republic*
Rhet.	Aristotle, *Rhetorica*
Rhet. Alex.	Rhetorica ad Alexandrum
Rhet. Her.	Rhetorica ad Herennium
Rust.	Columella, *De re rustica*
Sacr.	Philo, *On the Sacrifices of Cain and Abel*
Sanh.	Sanhedrin
Sat.	Horace, *Satires*; Juvenal, *Satirae*
Shev.	Shevi'it
Sel. Ps.	Origen, *Selecta in Psalmos*
Shabb.	Shabbat
Sim.	Shepherd of Hermas, Similitude(s)
Sobr.	Philo, *On Sobriety*
Spec.	Philo, *On the Special Laws*
t.	Tosefta
T. Abr.	Testament of Abraham
T. Dan	Testament of Dan
T. Iss.	Testament of Issachar
T. Job	Testament of Job
T. Naph.	Testament of Naphtali
T. Zeb.	Testament of Zebulun
Tg. Jer.	Targum Jeremiah

Tg. Neof.	Targum Neofiti
Vir. ill.	Jerome, *Lives of Illustrious Men*
Virt.	Philo, *On the Virtues*
Vis.	Shepherd of Hermas, Vision(s)
Vita	Josephus, *The Life*

Secondary Sources

AB	Anchor Bible
ABD	Freedman, David Noel, ed. *Anchor Bible Dictionary*. 6 vols. New York: Doubleday, 1992.
ABRL	Anchor Bible Reference Library
AnBib	Analecta Biblica
ANF	Roberts, Alexander, and James Donaldson, eds. *The Ante-Nicene Fathers*. 1885–1887. 10 vols. Repr. Peabody, MA: Hendrickson, 1994.
ANRW	Temporini, Hildegard, and Wolfgang Haase, eds. *Aufstieg und Niedergang der römanischen Welt: Geschichte und Kultur Rom sim Spiegel der neueren Forschung*. Part 2, *Principat*. Berlin: de Gruyter, 1972–.
ANTF	Arbeiten zur neutestamentlichen Textforschung
AUSS	*Andrews University Seminary Studies*
BBR	*Bulletin for Biblical Research*
BBRSup	Bulletin for Biblical Research Supplement
BDAG	Danker, Frederick W., Walter Bauer, William F. Arndt, and F. Wilbur Gingrich. *Greek-English Lexicon of the New Testament and Other Early Christian Literature*. 3rd ed. Chicago: University of Chicago Press, 2000.
BECNT	Baker Exegetical Commentary on the New Testament
BETL	Bibliotheca Ephemeridum Theologicarum Lovaniensium
BHGNT	Baylor Handbooks to the Greek New Testament
Bib	*Biblica*
BibInt	Biblical Interpretation Series
BJRL	*Bulletin of the John Rylands University Library of Manchester*
BNTC	Black's New Testament Commentaries
BRLJ	Brill Reference Library of Judaism
BRS	Biblical Resource Series
BTB	*Biblical Theology Bulletin*

BWANT	Beiträge zur Wissenschaft vom Neuen Testament
BZ	*Biblische Zeitschrift*
BZNW	Beihefte zur Zeitschrift für die neutestamentliche Wissenschaft
CBQ	*Catholic Biblical Quarterly*
CCS	Cambridge Classical Studies
CNTC	Torrance, David W., and Thomas F. Torrance, ed. *Calvin's New Testament Commentaries*. 12 vols. Grand Rapids: Eerdmans, 1959–1972.
ConBNT	Coniectanea Biblica: New Testament Series
CurBR	*Currents in Biblical Research*
CurBS	*Currents in Research: Biblical Studies*
CW	*Classical World*
CWE	*Collected Works of Erasmus*. Toronto: University of Toronto Press, 1974–.
DJD	Discoveries in the Judaean Desert
ECM	Editio Critica Maior
EDEJ	Collins, John J., and Daniel C. Harlow, eds. *Eerdmans Dictionary of Early Judaism*. Grand Rapids: Eerdmans, 2010.
ESEC	Emory Studies in Early Christianity
EvQ	*Evangelical Quarterly*
ExpTim	*Expository Times*
FC	Fathers of the Church
FF	Foundations and Facets
GBS	Guides to Biblical Scholarship
HBT	*Horizons in Biblical Theology*
HNT	Handbuch zum Neuen Testament
HThKNT	Herders Theologischer Kommentar zum Neuen Nestament
HTR	*Harvard Theological Review*
HvTSt	*Hervormde teologiese studies*
ICC	International Critical Commentary
JAC	*Jahrbuch für Antike und Christentum*
JAJ	*Journal of Ancient Judaism*
JBL	*Journal of Biblical Literature*
JETS	*Journal of the Evangelical Theological Society*
JSJ	*Journal of the Study of Judaism in the Persian, Hellenistic, and Roman Periods*

JSJSup	Supplements to the Journal for the Study of Judaism
JSNT	*Journal for the Study of the New Testament*
JSNTSup	Journal for the Study of the New Testament Supplement Series
JSPSup	Journal for the Study of the Pseudepigrapha Supplement Series
LB	Desiderius Erasmus. *Opera Omnia*. Edited by Jean Le Clerc. 10 vols. Leiden: van der Aa, 1703–1706.
LCL	Loeb Classical Library
LEC	Library of Early Christianity
LHBOTS	Library of Hebrew Bible/Old Testament Studies
LNTS	Library of New Testament Studies
LW	*Luther's Works*. American Edition. Original ed. 55 vols. New series 14 vols. St. Louis: Concordia; Philadelphia: Fortress, 1955–1986, 2010–.
NA[27]	Aland, Barbara, Kurt Aland, Johannes Karavidopoulos, Carlo M. Martini, and Bruce M. Metzger, eds. *Novum Testamentum Graece*. 27th ed. Stuttgart: Deutsche Bibelgesellschaft, 1993.
NA[28]	Aland, Barbara, Kurt Aland, Johannes Karavidopoulos, Carlo M. Martini, and Bruce M. Metzger, eds. *Novum Testamentum Graece*. 28th ed. Stuttgart: Deutsche Bibelgesellschaft, 2012.
NAC	New American Commentary
Neot	*Neotestamentica*
NIB	Keck, Leander E., ed. *The New Interpreter's Bible*. 12 vols. Nashville: Abingdon, 1995–2004.
NICNT	New International Commentary on the New Testament
NIGTC	New International Greek Testament Commentary
NovT	*Novum Testamentum*
NovTSup	Supplements to Novum Testamentum
NRSV	New Revised Standard Version
NTD	Das Neue Testament Deutsch
NTR	New Testament Readings
NTS	*New Testament Studies*
NTT	New Testament Theology
NTTS	New Testament Tools and Studies
NTTSD	New Testament Tools, Studies, and Documents
OCM	Oxford Classical Monographs

OTL	Old Testament Library
OTM	Oxford Theological Monographs
OTP	Charlesworth, James C., ed. *Old Testament Pseudepigrapha*. 2 vols. ABRL. New York: Doubleday, 1983–1985.
PBTM	Paternoster Biblical and Theological Monographs
PilNTC	Pillar New Testament Commentary
PTS	Patristische Texte und Studien
RB	*Revue biblique*
RBS	Resources for Biblical Study
RelSRev	*Religious Studies Review*
RevExp	*Review and Expositor*
RHR	*Revue de l'histoire des religions*
RIBLA	*Revista de Interpretación Bíblica Latinoamericana*
RSV	Revised Standard Version
SBJT	*Southern Baptist Journal of Theology*
SBLDS	Society of Biblical Literature Dissertation Series
SBLSBS	Society of Biblical Literature Sources for Biblical Study
SBS	Stuttgarter Bibelstudien
SC	Sources chrétiennes
SCHT	Studies in Christian History and Thought
SIG	Dittenberger, Wilhelm, ed. *Sylloge Inscriptionum Graecarum*. 3rd ed. 4 vols. Leipzig: Hirzel, 1915–1924.
SNTSMS	Society for New Testament Studies Monograph Series
SP	Sacra Pagina
ST	*Studia Theologica*
SSEJC	Studies in Scripture in Early Judaism and Christianity
STDJ	Studies on the Texts of the Desert of Judah
SUNT	Studien zur Umwelt des Neuen Testaments
SWBA	Social World of Biblical Antiquity
SymS	Symposium Series
TC	*TC: A Journal of Biblical Textual Criticism*
TCS	Text-Critical Studies
TDNT	Kittel, Gerhard, and Gerhard Friedrich, eds. *Theological Dictionary of the New Testament*. Translated by Geoffrey W. Bromiley. 10 vols. Grand Rapids, Eerdmans, 1964–1976.
THKNT	Theologischer Handkommentar zum Neuen Testament
TLZ	*Theologische Literaturzeitung*
TNTC	Tyndale New Testament Commentary

TSAJ	Texte und Studien zum antiken Judentum
TynBul	*Tyndale Bulletin*
UBS[5]	Aland, Barbara, Kurt Aland, Johannes Karavidopoulos, Carlo M. Martini, and Bruce M. Metzger, eds. *The Greek New Testament*. 5th ed. Stuttgart: Deutsche Bibelgesellschaft, 2014.
VTSup	Supplements to Vetus Testamentum
WBC	Word Biblical Commentary
WGRW	Writings from the Greco-Roman World
WLAW	Wisdom Literature from the Ancient World
WMANT	Wissenschaftliche Monographien zum Alten und Neuen Testament
WUNT	Wissenschaftliche Untersuchungen zum Neuen Testament
ZNW	*Zeitschrift für die neutestamentliche Wissenschaft und die Kunde der älteren Kirche*

Introduction

Darian R. Lockett and Eric F. Mason

Despite its lively examples and practical focus, the Epistle of James has had an uneven reception in both the church and the academy. Though purported to have been written by James, the brother of Jesus and early leader of the Christian movement in Jerusalem, there is surprising silence regarding its use in the earliest church. The first clear reference to James is found in the writings of Origen in the third century and even thereafter the letter is somewhat sparsely used. In the era of the Reformation, Martin Luther famously characterized James as a "strawy epistle" (*strohern Epistel*) in comparison to Paul's letters, which "show thee Christ" (preface to the New Testament, 1522; see *LW* 35:362). However, in practice Luther felt no scruples against preaching from James as Christian Scripture.

The letter's uneven reception continues in modern scholarship. In his recent commentary on James, Dale C. Allison (2013, 1) reflects upon the "unusually diverse" scholarly assessment of the letter. While some argue that the letter ranks among the earliest Christian texts and was written by the Lord's brother, others contend it was written perhaps several centuries later in the name of James. Readers will notice that the following essays take a range of views regarding the authorship of James. Whereas some will specifically argue for or against authorship by the historical James, the central insights of most of the essays are not dependent upon deciding this issue either way. Beyond the question of authorship, it is not uncommon for interpreters to lament any clear structure or plan in the letter, while others discern an intricate rhetorical or literary structure. Some argue that due to the letter's paraenesis there is no clear social-historical situation behind the letter, yet various commentators argue that the social situation of the first-century poor is vital for understanding the letter. Such diversity of assessment leads some interpreters to articulate a degree of skepticism regarding the letter, as explained in the opening two sentences of Andrew Chester's (1994, 3) work on the theology of James: "James presents a unique problem within the New Testament. The questions that loom over it are whether it has any theology at all, and whether it should have any place in Christian scripture." Perhaps such an assessment is most acute when expecting the theological message of James to conform to a Pauline matrix. In this context, some have puzzled over James as an "enigma" (Deissmann 1901, 52) and have even described the letter as "the 'Melchizedek' of the Christian canon" (Penner 2009, 257). This negative assessment of James might be summarized in the words of Martin Dibelius (1976), one of James's most influential interpreters of the twentieth century. He concluded that the disconnected sayings of the letter are so incoherent that the letter "has not theology" (21).

The past twenty-five years, however, have witnessed a renaissance in James scholarship, and many of the judgments that have dominated discussion of James have undergone fresh assessment. This new turn is a welcome development, especially as much of this fresh assessment has been committed to reading James on its own terms. An important group of newer commentaries embody this approach to James, including those by Luke Timothy Johnson (Anchor Bible [1995] and *New Interpreter's Bible* [1998]), Douglas J. Moo (Pillar New Testament Commentary [2000]), Scot McKnight (New International Commentary on the New Testament [2011]), and Dale C. Allison (International Critical Commentary [2013]). Each of these volumes approaches James with a fresh set of eyes intending to appreciate James's unique contribution to early Christian thought. Richard Bauckham's seminal investigation of the historical and literary contexts of James not only reads the letter on its own terms, but also sets the book within its canonical context within the Christian Scriptures (1999). Additionally, Karl-Wilhelm Niebuhr and Robert Wall (2009) have edited a collection of helpful essays that addresses the Catholic Epistles broadly and includes a section specifically on James. We hope that the present volume will continue this helpful trajectory of reading and appreciating James on its own terms.

The title of our book is *Reading the Epistle of James: A Resource for Students*. Both phrases in this title are very important and intentional. The first part reflects our task to address major issues in the interpretation of this epistle. Most members of our international team of contributors are leading scholars of James who have previously published numerous articles, monographs, and/or commentaries on the book, often including lengthy treatments of the very same topics they address more concisely in this volume. Other contributors have not normally published on James but bring fresh perspectives as experts in other related fields of study. In all cases the chapters reflect the most recent trends in contemporary scholarship, yet they are designed for classroom use by undergraduate, seminary, and graduate students, in accord with the second part of the book's title. We assume that most readers of this book will use it alongside one or more standard commentaries of James. We have sought to provide focused discussions of key interpretative issues in James that go beyond the discussions usually possible in commentaries, but in forms particularly designed for student readers in terms of content, length, and level of complexity. The editors are most familiar with the needs of undergraduate students in North America who are studying James closely in an academic context for the first time, but we trust the chapters here will also prove beneficial and illuminating for readers elsewhere and for those at more advanced educational levels.

The first section of the book includes four essays discussing possible sources and backgrounds utilized by the author of James. Though the words of Jesus are never quoted directly in James, the book clearly bears the influence of the Jesus tradition. Richard Bauckham considers the allusions to the sayings of Jesus in James in his chapter titled "James and Jesus Traditions." Bauckham argues that the data are best explained by recognizing the author of James as a wisdom teacher in the tradition of Jewish sages like Ben Sira. Such sages were deeply indebted to the wise sayings of their predecessors, but they did not merely repeat those sayings. Rather, they performed variations on them and crafted their own new aphorisms inspired by them. In a similar way, the wise sayings of Jesus were James's inspiration as he composed his own wisdom sayings in the tradition of Jesus's wisdom. Bauckham suggests that James is in fact more indebted to the teaching of Jesus than a few clear allusions would suggest.

The letter's connection to biblical and postbiblical Jewish tradition has also been long acknowledged. Eric F. Mason's "Use of Biblical and Other Jewish Traditions in James" reflects on this Jewish background of James, specifically considering the epistle's use of biblical and related traditions. Mason observes that whereas the Epistle of James includes only a few explicit quotations of Scripture, its contents are infused with biblical language. Also, the author appeals on several occasions to examples of biblical characters (including Abraham, Rahab, Job, and Elijah) as models for the ethical expectations presented in the letter. Mason notes especially the extended comments about Abraham in Jas 2, and he argues that the author assumes certain interpretative traditions about the patriarch that he expects are shared by the audience of the text.

Though the Letter of James is often considered one of the most Jewish works of the New Testament, its Hellenistic character has been no less obvious to critical scholars. The relatively polished Greek language and style, the apparent reflection of Hellenistic rhetorical conventions, and the familiarity with imagery and themes of the Greco-Roman moralists and philosophers all speak to a work as thoroughly embedded in the Greco-Roman as in the Jewish and Christian discourse of its time. In "The Letter of James and Hellenistic Philosophy," Matt Jackson-McCabe argues that Hellenistic philosophical concepts are entwined inseparably with Jewish and Christian ones within the very warp and woof of the epistle's fabric. In particular, a popular philosophical dichotomy between *logos* and desire lies at the heart of the theological worldview and ethical instruction of James, seamlessly integrated into its other central themes of faith and works, rich and poor, wisdom and perfection, and even speech and prayer.

Benjamin Wold considers the intersection of sapiential (or wisdom) instruction and eschatology in his chapter titled "James in the Context of Jewish Wisdom Literature." One of the questions that has transformed the study of early Jewish sapiential traditions is how eschatology, and especially issues of future reward for the righteous and punishment for the wicked, came to be part of wisdom literature's discourse. Wold addresses the cosmology of James alongside that of other early Jewish literature to better understand how such literature informs and shapes exhortations and ethics. Wold concludes that eschatology has come to be seen as part of a larger cosmology that shapes ethical instruction and that the integral combination of wisdom and eschatological concerns in ethical instruction is something demonstrated in James itself.

The next section of the book includes two chapters reflecting on the genre and structure of James. Luke L. Cheung and Kelvin C. L. Yu consider the genre of James in light of Jewish wisdom traditions in "The Genre of James: Diaspora Letter, Wisdom Instruction, or Both?" They note several proposals for the genre of James (including an allegory on Jacob's farewell address patterned on the Testament of the Twelve Patriarchs, Greek diatribe, Hellenistic-Jewish homily, protreptic discourse, and Hellenistic paraenesis) but argue that James fits in well with diaspora letters and Jewish wisdom instructions in terms of form, content, and function. Furthermore, they contend that the Letter of James should be understood as an example of blending the genre of diaspora letter and wisdom writing.

Identifying rhetorical features in New Testament letters has been a helpful way of understanding how the original authors of the texts sought to give shape to their arguments and to ensure that the letter would be persuasive. Focusing on the rhetorical context of James, Duane F. Watson's "The Rhetorical Composition of the Epistle of James" argues that James exhibits a unique blend of rhetoric common to the Jewish rhetorical tradition and Greco-Roman rhetorical instruction. James has sections of traditional exhortation that use many rhetorical figures, but the book also contains portions constructed according to the Greco-Roman instruction for development of a particular thesis. Though James does not precisely conform to Greco-Roman rhetorical convention, Watson concludes that the author of James comes from a Jewish background influenced by Hellenistic rhetoric. Furthermore, he argues that the rhetoric of James helps the audience understand their newfound status, both in continuity and discontinuity with their former lives.

As noted above, the modern scholarly view of James has been heavily influenced by Dibelius's assertion that the letter is void of any theology. Resisting this assessment, Peter H. Davids, Mariam Kamell Kovalishyn, Ryan E. Stokes, and Scot McKnight reflect on the theology of James in our volume's next section. Davids begins "The Good God and the Reigning Lord: Theology of the Epistle of James" by focusing on the most prominent divine figure in the letter, God the Father. He notes how James presents God as creator and the good giver whose gift is life. Furthermore, when James speaks of Jesus, it is always in regal terms: glorious Lord, coming judge, and, possibly, royal lawgiver. Davids argues that speaking in such terms gives James a unique texture among early Christian writings in its depiction of God and of Jesus Christ. He concludes that James expresses a kind of binitarian theology with God the Father functioning as creator and giver of good gifts and with Jesus as the exalted Lord, who rules now and whose teaching is the law of the community.

In "Salvation in James: Saved by Gift to Become Merciful," Kovalishyn seeks to reveal the soteriology of the letter. She argues that the epistle presents the full story of salvation, from initial birth into the new creation, to the life lived in keeping with God's character and law, to the final judgment before God. As in the story of Israel, the work of salvation in James begins with the prior work of God. Salvation, understood as reconciliation with God, is the ultimate good gift of God (1:16–18), the God who is the unchangingly good and generous giver, and this gift is implanted by God in his people (1:21, with echoes of the new covenant promises of Jer 31). Kovalishyn's overarching point is that the picture of salvation in James is holistic, arguing that, in the end, sanctification is inseparable from salvation.

Stokes's "The Devil and Demons in the Epistle of James" situates James's understanding of sin within the context of early Jewish debates regarding moral evil. Stokes notes that while James's concern in 1:13–18 is to exonerate God of any part in human transgression, he nevertheless allows for humans to be led astray by demons and by the devil (3:15; 4:6). In doing so, James charts a middle course between the two alternatives of divine sovereignty and human responsibility. This discussion takes place within James's developing notions of evil superhuman beings. Stokes suggests the possibility that James's thinking about demons resembles that of the Book of Watchers, where the devil and demons are the proponents of sin and the enemies of God.

Stressing that any Bible reading is an exercise in seeing and making connections, McKnight's "Poverty, Riches, and God's Blessings: James in the Context of the Biblical Story" offers a reading of James in the context of the Bible's story about justice, wealth, and poverty. Rather than a historical-critical reconstruction of these themes in the Jewish Scriptures, McKnight describes the narrative resources the author of James would have had when speaking about poverty and wealth. He concludes that James brings the biblical story correlating obedience with material flourishing and disobedience with material diminishment into relationship with the identification of God with the oppressed poor and God's use of testing. McKnight argues that James functions like one of the prophets lifting up the poor with words of encouragement and castigating the rich for their injustice against the poor.

In the renaissance of James scholarship mentioned above, several important insights into the letter's social, cultural, and narratival meaning have emerged through the application of new methodologies to the study of James. In the next section, chapters by Alicia J. Batten, Elsa Tamez, and Peter J. Gurry and Tommy Wassserman consider various methodologies for reading and interpreting James.

In her chapter titled "Reading James with the Social Sciences," Batten describes the general features of Mediterranean economic life with the aid of anthropological and sociological models, and then pays specific attention to the characterization of the rich, of the poor, and of the deity in James. Batten notes how the use of the social sciences illuminates how the author of James contrasts the rich and poor throughout the letter, especially when one takes into account the centrality of honor and shame concepts and the importance of ideas about what it meant to be masculine and noble.

Tamez reads the letter of James from the perspective of immigrants and the marginalized. In "Don't Conform Yourselves to the Values of the Empire," she argues that the letter's recipients suffer economic problems and persecution and that the author recognizes the danger of living in an attractive and seductive Greco-Roman society. The author, therefore, urges the recipients not to follow certain cultural and moral values that are contrary to the prophetic tradition and the Jesus movement, such as the system of patronage and the desire to accumulate money. The author tries to comfort his readers in their situation of oppression and discrimination, but at the same time he invites them to exemplify a genuine and integral spirituality and faith, which is made visible through solidarity with those most in need and through personal integrity. Such behavior includes the wise use of the tongue.

The discipline of textual criticism certainly is not new, but new methodologies in this field have influenced particular readings of the Greek New Testament. The publication of the first installment of the Editio Critica Maior (ECM) of the Epistle of James in 1997 was a milestone in the history of New Testament Textual Criticism. In "Textual Criticism and the Editio Critica Maior of James," Gurry and Wasserman consider these new developments and how they have shed new light on our understanding of James. A new method—the Coherence-Based Genealogical Method—was applied in the reconstruction of the "initial text" of James, in particular for the second edition of the ECM (ECM2). This method resulted in the detection of several significant textual witnesses in James that were previously relatively unknown and thus a reevaluation of the critical text of James as compared with that printed in the 27th edition of the Nestle-Aland *Novum Testamentum Graece*. Gurry and Wasserman briefly introduce the ECM2 and the Coherence-Based Genealogical Method, then examine a number of significant textual issues in James.

The final three chapters in this volume examine how James has been interpreted and received. John Painter considers the sometimes conflicting appraisals of whether the historical James was associated with our letter at all. Next, Darian R. Lockett and Stephen J. Chester consider the history of James's reception in the patristic and Reformation eras, respectively.

Painter's "James 'the Brother of the Lord' and the Epistle of James" considers traditions about the historical James and his relationship to the letter that bears his name. Painter argues that whereas the historical James focused his attention on the Jewish church in Jerusalem, the book's author was a Greek-speaking diaspora Jew who inherited the Jamesian tradition sometime after the Jerusalem-centered Jewish mission had ceased. Thus, the Epistle of James is best understood as the adaptation of the Jamesian transmission of the Jesus tradition that is intended for the needs of Greek-speaking Jews of the diaspora. Painter also discusses biblical and interpretative traditions relevant to understanding the figure of James and other siblings of Jesus.

Lockett takes up the issue of early use of the Epistle of James (or the lack thereof) in the patristic period in "Use, Authority, and Canonical Status of James in the Earliest Church." He considers the reception history of the epistle through the end of the fourth century, by which time the letter had been received as canonical. Specifically, Lockett sifts through the epistle's literary relationships with 1 Peter, 1 Clement, and the Shepherd of Hermas for hints about the date of composition of James. Then, starting with the use made of the letter by Eusebius, Lockett works backward to weigh evidence of early knowledge and use of James in patristic citations and in early canon lists. Attention finally turns to the manuscript tradition and what such early Christian artifacts might suggest about the use and authority of James.

In the concluding chapter, "Salvation, the Church, and Social Teaching: The Epistle of James in Exegesis of the Reformation Era," Chester addresses a question that was especially acute during the Reformation: how was James to be read in relation to the soteriology expressed in the Pauline epistles? Here the contents of the second chapter of James were of crucial significance. James 2:19 ("even demons believe—and shudder") was read by medieval exegetes in concert with Gal 5:6 ("in Christ Jesus … the only thing that counts is faith working through love") to suggest that for faith to rise above the level of cognitive assent to historical facts, it must be formed by love so that it might become living and active in good works. Similarly, the assertion of Jas 2:24 that "a person is justified by works and not by faith alone" indicated for medieval exegetes that Paul's assertion that justification is "not by works of the law" must exclude only those works performed before baptism. Chester explores the arguments presented by both Protestant and Catholic proponents to establish alternative ways of coordinating these texts and examines the responses they received from their opponents.

James and Jesus Traditions

Richard Bauckham

The letter of James contains no attributed citations of Jesus's teaching, though in one case it does come close to reproducing a saying of Jesus that occurs in one of the gospels (cf. Jas 5:12 and Matt 5:33–37). But most scholars have recognized that there are some close affinities with traditions of the sayings of Jesus that we know from the Synoptic Gospels, and some would go so far as to say that the Letter of James looks more like the Synoptic teaching of Jesus than anything else in the New Testament. Yet the precise way in which James is related to Jesus traditions remains somewhat elusive.[1]

Most commonly, it has been supposed that James alludes to sayings of Jesus, and scholars have attempted to identity such allusions by assessing the degree of resemblance between sayings of Jesus in the gospels and passages in James. Partly because there has been no agreement as to the nature and degree of resemblance that is required to constitute an allusion, the number of allusions identified by various scholars has varied widely. The most thorough study, by Dean Deppe, lists the 184 parallels that were suggested by sixty writers on James up to 1985 (Deppe 1989, 231–38). Deppe's (1989, 219–23) own careful and cautious study of the most often cited parallels concludes that there are in James eight "conscious" or "deliberate allusions" to Synoptic sayings of Jesus, thus:

Jas 1:5	Matt 7:7; Luke 11:9
Jas 2:5	Matt 5:3; Luke 6:20b
Jas 4:2	Matt 7:7; Luke 11:9
Jas 4:9	Luke 6:21, 25b

---

1. See Kloppenborg 2009, 72–80, for a description of six models that various scholars have proposed.

Jas 4:10   Matt 23:12; Luke 14:11; 18:14b
Jas 5:1   Luke 6:24
Jas 5:2–3a   Matt 6:19–20; Luke 12:33b
Jas 5:12   Matt 5:33–37

Significantly, Deppe (222–23) also concludes that "the primary parallels are those of common theme or subject matter rather than intended allusion or citation." His own list of nine "ethical themes" that "are paralleled emphatically in the Synoptic gospels" is this:

+ joy in tribulation: Jas 1:2; 5:10–11a; Matt 5:11–12a; Luke 6:22–23a;
+ faith and doubting: Jas 1:6; Matt 21:21; Mark 11:23;
+ exhortations against anger: Jas 1:19–20; Matt 5:22;
+ hearing and doing: Jas 1:22–25; Matt 7:24–26; Luke 6:46–49; 8:21; and faith and action: Jas 2:14; Matt 7:21; Luke 6:46;
+ the love commandment: Jas 2:8; Matt 22:39; Mark 12:31; Luke 10:27;
+ mercy: Jas 2:13; Matt 5:7; 9:13; 12:7; 18:33–35;
+ serving God versus loving the world: Jas 4:4; Luke 16:13; Matt 6:24;
+ refraining from judging: Jas 4:11–12; 5:9; Matt 7:1; Luke 6:37;
+ those who persevere in trial will receive a blessing: Jas 1:12; 5:10–11a; Matt 5:11–12a; 10:22; Luke 6:22–23a (Deppe 1989, 222–23).

Deppe has probably taken this method of approach to the relationship between James and the gospels as far as it can be taken. But subsequent scholars have continued to differ widely as to which parallels constitute allusions.[2] A fresh approach to the issue is required, which might well begin by questioning whether allusion is really the most helpful category with which to approach the issue. I myself doubt that even Deppe's eight "deliberate allu-

---

2. See the following lists of parallels given by scholars writing since Deppe's work (the figure in parenthesis gives the number of passages in James that are considered possible allusions to sayings of Jesus): Hartin 1991, 141–42 (28); Painter 2004, 261–62 (33); Popkes 2001, 33–34 (40); Kloppenborg 2007b, 148–50 (16); McKnight 2011, 25–26 (14); Allison 2013, 56–57 (13). P. Foster (2014) examines what he considers to be the eight strongest parallels, concludes that very few of them "provide a compelling case" for James's dependence on Jesus tradition (30), but admits that the cumulative case is stronger (30–31).

sions" should all count as such, if deliberate allusions means that the implied readers of James are expected to recognize these as allusions to sayings of Jesus or that such readerly recognition of allusions is part of the literary strategy of the text. In my view, while Deppe's categorization of the material as either intended allusion or thematic parallel has the advantage of extending the scope of James's indebtedness to Jesus beyond a narrowly defined notion of allusion and highlights impressive parallels that cannot truly be called allusions, it is also somewhat misleading. The category of thematic parallels downplays the role of specific sayings of Jesus in informing James's own formulations of the themes. We need to consider the parallels in a way that transcends the alternative of allusion and thematic parallel, and that avoids the inconclusive attempt to decide which parallels constitute allusions.

I think the way to do so is to focus on the literary genre of James, which is wisdom instruction. The book can be seen as a compendium of James's wisdom, and James himself may be understood as a wisdom teacher in the tradition of Jewish wisdom and also in the tradition of Jesus's sayings, most of which also fall generically into the category of Jewish wisdom instruction. My proposal is that as a disciple of Jesus, James was deeply informed by the teaching of his master and made it his own, but, as a wisdom teacher in his own right, he reexpressed it and developed it as his own teaching, both profoundly and broadly indebted to Jesus's teaching and also at the same time characteristically his own.[3] This makes available to us a perspective on the relationship of James to the Jesus traditions that is both deeper and broader than the category of allusion allows. James does not, for the most part, *allude* to sayings of Jesus, in the sense that the implied readers are expected to find that specific passages of James recall to their minds specific sayings of Jesus. This may happen, but it is not the main point. Rather James's relationship to the teaching of Jesus is one of creative indebtedness that makes all of James's teaching a wisdom in the style and tradition of his master Jesus.

Tradition and Creativity in the Work of a Wisdom Teacher: Ben Sira as a Model

James is a wisdom teacher deeply indebted both to the Jewish wisdom tradition, which he knew in its biblical instantiations and probably also

---

3. This proposal is developed in detail in Bauckham 1999.

in other written forms, and especially to the wisdom of his master and teacher Jesus. Like other Jewish wisdom teachers and like Jesus, James evidently formulated his wisdom especially in aphorisms. These are to be found throughout his work, often serving to encapsulate teaching that he also presents in more discursive forms. Importantly, resemblances to the sayings of Jesus are almost all to be found in these aphorisms of James, which seem to recall—but not to reproduce—aphorisms of Jesus. So how can we understand more precisely this relationship between the aphoristic wisdom of Jesus and the aphoristic wisdom of James?

In a longer treatment of this issue (Bauckham 1999; cf. also Bauckham 2004), I have suggested that a valuable model can be found in James's distinguished predecessor, the Jewish sage of the second century BCE Jeshua (Jesus) ben Eleazar ben Sira, usually known as Ben Sira. The way in which Ben Sira related to the tradition of Jewish wisdom and especially to the book of Proverbs, for him an authority as Jesus was for James, is very instructive.

Ben Sira saw himself standing at the end of a long line of wisdom teachers:

> Now I was the last to keep vigil;
> I was like a gleaner following the grape-pickers;
> by the blessing of the Lord I arrived first,
> and like a grape-picker I filled my wine press. (Sir 33:16–17)[4]

In the initially modest role of gleaner, gathering up, through his study of the Scriptures and other wisdom traditions, what his predecessors had left behind them, Ben Sira made such progress that he succeeded—as gleaners usually do not—in filling a wine press himself, just as his predecessors had done. In other words, from his study of the tradition he was able, by God's blessing, to produce his own wisdom teaching, indebted to the tradition, but very much his own contribution. In a parallel image (24:30–31), he sees his role as a student and teacher of wisdom in the first place as a water channel, irrigating his garden with water channeled from the river of traditional wisdom, but his channel then becomes itself a river and finally a sea.

The scriptural sources of wisdom, not only in what we know as the wisdom literature of the Hebrew Bible, but also in the Torah and the Prophets, Ben Sira studied intensively, as he depicts the ideal scribe doing:

---

4. Unless otherwise indicated, all quotations from the Bible and Apocrypha in this essay are from the NRSV.

> He seeks out the wisdom of all the ancients,
> and is concerned with prophecies;
> he preserves the sayings of the famous
> and penetrates the subtleties of parables....
> If the great Lord is willing,
> he will be filled with the spirit of understanding;
> he will pour forth words of wisdom of his own. (Sir 39:1–2, 6)

The role therefore involves passing on the accumulated wisdom of the tradition, but also penetrating its meaning, drawing out its insights, and developing it in new ways. Truth is fundamentally what is inherited, but the student who has entered thoroughly into the tradition and himself become a sage (cf. 6:32–37; 18:29), inspired with the divine gift of understanding (cf. 24:33), is a *creative* exponent of the tradition, interpreting it in fresh formulations of his own. What Ben Sira did himself on a grand scale is what he says of the wise person:

> When an intelligent person hears a wise saying,
> he praises it and adds to it. (Sir 21:15a)

It is in keeping with this conception of his role as a sage that Ben Sira, despite his enormous indebtedness to the book of Proverbs, never *quotes* a saying (a verse) from it. Only three times does he reproduce word-for-word as much as half a verse from Proverbs, leaving himself free to develop it creatively (Sir 1:14a = Prov 9:10a; Sir 27:26a = Prov 26:27a; Sir 28:8b = Prov 15:18a). Elsewhere sayings clearly inspired by Proverbs may take over a word or phrase from their source, but, even when they reproduce precisely the idea in the source, they reformulate it in a fresh way. Sometimes a new saying corresponds in concept quite closely to one in Proverbs without any verbal resemblance. Or a saying of Ben Sira may give a further twist to an idea found in Proverbs. Sometimes a number of different passages in Proverbs or other sources have come together in Ben Sira's study and contributed to a passage indebted to them all. Often a saying from Proverbs or elsewhere provides a theme that Ben Sira develops at greater length (for examples of these relationships, see Bauckham 1999, 77–79; 2004, 80; Skehan and Di Lella 1987, 40–44). While Proverbs forms the major repository of wisdom on which he draws, other sources are treated in much the same ways.

In summary, since the appropriate response of a sage to a wise saying is to add to it (21:15a), since a sage's skill is shown in creating apt proverbs (18:29), since the role of a sage is to express *as his own wisdom in his own formulation* the wisdom he has gained from his intensive study of the tradition, Ben Sira transmits and develops the tradition *without simply repeating it.* This reformulation and development of the tradition is, of course, in part contextual. Old wisdom needs to be adapted to new contexts and to be developed in line with fresh developments of thought. But it is important to notice that Ben Sira's avoidance of repetition cannot by any means be fully explained by such contextual adaptation and development. Even where the old wisdom would, in his eyes, have been wholly applicable as it stands, still he reformulates the old wisdom, because it is the role of the sage to make the old wisdom his own and to express it as his own wisdom. Many of the proverbs in Ben Sira seem so traditional we might easily suppose they must have come down to him in the tradition, but in reality they are traditional in content, traditional in style of formulation, but in their actual formulation newly minted by Ben Sira himself.

It follows that in most cases where verbal echoes of his scriptural sources occur, we should probably not regard these as *allusions* to Scripture, in the sense of deliberate intertextual pointers, meant to call the scriptural text to the reader's mind. Only in a very few cases should we identify something like a citation of Scripture intended to be recognized as such (notably 1:14a). Informed readers, students of wisdom like Ben Sira himself, would recognize the profound continuity between scriptural wisdom and his work, but not more so when he happens to pick up words from his source than when he does not.

The analogy with Ben Sira can now help us appreciate the similar way in which James relates to the wisdom tradition before him, both Jewish wisdom in general and in particular the sayings of Jesus, which to some extent occupy for James the position that Proverbs occupies for Ben Sira, as the major source of his wisdom. It is true that there are in James some formal citations of Scripture (2:8, 11, 23; 4:6; cf. 4:5), but these occur in argumentative sections in which James is establishing a point in debate. In the parts of his letter that are more typical of traditional Jewish wisdom teaching in style, he does not quote. Like Ben Sira, James, even at his most traditional, does not repeat; he reformulates.

This perspective puts the question of the relation of James to the sayings of Jesus in a new light. Rather than thinking in terms of allusion, which makes verbal correspondence the center of attention, we can think of James as a sage who has made the wisdom of Jesus his own. He does not repeat it; he is inspired by it. He creates his own wise sayings, sometimes as equivalents of specific sayings of Jesus, sometimes inspired by several sayings, sometimes encapsulating the theme of many sayings, sometimes based on points of contact between Jesus's sayings and other Jewish wisdom. The creativity and artistry of these sayings are missed when they are treated as allusions to sayings of Jesus. But the indebtedness of James's wisdom to Jesus is much greater than verbal resemblances would show. His sayings bear relationships to the teachings of Jesus even when there is no verbal resemblance; the range of themes his wisdom treats resembles that of Jesus's teaching; and the way he relates to other traditional Jewish wisdom is guided by his special attentiveness to Jesus's wisdom as his major authoritative norm.

New Aphorisms for Old

My suggestion is that, instead of looking for allusions to sayings of Jesus, we should look for the ways in which James has worked creatively with the sayings of Jesus. In every case we must respect both the form of the wisdom sayings he knew and the form of his own wisdom sayings. Precisely how James's aphorisms relate to those of Jesus differs, as we shall see, from case to case. Since we are proposing to approach the material from this fresh perspective, we cannot rely on the lists of parallels or the categorizations of them provided by other scholars. But neither can we do more than sample the material. In what follows then I shall adduce just a few examples of the way James creates new wisdom sayings indebted to the sayings of Jesus (another example is discussed in Bauckham 1999, 88–91; another in Bauckham 2004, 88–90). They are chosen with a view to illustrating the variety of kinds of relationship that occur.

We begin with the nearest James comes to actually quoting a saying of Jesus:

Again, you have heard that it was said
to those of ancient times, "You shall not
swear falsely, but carry out the vows you
have made to the Lord." But I say to you,　　Above all, my brothers and sisters,
Do not swear at all,　　do not swear
either by heaven,　　either by heaven
for it is the throne of God,
or by the earth,　　or by earth
for it is his footstool,
or by Jerusalem,　　or with any other oath,
for it is the city of the great King.

And do not swear by your head, for you
cannot make one hair white or black.

Let your word be "Yes, Yes"	but let your "Yes" be yes
or "No, No";	and your "No" be no,
anything more than this comes from	so that you may not fall under
the evil one. (Matt 5:33–37)	condemnation.
	(Jas 5:12, NRSV modified)

It is possible that Jas 5:12 is closer to the form in which James knew the saying of Jesus than it is to the form in Matthew (Schröter 2008, 247), but we should certainly not assume that James reproduces *verbatim* the form of the saying of Jesus he knew. However, the degree of verbal resemblance to the saying in Matthew makes it reasonable to think that readers familiar with this saying of Jesus would find a clear allusion to it in James. In my view, it is the only case in which we can confidently speak of allusion, meaning that reader recognition of an echo of Jesus's teaching belongs to the literary strategy of the text. Even here James has expanded the saying by adding a motive clause of his own ("so that you may not fall under condemnation").[5]

In other cases, by contrast, a relationship is very plausible, but it would be misleading to speak of allusion. For example:

	So I say to you,	If any of you is lacking in
Ask,	Ask,	wisdom, ask God, who gives to all generously and ungrudgingly,
and it will be given to you; search, and you will find; knock, and the door will be opened for you.... If you then, who are evil, know how to give good gifts to your children, how much more will your Father in heaven give good things to those who ask him! (Matt 7:7, 11)	and it will be given to you; search, and you will find; knock, and the door will be opened for you.... If you then, who are evil, know how to give good gifts to your children, how much more will the heavenly Father give the Holy Spirit to those who ask him! (Luke 11:9, 13)	and it will be given you.

---

5. In Bauckham 1999, 92–93, I explain why it is appropriate that in this case uniquely James makes a clear allusion to a saying of Jesus.

	Have faith in God.	
Truly I tell you, if you have	Truly I tell you,	But ask in faith,
faith and do not doubt …		never doubting,
even if you say to this	if you say to this	for the one who doubts
mountain,	mountain,	is like a wave of the sea,
"Be lifted up and thrown	"Be taken up and thrown	driven and tossed by the
into the sea,"	into the sea," and if you do	wind.
	not doubt in your heart,	(Jas 1:5–6)
	but believe that what you	
	say will come to pass,	
it will be done.	it will be done for you.	
Whatever you	So I tell you, whatever	
ask for in prayer with	you ask for in prayer,	
faith, you will receive.	believe that you have	
(Matt 21:21b–22)	received it, and it will be	
	yours. (Mark 11:22b–24)	

The way in which James in these two verses reexpresses the teaching of Jesus on prayer is very similar to the way in which Ben Sira frequently reexpresses the wisdom of Proverbs. In verse 5 James has taken the first line of Jesus's threefold parallelism and expanded it into a new saying, by (1) specifying what is asked as wisdom, and (2) introducing reference to God's generosity in giving to all. Expansion (2) in effect incorporates into this saying the point that Jesus makes by an *a minore ad majorem* ("from the smaller to the greater") argument in Matt 7:11 // Luke 11:13. Expansion (1) no doubt results from the reflection that, if God gives good gifts to those who ask (Matt 7:11 // Luke 11:13), then preeminent among these gifts must be the most needed gift of all: the wisdom from above that enables people to live according to God's will (Jas 3:17). In this way James is able to connect the saying of Jesus with the wisdom tradition that speaks of wisdom as the gift of God (Prov 2:6; Sir 51:17; Wis 8:21; 9:17; 4Q185 II, 11–12) and emphasizes God's generosity in lavishing wisdom on those who love him (Sir 1:9–10). James's two verses together succeed in expressing very concisely the major elements in Jesus's teaching about prayer. They are not *allusions* to the sayings of Jesus so much as a *creative reexpression* of the wisdom of Jesus by his disciple the sage James.

James evidently had this saying of Jesus in mind also in 4:3: "You ask and do not receive, because you ask wrongly, in order to spend what you get on your pleasures." Wisdom sayings are characteristically general, stated without qualifications or exceptions, and this is true of this saying of

Jesus. But, to explain why prayers are not always answered, James sees the need to introduce a qualification and develops Jesus's saying in such a way as to relate it to the situation he envisages. Other kinds of qualifications are made to this saying of Jesus in the Johannine literature (John 15:16; 16:24; 1 John 5:14–15). Evidently the saying was well known (see also John 4:10; 1 John 3:22) and so it may well be that readers of James would have recognized his creative variations on it as such.[6] But his literary strategy does not depend on their doing so.

A somewhat different example comes in Jas 2:5b:

Blessed are the poor in spirit, for theirs is the kingdom of heaven. (Matt 5:3)	Blessed are you poor, for yours is the kingdom of God. (Luke 6:20)	Has not God chosen the poor in the world to be rich in faith and to be heirs of the kingdom that he has promised to those who love him? (Jas 2:5b)

James does not quote the gospel beatitude, but has been inspired by it in composing his own saying. To the thought of the gospel saying he has added the notion of God's election of the poor and especially the paradox that "the poor in the world" (probably meaning poor with respect to those material goods that the world considers wealth) are "rich in faith" (i.e., in the sphere of faith). This paradox brilliantly encapsulates the Jewish tradition of regarding the pious poor as the paradigms of faith: due to their poverty they cannot rely on their own resources and thus must exemplify the utter dependence on God that true faith is. In this case, then, James has drawn both on Jesus's saying and also on the kind of Jewish teaching to which Jesus himself was indebted.

Different again is the relationship to Jesus's teaching in Jas 2:13:

Do not judge, so that you may not be judged. For with the judgment you make you will be judged, and the measure you give will be the measure you get. (Matt 7:1–2)	Judge not, and you will not be judged; condemn not, and you will not be condemned;… For the measure you give will be the measure you get back. (Luke 6:37a, 38b)	Judgment will be without mercy to anyone who has shown no mercy. Mercy triumphs over judgment. (Jas 2:13, NRSV modified)

---

6. For the many variations and developments of the saying Matt 7:7 // Luke 11:9 in the New Testament, see Minear 1972, 113–31.

Blessed are the merciful,
for they will receive
mercy. (Matt 5:7)

Show mercy, so that you may receive mercy ... As you judge, so shall you be judged ... With the measure you use, it will be measured to you. (Jesus, according to 1 Clem. 13:2, trans. Holmes 2007, 63)	Do not judge, so that you may not be judged.... Show mercy, so that you may be shown mercy ... With the measure you use, it will be measured back to you. (Jesus, according to Polycarp, Phil. 2:3, trans. Holmes 2007, 283)

James 2:13 consists of two carefully crafted aphorisms. They do not allude to a specific saying of Jesus, but put into memorable forms of their own an insight that is very characteristic of the teaching of Jesus (see also Matt 6:12, 14–15; 18:23–35; Mark 11:25; Luke 11:4). Statements of the same or similar ideas could easily be quoted also from other Jewish literature (Sir 28:1–4; Prov 17:5 LXX; b. Shabb. 151b; Tg. Neof. Gen 38:25). James would have known this idea as a traditional insight of Jewish wisdom, but one that Jesus had made especially his own, and so James in turn has made it his own by coining his own aphoristic expressions of it.

We can also consider two examples which could not conceivably count as allusions, since James does not echo the words or even the image used in the corresponding sayings of Jesus, but in which, once we recognize James's close and creative relationship with Jesus's teaching, we can easily imagine inspiration from the latter. One such example is Jas 4:4b:

Do you not know that friendship with the world is enmity with God? Therefore whoever wishes to be a friend of the world becomes an enemy of God.

Compare Luke 16:13 (// Matt 6:24):

No slave can serve two masters; for a slave will either hate the one and love the other, or be devoted to the one and despise the other. You cannot serve God and wealth.

The images used are quite distinct. But they are closely parallel: In each case the person cannot love both, but must love one and oppose the other. Devotion to one is incompatible with devotion to the other because each demands an exclusive loyalty. The reference in both cases is to the exclusive devotion that God requires of his people, such that devotion to what is opposed to him (the world or mammon) constitutes idolatry. It looks very much as though James has reexpressed Jesus's thought in a fresh image. Whether or not James's readers would recognize the resemblance is beside the point. Nothing about the effectiveness of James's teaching depends on its being recognized, but when we do see it we gain an insight into the way James's teaching has developed as that of a wise disciple of his wise master Jesus.[7]

A similar case is Jas 1:23–25 in relation to Matt 7:24–27 // Luke 6:47–49. In each text there is a pair of short narrative parables. They are so-called geminate parables, that is, each of the pair is the mirror opposite of the other. In the passage in James this is not quite explicit, because the second parable has been subsumed into its interpretation ("But the one who looked into …"), but the parable in the first two sentences evidently has an implicit twin only partly expressed: If anyone is a doer of the word, he is like a man who looked intently into a mirror and remained and did not forget. This is the opposite of the first parable, just as Jesus's parable of the foolish man is the opposite of his parable of the wise man. The two pairs of parables, Jesus's and James's, are quite different stories, but the message each pair conveys is precisely the same. Moreover, they share the same formal structure, one of several different forms of similitude that occur in both James and the sayings of Jesus (see Bauckham 1999, 51–52). Again it looks as though James has reexpressed Jesus's teaching in a way he has freshly devised.

Emulating the Sayings of Jesus?

John Kloppenborg, while agreeing with my argument that the way the wisdom sayings of Ben Sira relate to earlier Jewish wisdom illuminates James's relation to the sayings of Jesus, also argues that both belong within a wider practice of literary paraphrase that was taught in the initial stages of rhetorical education (*progymnasmata*) in the Greco-Roman world. He

---

7. Batten 2014b, 90–92, suggests that James's saying is more appropriate to an urban environment in the Jewish diaspora.

analyzes examples from James that show how his treatment of the sayings of Jesus corresponds to such rhetorical practice (Kloppenborg 2009, 84–100; 2007b, 129–42).

Thus Quintilian indicates that students at the beginning of their rhetorical education

> should learn to paraphrase Aesop's fables … in simple and restrained language and subsequently to set down this paraphrase in writing with the same simplicity of style: they should begin by analysing each verse, then give its meaning in different language, and finally proceed to a freer paraphrase in which they will be permitted now to abridge and now to embellish the original, so far as this may be done without losing the poet's meaning. (*Inst.* 1.9.2; trans. Butler)

Similar exercises applied to maxims, *chreiai*, and passages from Homer, from the speeches of the great orators, and from the historians.[8] Theon defined paraphrase as "changing the form of expression while keeping the thoughts." This could be achieved by varying the syntax, by expanding the original, by abridging it, and by substituting different words. The aim was to learn to paraphrase a whole speech. He also writes about the related practice of elaboration, which is "language that adds what is lacking in thought or expression." This is done

> by filling gaps in the language or content; by saying some things more strongly, or more believably, or more vividly, or more truly, or more wordily … or more legally, or more beautifully, or more appropriately, or making the subject pleasanter, or using a better arrangement or a style more ornate. (*Prog.* 15–16; trans. Kennedy 2003, 70–71)[9]

There is no doubt that training of this kind explains the widespread habit of ancient writers who regularly paraphrase their sources, rather than quoting their words. Since James does show some acquaintance with rhetorical techniques, such as diatribe (Watson 2007, 110–11), it is not improbable

---

8. For examples of rhetorical exercises in paraphrase in papyri from Egypt, see Morgan 1998, 202–26, and note how Morgan describes the limitations of this kind of paraphrase (225).

9. For an exercise on papyrus, paraphrasing Demosthenes, that exemplifies Theon's instructions, see Cribiore 2001, 235–37.

that he was influenced by a basic rhetorical education that taught para-phrase and elaboration.

Nevertheless, I am not convinced that James's practice of variation, elaboration, and creative reexpression of the sayings of Jesus is illuminated as much by the general rhetorical practice of paraphrase as it is by the more specific practice of the Jewish wisdom tradition. We should note that James's paraphrases always take the form of short aphorisms, the literary form most characteristic and traditional in the Jewish wisdom tradition. His passages of argumentation (e.g., 2:1–13) are not paraphrases, though they may include aphoristic reexpressions of sayings of Jesus (e.g., 2:5) and may conclude with summarizing aphorisms of that kind (e.g., 2:13). Moreover, James does not, as a rhetorical training would have encouraged him to do, paraphrase the long narrative parables of Jesus or the extended passages of teaching that he would have known had he known Q or our gospels. He works within a tradition of aphoristic reexpression that begins in the Hebrew Bible, though it was practiced most skillfully and exten-sively by Ben Sira.[10]

Kloppenborg stresses that, in the rhetorical tradition, the purpose of paraphrase was "to rival and vie [*certamen atque aemulationem*] with the original in the expression of the same thoughts" (Quintilian, *Inst.* 10.5.5, quoted by Kloppenborg 2007b, 133). This certainly implies that the para-phrase should attempt to improve on the original, but I am not so sure as Kloppenborg that audiences would commonly be expected to recognize the text being paraphrased and admire the skill of the rhetorical reexpres-sion. In the case of James, I do not agree that we should think of his work as emulation of the Jesus tradition in that sense (Kloppenborg 2009, 100). On the contrary, for the most part James does not *allude* to the sayings of Jesus as he would have had to have done if his literary strategy depended on his audience recognizing the sayings of Jesus that inspired his own wisdom.

The Wisdom of James and the Wisdom of Jesus

If James was a wisdom teacher engaged in the creative reexpression and development of the wisdom of Jesus, we might expect that he was inspired,

---

10. See, e.g., Prov 30:6 in relation to Deut 4:2; Eccl 10:8–9 in relation to Prov 26:27; and Job 28:28 in relation to Prov 1:7; 9:10; 15:23.

not merely by specific sayings of Jesus, but also more broadly by the general character of Jesus's teaching.[11] Given that both are indebted to the Jewish wisdom tradition, are there features of James's wisdom that resemble the specific characteristics of Jesus's distinctive wisdom?

We may begin with a negative indication that the wisdom of Jesus differs significantly from the main tradition of Jewish wisdom instruction and that the wisdom of James can be aligned with that of Jesus in this difference. A remarkable number of features and topics of traditional Jewish wisdom are wholly absent from the wisdom of both Jesus and James.[12] Purely prudential advice on how to behave so as to avoid suffering disadvantage, which appears in traditional wisdom alongside moral instruction, is absent from both Jesus and James. Exhortations not to be idle, to work hard, and to earn one's own living and advice about friends, on good and bad wives, upbringing of children and management of daughters, and on the treatment of slaves are examples of topics prominent in traditional wisdom but wholly absent from the teaching of both Jesus and James. Discussion of family relationships in general, and discussion of rulers and government, are both rare in the sayings of Jesus and completely absent from James. Neither, it seems, has much to say about how to exercise or to live under the conventional authority structures of society.

By this criterion of topics omitted, James is scarcely any closer to the concerns of the mainstream Jewish wisdom tradition than Jesus is, while the range of topics omitted by each corresponds rather closely. But this purely negative point, striking as it is, does not take us very far in understanding what is distinctive about the teaching of Jesus, or the extent to which James reflects this distinctiveness. The negative point could well be complemented by a positive demonstration of the extent to which the themes that do feature in the sayings of Jesus are, for the most part, traditional concerns of the Jewish religious tradition, many of them found in wisdom instruction. However, all that is possible here is a brief indication, in the following five points, of the positive characteristics of James's wisdom that align it with that of Jesus.[13]

---

11. This is also argued by Hartin 2009.

12. On Jesus in this respect, see Carlston 1980.

13. I have attempted a much more detailed comparison of the broad characteristics of Jesus's wisdom with that of James in Bauckham 1999, 93–108; cf. also Bauckham 2001, 123–31.

(1) The teaching of James, lacking the moderation and practical compromise often to be found in Jewish wisdom, resembles that of Jesus in its extreme—sometimes hyperbolic—demands for total and uncompromising obedience from the heart. (2) The teaching of James is directed to the formation of a countercultural community in which key values of the dominant society, such as honoring the rich and competitive ambition for status, are radically reversed. (3) The eschatological judgment of God is the overriding sanction and motivation of righteous living, to the exclusion of the other kinds of consideration that often feature in wisdom instruction. Like the wisdom of Jesus, that of James is radicalized by its eschatological and theocentric concentration. (4) The God of James, like the Abba of Jesus, is emphatically the giving, generous, merciful, and compassionate one. (5) The uncompromising demand for wholehearted obedience to God in a countercultural community entails a certain sort of dualism, in which God and the world stand for opposed value systems, and it is not possible to divide one's allegiance between the two.

In conclusion, James is a Jewish sage who has deeply appropriated the wisdom of Jesus the Jewish sage and has creatively reexpressed and developed it in his own wise teaching. This can be seen both in the way in which many specific aphorisms of James are creatively indebted to those of Jesus and also in the way the characteristics of the whole of the wisdom gathered in James's compendium match those of Jesus's wisdom as we have it in the synoptic sayings of Jesus.

The Source of James's Knowledge of the Sayings of Jesus

Scholars who work with the category of allusion for the way in which James relates to the sayings of Jesus have often attempted to specify in what form, oral or textual, James was acquainted with the sayings of Jesus. Some have concluded that James knew oral traditions of Jesus's sayings (e.g., Davids 1982, 49–50; Deppe 1989, 223–25), or, more specifically, the traditions of the Matthean community (Martin 1988, lxxiv–lxxvii); some that he was dependent on the hypothetical document Q or, more precisely, a redaction of Q close to the form in which Matthew knew it (QMatt; Hartin 1991; Kloppenborg 2007b; 2009; cf. also Hartin 2014, who argues for general theological resemblances between Q and James); some that he knew Matthew's Gospel (Shepherd 1956; Allison 2013, 61–62; 2014, 63–69) or both Matthew's and Luke's Gospels (Tuckett 2016). These judgments are based on the expectation that James makes deliberate allusions that should be recognized by readers. I have suggested that, except in one or two instances (2:5?; 5:12), this is not the case. Generally, James is engaged in creative reexpression of the sayings of Jesus. This means that, on the one hand, there may be more passages in which James was inspired by sayings of Jesus than the search for allusions, conducted with rigor, will detect. But it also means, on the other hand, that identifying such passages is bound to be insecure, since James did not write in such a way as to enable such identification.

However, New Testament scholars are inevitably interested in what James may show us about the Jesus tradition, and so I offer, with the warning that in the nature of the case this exercise cannot be done with methodological rigor, my own list of passages in which it seems to me likely that a saying of Jesus lies behind the text of James:

Jas 1:2	Matt 5:11–12; Luke 6:22–23
Jas 1:4	Matt 5:48
Jas 1:5	Matt 7:7; Luke 11:9
Jas 1:6	*Mark 11:23; Matt 21:21*
Jas 1:22–23	Matt 7:24–27; Luke 6:47–49
Jas 2:5	Matt 5:3; Luke 6:20
Jas 2:8	*Matt 22:39–40; Mark 12:28–34; Luke 10:27*
Jas 2:13	Matt 5:7; 7:1–2; Luke 6:37–38
Jas 3:18	Matt 5:9
Jas 4:2–3	Matt 7:7; Luke 11:9
Jas 4:4	Matt 6:24; Luke 16:13
Jas 4:10	*Matt 23:12; Luke 14:11; 18:14b*
Jas 4:11–12	Matt 7:1–2; Luke 6:37–38
Jas 5:2–3a	Matt 6:19–20; Luke 12:33b
Jas 5:6	Matt 5:39
Jas 5:7b	*Mark 4:26–29*
Jas 5:9	*Matt 24:33; Mark 13:29; cf. Luke 12:35–36*
Jas 5:12	Matt 5:33–37.

I have italicized the passages where the saying of Jesus is *not* to be found in the Matthean Sermon on the Mount. The predominance of parallels in James to the Sermon on the Mount/Plain has often been observed and is part of the evidence for supposing James to be dependent either on Q[Matt] or on the Gospel of Matthew. But my list also includes four parallels to sayings in other parts of Matthew (that appear also in Mark and/or Luke) and one parallel to a saying in Mark alone. These would not normally be assigned to Q (assuming for the sake of argument the Q hypothesis) and probably few Q scholars would assign to Q or even Q^Matt all the sayings in this list that occur only in Matthew. So, James's knowledge of sayings of Jesus could not have been confined to Q or even (in view of Jas 5:7) to Matthew's Gospel.

But did he know, among the sayings he knew, something like the Sermon on the Mount/Plain as a collection? I do not think this is as clear as many scholars have thought. In the first place, we must take account of the topics James treats, which in chapters 1–4 largely correspond to the ethical teaching of Jesus. Matthew's Sermon on the Mount is precisely a collection of such teaching. It includes, in fact, most of the ethical teaching of Jesus to be found in the Synoptic Gospels. The same reasons that led Matthew to collect this material would have led James to focus on such sayings, even if he did not know them as a collection. He drew on them because they were relevant to ethical paraenesis. We should also note that, when James in chapter 5 turns to eschatological exhortation (5:7–9), the parallels are with sayings not included in Matthew's Sermon on the Mount. If scholars had paid more attention to these parallels (as well as to Jas 1:6; 4:10), the predominance of parallels to the Sermon on the Mount would not have seemed so remarkable.

The other issue relevant to James's source is whether he can be shown to know the specifically Q redaction of sayings or the Matthean or Lukan redaction.[14] But attempts to show this seem to me to be far too speculative, both in their distinction between what is original and what is redactional in the sayings of Jesus and in the confidence with which they deduce from James the forms of the sayings as he knew them. On the other hand, we cannot claim, as some have, that the divergences between the sayings as we have them in the gospels and James's "allusions" to them shows that he knew them in oral rather than textual form (e.g., Rendall 1927, 101–2). Since James is not alluding but reformulating or reexpressing, there is no basis for supposing he knew sayings of Jesus in forms we do not. In conclusion, while James was acquainted with quite a wide range of sayings of Jesus relevant to his subject matter, it is probably not possible to know in what form he knew them.

---

14. Kloppenborg 2009, 92–94, argues that Jas 1:5; 4:2–3 depend on the Q redaction of a saying of Jesus that did not originally apply to prayer; but for arguments against Kloppenborg, see P. Foster 2014, 19; Tuckett 2016, 239–40.

Use of Biblical and Other Jewish Traditions in James

Eric F. Mason

Scholars have long been fascinated with questions about possible literary and textual sources used by the author of the Epistle of James.[1] Such questions certainly are typical in New Testament scholarship on many books, but James is especially fertile—and complex—ground for these investigations. It is common for scholars to discuss connections between James and five different kinds of possible sources: Jesus traditions, especially words of Jesus from the gospels saying source Q (as utilized by the authors of the Gospels of Matthew and Luke); Greco-Roman philosophical traditions; other New Testament texts, not just concerning the persistent question about whether James is in dialogue with Paul or Pauline tradition about faith and works, but also queries about literary relationships between James and other texts of the Catholic Epistles like 1 Peter (especially if James is a composition of the second century or later); biblical texts, that is, use of the Jewish Scriptures; and other Second Temple period (and perhaps also later) Jewish literature. The chapters in this volume by Richard Bauckham, Matt Jackson-McCabe, and Darian R. Lockett address the first three of those possible sources, respectively, but the latter two are the subject of my investigation.[2]

---

1. I use *James* and the term *epistle* in this chapter for ease of discussion, with no intent to imply particular interpretative decisions about the identity of the historical author of the book or its genre classification. I use the words *biblical* and *Scripture* to refer to texts of the Jewish Bible, usually read by the author of James in Greek translations of the LXX tradition.

2. Note that Bauckham also gives significant attention to Ben Sira, and Benjamin Wold considers James in the broader context of wisdom literature in the Second Temple period. In this chapter I normally limit discussion of postbiblical Jewish texts to those of the Second Temple period. This is not to deny that materials from rabbinic texts might be valuable for understanding the context of James, but the thorny ques-

A comprehensive attempt to catalog here every use in James of biblical and other ancient Jewish texts would be both overwhelming and tedious, as virtually every passage in the book is marked by biblical language and/or resonates with broader themes in nonbiblical Jewish literature.[3] Even the opening address of the epistle, "to the twelve tribes in the Dispersion," evokes both the biblical images of the familial confederation of God's chosen people, the children of Israel, and the later experiences of scattered exiles striving to maintain their identity in strange and foreign circumstances.[4] The author's thoughts and language are saturated in biblical imagery, and he assumes that his audience imbibes and inhabits a similar contextual world shaped by the words and ethos of Scripture and a rich, vibrant interpretative tradition. For the author of James, however, *interpretative* does not necessarily equate to *exegetical*, certainly not if the latter implies that an author cites a biblical text (or multiple texts read in conjunction) in order to unpack or argue for some theological or ethical implications in a formal, logic-driven manner.[5] Instead, one might say that the author of James works in tableaus. Rather than articulate how and why this means that in a systematic way, he uses images drenched in Scripture and interpretative tradition that prod, shape, evoke, remind, and illustrate. The images may be so refracted through the traditions that one can scarcely delineate where the Scripture reference itself ends and the tradition begins. Unlike many modern interpreters who are inclined to draw sharp lines between texts that eventually were deemed canonical and noncanonical, ancient exegetes highly valued traditional narrative (re)interpretations of biblical texts and characters that contextualized how such things in the sacred texts themselves should and would be understood.[6]

---

tions of dating for such literature prompts many contemporary scholars to be cautious about their utilization.

3. Cf. the assessment of Allison 2013, 52, who writes that James is "full of scriptural and LXX idioms, and every single paragraph carries forward themes at home in the Jewish Bible."

4. Unless noted otherwise, all biblical translations are from the NRSV.

5. Johnson (1995, 243) notes that even the statement that Scripture is "fulfilled" or "completed" (passive form of *plēroō*) is rare in James, appearing only in 2:23 (discussed below). Even there the interpretation occurs by means of example rather than exegesis.

6. It is in this vein that James L. Kugel, a leading modern scholar of ancient biblical interpretation, could use the title *The Bible as It Was* (1997) for a handbook illustrating ancient Jewish and early Christian interpretations of key passages in the first

This is not the place to discuss the genre of the book of James, but most scholars agree that it has strong affinities with the Hebrew wisdom tradition. As such, it is little surprise that James has many allusions to and/or points of contact with passages from Proverbs, but also Job (sometimes read in light of the pseudepigraphical Testament of Job) and Ecclesiastes, as well as later wisdom traditions in books like Ben Sira (e.g., Sirach or Ecclesiasticus), Wisdom of Solomon, and Pseudo-Phocylides. Influences from Psalms likely also are present. Texts from the books of the Torah (Pentateuch) also figure prominently; several of James's biblical quotations come from this corpus, as do the example of Abraham and numerous cases of minor textual borrowing and allusions. Rahab and Elijah also appear as exemplars and highlight James's use of the Former Prophets, but language and themes from the Latter Prophets abound (including contacts with Isaiah, Jeremiah, Ezekiel, and several texts from the Book of the Twelve).[7]

Normally James appears to know the Jewish Scriptures in Greek translations today called the Septuagint (LXX). Likewise, correspondences (if not dependence in some cases) with multitudes of passages in the Testaments of the Twelve Patriarchs and especially the voluminous writings of Philo of Alexandria illustrate that James (and the other authors) drew "from the common river of Hellenistic-Jewish tradition" (Allison 2013, 55).[8] Yet James also has numerous links to Palestinian Jewish texts (including some Dead Sea Scrolls, Jubilees, and 4 Ezra) and to later rabbinic literature. Again, *correspondences* is the key term: it is not always possible to know with certainty that James had access to these books—and some he certainly could not because issues of dating make that prohibitive—but still James engages with traditional ideas that ultimately found fruition in a vast range of Jewish texts.[9]

---

five books of the Hebrew Bible. See the discussion below of James's understanding of Abraham for an example from this epistle.

7. Multiple examples of links between James and other texts are addressed later in this chapter. See also n. 10 for references to several detailed lists of quotations, allusions, and parallels.

8. Davids (1982, 10) urges caution about the assertion that James relied on the LXX and considers the evidence usually cited as inconclusive. See Dibelius (1976, 27) for a defense of use of the LXX. The date and provenance of the Testaments of the Twelve Patriarchs are very difficult to determine. Many argue that the text as preserved is a second-century CE Christian document, though it appears to draw (heavily, in some cases) from earlier Hebrew and Aramaic traditions. See Kugler 2010, 1296–97.

9. See Davids 1978b, 1993 for especially rich discussions of connections between James and numerous texts of the Pseudepigrapha.

As such, we can affirm the following with Allison:

> One's general impression ... is that our author was well-versed in the scriptures.... That he was familiar with most of what we think of as the LXX is a reasonable inference. He assumes such familiarity on the part of his audience.... [James] nowhere pretends to dispense novelties, and its extensive intertextuality, which is often on the surface, at least for the biblically literate, prohibits the thought. James consistently interacts with a large network of authoritative texts. Biblical stories, wisdom, and prophecy are its chief memories and its dominant linguistic idiom. The upshot is an implicit claim faithfully to represent and reinscribe the divine revelation in the Jewish scriptures. (2013, 52)

Despite James's rich use of biblical language and traditions—but perhaps consistent with how such materials are actually used in the book—the epistle includes a relative lack of explicit citations of scriptural (or other) texts. Many scholars (including, e.g., Dibelius 1976, 27; Johnson 1995, 230; Allison 2013, 51) find just four explicit biblical quotations, each of which is introduced with what *may* be a citation formula of some sort.[10] These quotations are Lev 19:18 in Jas 2:8; Exod 20:13–15 = Deut 5:17–18 in Jas 2:11; Gen 15:6 in Jas 2:23; and Prov 3:34 in Jas 4:6.[11] Similarly, James cites four biblical characters as exemplars of particular virtues for his audience. These are Abraham (2:21–23), Rahab (2:25), Job (5:11), and Elijah (5:17).

Two of the biblical quotations appear within the same discussion in Jas 2:1–13, in which the author condemns favoritism of the rich over the poor. The third quotation follows in the discussion of faith and works in

---

10. Compare the very extensive list of verbal ties in Mayor 1913, cx–cxvi; the more restrictive list in Allison 2013, 51; and the marginal notations of quotations and allusions in NA[28]. Scholarly assessments of what constitutes a quotation or allusion can differ. E.g., the editors of NA[28] identify two additional quotations in James beyond the four commonly noted (five words from Isa 5:9 in Jas 5:4 and three words from Jer 12:3 in Jas 5:5), but Allison considers these cases of "borrowed language" rather than quotation. See Carson 2007 for focused discussion of James's use of select biblical quotations and allusions.

11. A fifth text may also be cited in Jas 4:5 and prefaced as Scripture. This verse, however, presents numerous difficult textual, translational, and interpretative problems. If one indeed finds a quotation here that the author considers scripture—something about which scholars are divided—it cannot be identified with any text from the Jewish Bible, and presumably it instead comes from a lost apocryphal book such as Eldad and Modad. See the extensive discussion in Allison 2013, 611–22.

Jas 2:14–26, which also includes appeals to the examples of Abraham and Rahab.[12] Though, as noted already, explicit quotations are not the typical way the author of James utilizes biblical language in the epistle, and mention of particular biblical characters is likewise limited, closer examinations of Jas 2:1–13 and 2:14–26 offer focused opportunities to see the author at work as he engages these sorts of materials in combination with his abundant allusions to other texts and themes.[13]

James 2:1–13, Favoritism, and the Importance of Leviticus 19

The author of James opens this critique of acts of favoritism by declaring such behavior incompatible with the faith of Jesus Christ.[14] Jewish criticism of the practice of favoritism was strong (e.g., Lev 18:15; Sir 7:6–7; Ps.-Phoc. 10), as were affirmations about God's own impartiality (as in Deut 10:17; Sir 35:10–18; also, frequently in the New Testament; Johnson 1995, 221; Hartin 2003, 117; Allison 2013, 380). Though Lev 19:15 (unlike Lev 19:18) is never explicitly cited in James, scholars commonly relate the epistle's critique of favoritism to the commands in Lev 19:15 against partiality and unjust judgments (see further below), even if the terms used in James for favoritism (*prosōpolēmpsia*, 2:1) and the act of expressing it (*prosōpolēmpteō*, 2:9) do not appear in the LXX (Hartin 2003, 117; but see T. Job 43:10 per Allison 2013, 379).

---

12. This division of the text is typical in contemporary scholarship (so, e.g., Allison 2013; Hartin 2003; McKnight 2011; Painter 2012) even among those who find these topics closely related (so Davids 1982, 105: "the first part argues that one must honor the poor and the second that one ought to share with them"). Cf. Johnson (1995, 219), who argues that 2:1–26 forms "a single argument" on "faith and its deeds." Elsewhere (246) he notes numerous structural parallels between 2:1–13 and 2:14–26.

13. Because the purpose of the present chapter is to discuss James's use of Scripture and other Jewish traditions (and direct readers to appropriate resources for further study), in the following discussion I chiefly engage four commentaries that give exemplary attention to such textual questions: those of Davids (1982), Johnson (1995), Hartin (2003), and Allison (2013).

14. The NRSV translation of *mē ... echete tēn pistin ... Iēsou Christou* as "do you ... really believe in ... Jesus Christ" effectively reads the phrase as a subjective genitive emphasizing the faith of the audience itself, an interpretation sometimes embraced by commentators (Mayor 1913, 79; Ropes 1916, 187; McKnight 2011, 176–77; Allison 2013, 381, due to textual emendation discussed on 382–84), but an objective genitive reading that understands the faith(fulness) as that of Jesus Christ is preferable (Hartin 2003, 116–17; Johnson 1995, 220).

Next, in 2:2-7 James presents a series of rhetorical questions rooted in a hypothetical (yet very realistic; Allison 2013, 377, 384) scenario of responses to socioeconomic disparity: does one not demonstrate such illicit partiality if a rich person and a poor person (both readily identifiable by their attire) were to enter the assembly and be treated differently by those present?[15] If so, James levels the charge that those who behave in such a way are "judges with evil thoughts" (2:4). Indeed, such inequitable behavior conflicts with God's own evaluations of the rich and the poor. The author prefaces this charge in 2:5 with the imperative *akousate* ("Listen!"), a term that often appears in the LXX and elsewhere to signal the importance of words that follow (see extensive lists of examples in Hartin 2003, 119; Johnson 1995, 224; Allison 2013, 394–95). Next come two rhetorical questions. In the first, the author calls his audience to see that the rich are those who oppress, exploit, and blaspheme (2:6-7).[16] On

---

15. The described response to the rich and poor in 2:3 concerns their seating: the rich person is offered a place of honor and comfort, whereas the poor person is disrespectfully told to "stand there" or "sit at my feet" (so NRSV; cf. the image of subjugation of enemies in Ps 110:1). Interpreters disagree about how to understand the nature of the *synagōgē*, "assembly" (NRSV), in which the scene is set. Does the term here denote chiefly a gathering of people or else a physical building in which people met? (The latter is perhaps implied in those manuscripts that include a definite article before *synagōgē*.) Should the context be understood as one of worship, whether a Jewish synagogue or Christian church (if such a distinction can yet be made), or is the setting more akin to a judicial court or a communal gathering for resolution of disputes? (Both worship and communal activities commonly occurred in Jewish synagogue buildings.) Likewise, what kind of rich person is envisioned: an "insider" (whether Jewish or Christian) such as a wealthy patron, or a visiting "outsider"? These options are much discussed in standard commentaries and need not be detailed here, but Johnson (1995, 228) notes a rabbinic tradition in 'Avot R. Nat. 1:10 that identifies inequitable arrangements of seating and standing for litigants with judicial injustice (cf. the similar comments in Sifra Lev 200 and b. Shev. 30a–b noted by Allison 2013, 378). In recent decades Ward (1969) collected numerous rabbinic texts to support this kind of judicial approach within a Jewish synagogue and has convinced many; Allison (2013, 370–72) finds this proposal already in commentaries dating to the seventeenth century and suggests that it accords well with architectural considerations implied in the text of James (386–88).

16. Similar characterizations of the rich appear elsewhere in James and are common in the LXX and other Jewish texts, e.g., Prov 14:21, "the one who dishonors the poor commits sin"; Sir 10:23, "it is not right to dishonor one who is poor but intelligent"; numerous others are noted by Johnson 1995, 225–26; and Hartin 2003, 117. For biblical and later Jewish ideas about the name of God, see Allison 2013, 399.

the other hand, the *poor*—deemed worthless by the "world" (Hartin 2003, 117; this understanding of *tō kosmō* is preferable to the NRSV's "in the world," which implies geographical location)—are *rich* in faith and heirs of God's kingdom (cf. biblical promises of "inheritance" in Gen 28:4; Ps 15:5 LXX; 36:18; Johnson 1995, 225). The poor are beloved and blessed by God because of their pious reliance upon him (2:5), a theme with strong biblical precedents (see Davids 1982, 111, for extensive references to biblical and other texts). Even the question "has not God chosen the poor" exudes biblical language, because the same verb (*eklegomai*) is used frequently in the LXX for God's election of Israel as his people (Johnson 1995, 224). This preference for the poor does not violate the impartiality of God because God acts to correct prevailing injustices (Allison 2013, 395).

James continues in 2:8, "You do well if you really fulfill the royal law according to the scripture, 'You shall love your neighbor as yourself.'" The quotation reflects the LXX translation of Lev 19:18, and in Jewish exegetical tradition the command was held in especially high esteem as a summary either of the torah as a whole or of the sixth through tenth commandments of the Decalogue (Allison 2013, 406–8).[17] The designation "royal law" (not used in the LXX, but cf. Esth 3:8 and 4 Ezra 7:26; Allison 2013, 402) raises several questions for interpreters, including the meaning of "royal" (*basilikos*) and whether this appellation is applied to the specific Levitical command quoted or else to a broader, more encompassing understanding of torah; these options need not be detailed here, but note that Philo of Alexandria called the word of God "the royal road" (*Post.* 101–102; cited by Allison 2013, 404). Allison (2013, 402) observes, "Given the conventional status of Lev 19.18 as the most important principle in the Torah, that verse is a part that stands for the whole, and James seems to be writing about both part and whole simultaneously." Likewise, interpreters debate whether *kata tēn graphēn* ("according to the scripture") functions to identify the quotation of Lev 19:18 explicitly as a biblical citation (Ropes 1916, 199; Hartin 2003, 121; Allison 2013, 408) or else is another way (perhaps in addition to "royal") to speak broadly about the Mosaic law as

---

17. Allison also notes the observation of Jackson-McCabe 2001, 169–76, that Jas 2:10 demands fidelity to "the whole law," and that of Kloppenborg 2005, 210–11, that both this quotation and the subsequent use in Jas 2:19 of language from Deut 6:4, often viewed as a summary for the first five commandments, are followed in James with the affirmation *kalōs poieite*, "you do well."

a whole, with the implication that the command of Lev 19:18 accords with the thrust of the entire scriptural message (Johnson 1995, 231).

After this quotation, the author of James then notes that one who shows partiality commits sin and thus is a transgressor of the law (2:9). Acts of favoritism are not minor issues that can be separated from one's ethics and obedience overall: one who "really" (*mentoi*) fulfills the royal law (2:8) does not show partiality (Johnson 1995, 236). The implication is that acts of favoritism violate not only the particular teaching of Lev 19:18 but even the entire law, perhaps because of the representative importance of this particular command (as suggested by Allison 2013, 410–11). Regardless, the author of James is quick to rule out compartmentalization of sins by adding in 2:10 that "whoever keeps the whole law but fails in one point has become accountable for all of it." Davids (1982, 116) traces this "unitary conception of the law" to Deut 27:26 LXX and (like Johnson 1995, 232; Hartin 2003, 122) finds it expressed frequently in later Jewish texts. Also, it is likely that the author of James here (and already in Jas 2:1, with the first mention of favoritism) has the broader context of Lev 19 in mind, as Lev 19:15 reads, "You shall not render an unjust judgment; you shall not be partial to the poor or defer to the great: with justice you shall judge your neighbor." Regardless, this understanding of accountability for law disobedience prompts the second biblical quotation in Jas 2:11, now of two divine commands from the Decalogue, those forbidding adultery and murder. These words are introduced implicitly but clearly as the words of God ("For the one who said … also said"), so again we find something of a citation formula, indeed an especially personal one emphasizing that "to break a commandment is to sin against its divine source" while it also evokes the tradition of God speaking the laws directly at Sinai (Allison 2013, 414–15). The precise wording of the individual parts of the quotation may reflect either Exod 20:13–15 or Deut 5:17–18, but the Greek translation differs slightly from the wording of the LXX in that James uses aorist subjunctives for the prohibitions rather than the future tense, even if the epistle follows the LXX sequence for these two commands.[18] Again the ultimate point is that violation of one divine command (here murder)

---

18. Interpreters routinely note that the sequence of these (and the command against theft) differs in the MT (of both Exodus and Deuteronomy), the LXX of Exodus, and the LXX of Deuteronomy. These differences also extend to the traditional verse numbers assigned to each command, such that the versification of this section of Exodus differs in the MT and LXX. Allison (2013, 415) provides details on the differ-

while upholding another (here adultery) nevertheless makes one a law-breaker (2:11).[19]

The author concludes in 2:12–13 with a challenge for those in his audience to consider their speech and behavior in light of their own impending judgment. They will be judged by God according to the "law of liberty" (2:12; cf. Jas 1:25).[20] Those who show no mercy will themselves be denied mercy. Translation of the concluding phrase of verse 13 is complicated by numerous textual variants, but the NRSV's rendering "mercy triumphs over judgment" is typical. The importance of mercy (*eleos*, used in the LXX to translate the Hebrew *hesed*, God's loving kindness for humanity), including the relationship between mercy and one's own future judgment, is a common theme in Jewish wisdom literature (e.g., Sir 3:20; 27:30–28:7; Tob 4:9–11; 14:9; Ps.-Phoc. 11; T. Zeb. 5:3; 8:1–3), and mercy has a close association with concern for the poor (including almsgiving, a major topic in Tobit; cf. Sir 29:1; 18:13; Johnson 1995, 234; Davids 1982, 119; Allison 2013, 423).

We have noted already the importance of Lev 19 for this discussion of favoritism in James, particularly the use of the explicit citation of Lev 19:18 and the implied but very significant impact on the entire topic wielded by Lev 19:15. Johnson (1982) builds on earlier but underdeveloped observations of several previous scholars to argue that the tentacles of Lev 19 extend even further into this epistle, and in a way that parallels the very similar usage of the biblical materials in the Jewish wisdom text Pseudo-Phocylides.[21] Brief consideration of his argument here is helpful to demonstrate yet again how rooted James is in Jewish exegetical traditions.

Like James, Pseudo-Phocylides is a text marked by its focus on issues of practical life, presented in the form of poetic "sentences." Ber-

---

ent arrangements but also downplays the significance of the variation in James, which may "just be paraphrasing, so that the order means little or nothing."

19. Note the later accusations that some commit adultery in Jas 4:4 and murder in Jas 5:6.

20. Cf. the description of the "law of liberty" as "perfect" in Jas 1:25. Johnson (1995, 209) notes frequent comments in praise of God's law in Scripture and subsequent Jewish texts.

21. See the recent assessment of Pseudo-Phocylides by Derron (2010), who notes that most scholars now date the book between the first century BCE and the first century CE (before 70 CE). See also the introduction and translation by van der Horst (1985) in *OTP*. Johnson does not argue that the author of James utilized Pseudo-Phocylides as a literary source. Instead, he describes their similar use of Lev 19 as "analogous" (1982, 391).

nays argued in 1856 that Ps.-Phoc. 9–21 reflects a poetic recasting of Lev 19:12–19, even if no explicit quotations appear, and more recently van der Horst (1978) has affirmed the relationship. The author of Pseudo-Phocylides seems not to have used the portion of Lev 19:18 cited in Jas 2:8, but the impact of Lev 19:15 is evident when the author discusses the issue of judging others. Overall the use of material from Leviticus in this text is quite subtle and perhaps does not demand that one acknowledge the connection between the texts when only individual points of contact are considered, but Johnson (1982, 392–93) argues that the dense cluster of thematic correspondences between Lev 19 and Ps.-Phoc. 9–21 (including topics that seem unrelated otherwise, such as perjury, partiality, and oppression) indicates that such a connection is indeed warranted.

Dibelius (1976, 142, 238, 248) had suggested certain parallels between James and Pseudo-Phocylides in his commentary on James that first appeared in German in 1921. Prompted by this and similar observations, Johnson argues that James's significant dependence on Lev 19 can be demonstrated in the same way others presented such in Pseudo-Phocylides: by identifying clusters of relationships that collectively prove decisive. Ultimately Johnson argues for the following seven correspondences (adapted from 1982, 399):

Leviticus	James
19:12	5:12
19:13	5:2
19:15	2:1, 9
19:16	4:11
19:17b	5:20 (tentative)
19:18a	5:9 (tentative)
19:18b	2:8

He concludes that

> the only verse from this section of Leviticus which is missing is 19:14. The evidence, therefore, strongly suggests that James made conscious and sustained use of Lev 19:12–18 in his letter … the clear thematic connections, together with the formal characteristics involving law, judgment and prohibition shared by many of these passages, point this way: that James regarded the "Royal Law" by which Christians were to live, and the "Law of Liberty" by which they were to be judged, as explicated concretely and specifically not only by the Decalogue (2:11),

but by the immediate context of the Law of Love, the commands found
in Lev 19:12-18. (1982, 399)

If so, this demonstrates yet again how fully enmeshed James is with biblical thought and Jewish traditions.

James 2:14-26, Genesis 15:6, and Abraham Traditions
Concerning Faith and Works

James 2:14-26 also features a direct biblical quotation, but it adds appeals
to biblical characters that are shaped by centuries of reflection in Jewish
tradition. This passage has often been read from perspectives that privilege understandings of faith and works rooted in interpretation of Paul,
with the result that James is assumed to contradict the more familiar theological insights of that prolific apostle. Admittedly what follows will note
some differences in James and Paul, but the purpose is not to cast the two
perspectives in conflict.[22] Rather, the goal is to appreciate more fully how
James understands the story of Abraham (in particular) in the context of
traditional Jewish interpretation.[23]

Scholars debate the intrinsic connection (if any) between this passage
and the previous 2:1-13, but the opening scenario in 2:14-17 certainly
resonates with the prior context of social needs, and overall the literary
structures of the two texts have several parallels. Reminiscent of the initial
comment in 2:1 about whether acts of favoritism are consistent with the
faith of Jesus Christ, here in 2:14 the author opens by asking his hypothetical diatribe partner what benefit comes if someone claims faith but lacks
corresponding works.[24] Then, as in 2:2, the author moves immediately

---

22. See Allison 2013, 426-28, for a brief summary of major positions on the relationship between Paul and James (followed subsequently by detailed discussion of
several specific interpretive debates). Unlike many recent commentators, Allison
(444-57) argues that numerous textual factors imply that James indeed is a response
to Paul. DeSilva (2012, 49-52) also proposes that James is a response to Paul, but a
very early one "quite plausibly written before the issues in the debate are fully clarified,
indeed in the heat of the debate" (51).

23. See Hansen 1989 for a helpful survey of Abraham traditions in postbiblical
Jewish literature. On Abraham in the Hebrew Bible, see esp. Blenkinsopp 2015.

24. Johnson (1983, 238) aptly notes: "It is God who saves humans (4:12) but the
person who has received the word from God that saves and puts it into action in deeds
of mercy (2:18-26) and prayer (5:15) and mutual correction (5:20) 'saves his soul from

to present a realistic, socially conscious, hypothetical scenario: a brother or sister in need of essential clothing and food encounters someone who offers only well-wishes and no tangible assistance.[25] The author enhances the cultural plausibility of the scene when the unwilling benefactor says, "Go in peace; keep warm and eat your fill." "Go in peace" was a common and respectable Hebrew farewell often noted in biblical and subsequent literature (Judg 18:6; 1 Sam 29:7; Jdt 8:35; Davids 1982, 122; Hartin 2003, 150; Johnson 1995, 239), but when combined with hollow wishes of fulfillment of one's explicitly unmet needs (here warmth and satiation), it rang comparable to the much-disdained "thoughts and prayers" response (without accompanying tangible actions) to the modern American plague of gun violence. Such a response would strike James's biblically formed audience as hypocritical (Hartin 2003, 150) and would be crassly offensive for those rooted in the Hebrew prophetic tradition and Jewish emphasis on the importance of charity (Davids 1982, 122). The author of James forcefully mocks such a response ("What is the good of that?"); he then declares in 2:17, "So faith *by itself*, if it has no works, is dead" (NRSV, emphasis added).

The voice of an interlocutor then declares in 2:18, "You have faith and I have works." Scholars find this perplexing: normally interlocutors voice positions that *oppose* those held by the author, but here the speaker seems to claim for himself the "works" so prized in James (thus Johnson 1995, 240: "the positions appear illogically reversed"; Allison 2013, 468–71, summarizes twelve possible interpretative approaches). Yet in the next verse it seems that James charges him with an empty claim of faith instead. Even though the Greek of verse 18 specifies that the contrasting positions are held by "you" (*su*) followed by "and I" (*kagō*, contracted from *kai egō*), a popular solution to this interpretative dilemma (proposed by, e.g., Ropes 1916, 208–14; Dibelius 1976, 155–56; and endorsed by numerous others) is to read the statement as if to mean "someone claims to have faith and

---

death.'" He compares the perspective in James to approaches in 2 Bar. 14:12; 24:1; 51:7; and 4 Ezra 7:77; 8:32–36; 9:7; 13:23.

25. Allison (2013, 464) lists numerous Jewish texts urging care for those lacking clothes and food. Note that both "brother" and "sister" are named explicitly in this scene; this mention of persons of both genders is not the result of gender-inclusive translation. Normal practice in ancient literature would be to use just a masculine example. Allison (2013, 463) suggests that James specifies both brother and sister to heighten the emphasis on the "human objects of compassion" and because women were especially numerous among the needy in James's world.

someone else claims to have works." If so, the statement simply points to differing positions without ascribing one to the interlocutor particularly and the other to the voice of James. While admittedly the author could have articulated that meaning more clearly in Greek, this interpretation does allow one to read the statement as a (false) claim that faith and works are not intrinsically related. This indeed seems to be the position that is rebutted immediately by James: "Show me your faith apart from your works, and I by my works will show you my faith" (2:18).

James is not yet finished with the interlocutor. He now charges in response, "You believe that God is one; you do well. Even the demons believe—and shudder" (2:19).[26] The interlocutor's intellectual nod to doctrinal orthodoxy—which James considers to be insufficient—is affirmed with words reminiscent of the Shema, the foundational Jewish affirmation of monotheism from Deut 6:4 (Davids 1982, 125; Johnson 1995, 240; see both for subsequent references in Jewish literature).[27] James then offers two biblical examples to illustrate his point "that faith apart from works is barren" (2:20).[28]

Abraham provides the major example (2:21–24), followed by Rahab (2:25). The author of James presumes that his audience will know both their biblical stories and the ways these have been interpreted in widespread Jewish tradition. Indeed, both characters came to be praised in such traditions for their hospitality (Abraham, toward the angelic visitors at Mamre in Gen 18; Rahab, toward the Hebrew spies at Jericho in Josh 2)

---

26. Davids (1982, 125–26) notes Jewish texts that describe various figures "shuddering" before God but that such demonic responses are significantly more common in later Christian compositions. Allison (2013, 477) discusses similarly and notes that James seems to be the first author to associate such shuddering of demons with faith. Originally *daimonion* could refer to both good and evil spiritual beings, but in Second Temple period Jewish texts and the New Testament only the latter was the norm. See also Stokes, ch. 10 in this volume, for discussion of how James understands evil spiritual powers.

27. Note again the statement "you do well," used earlier in 2:8 when James states that assent to the teaching of Lev 19:18 is similarly inadequate if not expressed tangibly.

28. Here faith without works is *argē* (feminine form of *argos*; BDAG "useless," "worthless"; NRSV "barren"). Such faith is instead deemed *nekra* ("dead") in 2:17, 26. Surely this is the reason a significant number of manuscripts have the variant reading *nekra* in 2:20, despite the attractive wordplay of *argē* and *ergōn* ("works"; Davids 1982, 126). Johnson (1995, 242) notes a different kind of wordplay: *argos* sounds like a negation (performed in Greek with the prefix *a-*) of *ergon*, "work" or "deed."

and embrace of God as proselytes from their pagan backgrounds (Abraham left Mesopotamian traditions when called by God, Gen 11:31; 12:1, a topic for significant expansion and elaboration in texts including Jub. 11–12 and Apoc. Ab. 1–8; Rahab was a Canaanite of Jericho). Presumably these two factors contribute to their linkage here in James (Davids 1982, 132–33; see esp. 128 on traditions about Abraham's conversion; and Hartin 2003, 156, 161 for those concerning Rahab).[29]

James introduces and concludes his discussion of these figures by asserting that they prove his thesis that faith without works is "barren" (2:20) and "dead" (2:26; cf. 2:17). Yet, along the way he introduces the language of justification (with the verb *dikaioō*), such that both Abraham (2:21) and Rahab (2:25) are said to have been "justified by works," and the intermediate summary statement between their two stories affirms the principle that "a person is justified by works and not by faith [*pisteōs*] alone." Thus, the point comes into even sharper focus: the issue is not just the *correlation* of faith and works that benefit others, but also the *effective function* of works as proof and validation of true faith (so Johnson 1995, 242, who reads *dikaioō* in this passage as "shown to be righteous"). This language shift happens because in 2:23 James utilizes a prominent biblical quotation from Gen 15:6, "Abraham believed [*episteusen*] God, and it was reckoned to him as righteousness [*dikaiosunēn*]." The verbal links between Gen 15:6 and James's thesis concern themes of faith and believing (noun *pistis*, verb *pisteuō*) and of righteousness and justification (noun *dikaiosunē*, verb *dikaioō*). James uses this quotation in a way that accords strongly with traditional Jewish interpretation but differs significantly from Paul's use of the same words in Gal 3:6 and Rom 4:3.[30]

James begins the discussion of Abraham in 2:21 by asking, "Was not our ancestor [literally "father"] Abraham justified by works when he offered his son Isaac on the altar?" Here Abraham is called "father," a term

---

29. Some scholars question the hospitality link, including Ellis (2015, 199–210) and R. Foster (2014, 59–103), who argue instead that the two characters exemplify endurance through trials. See additional discussion in Kamell Kovalishyn 2018b, 1039–40. Allison (2013, 500–501) notes that discussion of Rahab in Second Temple period texts is rare, perhaps because of her shameful occupation; Josephus, *A.J.* 5.5–30, is an exception and presents her as an innkeeper. Allison also surveys *fifteen* suggestions for why James links Abraham and Rahab (501–4).

30. It seems likely that the author of Hebrews also has Gen 15:6 in mind when he discusses Abraham in 6:13–15 and esp. 11:8–22, but the verse is not cited explicitly.

of endearment that likely sprang from Gen 17:4–5 ("ancestor [father] of a multitude of nations") and became prominent in later Jewish tradition (see Davids 1982, 126; Hartin 2003, 153 for details). Similarly, Abraham is called "friend [*philos*] of God," another idea with biblical roots (Isa 41:8; 2 Chr 20:7) that figured prominently in later Jewish thought (e.g., T. Abr. 15:13–14 A; Davids 1982, 130; Hartin 2003, 155).[31] More significantly, though, James links Abraham's justification by works with the account in Gen 22:1–19, when he responded willingly to God's call that he sacrifice his son.[32] This story, called the Akedah (or Aqedah; "binding") in Jewish tradition, was utilized in numerous ways in a vast multitude of Jewish texts in the Second Temple and rabbinic periods (Ripley 2010).[33] It came to be hailed as the great example of Abraham's faithfulness to God as demonstrated through a series of ten tests (see, e.g., Jub. 17:17–18; 19:2–8; m. Avot 5:3; cf. Heb 11:17–19; Kugel 1997, 167–68; Davids 1982, 127; see the extensive list of texts discussing the tests in Allison 2013, 288–89 n. 367).[34] Despite the fact that language of justification does not appear in the Gen 22 account itself, it was read as the preeminent explanation of how Abraham demonstrated that he "believed God" with the result that "it was reckoned to him as righteousness" (Gen 15:6).[35] As the author of 1 Macc 2:52 states clearly but concisely, "Was not Abraham found faithful when tested, and it was reckoned to him as righteousness?"[36]

---

31. Johnson (1995, 244) observes that the LXX does not use *philos* in either Isa 41:8 or 2 Chr 20:7, but Philo uses the term in his paraphrase of Gen 18:17 in *Sobr.* 56 and elsewhere calls Abraham *theophilēs* ("friend of God") in *Abr.* 19.9. See also the extensive list of "friend" references in Allison 2013, 494 n. 403.

32. Hartin (2003, 154) notes several verbal correspondences between the Greek of Gen 22:1–19 LXX and Jas 2:21–23.

33. The Akedah is especially prominent in 4 Maccabees (esp. 16:16–21 but also frequently elsewhere), a text in praise of faithfulness in martyrdom and an expansion of 2 Macc 6:18–7:42. Perhaps surprisingly in light of the context, emphasis is placed on Abraham's faithful willingness to *kill* his son, though Isaac is also hailed for his bravery.

34. Commentators on James debate whether the plural "works" of Abraham in Jas 2:21 intentionally alludes to such a series of tests.

35. See Allison 2013, 491–92, for discussion of interpretations of Gen 15:6 in Second Temple period Jewish texts. Also, though comments about God's faithfulness to Abraham are common in the Jewish Scriptures, only one text in the Hebrew Bible outside of Gen 12–25 praises Abraham for his own faithfulness to God. This occurs in Neh 9:7–8, a prayer directed to God!

36. Compare Sir 44:19–21. Admittedly this is a poetic text, but it may imply the idea that the promises of God about Abraham's descendants (uttered at various points

For James, then, the answer to the question "Was not ... Abraham justified by works?" is "yes!" As such, the author writes in Jas 2:22, "You see that faith was active along with his works, and faith was brought to completion [*eteleiōthē*] by the works." This is thus proved—and Scripture is fulfilled [*eplērōthē*]—because Gen 15:6 affirmingly states that "Abraham believed God, and it was reckoned to him as righteousness." As noted above, Paul used this same quotation in Gal 3:6 and Rom 4:3, but he does so to support his arguments that both gentiles and Jews are deemed righteous on the basis of faith. Interpreters debate whether the dimension of faith Paul so emphasized should be understood as the believer's own trusting response to God or else reliance on the faith(fulness) of Jesus, exemplified by his death on the cross. Either way, though, for Paul the point is that God ultimately is concerned with faith rather than "works of the law," which in recent decades are increasingly understood by scholars as particular social "boundary" aspects of the Jewish law (like circumcision and observance of dietary laws) that functioned positively to identify publicly practicing Jews as devoted to God, but negatively if such things were viewed as essentials in addition to faith for non-Jews who were also believers in Christ.[37] Thus Paul makes chronologically based arguments that center on Gen 15:6—God considered Abraham to be righteous (i.e., God justified him) simply because Abraham believed (i.e., had faith), long before the biblical narrative mentions anything about circumcision (Gen 17:9-14, so Paul's argument in Rom 4:1-12) or the Sinai law (Exod 20 and beyond, so Paul's argument in Gal 3:6-18). Paul's methodologies for making such arguments certainly fit in the context of Jewish exegetical methods, but his results do not when applied specifically to the figure of Abraham, because Jewish tradition overwhelmingly read Gen 15:6 as ultimately demonstrated and fulfilled when the patriarch is willing even to sacrifice his promised son in Gen 22 in the Akedah. This is also how

---

in Gen 12-17) were offered *after* Abraham demonstrated his faithfulness: "Abraham was the great father of a multitude of nations, and no one has been found like him in glory. He kept the law of the Most High, and entered into a covenant with him; he certified the covenant in his flesh, and when he was tested he proved faithful. Therefore the Lord [literally "he"] assured him with an oath that the nations would be blessed through his offspring; that he would make him as numerous as the dust of the earth, and exalt his offspring like the stars, and give them an inheritance from sea to sea and from the Euphrates to the ends of the earth."

37. Dunn (1983) is most associated with this approach. As such, Paul's "works of the law" are very different things than James's "works."

James reads that quotation: Abraham's faith is proved by his proper behavior. So, the author can assert in Jas 2:24 (with interpretive expansions added), "You see that a person is justified by works [i.e., obedient actions of mercy and justice that are consistent with one's claim to faith] and not by faith alone [i.e., claims of devotion to God that are not substantiated by actions consistent with such a profession]." To this James can briefly add the example of Rahab, the prostitute of Jericho who in Josh 2 sheltered the Hebrew spies (called "messengers" in Jas 2:25) sent to scout the city before the Israelite attack. James concludes, "For just as the body without spirit is dead, so faith without works is also dead."[38]

Conclusion

My goal has been to demonstrate some of the rich and permeating ways that Scripture and other nonbiblical Jewish interpretive traditions are utilized by the author of James in this epistle. James can quote Scripture, but even more frequently he seamlessly weaves biblical words or ideas into his own exhortations to Christian faithfulness. Likewise, he can point to biblical figures that exemplify particular ethical virtues that model the way of life he commends for followers of Jesus. None of this diminishes the distinctive voice or profound contributions of the author of James himself, but rather it highlights how he uses Scripture and other traditions as vital foundations (along with Jesus traditions and other sources) of his own exhortations.

---

38. Davids (1982, 133) suggests that this language of "body" and "spirit" may reflect Gen 2:7.

The Letter of James and Hellenistic Philosophy

Matt Jackson-McCabe

While the Letter of James is often considered one of the most Jewish works of the New Testament, the implied alternative is not so much Hellenism as Christianism.[1] In fact, James's Hellenistic character is no less obvious than its Jewish character. Scholars have long noted the relative polish of its Greek language and style, its reflection of Hellenistic rhetorical conventions, and its appeal to imagery and ideas typical of Greco-Roman moralists and philosophers. Such a synthesis of Judean and Hellenistic cultures is of course far from surprising in a text of this era, which saw the production of any number of such syntheses in works ranging from historiography and scriptural interpretation, to oracular and testamentary literature, to wisdom writings and letters (Hengel 1974; Collins 2000). The question where the Letter of James is concerned, then, is not whether it is Hellenistic, but the nature and extent of its Hellenism.

The question is complicated by its intersection with the classic problems of James's authorship and literary character, and, more subtly, by its canonical status. For those inclined to affirm the letter's traditional ascription to the brother of Jesus, its Hellenistic character is a cause of consternation.[2] How likely is it that an artisan-class man from Nazareth would have become sufficiently at home in the literary culture of the Greco-Roman

---

1. E.g., Ropes 1916, 27–28: "The most striking fact about this epistle is the paucity in it of allusions and ideas and interests which were peculiar to any particular phase of early Christianity.... The writer's position is fundamentally that of later Judaism." See already Luther's assessment (*LW* 35:395–97); more recently Allison 2013, 88–94; Kloppenborg 2007a. Some late nineteenth- and early twentieth-century interpreters concluded that the text's references to Jesus (1:1; 2:1) must have been later additions (Massebieau 1895; Spitta 1896; Meyer 1930). I am grateful to Dale Walker for very helpful comments on an earlier draft of this essay.

2. In my view, the text of James is more easily explained as the work of a pseud-

world to produce a text such as this? While some are content to argue for the possibility, the lingering problem of probability has led others to hypothesize the existence of a mediating hand that added a Hellenistic veneer to James's own, more purely "Jewish-Christian" material (e.g., Mayor 1913, cclxiv–xv; Sevenster 1968; see further Jackson-McCabe 2009). A different version of this "superficial Hellenism" thesis was advanced by Dibelius. He also posited the compilation and editing of source materials by a native Greek speaker (Dibelius 1976, 17). But in his view, that earlier material consisted of traditions the editor pseudonymously attributed to James—traditions that already included philosophical concepts (Dibelius 1976, 1–26). Nonetheless, Dibelius insisted that this told us nothing about the writer's own thinking; on the contrary, the author "used various materials whose provenance was unknown to him, or even intrinsically alien to him" (1976, 21). Consequently, the philosophical terms in James are taken as little more than fossilized shells, emptied of their original significance and filled with an entirely new and uniquely Christian meaning.[3]

While these theses regarding a postulated original layer of material behind the Letter of James could scarcely be more different, the end result is strikingly consistent. On either reading, James's Hellenistic character is effectively reduced to a matter of mere form—the discursive flesh, as it were, in which a uniquely Christian content becomes incarnate. The not incidental outcome of both theories is the creation of space for a hermeneutical assumption that the real, generative heart of the letter is something that cannot be found in Greco-Roman (or for that matter, Jewish) culture: a distinctly Christian essence that links James fundamentally to other New Testament works while simultaneously separating it (and them) from their wider cultural environment—a postulated essence, however precisely understood, for which the term *gospel* often serves as cipher.

Though fundamental to much of the history of the letter's interpretation, this assumption has become increasingly untenable for scholars who approach the study of early Christianity not as theologians, but as historians of culture. In an academic climate where Judaism, Hellenism, and

---

onymous author (Jackson-McCabe 2009, 613–23). In what follows, then, references to *James* are to the letter, not the brother of Jesus.

3. James's concept of *emphytos logos* is especially singled out at this point: "Even if 'the implanted word' … in 1:21 should actually prove to be an echo of Stoic terminology, the expression as James used it had obviously already been given a new meaning by the Christians" (Dibelius 1976, 21).

Christianism are analyzed as socially constructed terms of identity rather than distinct ontological realities (e.g., Hall 2002; Lieu 2002; Collins 2017), the question of the relationship of the Letter of James to Hellenistic philosophy is ripe for reconsideration. In what follows, I will suggest that the Hellenistic traits long noted by James's readers signal a work as thoroughly embedded in the Greco-Roman as in the Jewish discourse of its time. The influence of popular Hellenistic philosophy in particular is reducible neither to superficial matters of form and style, nor to the presence of discrete terms somehow drained of their original significance. As in so many other texts of its era, Greek philosophical concepts and elements of Judean culture are mutually interpretive in the Letter of James, fused inseparably within its ethical vision.

Judaism and Hellenism in James

Interpreters of James routinely emphasize its Jewish character, and with good reason. It assumes the existence of the God of the Jewish Scriptures, portraying him as the creator of the world (1:17–18; 3:9), as "lawgiver and judge" (4:12), and as one whose elect "poor" would be the "inheritors" of a "kingdom he promised to those who love him" (2:5).[4] It also assumes the existence of the devil as God's superhuman nemesis (4:7–8), and a messiah, Jesus, who will come from heaven at an impending final judgment (1:1; 2:1; see also 5:7–9). Its ethical instruction is issued in light of this judgment, which is to be executed according to the standard of the torah (2:8–13; see also 4:11; 5:1–6, 7–9). The audience of this instruction, identified as "the twelve tribes in the diaspora" (1:1), is imagined as fellow descendants of "Abraham our father" (2:21), and its paradigmatic heroes are likewise taken from the Jewish Scriptures (2:21–25; 5:10–11, 17–18). The letter, in fact, contains no obvious signs that it was produced by someone who considered being a "slave of the Lord Jesus Christ" (1:1) or part of God's elect "poor" (2:5) to be in any way implicated in the sort of disavowal of Judaism advocated by Ignatius of Antioch and other early proponents of "Christianism."[5]

---

4. Translations of James are my own unless otherwise noted. Translations of Philo and classical sources are from LCL unless otherwise noted.

5. The concept of "Christianism" (*Christianismos*) is first evident in the letters of Ignatius, who formulates it precisely in antithesis to "Judaism" (*Magn.* 10.1–3; 8.1; *Phld.* 6.1). Compare Hartin 2003, 204: "The writer of [James] clearly sees himself as

James's Hellenistic character is equally clear. It was composed in Greek, not translated into it, in a manner that has been described as "approaching more nearly to the standard of classical purity than that of any other book of the New Testament with the exception perhaps of the Epistle to the Hebrews" (Mayor 1913, ccxliv; see also Ropes 1916, 24–27; Dibelius 1976, 34–38; Johnson 1995, 7–10). While its instructional character and fondness for aphorisms have generated frequent comparisons to Jewish wisdom literature, James's formal composition is more akin to Greco-Roman prose than to the poetic structures that often characterize wisdom texts.[6] In particular, scholars have long noted its formal similarities to the Hellenistic diatribe (e.g., Ropes 1916, 6–18; Dibelius 1976, 1, 38; Johnson 1995, 9–10), an instructional style especially characteristic of the philosophical moralists of the era (Stowers 1988). Interpreters in recent decades have also shown how particular sections of the letter conform to patterns of elaboration advocated by Hellenistic rhetoricians (Watson 1993a; 1993b; Wachob 2000).

James's Hellenistic character, moreover, extends well beyond mere form. Luke Timothy Johnson's commentary, for example, provides "overwhelming evidence that at the level of individual themes, James shares substantially in the moral teaching of the Greco-Roman world" (1995, 27).[7] Such themes, moreover, are integrated seamlessly into those derived from Jewish tradition. The ruminations on the dangers of uncontrolled speech in Jas 3:1–12, which is among the clearest examples of James's conformity to ancient rhetorical practice (Watson 1993b), is a prime example. Speech ethics were as prevalent among Greco-Roman moralists as in the Jewish wisdom literature (e.g., Baker 1995), making it a natural and perhaps par-

---

part of Second Temple Israelite religious thought and traditions while at the same time being a follower of Jesus. The writer did not see a contradiction between these two groups."

6. Jewish wisdom is at any rate less a well-defined genre than "a tradition, held together by certain family resemblances rather than by a constant essence" (Collins 1997, 1).

7. While Johnson's commentary is particularly good on this score, the reader will find a variety of such evidence in most critical commentaries; compare Allison 2013, 55: "as this commentary confirms again and again, James and Philo have so much in common because they draw from the common river of Hellenistic-Jewish tradition." Also noteworthy in the present context is the more specific finding of Mayor (1913, cclxv): "the writer was acquainted ... with the principles of the Stoic philosophy"; see also Boyle 1985.

ticularly appealing topic in a work like James. The section is developed with reference to ideas derived unmistakably from Jewish culture. A passing allusion is made to gehenna as a place of mythological fire (3:6); and the notion that people were made "according to the likeness of God" (3:9, *kath' homoiōsin theou*) clearly echoes Gen 1:26–27 LXX (*kath' homoiōsin*), as apparently does the immediately preceding catalogue of animals (3:7; see also Allison 2013, 543). Nevertheless, the principal metaphors illustrating the section's core theme—the relationship between controlling the tongue and the ability "to bridle the whole body" (3:2)—are stock images of Hellenistic ethical discourse (e.g., Johnson 1995, 257–58): bridling horses (3:3), controlling ships (3:4), and blazing fires (3:5–6). These images are found repeatedly, for example, in Philo's voluminous writings, particularly in illustrations of reason's mastery over the soul; all three, in fact, are adduced side-by-side when Philo interprets the punishment of Adam in Gen 3:17 as an allegory of what happens when the soul is ruled by sense perception rather than the rational mind.[8] Plutarch similarly juxtaposes the metaphors of controlling ships and setting big fires with small flames precisely in his own essay on the problem of controlling speech (*Garr.* 507 A–B).

Nor, moreover, are such Jewish and Greek ideas merely juxtaposed to each other in James. As for Philo, rather, they are mutually interpretive. The otherwise undeveloped allusion to gehenna is adduced specifically to identify the ultimate source of a fire said to characterize an equally allusive "cycle of creation" (3:6, *ton trochon tēs geneseōs*). The latter phrase, which is as obviously derived from Greek philosophy as gehenna is from Judean culture, is apparently used with reference to the entirety of the transitory, material world (Dibelius 1976, 196–98; Allison 2013, 539–40).

---

8. *Leg.* 3.222–224 (Colson, slightly modified): "Let us observe ... [how Moses] discourses [in Gen 3:17] respecting Mind itself when acted upon in violation of right reason [*para ton orthon logon*] ... it is always right that the superior should rule and the inferior be ruled; and Mind is superior to Sense-perception. When the charioteer is in command and guides the horses with the reins, the chariot goes the way he wishes.... A ship, again, keeps to her straight course, when the helmsman grasping the tiller steers accordingly, but capsizes when a contrary wind has sprung up over the sea, and the surge has settled in it. Just so, when Mind, the charioteer and helmsman of the soul, rules the whole living being ...the life holds a straight course, but when irrational sense gains the chief place, a terrible confusion overtakes it ... for then, in very deed, the mind is set on fire and is all ablaze, and that fire is kindled by objects of sense which Sense-perception supplies."

The assertion of a causal connection between the present, transitory world and gehenna, via the human tongue, places both concepts in new light. Similarly, while James alludes to the story of God's creation of humanity in Genesis, it interprets that story on the patently Greek assumption that there is such a thing as a "human nature" (3:8, *tē physei tē anthrōpinē*) distinct from that of other animals (3:7, *pasa physis thēriōn*)—an assumption that was as foundational to Hellenistic philosophy and ethics as it was alien to pre-Hellenistic Judean discourse (Koester 1975, 251–77). Analogous refractions of Jewish scriptural tradition through the lenses of popular Hellenistic philosophy are evident elsewhere in James, as in connection with its recurring theme of "friendship with God" (2:23; 4:4–6; Johnson 1995, 27 and 243–44; Batten 2010, 48–54; Kaden 2014, 106–12). As John Kloppenborg (2010) has demonstrated, the letter interprets Jesus tradition, too, from this same point of view.

James, in sum, is both thoroughly Jewish and thoroughly Hellenistic. It is in this respect comparable to other texts of its era that were similarly concerned to convey a certain ethical wisdom to an audience of Jews living within the social and cultural order of the Roman Empire. While one can of course distinguish elements derived from Jewish and Greek cultures for analytical purposes, the substance of James's instruction, to use a chemical metaphor, is more akin to a compound than a mixture. Neither its ethical outlook nor the wider worldview in which it is bound up is finally resolvable into a simplistic dichotomy of Jewish or Hellenistic. The Letter of James, rather, is both/and.

Theology and Anthropology

There is widespread agreement among contemporary interpreters that James's ethical exhortations are informed by a more or less coherent worldview (e.g., Batten 2009, 54–64). Despite the absence of themes and ideas that feature prominently in, for example, the letters of Paul, James's ethical instruction is rooted in a basically coherent understanding of the human condition and its relationship to superhuman realities. As signaled already by the fact that humanity is understood to be both in the "likeness of God" and defined by a distinct "nature," the letter's theological and anthropological views represent a creative blending of ideas derived from Jewish culture on one hand and popular Hellenistic philosophy on the other.

Theology

The reality of the God of the Jewish people is among the most fundamental of the letter's assumptions. It surfaces repeatedly throughout the text, nowhere more obviously than in its allusions to the oft-cited Shema (2:19; 4:12; see also Deut 6:4 LXX; further Allison 2013, 473–74). As in these Scriptures, this God is identified as the creator—and thus in James's usage, "Father" (1:17–18; 3:9)—of the world. His relationship to the world, however, is seen through James's own interpretive lenses, which are colored in part by Jewish apocalyptic tradition. That relationship, accordingly, is not merely one of creator and created but involves a stark ethical opposition: God is characterized by righteousness (1:20, *dikaiosynēn*), and the world by "injustice" (3:6, *ho kosmos tēs adikias*). To be a "friend of the world" (*philos tou kosmou*), therefore, is to be an "enemy of God" (4:4; see also 2:23), while being "the poor with respect to the world" (*tous ptōchous tō kosmō*) means being "rich" in a higher sense, and indeed the elect "inheritors" of God's promised kingdom (2:5). This opposition is further reinforced by James's association of the world with evil superhuman beings—the devil and demons (2:19; 4:7)—and the correlation of these, in turn, with an "earthly" (*epigeios*) and "demonic" (*daimoniōdēs*) pseudo-wisdom marked by jealousy, instability, and social conflict (3:15–16). This contrasts with the true wisdom that "comes down from above" (3:15; see also 3:17), which is to say from God (see 1:17), and that is marked by purity, gentleness, and peace (3:17). Keeping oneself "untainted by the world" is thus of the very essence of "pure and undefiled piety before God" (1:27).

James's formulation of an opposition between God and the world is also, however, filtered through Hellenistic philosophical ideas. Some of the above-mentioned apocalyptic themes were themselves ripe for combination with the latter, such as the contrast between true and false wisdom and divine versus merely material riches.[9] Other elements of James's theology are in any case much more reminiscent of Hellenistic philosophy than these Jewish traditions. If the unjust world, as we have seen, is likened

---

9. Both are found, e.g., in Plato's *Republic*, which contrasts the pseudowisdom of Sophists with that of the true philosopher (493A–494A), as well as "the divine gold and silver from the gods" that one might have in "the soul" with merely "human gold and silver" (*Resp.* 416E). The Stoics in particular were known for claiming that it was only the sage who was truly rich (Brouwer 2014, 59–60).

to a transient "wheel of creation" (*trochon tes geneseōs*, 3:6), its righteous creator, in contrast, is not subject to change: The "Father of lights," in stark contrast to the heavenly bodies he creates, is unswervingly constant (1:17). As Allison (2013, 277) notes, such insistence on the unchanging nature of God is particularly characteristic of Greek philosophy and, consequently, those purveyors of Jewish tradition whose theological thinking had been colored by it. It is found repeatedly, for instance, in the writings of Philo, not least in the treatise he devoted to this very theme, *On the Unchange-ableness of God*. Elsewhere Philo draws an analogous contrast between God and creation: "that which is unwaveringly stable is God, and that which is subject to movement is creation [*hē genesis*]" (*Post.* 23).[10] Philo does this, moreover, precisely to make the point that humans should aspire to be like God, specifically by living in accord with right reason (*orthos logos*) rather than pursuing the desire (*epithymia*) and pleasures (*hēdonai*) of the body (*sōma*) that render one as unstable as a ship tossed on a stormy sea.[11]

James's analogous commitment to a principled separation of a perfectly good and stable God from the ephemeral world of human desires and its evils, in fact, leads it into a literal contradiction of the very Jewish texts it otherwise regards so highly (see Kloppenborg 2010, 66–67). The bald declaration in 1:13 that God "himself tempts [or: tests] no one" (*ho*

---

10. See also *Opif.* 151: "no created thing [*ouden tōn genesei*] is constant"; also *Leg.* 2.33: "Now every created thing must necessarily undergo change, for this is its property, even as unchangeableness is the property of God"; further Allison 2013, 278 n. 159.

11. *Post.* 22–27 (Colson and Whitaker): "The lawgiver indicates that the foolish man, being a creature of wavering and unsettled impulses, is subject to tossing and tumult, like the sea lashed by contrary winds when a storm is raging, ... And as at a time when a ship is tossing at the mercy of the sea, it is capable neither of sailing nor of riding at anchor, but pitched about this way and that ... even so the worthless man, with a mind reeling and storm-driven ... is always tossing, ready to make shipwreck of his life.... Proximity to a stable object produces a desire to be like it and a longing for quiescence. Now that which is unwaveringly stable is God, and that which is subject to movement is creation. He therefore that draws nigh to God longs for stability, but he that forsakes Him, inasmuch as he approaches unresting creation is, as we might expect, carried about.... For it is the nature of the foolish man to be ever moving contrary to right reason, and to be averse to rest and quietness, and never to plant himself firmly and fixedly on any principle.... [But] hope, being an expectation of good things, fastens the mind upon the bountiful God [*tou philodōrou theou*], whereas desire [*epithymia*], infusing irrational cravings fastens it upon the body, which Nature has wrought as a receptacle and abode of pleasures [*hēdonōn*]."

gar theos ... peirazei de autos oudena) flatly contradicts the Jewish Scriptures at several points, including the very story of Abraham's sacrifice of
Isaac that James will later feature prominently (Jas 2:22–24; cf. Gen 22:1
LXX, *ho theos epeirazen ton Abraam*; see Allison 2013, 237). This remarkable characterization of the God of the Jewish Scriptures, which caused
so much disquiet among James's early interpreters (Johnson 1995, 134,
193, 203–4), is the logical consequence of its rigorous insistence on two
abstract principles: that God is the providential source of every good thing
(1:17; see also 1:5–8 and 4:2–6) and that he is unchanging. Strikingly, these
are the very theological principles upon which Socrates insists in Plato's
Republic (377–383)—principles that led him, too, into direct contradiction
with the scriptures of his own people.[12]

Within the logic of James, responsibility for evil in any event is not
directly traceable to God. This again is a common theme of Hellenistic
philosophical theology, where one finds "many texts ... [that] isolate the
deity from evil and/or blame humans for evil" (Allison 2013, 243). The
Stoic Cleanthes's *Hymn to Zeus* illustrates the matter well: "No deed is
done on earth, God, without your offices, nor in the divine ethereal vault
of heaven, nor at sea, *save what bad men do in their folly*" (Long and Sedley
1988, 1:326 [54I], emphasis added). Philo is similarly insistent: God "is the
cause of nothing evil, but of all that is good" (*Conf.* 161; see also 180–182).
Interpreting the Jewish Scriptures through these lenses, Philo identifies
two alternative sources of such real or apparent evils: punishing angels
on one hand (*Conf.* 168–182, esp. 181–182), and the human being's own
desire on the other—the latter of which, in particular, is said to "beget"
(*egennēsen*) both illicit deeds and death (*Opif.* 152 [cf. Jas 1:15!]; further
Wilson 2002, 151–52).

---

12. See esp. 380C (Emlyn-Jones and Preddy): "this would be one of the laws and
models concerning the gods which those telling the tales will have to use and follow,
and writers likewise saying that god is not responsible for everything, but for all good
things"; and for the "second point" (380D) esp. 381C: "it is impossible even for a god
to want to change himself." The latter principle is linked closely to the conviction that
a god would never mislead someone. While Socrates is explicitly critical of Homer
and Hesiod on these grounds, the author of James, who is not so overtly critical of
the traditions of his own people, would presumably have preserved their authority by
considering the contradiction merely literal, not actual. Note also, however, the theory
of "false pericopes" used to deal with analogous problems in the Pseudo-Clementine
Homilies, on which see Carlson 2013, 51–75.

James itself similarly identifies the source of evil as human temptation (*peirasmos*), driving the larger theological point home by declaring God himself both beyond temptation (*apeirastos*) and the tempter of no one (1:13–15; see also 1:2–4, 12). Given the impact of Jewish apocalyptic ideas on James, one might expect at this point an analogous appeal to angelic forces, specifically the devil, who is so often cast in the role of mythological "tempter" (e.g., Matt 4:3; 1 Thess 3:5, *ho peirazōn*; cf. Jas 4:7, *ho diabolos*). Be that as it may, the only culprit explicitly identified in 1:13–15 is one's own desire (*hypo tēs idias epithymias*), which, much as in Philo, is said to "give birth" to sin and, by extension, death (see Wilson 2002). To be sure, as with Philo this might seem merely to push the problem back insofar as God, as creator, is ultimately responsible for the existence of human desire. As Johnson (1995, 204) rightly explains, however, James "uses *epithymia* in the manner already widely attested in Hellenistic moral discourse. It refers, not to legitimate human desire, but to desire disordered by sinful passion"—what James elsewhere, when addressing the specific matter of anger (*orgē*), refers to as "evil excess" (1:21, *perisseian kakias*).[13] Even if, as we might fairly surmise, the text assumes some synergy between the devil and human desire, the result is the same sort of mutually interpretive merger of apocalyptic mythology and Hellenistic philosophy found in its linking of gehenna and the "wheel of creation" in 3:6. Analogous syntheses are found in the Testaments of the Twelve Patriarchs (Kloppenborg 2010, 43–47) and a host of early Christian writings, including Justin, Irenaeus, and Methodius (on which see below). James's understanding of God and his relationship to the world, in short, is both thoroughly Jewish and thoroughly Hellenistic.

Anthropology

James's understanding of what it, like other Hellenistic writers, calls "human nature" is bound up closely in its understanding of God, both in terms of similarity and, most especially, difference. While the text is not explicit as to what, exactly, constitutes humanity's likeness to God, the key differences are clear enough. In contrast to the unchanging God, humans—like the "wheel of creation" more generally—are ephemeral, likened to "mist

---

13. See, e.g., the Stoic treatment of the passions as discussed in Long and Sedley 1988, 1:419–23.

that appears for a little while, and then disappears" (4:14; see also 1:10–11). Indeed, humans with insufficient faith in God's stable providence become unstable (*akatastos*) in a still more problematic sense, "like a wave of the sea, blown and tossed about by the wind" (1:5–8; see also 3:16, *akatastasia*; 3:8, *akatastaton kakon*).[14] More emphatic still is the closely related contrast between a God who is *apeirastos*, which is to say entirely dissociated from temptation, and a humanity whose existence is fundamentally defined by it (1:2–4, 12–15). The *epithymia* or "desire" that James identifies as the source of this temptation is central to its understanding of the human condition, just as it was for the Hellenistic moralists.[15]

James includes a variety of terms plainly relevant to its understanding of human nature. While it is by no means obvious that each is used with an exacting definition—any more, say, than when American writers make popular use of terms such as "mind," "soul," or "spirit"—the outlines of a basically consistent anthropology are clear enough. James assumes in the first place a basic distinction between the body (*sōma*) and a spirit (*pneuma*) that animates it (2:26). This *pneuma* has an indeterminate relationship to the soul (*psychē*), which, as James's soteriological focus (1:21; 5:20), apparently comes closest to what we might today call the self.[16] The body, for its part, consists of many "members" (3:6; 4:1). It has its own particular needs (2:16, *ta epitedeia tou sōmatos*), like food and clothing, that are not only unproblematic in themselves, but merit active

---

14. See also Philo, *Conf.* 30–31: "But the wise man ... gains a privilege vouchsafed to him from God, who ever stands fast, a privilege which is the congener of His power which never swerves and never wavers. For [Deut 5:31 was written] to the end that he should put off doubt and hesitation, the qualities of the unstable mind, and put on that surest and most stable quality, faith [*pistin*]" (Colson and Whitaker); see also *Post.* 22–27, quoted above in n. 11. On the philosophical context of *akatastasia*, see Kloppenborg 2010, 50–52.

15. Compare the analysis of James's anthropology in Wilson 2002. Wilson's view that the framework of James's anthropology is supplied by apocalypticism *as opposed to* Hellenistic philosophy (158) forces a choice that is not only unnecessary, but rather odd given the larger thesis of his article, which is that the sexual imagery of Jas 1:12–15 must be understood in light of Philo and Hellenistic philosophy (148).

16. Cf. Gen 2:7: Adam becomes a "living soul" (*psychēn zōsan*) after God "breathes into his face the breath of life" (*enephusēsen eis to prosōpon autou pnoēn zōēs*). The Stoic view that *pneuma* ("breath") was the stuff of the *psychē* (Long and Sedley 1988, 1:315 [53G], 282 [47H]) as well as the stuff of God (274–75 [46A]) has potential for a creative interpretation of Genesis.

attention—particularly where vulnerable others are concerned (2:14–17; see also 1:27; contrast 5:4). Problems arise, apparently, only when such needs, unchecked, turn into an excessive acquisitiveness driven by lustful cravings James calls *hēdonai* (4:1, 3) or *epithymia* (4:2, *epithymeite*; 1:15, *epithymia*)—which is to say the kind of "evil excess" he associates with anger (1:21, *perisseian kakias*). When this happens, the various "members" that make up "the whole body" become subject to fierce internal conflicts (4:1–2). Following a "logic of envy" familiar from Hellenistic moralists (Johnson 1983), this internal discord inevitably spills over into the social realm when those cravings are, according to James, actively frustrated by God (4:1–3; see also 1:5–8).[17]

Given the destructive power of human desire, the "whole body" stands in need of "bridling" (3:2). It was human reason that was generally assigned this function by philosophical moralists (Johnson 1995, 257), and thus too, as we have seen, by Philo. In James, strikingly, it is "the tongue" that is said to have been "installed" (3:6, *kathistatai*) for this task, so much so that the man who is perfect with respect to speech (*en logō*) is said himself to be "perfect" (3:2, *teleios anēr*). Given James's general emphasis on the necessity of deeds both for salvation and for true wisdom, interpreters have long struggled with this idea. As one commentator has put it, "Can James seriously think that 'perfection in speech' can make a person perfect?" (Johnson 1995, 256). The key, however, lies in recognizing that the tongue itself, according to James, is emphatically in need of "taming" (3:7–8). The anthropological logic underlying the relationship between controlling the tongue, bridling the body, producing good deeds, and being perfect is greatly illuminated once again particularly by comparison with Philo.

Though James does not explicitly name what it is that might tame the tongue, the obvious answer in a philosophical context, at least, once again would have been human reason. Stoic psychology in particular posited an intimate relationship between the "reasoning faculty" (*logismon*) and "the tongue" (*glōtta*): reason represented a capacity for "internal speech" (*endiathetos logos*), which the tongue translated into "uttered speech" (*prophorikos logos*).[18] Philo portrays this distinction, in terms reminiscent of

---

17. "The rich," characterized by especially extravagant clothing and jewelry (2:2–3; see also 5:2–3), represent the epitome of such self-seeking at the expense of the elect "poor" and "righteous" in James (5:4–6; 2:6–7; see also 1:9–11).

18. See Aetius excerpted in Long and Sedley (1988, 1:315–16, 2:314 [53H]): "The Stoics say that the commanding-faculty is the soul's highest part [*tēs psychēs anōtaton*

Jas 3:11, as one between a spring (*pēgē*) and its outflow (*Migr.* 71; *Mos.* 2.127). So closely related are they, in fact, that Philo—portraying the *logos* as both charioteer and pilot over the human's spirited element (*thymos*) and desire (*epithymia*)—can similarly assume that control of speech will "render the whole soul [*holēn psychēn*] gentle."[19] In Philo's view, therefore, controlling speech is not only the antidote for anger, but the linchpin for attaining moral perfection more generally. Insofar as "perfection [*teleiotēs*] depends ... on both divisions of *logos*, the reason which suggests the ideas ... and the speech which gives unfailing expression to them" (*Migr.* 73), it is the one who succeeds "in bringing speech [*logon*] into harmony with intent, and intent with deed [*ergō*]" who is considered "perfect [*teleios*] and of a truly harmonious character" (*Post.* 88). This philosophical background illuminates not only—as James's ancient interpreters already recognized (Allison 2013, 525)— the logic of James's speech ethics, but its wider context in the letter's anthropology.

James's signature term for the person whose *psychē* is subject to these internal conflicts is *dipsychos* (1:8; 4:8)—one, that is, whose soul is divided and who is thus not "perfect and whole" (Jas 1:4, *teleioi kai holoklēroi*). Like a number of other key themes in James, the underlying idea, if not the term itself, has points of contact in both Jewish and Hellenistic literature. Plato's *Republic*, for example, had already characterized the person who fails to control "evil desires" (*kakas epithymias*) through reason (*logō*) as being subject to internal dissension (*astasiastos en heautō*) and thus, in a word, as "some kind of a twofold person [*diplous tis*]" (*Resp.* 554D–E; see Johnson 1995, 181).[20] As Kloppenborg and others have observed, analogous ideas recur in the Testaments of the Twelve Patriarchs, which themselves adapted Hellenistic and especially Stoic ethical theory to Judean cultural assump-

---

meros], ... They also call it the reasoning faculty [*logismon*] ... utterance [*phōnēn*] is breath [*pneuma*] extending from the commanding faculty to the pharynx, tongue [*glōttes*] and appropriate organs"; see also Philo, *Mos.* 2.127; further Long and Sedley 1988, 1:317–18, 2:319 (53T): "it is not uttered speech [*tō prophorikō logō*] but internal speech [*alla tō endiathetō*] by which man differs from non-rational animals [*tōn alogōn zōōn*]."

19. See Philo, *Leg.* 3.118–128; further Jackson-McCabe 2001, 226–28.

20. Porter (1990) argues that the actual term *dipsychos* was James's own coinage; Johnson (1995, 181) allows for at least the possibility. Allison (2013, 186), noting that "Greek literature ... portrays a keen interest in the divided self," rejects this thesis outright. It is frequent in any event in the second century, most especially in Hermas, but also Didache, Barnabas, and 1–2 Clement; for references see Goodspeed 1960, 55.

tions (Kloppenborg 2010, esp. 43–53). It seems not only unnecessary special pleading, but positively misleading to insist that the concept must be *either* Jewish *or* Hellenistic in a text like James (see Konradt 1998, 96–97).[21]

As in these texts, the cause of such internal division in James too, in a word, is *epithymia*—that is, the unbridled desires of the body. In this sense, then, the central existential threat facing humanity as understood in this text can be summed up as *peirasmos*, "temptation." It is not accidental that this theme, along with the closely related concerns regarding self-deception and proper understanding, is among the most prominent in the letter's introductory section (see Johnson 1995, 175; Wilson 2002, 160–61; Kloppenborg 2010)—a section that traces it emphatically to an individual's own desire rather than to a provident and unchanging deity (1:13–18), and imagines successful endurance of it, using athletic imagery familiar once again from Hellenistic moralists, being rewarded with a "crown" (1:2–4, 12; see Wilson 2002, 164–65). How though, according to James, can we overcome the destructive power of desire? If temptation by desire represents a chief point of contrast between God and humanity, how can one come to realize more fully that aspect of one's nature that *does* bear "the likeness of God" (3:9), and so become a "friend of God" like Abraham (2:23), rather than a "friend of the world" like the *dipsychos* (4:4–8). Undoubtedly it is God himself, as "the one lawgiver and judge who is able to save and to destroy" (4:12), who is imagined by James as providing the solution. But how, in the context of our letter, does the divine Lawgiver do this?

Soteriology

The preceding analysis of James's anthropology leaves several significant questions unanswered. James, after the fashion of Greek philosophers,

---

21. The underlying concept, both in James and in the Testaments, is sometimes interpreted with reference to the rabbinic notion of the "evil inclination" (e.g., Marcus 1982); against this, however, see Kloppenborg 2010, 44–46. Allison links it more generally to the common Hebrew notion of the "double heart" (Allison 2013, 187–90); note in this connection that James also imagines the "heart" as being in need of purification (4:8, "purify your hearts, *dipsychoi!*") and strengthening (5:8); see also 3:14 ("if you have bitter jealously and selfish ambition in your heart"); also 5:5, where "the rich" have "fattened [their] hearts for a day of slaughter"; and 1:27, where one who appears to be pious but does not "bridle his tongue" is only "deceiving his heart." Such potential convergences of Jewish and Hellenistic discourse were likely especially attractive in a text such as this; see Collins 2000, 14–16.

assumes there is a distinctly "human nature" and, like Philo, interprets Gen 1:26–27 in light of this assumption. But what exactly, in James's view, makes human nature different from that of other animals? And what, on the other hand, comprises humanity's likeness to God? Like Hellenistic moralists, James identifies desire as the central human problem, the cause of turmoil and division within the soul. But what is it, as understood in this particular text, that can bring harmony and unity to the divided soul? And if James, like Philo, considers control of the tongue to be a linchpin for such "bridling," what is it, in James's view, that can tame the notoriously problematic tongue itself?

For the philosophically minded writers who shared these ideas and concerns, the answer to all these questions would have been obvious, and one and the same. It is humanity's rational capacity that both differentiates it from other animals and comprises its special kinship with God (Inwood 1985, 18–27). Cleanthes's *Hymn to Zeus*, in fact, put this latter kinship in terms that would have especially resonated with readers of the Jewish Scriptures: "we [humans] are your offspring, and alone of mortal creatures … bear a likeness to god [*theou mimēma*]" (Long and Sedley 1988, 1:326, 2:326 [54I]). It was thus natural for Philo, who made sense of Greek philosophy and the Jewish Scriptures in light of one another, to interpret the "image" and "likeness" of God in Gen 1:26–27 precisely with reference to *logos*, or reason (e.g., *Her.* 230–231; *Plant.* 18–20; *Opif.* 25; cf. *Leg.* 3.95–96). As we have seen, moreover, it was this same *logos* that Hellenistic moralists generally understood to have the power to overcome desire, to control the tongue, and to render the human soul a stable unity. Is there evidence in the Letter of James to suggest it would answer any of these questions differently? Conversely, is there evidence that the philosophical influence on James included not only the identification of human desire as problem, but of reason, or *logos*, as solution?

As it happens, James not only identifies the individual's own desire as the cause of the soul's division and death, but a *logos* similarly internal to a person—an *emphytos* or "implanted" *logos*—as that which is able to "save your souls" (1:21). But what does this implanted *logos* refer to in the context of James? Is this concept, too, informed by Hellenistic philosophy?

In fact, scholars have long noted the Stoic ring of the phrase *emphytos logos*, even in isolation from the larger matter of James's anthropology (among others Dibelius 1976, 114; Meyer 1930, 150–55; Windisch 1951, 11; Boismard 1957; Laws 1980, 83–84; Vouga 1984, 63; Klein 1995, 135; Tsuji 1997, 108 n. 58). There is good reason for this. As I have shown at

length elsewhere, the description of either human reason itself or a natural law correlated with it as "implanted" is typical particularly of ancient
works influenced by Stoic ethical theory.[22] According to the Stoics, the
undeveloped *logos* with which people are born is intimately related to
ethical potentialities they called "implanted preconceptions" (*emphytoi
prolēpseis*), which comprise the human's natural ability to conceptualize
the distinction between good and bad. Often characterized as "seeds of
virtue" planted by God in human nature, the refinement of these preconceptions into proper notions of the *truly* good was understood to be central
to the development of the *logos* into the "right reason" (*orthos logos*) of the
sage, who alone lived in harmony with nature and the will of God. For the
Stoics, then, this *logos* was itself the true, divine law, the constitution of a
great World City ruled by God. Cicero's extensive account of Greek natural
law theory, accordingly, is built around a definition of true law as "highest
reason implanted in nature" (*Leg.* 1.18–19, *summa ratio insita in natura*).

A variety of early Christian writers adapted this theory to their own
ends. Justin took advantage of its developmental aspect in order to contrast
"the seed of the logos implanted in every race of humanity" (*to emphyton panti genei anthrōpōn sperma tou logou*) with the "whole *logos*" (*tou
pantos logou*) he believed to have been embodied by Christ, whose teaching could thus be described equally well as "right reason" (*orthos logos*) or
"natural law" (*ho tēs physeōs nomos*) (Justin, *2 Apol.* 8.1–3; see also 13.3–5
and 2.2–4).[23] The Apostolic Constitutions, on the other hand, in a manner
more reminiscent of Philo and 4 Maccabees, turned this philosophical
theory into an apology for the torah, framing it as a written expression
of the "implanted law" (*emphyton nomon*) given to Adam at creation as
"the seeds of divine knowledge" (Apos. Con. 8.12.18). The torah, according to this text, was given through Moses as an "aid" precisely because
humans had corrupted the implanted "natural law" (18.12.25, *ton physikon
nomon*). It is particularly this combination of the written and implanted
law, therefore, that now enables the human "to live as a rational [animal]"
(Apos. Con. 7.39.2).[24] Methodius, differently again, read Rom 7 and Gen

---

22. For what follows in the next several paragraphs, see Jackson-McCabe 2001,
29–133.

23. See further Jackson-McCabe 2001, 123–27. Thus Justin's striking description of Socrates and other idealized figures that lived even before the era of Christ as
"Christians" (*1 Apol.* 46; see also *2 Apol.* 10).

24. An analogous idea underlies the Pseudo-Clementine *Homilies*; see, e.g., 8.5.4

1–3 in light of an assumed contrast between two different logics simultaneously at work within a person. One arises "from the desire [*tēs epithymias*]
that lurks in the body," is also associated with the devil, and is the cause
of death. Another stems from our "impulse to the good," which Methodius associates with "the commandment that we received [from God]
to have as an implanted natural law [*hon emphyton elabomen exein kai
physikon nomon*]." According to Methodius, therefore, Christ brings not
a transformation of human nature, but rather a restoration of "its original
nature before its fall, when it was immortal" (see the fragment preserved
in Epiphanius, *Pan.* 60.5–6).

Though each of these texts adapts Stoic ethical theory to its own
peculiar purpose, the similarities in their language plainly result from the
common influence of the Stoic correlation of human reason with natural law. Seen in this light, what is striking about James is not merely the
isolated term *emphytos*, but its functional identification of an *emphytos
logos* precisely with a law—indeed, the "perfect [*teleion*] law," a divine law
associated emphatically with "freedom" (*eleutherias*) (1:21–25; 2:12). As is
widely acknowledged, this paradoxical and otherwise unexplained glorification of the law as a "law of freedom" is itself rooted in Stoic ethical theory,
which correlated true freedom with freedom from desire, and thus with
the sage's life in accord with God's natural law (e.g., Dibelius 1976, 116–20;
Konradt 1998, 93–99; further Jackson-McCabe 2001, 145–51). When one
considers that James's *logos*, too, functions in opposition to desire in the
context of an anthropology that was otherwise clearly shaped by Hellenistic moral philosophy, the idea that its own correlation of a "perfect law
of freedom" with an "implanted *logos*" was not also shaped by Hellenistic
philosophy strains credibility. James's early interpreters, at any rate, found
the implication to be obvious, taking its *emphtyos logos* straightforwardly
as that which makes humans "rational" (*logikoi*) and able to distinguish
good from bad, or simply as "natural law" itself.[25]

Nonetheless, the relevance of this collection of texts for the interpretation of James's *logos* remains a point of contention among contemporary
interpreters. While a number of recent scholars now interpret James's
logos along these lines (see Kloppenborg 2007a, 246–48; Overman 2008,

---

(ANF): "For there would have been no need of Moses, or of the coming of Jesus, if of
themselves they would have understood what is reasonable [*to eulogon*]."

25. See the early interpretations of Oecumenius, Theophylactus, and Dionysius
bar Salibi, on which see Jackson-McCabe 2001, 131–32.

266–69; Allison 2013, 311–15; Adam 2013), it is still here above all that one continues to find interpreters insisting that the Jewish and Hellenistic character of James be framed as an either/or proposition, or reduced at most to a distinction between real substance and superficial form. While several specific arguments have been raised, the underlying objection to the idea of significant Stoic influence on James's *logos* concept has always been its soteriological implications. Could a New Testament text really assume that God gave a potential power to "save souls" to all people rather than reserving it exclusively for Christians? Even those earlier scholars who recognized the Stoic character of the phrase thus typically interpreted it along the lines of the "superficial Hellenism" thesis, concluding that it had been entirely stripped of its original significance and reapplied to "the gospel."[26] Others go still further, explicitly (or implicitly) rejecting the idea even of superficial philosophical influence on James, at least where its *logos* concept is concerned (see discussion in Jackson-McCabe 2001, 20–24; for more recent examples see Konradt 2003; Whitlark 2010; Hartin 2003, 97–98; see also Marcus 2002; McKnight 2011, 142–44). A recent study by Jason Whitlark (2010) provides the fullest development of this position, arguing strenuously that James's phrase *emphytos logos* reflects Jeremiah's notion of a new covenant written by God on the hearts of his people (Jer 31:33) rather than Hellenistic philosophy. This debate, which gets to the very heart of the question of the Letter of James and Hellenistic philosophy, merits our attention. While a thorough consideration of the issues would be out of place here, I should at least explain Whitlark's recent argument, and why I consider such attempts to insulate James's *logos* from the philosophical influence otherwise evident in the letter to be problematic.

I emphasize at the outset that the debate should not be framed as a choice between "cosmological" and "soteriological" interpretations of James's *logos* (so Whitlark 2010, 144–46). Insofar as it is explicitly identified as that which "saves souls," James's *emphytos logos* can only be a soteriological concept on any interpretation. The question, rather, is whether James understands the potential for "saving the soul" to have been bestowed by God exclusively on Christians as a consequence of conversion, or on all people from the moment he created them. Nor is it the case,

---

26. Note, however, that while the term *logos* (and esp. "*logos* of truth") frequently leads interpreters to speak of "the gospel" in this connection, what is really in mind is something more akin to Paul's notion of a superadded *pneuma* than to the "good news" about how it came to be available to people through Christ; see below.

despite frequent assertions to the contrary (see Jackson-McCabe 2001, 9–11), that such a linking of an inborn *logos* to a notion of divine salvation of the soul would have been unheard of in antiquity. Philo, who like James was influenced by the language of the Septuagint as much as by Hellenistic philosophy, routinely talks about God's salvation of the soul, even in conjunction with reason's mastery of the passions.[27] In the *Allegorical Interpretation*, for example, Philo is careful to insist that though "it is necessary that the reason [*ton logon*] should be put and set firmly on the spirited element [*tō thymō*], as though it were a kind of charioteer keeping straight a stiff-necked and restive horse," one must nonetheless recognize that it is ultimately God who is the source of soul's salvation: "It is necessary that the soul [*tēn psychēn*] should not ascribe to itself its toil for virtue, but that it should take it away from itself and refer it to God, confessing that not its own strength or power acquired nobility, but he who freely bestowed also the love of it.... For only then does the soul begin to be saved [*hē psychē sōzetai*], when the spirited element has received reason [*logou*] as its charioteer, and toil has come to create in it, not self-satisfaction, but a readiness to yield the honour to God, the Bestower of the boon" (*Leg.* 3.136–137 [LCL, slightly modified]). The question, in other words, is not whether James's *logos* is soteriological, but whether its soteriological significance is more broadly akin to Philo's inborn *logos* or Paul's superadded *pneuma*.[28]

---

27. Philo's use of salvation language is derived from the Jewish Scriptures in *Leg.* 2.94, 101–102 (see Gen 49:18 LXX, *tēn sōterian kyriou*) and in *Cher.* 130 (see Exod 14:13 LXX, *tēn sōterian tēn para tou theou*); see also *Virt.* 47–49. Elsewhere it seems simply a function of the use of medical imagery in connection with care for the soul, which was again typical of Hellenistic moralists (*Deus* 66–67, 129–30; *Ebr.* 140; *Spec.* 1.239, 253). See also *Spec.* 1.222; 4.79–80; and *Sacr.* 123 (with which compare Jas 5:18–20). Philo, moreover, portrays this salvation in terms of God's redemption of the soul in *Conf.* 93: "Which of the wisely-minded ... would not ... cry aloud to God the only Saviour to lighten their tasks and provide a price of the soul's salvation to redeem it into liberty?" Compare also Cleanthes's *Hymn to Zeus:* "All-giving Zeus ... deliver [*rhyou*] mankind from its pitiful incompetence. Scatter this from our soul [*psychēs*], Father" (Long and Sedley 1988, 1:327, 2:327 [54I], slightly modified).

28. Note also in this connection that, again despite a widely repeated argument to the contrary, the idea of "receiving" something already "implanted" is equally paradoxical regardless of when the implanting took place—and equally mitigated by James's assumption that what is implanted correlates with some external discourse, whether the torah or a gospel. See further on this n. 40 below.

There are actually two distinct questions here. Is James's *logos* imagined as the common possession of all humanity, or as the exclusive possession of some divinely favored subset of it? Either way, was James's assumption of a correlation between an "implanted *logos*" and a "perfect law of freedom" informed by Hellenistic philosophy, or was it not? These questions are reflected respectively in the two main considerations Whitlark rightly recognizes as central to the debate. The first is basically an exegetical question, pertaining particularly to the letter's anthropology. Does James assume that people are fundamentally incapable of resisting desire unless something God did not provide when creating them is now superadded on an individual basis? The second is a matter of comparison. While any reader might of course choose to interpret James in light of whatever texts she likes, the historical question is whether one set of comparisons illuminates James's *logos* discourse more fully than another—or, let us not forget when considering a work like James, whether different sets of comparisons might prove equally if differently illuminating.[29] To argue persuasively against Hellenistic philosophical influence on James's *logos* concept, in other words, is not simply to argue that James *can* be read another way, but that Jeremiah's notion of a new covenant provides a *better* explanation of the evidence in the text.

Regarding the exegetical matter, Whitlark argues that "James's anthropological perspective is antagonistic to the Stoic-cosmological interpretation of the *emphytos logos*" (2010, 146). Put more positively, "the Letter of James embodies a pessimistic anthropological assumption," namely, that "intrinsic human ability is not adequate for living the Christian life as it is envisioned in the letter" (147). Two arguments are made in support of this claim, both of which are problematic. The first concerns James's declaration that despite the success of human nature in taming all other animals, "no one among humans is able to tame the tongue" (3:7–8). Highlighting Dibelius's observation that the Stoics in particular liked to demonstrate the superiority of the rational animal by citing its mastery over other species (1976, 199), Whitlark argues that James "turns this type of reasoning on its head" by subversively pointing out that humans nonetheless cannot even tame their own tongues (Whitlark 2010, 148). To take 3:8 as a statement of the theoretical impossibility of controlling speech,

---

29. Recall that Methodius, e.g., reads Gen 1–3, Paul's writings, and Stoic natural law theory all as mutually interpretive discourses; see further below on Irenaeus.

however, is to ignore what would seem to be the real point of the section, which immediately follows: "It is not necessary, my brothers, for things to be this way" (3:10)—a point the conclusion then develops with analogies from springs and fruit trees (3:10–11; see also Philo, *Migr.* 71; *Mos.* 2.127; Matt 7:16–20). We are left, then, with two possibilities. The first is that the concluding plea that things need not be this way—and thus the section's larger point about "bridling the whole body" by controlling the tongue (3:1–6), and even James's whole concept of true piety, which similarly depends on "bridling the tongue" (1:26–27)—was meant ironically. The second, and in my view much more likely, possibility is that the point that "no one is able to control the tongue" is less a statement of rigorous theoretical principle than a practical observation regarding the notorious difficulty of controlling speech.[30] As Dibelius (1976, 201) himself put it, "one must understand the exaggerated paradox of such statements [as 3:8]: precisely in the negation lies the incentive to continue in the effort to tame the tongue." Indeed, even on Whitlark's reading *some* human beings would seem to be at least *theoretically* capable of controlling the tongue and thus exhibiting true piety (1:26)—namely, those with the implanted *logos*. The question is simply whether this theoretical possibility obtains for all people, or exclusively to a divinely favored subset of converts.[31]

In further support of his thesis regarding James's Pauline-style pessimism, Whitlark also argues that James believes "humans lack the resources to master their desires" (2010, 149). This judgment is based primarily on the letter's opening exhortation that "if someone among you lacks wisdom, let that one ask of the God who gives to all simply and ungrudgingly, and it will be given to him" (1:4). Whitlark's conclusion: "for James, this wisdom is not intrinsic to the human condition like reason is for the Stoic" (150). This, however, is to compare apples with oranges. While the Stoics of course understood *reason* to be innate in the human being, they no more considered *wisdom* "intrinsic to the human condition" than James does. Quite the contrary: the Stoics were notorious for considering the actual attainment of wisdom, if possible in theory, to be as rare (if not rarer!) than the

---

30. See in this respect the immediately preceding claim that every species (*pasa physis*) of animal has been tamed by humans (3:7). This too seems less a wooden statement of literal fact than a hyperbolic exaggeration in the service of the exhortation (Allison 2013, 544).

31. Either way, James would presumably attribute this power ultimately to God (e.g., 1:18); compare Philo, *Leg.* 3.136–137, cited above.

Phoenix in actual practice (Brouwer 2014, 92–135, esp. 97–112).[32] Indeed, Stoic ethics—and in fact Greek philosophy more generally—was predicated on the assumption that the mass of humanity, despite its innate capacity for rationality and virtue, was quite far from wise. Prayer for divine aid in attaining what people scarcely if ever achieved in practice, moreover, was no less possible in a Stoic context than for James. Cleanthes closed his *Hymn to Zeus* with a petition not entirely out of step with that which opens James:

> Zeus, Giver of all [*pandōre*] ... deliver [*rhyou*] mankind from its piti-ful incompetence. Scatter this from our soul [*psychēs*], Father. Give us the power of judgment [*dos de kyrēsai gnōmēs*] by trusting in which you steer all things with justice, so that by winning honour we may repay you with honour, forever singing of your works, as it befits mortals to do. (Long and Sedley 1988, 1:327, 2:327 [54I], slightly modified)

The exhortation in Jas 1:4 is in any case conditional; "*if* someone among you lacks wisdom" would seem to imply at least the *theoretical* possibility that some do not. Once again, Whitlark's own analysis would also seem to imply this much insofar as the letter assumes an audience endowed with an *emphytos logos* that is able to "save souls." The question remains: For whom, exactly, does this theoretical possibility obtain?

We are thus brought back to the question of the *emphytos logos* itself, and particularly its relationship to Stoic ethical theory. Given the larger theme of this essay, we should not lose sight of the fact that Whitlark by no means denies that James's ethical outlook was significantly shaped by Hellenistic moral philosophy.[33] On the contrary, he seems to assume this as the broad context of James's anthropology—even apparently suggesting, as we have seen, that the letter had enough familiarity with Stoic anthropology to antagonistically tweak one of its typical tropes. His position instead is that James's *logos* concept in particular was somehow insulated from the philosophical anthropology that otherwise informed the letter. Nor does

---

32. No doubt this problem helped create an opening for Jewish and Christian claims that their own divinely revealed teachings represented further help in the matter.

33. See Whitlark 2010, 148: "The importance of self-mastery is not a concern peculiar to James. James represents a concern common to the larger ancient Mediter-ranean milieu." The parallels he cites are Plato, Xenophon, Plutarch, 4 Maccabees, and Philo (148–49). Note also his interpretation of *emphytos logos* in particular in light of Wilson's (2002) analysis of 1:12–15, on which, however, see above n. 15.

he reject the finding that the recurring notions of an implanted *logos* or law in the works discussed above resulted from Stoic influence. His thesis, rather, is that James's *emphytos logos* in particular is better understood in comparison with a different set of texts, namely the Epistle of Barnabas and Irenaeus's *Against Heresies*.

Barnabas imagines a divine spirit (*pneuma*) given to Christians in particular as an "implanted grace of the spiritual gift [*emphyton tēs dōreas pneumatikēs charin*]" (1:2–3), apparently correlating it further with "the implanted gift of the covenant" or (depending on the manuscript) "teaching" (9:9, *tēn emphyton dōrean tēs diathēkēs* [or: *didachēs*]). Irenaeus similarly uses forms of the term "implant" (Latin: *infigo*; cf. *emphyō*) with reference to God's "implanting" of a Pauline-like (see Rom 8:4) "righteous require-ment of the law" (4.13.1, *infigens*; cf. *emphyōn*), or superior piety (4.13.3, *infixam*; cf. *empephykuian*) in Christians in particular.[34] Arguing that "within the Christian context" of these two texts "*emphytos* and its cognates are adapted to new covenant thinking," Whitlark (2010, 162) concludes that Barnabas and Irenaeus "provide warrant for associating the language of *emphytos* with new covenant thinking within a Christian context" in James as well. Of course, given the fact that Justin, the Apostolic Constitutions, and Methodius also aligned themselves with Christ, the real question is why one "Christian context" should be considered more illuminating of James than another. Notably, Whitlark can point to no clear allusion to a new covenant idea in James beyond the disputed term *emphytos logos* itself.[35] The cen-tral rationale for emphasizing Barnabas—the text to which Whitlark (2010, 153–61) devotes the bulk of his attention—over Justin and these others is its inclusion among "the corpus of the Apostolic Fathers," "certain texts" of which contain other lexical and thematic similarities with James (153).[36] This is a curious argument on the face of it since this corpus was not actu-ally assembled until the seventeenth century.[37] In any case, what Whitlark

---

34. Here and elsewhere the Latin text and Greek reconstruction of Irenaeus are those of Rousseau 1965.

35. See Whitlark 2010, 162: "the language of implantation is how new covenant thinking finds expression in the Letter of James."

36. Whitlark 2010, 155: "When we take together the clustering of terms and simi-larity of concerns between the Letter of James and some of the documents of the Apos-tolic Fathers, an analysis of the use of *emphytos* in the *Epistle of Barnabas* proves both warranted and relevant for understanding its use in the Letter of James."

37. See Ehrman 2003, 1:1–14, noting that modern scholars debate the utility of the collection at all, characterizing "the most widely accepted view" of it as "a rather arbi-

(2010, 153–54) has in mind is above all the oft-noted similarities between James and the Shepherd of Hermas—similarities that do not include the term *emphytos*, let alone an *emphytos logos* that is also the perfect law. With respect to Barnabas itself, the main such similarities adduced beyond the term *emphytos* are their common use of the word *dipsychos* (Barn. 19:5) and of the *haplo-* root (Barn. 19:2; cf. Jas 1:5). Why this outweighs the complex of ideas James shares with Stoic ethical theory is unclear.

The comparison with Irenaeus, while substantially less developed (Whitlark 2010, 161–62), is actually more potentially compelling. As noted above, Irenaeus uses similar implanting language not only in association with law, but a law, as in James, that is correlated explicitly with "freedom" (*Haer.* 4.13.2, *decreta libertatis* [cf. *ta dogmata tēs eleutherias*]; see also 4.34.4, *libertatis lex* [cf. *ho tēs eleutherias nomos*]). What is particularly striking in this case, however, is that Irenaeus, even if he also has Jer 31:33 (see *Haer.* 4.34.4) and Paul in the back of his mind, is clearly interpreting them here in light of natural law theory (further Schoedel 1963, 435–43). The implanting by God cited by Whitlark, in fact, only builds on (rather than abrogates, Irenaeus insists), the "natural precepts of the law" (4.13.1, *naturalia legis*; cf. *ta physika tou nomou*) which, Irenaeus says, were themselves "implanted [*infixa*; cf. *emphytous*] within human beings from the beginning [*ab initio*]," and subsequently given in verbal form to Israel in the Decalogue before finally being brought to fulfillment by Christ (4.15.1). The notion of a specific implanting in Christians, in other words, is patterned after the notion of a first such implanting of natural law in all humanity at creation. In fact, though Irenaeus claims that his own cult group alone has experienced this second implanting, resulting in a "more complete subjection and affection towards our Liberator" than all other peoples (4.13.3), it is nonetheless the "natural precepts" themselves "by which man is justified," and "which also those who were justified by faith, and who pleased God, did observe" even "previous to the giving of the law" (4.13.1).[38] The general strategy, if not the precise language, is reminiscent of the one pursued by Justin. Irenaeus projects the developmental aspect of Stoic natural law theory onto the stage of human history

---

trary collection of writings made for the sake of convenience and based on (modern) tradition" (12, parenthetical caveat his); further Rothschild 2017, 7–33.

38. Note in this connection that later Stoics, at least, argued that a natural affection for God was also part of the "implanted preconceptions" (Jackson-McCabe 2001, 67–72).

in order to present the teaching of Christ as the full expression of a natural law identified by the Stoics as the moral ideal, the true law of freedom. To this end he postulates, in addition to God's initial implanting of natural law in humanity in general, a subsequent, supplementary implanting in members of his own group in particular, while still allowing the possibility that some had basically observed it even prior to Christ. Even if one were inclined to compare James's *emphytos logos* specifically with Irenaeus's notion of a second implanting, then, we are still led back to Stoic ethical theory as the source of their similar language.

But in fact there is little reason to conclude that James's *logos* is to be interpreted with reference to Irenaeus's idiosyncratic theory of a second implanting rather than in light of its more usual association, even in other Christian texts, with a *logos* or law implanted in humanity in general at creation.[39] While James quotes or otherwise alludes to Jewish scriptural texts to a "striking" extent, Jer 31:33 is not among them (Allison 2013, 51). To be sure, like all other Jewish and Christian authors who adapted Stoic ethical theory for their own apologetic ends, James correlates the implanted *logos* specifically with the law that defines his own group.[40] But

---

39. The description of it as a "law of freedom" scarcely implies such a contrast in itself. For example, 4 Maccabees exploits the Stoic association of law with freedom as an apology for Jewish law, not a criticism of it (14:2); see also Philo's *Every Good Man is Free*, esp. 45–47; also *Conf.* 93, where he equates such freedom (*eleutherian*) with the redemption of the soul by "God the only Saviour"; see Allison 2013, 91.

40. This results in some expressions that would have sounded peculiar to a traditional Stoic, as, e.g., the notion of a *logos* "doer" in 1:22–25. See in this respect Philo's interpretation of a standard Stoic definition of law in light of Deut 33:3–4 LXX: "'Law' being evidently nothing else than the divine *logos* enjoining what we ought to do and forbidding what we should not do, as Moses testifies by saying 'he received [*edexato*] a law from his words [*apo tōn logōn*]'.... If, then, the law is a divine *logos*, and the man of true worth 'does' the law [*poei ton nomon*], he assuredly 'does' the *logos* as well [*poiei ... kai ton logon*]" (*Migr.* 130 [Colson and Whitaker, slightly modified]). James's enjoinder to "receive" (*dexasthe*) a *logos* that is already implanted is apparently another result of its apologetic correlation of the internal law posited by Stoics with the authoritative texts and ethic of his own group. Note also in this connection, however, Wilson's observations (2002, 156–57) regarding Philo's use of the term "receiving" (*dexomai*) in the context of sexual metaphors for attaining virtue with which he compares Jas 1:14–15, 18. In *QG* 4.99, e.g., Philo portrays the virtuous man as one who "receives the unadulterated seeds of divinity which the Father of all is wont to sow in us from above." Note that such "receiving" of something "from above" is necessary despite the fact that humans, according to Philo, already

here, as for Philo, 4 Maccabees, and the Apostolic Constitutions, the ethic in question is that defined by the scriptural torah (2:8–12; see Kloppenborg 2007a, 247–48). If James assumes that this law has been somehow modified (rather than merely interpreted) by Jesus so as to now stand in contrast to Jewish law—or assumes, more generally, a Christianism that stands in contrast to Judaism—such assumptions are so tacit as to be beyond subtle.[41]

Conclusion

The Jewish and Hellenistic characteristics of the Letter of James are not reducible to a dichotomy of substance and form. James interprets the literary culture of the Jews in light of that of the Greeks, and vice-versa. As in so many other works of its era, central themes and concepts of Hellenistic philosophy are read into Judean tradition, rendering the latter the very embodiment of elite Greek values in what was effectively an apology for Jewish culture and piety (Collins 2000, 14–16). In James's creative fusion of Greek and Judean culture, the moral philosophers' central problem of mastering desire is integrated into a conceptual worldview in which humanity was created by the God of the Judeans in his own image, is subject to the wiles of a devil and his demons, and will ultimately face a final

---

have a natural capacity for virtue. See in this respect Philo's allegorical interpretation of the injunction regarding leprosy in Lev 13:12–13 in *Plant.* 110–111, with which one might also compare Jas 1:21: "But while we, even under teachers, fail to make progress and become apt pupils, some, taking advantage of a nature which is its own teacher, have released the good in them from the hurtful growths which had fastened upon it.… The aim of this ordinance [about leprosy] is that, by way of leaving behind [*methemenoi*] us bodily concerns, we may abandon the condition of mind which is changeful and vacillating … and may receive the plain hue of truth [*alētheias haploun chrōma dexōmetha*] with its freedom from changefulness and indecision." The mixed metaphors of "releasing the good in them" and "receiving … the truth" result from Philo's simultaneous views that humans have an innate potential for goodness and that God is nonetheless the one who actually accomplishes it in them; see *Mut.* 141, and further *Leg.* 3.136–137, quoted above.

41. Allison (2013, 88) suggests that the absence of such "unambiguously Christian beliefs" is a function of the author's desire for "his group to be perceived as conventional … he wanted Christian Jews to be perceived as Jews"; similarly Kloppenborg 2007a. The other possibility, of course, is the whole perception of absent ideas is a function of problematic modern expectations rather than some deliberate rhetorical strategy on the part of the author.

judgment in accord with God's law. This sharpens the classic questions of the letter's authorship and social-historical context, and even its literary structure and composition (Jackson-McCabe 2014). More generally, it reminds modern, critical readers to be both aware and wary of facile assumptions regarding the relationship of the subcultures created by Jesus groups both to one another and to the wider cultures they inhabited, and thus what it means, more generally, to talk about a "Christian context" in the ancient world.

James in the Context of Jewish Wisdom Literature

Benjamin Wold

Before seeking to contextualize the letter of James within Jewish wisdom literature, it is first necessary to articulate how this category is used.[1] The wisdom traditions of the Hebrew Bible—Job, Psalms, Proverbs, Qoheleth (Ecclesiastes), Song of Songs—belong more precisely to Israelite wisdom, whereas the focus here is on postbiblical tradition and especially texts that belong to early Jewish writings from the second century BCE to first century CE. Some compositions, especially Sirach (Ecclesiasticus) and the Wisdom of Solomon, are well known as they are transmitted in both canonical and apocryphal collections by different religious communities. The discovery of the Dead Sea Scrolls is still in the process of transforming our understanding of Jewish wisdom in the period. In addition to fragmentary manuscripts of Psalms, Proverbs, Qoheleth, and Ben Sira (the Hebrew original of Greek Sirach), several previously unknown wisdom compositions were found at Qumran. These are: Instruction (1Q26, 4Q415, 4Q416, 4Q417, 4Q418, 4Q423), Wiles of Wicked Woman (4Q184), Beatitudes (4Q525), and a variety of sapiential works and hymns (4Q410–413, 4Q424, 4Q426, 4Q473, 4Q474–476, 4Q498).

Literature discovered at Qumran is by no means monolithic, but rather it represents religious traditions from a multiplicity of authors and a variety of communities. Although the eleven caves that held scrolls were found in the late 1940s and early 1950s, the materials from Cave 4, where 574 manuscripts were discovered in 1952, were not published in critical editions until the mid-1990s through to the early 2000s. Many of these compositions, including many wisdom texts, are not products of the Yahad (the Jewish community at Qumran) and should not be labeled sectarian. The relevance of these previously unknown wisdom compositions for the assessment of

---

1. Portions of this chapter appear in a different form in Wold 2019.

wisdom traditions in the New Testament has only been the subject of a few preliminary studies (e.g., Brooke 2005; Lichtenberger 2003).

Of the sapiential writings discovered at Qumran, Instruction has had the largest impact on the reassessment of Jewish wisdom because revelation, cosmology, and eschatology (i.e., apocalyptic perspectives) are part of its discourse. This is especially important for the study of James because similar apocalyptic views also occur in that letter. Both James and Instruction are widely considered to be sapiential documents because they are interested in well-known wisdom topoi (e.g., poverty) and teach using standard wisdom forms such as aphorisms and admonitions. To a large extent, before the discovery of Instruction wisdom and apocalyptic were considered incompatible, like oil and water, but since the publication of this composition in 1999 these once impermeable categories have been eroded. Although wisdom and apocalyptic have been discussed in relationship to other sapiential texts, such as the Wisdom of Solomon (Burkes 2002), Instruction has had the most significant impact on the study of Jewish wisdom in the last decade. In recent years, it has become commonplace to discuss conflicted boundaries between wisdom and apocalyptic, which is to say that this-worldly and otherworldly perspectives do not assume competing worldviews.

Instruction was originally about thirty columns in length and is the largest and most substantive wisdom composition discovered at Qumran. It is partially preserved in at least eight copies, from which we may infer its significance. Moreover, Instruction is not a product of the Qumran community, is not sectarian, and cannot be relegated to a perceived fringe movement. Although the surviving manuscripts date to the late first century BCE and early first century CE, it is most likely that Instruction was composed by at least the mid-second century BCE because it appears to be cited by the Hodayot (1QH^a XVIII, 29–30; 4Q418 55, 10). Instruction has often been translated and interpreted as a text with deterministic assumptions and a dualistic view of humanity (Goff 2013); however, in a recent study I have argued against this view and concluded instead that all humanity are created the same, they are universally given the ability to differentiate between good and evil, and one's fate relates to lived-out wisdom and individual merit (Wold 2018).

One of the most striking features of James's paraenesis is the nature of wisdom as revealed (1:5) and given by God from above (3:15); this feature indicates an apocalyptic transcendence whereby understanding is derived from the heavenly realm as opposed to the earthly. James acknowledges otherworldly beings, namely the devil (4:7; cf. Wis 2:24) and demons (2:19; 3:15), which reflects his cosmology. James's teaching about wisdom has an eschatological aspect: the consequences for wise and ethical behavior are not only found in the here and now, but also reward and punishment are future. This stands in contrast, for example, to Sirach, who understands act and consequence in this life rather than the afterlife. Below the letter of James is contextualized within Jewish wisdom literature by focusing on these three topics: revelation, cosmology, and eschatology.

Revelation

James 1:5 exhorts that anyone who lacks wisdom should petition God, who will bestow it. Two types of wisdom are contrasted in 3:15–17. One is earthly, unspiritual, and devilish, but the other comes from above and is pure. Although wisdom comes from above, James does not personify wisdom (cf. 1 En. 42). The reason revelation is needed is because a person "lacks," which likely relates at least in part to a negative anthropology (Jas 2:4; 3:8; 4:16). The notion that any quest for wisdom will fail unless God gives understanding undergirds ideas about the pursuit of wisdom in early Jewish literature generally (e.g., 4Q299 8, 5–7). What is the nature of revealed wisdom, and how should we understand it in relationship to other early Jewish traditions? One way to address this question is to consider the relationship between revealed wisdom and the Mosaic torah. James roots his teachings in exegetical tradition and therefore views Scripture as authoritative, however he never thematizes the torah nor identifies wisdom with the torah (cf. Sir 15:1; 24:8; 24:23). The only occasion where the Greek word *nomos* (i.e., "law") may refer to the torah is in the "law of freedom" (Jas 2:12). The other occurrences of *nomos* in Jas 4:11 are likely about the law of Christ and intentionally evoke Jesus's teaching in Matt 7:1–5. In a study devoted to law and the torah in James, Matt Jackson-McCabe (2001) concludes that God implants the *logos* ("implanted word," 1:21) in humanity, which finds written expression in the torah, but that 2:12 is concerned to associate *nomos* with a Stoic conception of freedom and natural law and not to the Mosaic torah. Therefore, while Scripture informs James's teaching and is both alluded to and cited, there is no explicit mention of the torah vis-à-vis the Greek term *nomos*.[2]

---

2. I use *Scripture* here to denote traditions that were not yet defined or necessarily canonical when James was written.

A hallmark of Instruction is the repeated (about twenty-five times) exhortation for the audience to seek and understand the *rāz nihyeh* ("mystery of existence"). This Hebrew expression has temporal connotations and refers to God's ordering of the cosmos and encompasses everything from creation to end-time judgment. Both James and Instruction make revealed wisdom central to their ethical exhortations. Apart from Instruction the mystery of existence is found in the Rule of the Community (1QS XI, 3–4) and the Book of Mysteries (1Q27 1 I, 3–4); the notion of "mystery" is frequent in Qumran discoveries as well as in Pauline writings, but occurs nowhere in James. Instruction never thematizes the torah, the torah is not associated with wisdom, and indeed the Hebrew word *torah* never occurs. Moreover, the mystery of existence in Instruction is not a cipher for the torah, but rather the torah is likely subordinate to the mystery (Wold 2018). Instruction, like James, relies upon Scripture when admonishing and exhorting his audience, which differs from Sirach who is uninterested in interpreting the torah and never cites it, preferring instead to write in the form of proverbs.

In one passage of Instruction, often referred to as the Vision of Hagu (4Q417 1 I), meditation on revelation called "Hagu" appears to be given to all humanity at creation ("this is a vision of meditation to a book of memorial, and he made humanity, a people with a spirit, to inherit it," line 16).[3] Hagu and the mystery are closely related and express revelation in similar ways. Fundamentally, revelation in Instruction enables one to distinguish between good and evil, however this is only the beginning point as the pursuit of the mystery is a life-long endeavor. By seeking the mystery and living according to it, one may be appointed a "firstborn son" to God (4Q416 2 II, 19–23; 4Q418 81+81a, 5) and become one who "actualizes wisdom" (4Q418 81+81a, 15–20).

One difference between revealed wisdom in James and Instruction relates to when and why it is bestowed. In James, wisdom is revealed at an individual's request and helps one to overcome one's own deficiencies. James's emphasis is on right action, and revelation enables one to live out wisdom. Instruction's beginning point is the creation of humanity, who have inherited the ability to meditate on the order of the cosmos, and if one fails to act appropriately by distinguishing good from evil then access to meditation is removed ("Hagu is no longer given to a fleshly spirit

---

3. Translations are those of the author unless otherwise noted.

because it did not know the difference between good and evil," 4Q417 1 I, 17–18). Therefore, the relationship of right action and revelation in James and Instruction is inverse: in James wisdom is revealed and enables right living, in Instruction it has been revealed to one how to live rightly and one is accountable to do so. Revealed wisdom in James helps to resolve a negative anthropology; revelation is given from above to help a person overcome sin. Instruction does not share the same view of humanity; from the beginning humankind has it within their remit to distinguish right from wrong, and one who fails to do so loses this privilege.

Instruction associates revelation with creation and the structure of the cosmos. The implanted *logos* (1:21) and the "law of freedom" (2:12) in James have been discussed by Matt Jackson-McCabe (in this volume) as relating to the natural order vis-à-vis Stoicism, however there is also an analogue in the Jewish sapiential tradition. Both James and Instruction understand, albeit in their own terms, the cosmic order and an inherent aspect of creation as informing humanity when making ethical choices.

Cosmology

James's cosmology is apparent in his belief in otherworldly actors, namely the devil and demons, and yet it has been argued that these beings only function rhetorically. In this view, James acknowledges external evil, but this is ultimately a pragmatic mechanism to motivate his audience to live rightly (Wischmeyer 2016, 163). This conclusion may be challenged by the discovery of Instruction, because the first column (4Q416 1) introduces its wisdom teachings by explicitly setting it within a cosmological framework. Moreover, Instruction has a lively interest in otherworldly actors too, namely angelic beings.

One might assess whether the devil and demons in James are only rhetorical—or, alternatively, an integral aspect of his cosmology—by exploring how sin and evil are understood. The human capacity to sin is the subject of Jas 1:13–15. Within scholarship on this composition is a wider tendency to infer that the author has a pessimistic anthropology and that humans by nature are inclined to do evil, but is evil confined to a human capacity to sin? In Jas 2:4 thought is described as evil; in 3:8 the tongue is a "restless evil" full of deadly poison; and in 4:16 human boasting is evil. Human nature in Jas 1:13–15 includes desire, which entices and lures one down a path which ultimately leads to death: "No one, when tempted, should say, 'I am being tempted by God'; for God cannot be tempted by evil and he himself tempts no one. But one is tempted by one's own desire, being lured and enticed by it; then, when that desire has conceived, it gives birth to sin, and that sin, when it is fully grown, gives birth to death" (NRSV).

"Desire" (Greek *epithymia*) has been identified by Joel Marcus with the Jewish notion of the "evil inclination," which in Hebrew is *yētser ra*. His identification of "desire" with *yētser* ("inclination") is made in reference to Sir 15:11–20; he concludes that Jas 1:14–15 is similar to Sirach in that a "human being's own evil desire" is the source of evil (Marcus 1982, 608). Greek Sirach translates the Hebrew *yētser* of Sir 15:14 as "He placed humanity into the hand of their own *counsel* [*diaboulion*]." Marcus observes that the Greek term *epithymia* is never used in the Septuagint to translate the Hebrew *yētser*, but he seeks to strengthen the link between *yētser* and *epithymia* by drawing upon the writings of Philo of Alexandria. When considering Philo and Sirach to inform how *yētser* is understood, it is noteworthy that both ancient authors reject the notion that the source of evil is external to a human being. Most likely this is because their philosophically educated Greco-Roman audience was skeptical about the existence of such demonic powers.

The Qumran scrolls are our earliest witness to *yētser*, and these materials are still in the process of changing how we map the history of this idea. Qumran literature studied by Marcus is limited to the Hodayot, Rule of the Community, and Damascus Document, however several instances of *yētser* in scrolls from Cave 4, not available to him in the 1980s, update his study. When Marcus concludes by identifying "desire" with an "evil inclination," he states that "there are no specific references to a good inclination" (Marcus 1982, 621) and that it may not be accidental that the concept of the good inclination is absent. Late rabbinic concepts of *yētser* assume that there is a good *yētser* and an evil *yētser* in every person, and scholarship on James has accepted that this rabbinic notion was in operation when the letter was composed. But studies by Ishay Rosen-Zvi (2008, 2011) demonstrate that it does not operate within a binary model in early Judaism and that this is a much later development. Rosen-Zvi (2008, 27) gives significant attention to Qumran discoveries, as well as other early Jewish literature, and concludes that a monistic model of, specifically, an *evil* inclination was dominant in early Judaism.

In the Jewish literature of this era there is no undisputed occurrence of evil inclination outside of previously unknown documents from Qumran— the scrolls are the only place before rabbinic literature where the Hebrew term *yētser* qualified by *ra* ("evil") occurs. In the Qumran literature, the set phrase *yētser ra* is found on five occasions in four texts: the Plea for Deliverance (11Q5 XIX, 15–16); Instruction (4Q417 1 II, 12); Barkhi Nafshi (4Q436 1 I, 10); and the so-called 4QSectarian Text (4Q422 I, 12). Before the publication of these materials, studies on *yētser* in Qumran discoveries focused mainly on the Hodayot, where the term is so frequent (about seventy times). The negative *yētser* in the Rule of the Community and the Hodayot relate in one way or another to the activities of Belial. Occurrences of *yētser* in several of the scrolls not discussed by Marcus take this a step further when they convey that *yētser* has demonic connotations; indeed, in the Plea for Deliverance (11Q5 [11QPsª] XIX, 15–16) the *yētser* appears to move from within the human being to an outward force. The Plea for Deliverance has attracted considerable attention because "evil inclination" occurs in a context alongside "satan" and an "unclean spirit," and it could be interpreted as personified external evil. The Plea for Deliverance is structured on Ps 51 and at lines 15–16 alludes to Ps 119:133 ("let not iniquity rule over me," replacing "iniquity" with both "satan" and "unclean spirit"). Plea for Deliverance (11Q5 XIX, 15–16a) reads: "let not a satan rule over me, or an unclean spirit, let not pain or an evil inclination rule over my bones."

In the Plea for Deliverance, the coupling of "satan" and "unclean spirit" in parallel with "evil inclination" makes clear that these are not a state of mind, but rather outward forces and demonic in nature. Such personification is part of a broader development demonizing sin, perhaps similar to Barkhi Nafshi (4Q436 1 I–II), where "evil inclination" is rebuked. On the one hand, the reference in Barkhi Nafshi may be describing the warding-off of a demonic being or evil spirit. On the other hand, it is described along with negative tendencies (e.g., stiff neck, haughty eyes) and may simply be a personification of vices.

In Instruction, excluding overlaps, the noun *yētser* may occur as many as six times; five times with at least some discernible context (4Q416 1, 16; 4Q417 1 I, 9, 11, 17; 4Q417 1 II, 12) and once without any meaningful context (4Q418 217, 1). Only one of these uses in Instruction is qualified with "evil." In comparison with the Hodayot and Plea for Deliverance, occurrences of the term in Instruction have received little attention. Rosen-Zvi sees this instance of *yētser ra* in Instruction as innovative because it is an active misleading agent and is closer to what we find in the Plea for Deliverance (and perhaps Barkhi Nafshi) than the Hodayot. Rosen-Zvi (2011, 48) is particularly interested in whether it is reified and concludes that it features "in a demonological semantic field" even if its precise meaning is rather fluid.

While Instruction frequently refers to angelic beings, there are no explicit references either to demons or the devil. 4Q416 1 preserves the opening column of the document and has the broken line: "[fo]r inclination of the flesh [*yētser baśar*] is he, and from understand[ing" (4Q416 1, 16). John Strugnell and Daniel Harrington (1999, 8), the editors of the critical edition of Instruction, describe this passage as speaking "about God's orderly rule over the cosmos—the heavenly hosts and the luminaries (ll. 1–10)," as well as the proper response of all creation to the order of the cosmos. Therefore, a negatively qualified *yētser*, here called "fleshly" and later described as "evil," may be part of the cosmological framework that begins this composition.

In 4Q417 1 II it appears that "evil inclination" may be in synonymous parallel with "understandings of the flesh," both of which lead the addressee astray. What is striking about this passage of Instruction, especially if desire in James is related to the Hebrew notion of inclination, is the similar activity of misleading and enticing associated with it. These lines of 4Q417 1 II (par. 4Q418 123 I, 1–2) read:

12   do not let the thought of an evil inclination entice you[
13   by truth you will seek, do not [*let the thought of an evil inclination*] entice you [*and do not do anything*]
14   without his commanding. *By* understandings of the flesh do not be led as[tray

The expression "thought" in construct with the *yētser*, were it to occur without "entice," would seemingly locate the inclination within the interior of a human being (cf. 1QS V, 5; 4Q370 1 I, 3; 4Q422 I, 12). The Hebrew word translated "enticed" (*patah*) could be rendered as "misled," "deceived," or even "seduced." The only other occurrences of this term in the Qumran literature are in (1) 4Q184 1 line 17 (Wiles of the Wicked Woman), and (2) the Temple Scroll (11Q19 66, 8; par. 4Q524 15, 22). In 4Q184 the seductress, or perhaps demonic figure, "entices" human beings, and in the Temple Scroll a man "seduces" a virgin. The language of enticement has strong sexual as well as demonic connotations, which is noteworthy because Jas 1:14–15 uses highly sexualized terms ("conceive," "give birth") to describe enticement to sin. Here in Instruction, the activity ascribed to evil inclination in line 12 makes it an alien and independent force. This evil inclination, as an alien threat, refers to active evil whose field of play is the human mind, emotions, and perceptions; this is particularly threatening because one can no longer trust one's self. Moreover, reflected in this mechanism is the generation of a more highly attuned sense of interiority.

4Q417 1 II lines 13–14 emphasize keeping God's commandment, which has similarities with the language of the original Hebrew of Sir 15:14–15 preserved in MS A.

> 14 From the beginning God created man,
>   and He placed him in the hand of one lying in wait,
>   He gave him into the hand of his inclination [yētser];
> 15 if you desire, keep the commandment,
>   and (with) understanding do his will.

Both here in Ben Sira ("keep the commandment") and Instruction ("do not do anything without his commanding") associate God's command-ment with yētser. In Ben Sira, keeping a commandment is qualified with "if you desire," which sets obedience as a choice to be made according to one's inclination (cf. 15:17, "before man is life and death, whatever he desires will be given to him"). Instruction does not associate obe-dience to God's commands with one's thoughts, and certainly not the evil inclination, but rather stringently instructs not to do anything that God has not commanded. Ben Sira (MS A) exhorts one to do God's will in relationship to "understanding," whereas Instruction warns that "understandings of the flesh" can mislead. Instruction at these points reflects concern about being led astray by thoughts of an evil inclination, whereas Ben Sira has a more positive view that people can choose to do God's will without alien influence.

Like Instruction (4Q417 1 II), Jas 1:14–15 denotes active agency when desire is described as "luring" and "enticing" (deleazo). The only other occurrence of the Greek verb deleazo in the New Testament is in 2 Pet 2:14, 18, where false teachers "entice" others to indulge in sinful passions of the flesh. This section of 2 Peter emphasizes sexual sin and gives sus-tained attention to comparing those who deceive with the fallen angels (2:4–5). The only other occurrence of deleazo is in the Greek versions of early Jewish pseudepigraphical writings, namely the Greek Apocalypse of Moses. In 19:1 the activities of the serpent trying to deceive Eve in the garden of Eden are described as: "He said these things, wishing in the end to entice [deleazo] and kill me." Later in 26:3, the serpent is cursed, and the reason given is that "you ensnared [deleazo] them in your evil." There-fore, deleazo is clearly associated with the activity of evil actors enticing one to sin, and in the Greek Apocalypse of Moses this is even to death (cf. Jas 1:14–15). The Hebrew verb "entice" (*patah*) and Greek verb "entice" (*deleazo*) are both used for *yētser/epithymia* and have both demonic and sexual overtones.

James and Instruction share a combination of expressing an internal process—that is, in Instruction it is the "thought" of an evil inclination and in James it is "one's own" desire—while coupling it with active agency. The activity ascribed to both "thought" and "desire" is alien; the human mind and emotions are within the demonic force's field of play, which is particularly frightening because one cannot trust one's own judgment. In both Instruction and James, the ability to overcome this active and alien force operating within a person's interior is revealed wisdom (i.e., Jas 1:5; "mystery of existence" in Instruction). Revelation comes from above and outside of humanity and enables one to act wisely.

Although James avoids explicitly detailing his cosmology, he is interested in what is above and below (3:15): heavenly wisdom stands in contrast to what is earthly and devilish. From 1:16–18 we learn that God the Father is above in the heavens, which is a place of light where there are no shadows and from where he gives gifts to his children. Those below are exhorted not to become stained by this world; we read in 1:27: "Religion that is pure and undefiled before God" is "to keep oneself unstained by the world." Noteworthy is that Instruction understands that the spirit with which humanity is created may be corrupted and become "*fleshly* spirit" (*ruaḥ baśar*, emphasis added). In James, the terms *kosmos* ("world") and *sarx* ("flesh") describe what is impure and below while God and light describe what is above. This contrast is particularly salient in 4:4, where "friendship with the world" is "enmity with God." This description anthropomorphizes the "world": those who are friends with it are God's enemy. One possibility is that the personified world is a way to express a power that is in opposition to God. The association of the world with what is "devilish" (3:15) suggests such a characterization. Indeed, when James mentions demons and the devil, they are not—within early Jewish and Christian literature—esoteric ideas or rhetorical devices.

In Jas 4:7, the author instructs: "Submit yourselves to God, resist the devil and he will flee from you." Submitting and drawing near to God is an integral and instrumental part of resisting the devil; how humanity approaches God is mainly conceivable through acts of prayer and worship. Indeed, when prayer is mentioned later in 5:16, in reference to confessing sins in order to be healed (cf. 5:13), James comments that "the prayer of a righteous man has great power in its effects." The devil is regarded in 4:7 as an actual being, and yet the opposition portrayed in this verse is not between God and the devil, but rather the devil is humanity's opponent. The devil is not described as fleeing from God, but rather from the person who resists him. Humanity in this verse stands between God and the devil, who are part of the fabric of James's cosmological framework in which humanity is located and instructed. The author's emphasis is not on negotiating cosmological dualism, per se, but rather addressing pervasive and variegated evil. Rather than describing the conflict between two cosmic powers, James is interested in locating humanity between them and offers solutions to a complex problem of evil: revelation, given by human petition (1:5), provides wisdom from above (3:15) and is key to overcoming evil.

The example of correct belief in Jas 2:19 is the oneness of God—a clear reference to the Shema Israel (Deut 6:4)—and holds further clues about the place of demons within the author's cosmology. The reference in James to the Shema in the phrase "God is one" is found within a demonological context ("even the demons believe—and shudder") and therefore resonates with the liturgical practices involving phylacteries and mezuzot in the period. Esther Eshel, Hanan Eshel, and Armin Lange (2010, 48) conclude that the inclusion of Deut 6:4 in 4Q150–152 (4QMezuzot[b-d]) demonstrates that since the first century BCE, the Shema was "understood as a powerful protection for the houses of Jewish families" and that "already in the late Second Temple period … mezuzot containing the Shema Israel were used for apotropaic purposes." In addition to mezuzot from Qumran, the Nash Papyrus, containing the Shema, may also have been intended for use as a Jewish amulet, either a tefillah or a mezuzah. Furthermore, there are echoes of the Shema in Testament of the Twelve Patriarchs when "loving the Lord with all one's strength" results in the "spirit of Beliar" fleeing (T. Iss. 7:6–7). The response of demons to the Shema in Jas 2:19 is to shudder; a similar response to the use of phylacteries is observed by Graham Twelftree (2007, 179–80) in the Greek Magical Papyri (4:3014–3019, in Betz 1992), which reads: "Write this phylactery upon a sheet of tin and hang it on the patient. It is for every demon a thing to be trembled at, as he fears it."

James 2:19 is not offering instruction in the practice of apotropaic prayer or use of amulets, however this verse reflects James's cosmology when it discursively alludes to a well-known practice of countering demonic evil. To depict demons as shuddering in response to the declaration of the oneness of God found in the Shema is to evoke an apotropaic practice known to and accepted by the audience. This resonates with Jas 5:14, where the "name of the Lord" is used when healing the sick (cf. 11Q11 V; 4Q560 I-II; Jub. 10:3-6). Therefore, in James, drawing near to God in prayer is a practice wherein the devil and demons may be resisted.

Instruction reconfigures our understanding of sapiential discourse because of its explicit cosmological framework. The occurrence of "evil inclination" in Instruction (4Q417 1 II) has an important parallel with Jas 1:14-15; both passages share the similarity of expressing alien activity operating within the human interior. The assessment of *yētser*, as it relates to *epithymia* in Jas 1:14-15, opens up wider questions about the presence of evil actors external to human beings in the letter. The problem of sin and evil in James is multifaceted: it is not only that people cannot trust themselves, which seems to be the case, but also demonic forces are at play both within and without. The absolute purity of "wisdom from above" (3:17) is the solution to this wide-ranging problem of evil. While James does not spell out his cosmology like Instruction does, when this composition is set among early Jewish writings it comes more clearly into view.

Eschatology

Eschatology is one aspect of the broader phenomenon of ancient apocalyptic. As we have seen, the otherworldly perspectives of Instruction and James cannot be reduced merely to discussions about temporal axis. James reflects not only an eschatological urgency, but also a greater concern about how to deal with sin and evil in the present time. The eschatological dimensions to James's teachings have received attention from several scholars, notably Todd Penner (1996) and Patrick J. Hartin (2005), however Darian Lockett (2005) is alone in offering a study specifically on eschatology in both James and Instruction. While eschatology is a subject treated in nearly every study on Instruction, Jean-Sébastien Rey (2009) in his book titled 4QInstruction: Sagesse et eschatologie ("wisdom and eschatology") makes it the focal point.

The imminent expectation of punishment for the wicked and reward for the righteous in James is located within a hope that the Lord will return as judge (5:8-9). Whereas in Instruction the mystery of existence reveals God's justice as framed within cosmology, in James the emphasis is on the Lord who brings justice. The sinner's fate in James is "death" (5:20). While gehenna is mentioned, it is not as a place where sinners go after death, but rather as something that sets the human tongue afire (3:6; cf. "Hades" in Wis 1:14, 2:1). James promises future reward, a "crown of life," to those who are steadfast in trials (1:12) and says that they will inherit the kingdom (2:5). The present time is also called the "last days" (5:3).

James and Instruction both envisage eschatological reward for the righteous and destruction for the wicked. In the opening column of Instruction, God pronounces judgment from heaven upon works of wickedness while accepting his faithful children with pleasure (4Q416 1, 10). It seems that a day of judgment and destruction of the wicked is anticipated (4Q416 1, 12–13; cf. "day of judgment," Wis 3:18), a time when iniquity comes to an end and truth is perfected forever. 4Q417 1 I instructs that from the mystery of existence one may know good and evil and their respective ways. This column emphasizes that the ways of iniquity result in future punishment (4Q417 1 I, 6–8) and the righteous are rewarded for their faithfulness (4Q417 1 I, 14, 26; cf. 1 En. 104:1–5; Wis 4–9). The order of the cosmos, right and wrong, is engraved in the heavens and is the basis for judgment against humanity (4Q417 1 I, 13b–18). Future judgment and reward are found elsewhere (4Q418 55 11–12; 4Q418 69 8); destruction (4Q418 162, 4; cf. 4Q418 177, 2, "the pi]t and Abaddon is his end") awaits the unfaithful while "glory everlasting and peace eternal" are promised to the righteous (4Q418 126 I–II, 6–7).

Instruction is concerned about guarding one's spirit from contamination (4Q416 2 I, 1–6; 2 II, 6; 2 III, 17–18; 4Q418 126 II, 8, 77). As we have seen, the unfaithful are referred to as "fleshly spirit" because they have not lived in accordance with the created order. In 4Q418 127, the addressee is directly warned that one's soul becomes faint from failing to do good, which results in death. Instruction presents judgment and destruction for those who fail to act wisely; one's fate is dependent upon right action and readers are urged to live faithfully in accordance with the mystery that results in eternal life. Instruction does not express imminent anticipation of the end of time, but rather is interested in locating consequences for present actions in the eschaton. Indeed, when the Hebrew term qets ("end") occurs in Instruction, it refers to a time or period, but not to the "end" as found in Yaḥad literature (e.g., "end of days").

Both James and Instruction use farming imagery in relationship to understanding periods of time. James 5:7–8 exhorts one to be patient while awaiting the Lord's coming and presents a simile: This is like a farmer who tends crops and waits for both the early and late rains before the harvest. Instruction uses farming and agriculture to teach about observing times and understanding the created order. 4Q423 5 lines 5–6 state that "if you are a f]armer, observe the appointed time … meditate on your crops, in your labor give attention[n to the knowledge of] good and evil."

The fragmentary nature of Instruction has resulted in different interpretations of its eschatology. Disagreement centers primarily on whether Instruction reflects a realized eschatology. When the addressee is said to be seated among "nobles" (4Q416 2 III 11) and "holy ones" (4Q418 81+81a, 1–14), terms denoting angelic beings, some scholars view this as anticipation of future glorification, while others understand that the community participates with an angelic community in the present through acts of worship and veneration (e.g., 4Q400–407 [4QShirShab]). One leitmotif of Instruction is the notion of inheritance, which appears most frequently to refer to allotment or one's place within the community, and it is unlikely that this language is used regarding one's predetermined fate in the hereafter.

Conclusion

Reading James in the context of early Jewish literature may find any number of departure points. The focus here has been a relatively newly discovered composition—Instruction—because it has had such a profound influence on how Jewish wisdom of the Second Temple era is understood. An observation that does not fit within the three subsections above is that both James and Instruction also share an interest in poverty and the poor. While this is a common topos in ancient wisdom literature, James and Instruction—in contrast to the elitism of Sirach (e.g., 38:24)—positively associate poverty with humility and the pursuit of wisdom, and on occasion they even use poverty language figuratively for their communities (Jas 2:5; 4Q416 2 II–III). Much remains to be done contextualizing James within early Jewish wisdom literature as the significance of previously unknown Qumran discoveries become more familiar to scholars of early Christianity. Most importantly, the reconfiguration of how we understand the relationship of wisdom to apocalypticism, which has defined the study of early Jewish literature in the last two decades, is still in the process of transforming our understanding of wisdom in the New Testament.

The Genre of James:
Diaspora Letter, Wisdom Instruction, or Both?

Luke L. Cheung and Kelvin C. L. Yu

Eric D. Hirsch (1967, 93) regards genre as "less like a game than like a code of social behavior." In this spirit, the literary critic Heather Dubrow (2005, 31) explains that by adopting a certain genre, the author "is in effect telling us the name and rules of his code, rules that affect not only how he should write the work but also how we should read it." This literary character with regard to the entire document is what we refer to as literary genre. By use of a particular genre, the author establishes with the reader a kind of generic contract that stabilizes and enables interpretation. As distinct from the shorter literary forms such as pronouncement story or aphorism, genre refers to the longer, larger, more encompassing literary types like apocalypse, gospel, wisdom instruction, and letter. It refers to the work as a whole, viewed in comparison with other contemporary literary works.

Over the years James has been classified in various ways, including as an allegory on Jacob's farewell address (Meyer 1930), as a Greek diatribe (Ropes 1916, 12–14), and as a homily or a collection of homilies (Luther, *LW* 35:397; Wessel 1953, 80–96).[1] None of these suggestions has received wide acceptance.[2] In recent decades, however, scholars have arrived at a partial consensus. Many have argued that James belongs to the genre of Jewish diaspora letter.[3] Also, James's characteristics of wisdom instruction have been recognized. In the following discussion, we will first examine

---

1. Other scholars who classify James as a homily include Moo 2000, 6–9; and Witherington 2007, 11.

2. See the critique of those classifications in Cheung 2003, 6–11.

3. Scholars who read James as a diaspora letter include Adamson 1989, 116–18; Jackson-McCabe 1996; Tsuji 1997, 23–37; Niebuhr 1998; Verseput 2000; Allison 2013, 73; Painter 2012, 42; and Vlachos 2013.

the letter form of James and see how well it fits into the genre of Jewish diaspora letter. We will then consider if the work can also be categorized as a text of wisdom instruction.

James as a Diaspora Letter

Although in its present form James has a clear letter opening in 1:1, the epistolary classification of James has been debated and rejected by some. One of the main reasons for rejecting James as a letter is the lack of a formal letter ending, which usually includes a farewell wish, a health wish, secondary greetings, and an autograph.[4] The absence of greetings and other formal ending components, however, is not the only reason that prompts scholars to question the epistolary nature of James. Martin Dibelius (1976, 2) argued that "it is impossible to consider [James] an actual letter." His conclusion is based on the assumption that James is a paraenesis that lacks design and coherence, a kind of literature that addresses a general Greco-Roman context rather than a specific situational setting. Stephen R. Llewelyn (1997) also rejects the epistolary classification of James on the ground that 1:1 is a pseudepigraphic designation added to the work at a later date. He argues that the name of the actual author is missing and that the identity of the recipients is obscure. Llewelyn's argument is based on a hypothesis that has no support from any textual tradition or the letter itself.

Fred O. Francis (1970), in his influential study on the structures of Hellenistic Jewish epistolary literature, considers the forms of Jewish letters embedded in historical narratives (1 Macc 10:25–45 and Josephus, A.J. 8.50–54). Arguing from these examples, he notes that both James and 1 John have a doubling of opening formulae that state and restate the theme of the letter. In James, following the greeting, the double letter-opening twice (1:2–11 on joy [chara], and 1:12–15 on blessing [makarios]) introduces the subject matter of the letter. Though this perspective is endorsed by Peter Davids (1982, 22–28), the exhortation to rejoice in James is very different from the usual expression of the sender's joy in the opening of Hellenistic letters.[5] Instead of expressing joy on behalf of the recipients,

---

4. For the form of Hellenistic letter endings, see Exler 1923, 69–77, 113–27; Weima 2010, 310.

5. Typical expressions of joy on behalf of the recipients in the letter opening can be seen, e.g., in 1 Cor 1:4–9 and 1 Thess 1:2–10.

James asks them to consider their testing as joy. In addition, the beatitude in 1:12 corresponds neither with the blessing in Aramaic letters (Pardee 1978, 338) nor the thanksgiving section of the Pauline epistles. Thus Francis's notion of a double opening has been challenged.

Regardless, the letter opening of James is still clearly recognizable. It consists of a prescript (1:1) and a prologue (1:2–17). The prescript provides information concerning the sender and the addressee of the letter and functions like the greeting in a personal speech dialogue. The prescript of many Jewish letters in the Second Temple period basically followed the Greek letter form (e.g., 2 Macc 1:10). James opens with the customary Greek formula of address: A (the sender) to B (the recipient). The use of the single salutation, "greeting" (*chairein*), as the opening formula accords with the common convention of the Greek letter as well (cf. 2 Macc 1:10; Acts 15:23; 23:26; White 1984, 1734).

On the other hand, whether James's closing section qualifies it as a letter is not so clear. Some regard James as having no formal letter closing (Bauckham 1999, 12). In particular, no greetings or farewells are found at the end of James. Others, however, argue that the letter closing begins with 5:12, introduced by "above all" (*pro pantōn*) and followed by a direct address with an imperative (Francis 1970, 125; White 1986, 200–201; Moo 2000, 232). This section functions more or less in the same way as "finally" (*loipon*) at the close of Pauline letters (1 Thess 4:1; 2 Thess 3:1; 2 Cor 13:11; Phil 4:8). Many scholars agree that James is a letter since it exhibits formal epistolary features (in addition to those mentioned above, see Pearson and Porter 2002, 155), yet there is debate regarding whether the letter was ever actually sent and, if it was intended for actual delivery, what exact kind of letter it represents.

Function: Literary or Real Letter?

Adolf Deissmann (1901, 1–59) distinguishes between a "literary" or "artistic" epistle and a "real" letter. The former is not a real private letter sent to the readers, but instead it is public literature with an epistolary format that was never actually sent to the named recipients. Some regard James as a literary letter rather than a real one (Francis 1970; Davids 1982, 24; Johnson 1995, 24; Wachob 2000, 2–8). Richard Bauckham (1999, 13), however, rightly points out that in form and content it is a real letter that could have been sent from the author to a community or groups of communities, but it is not clear whether it *functioned* as a real letter. Though we cannot be sure from the form and content of the work whether the letter of James was actually sent from its purported author to its recipients, Darian R. Lockett (2008, 69) insists that "James is set within an epistolary framework and must be read and interpreted as a letter." In this regard, analyzing the genre of Jewish diaspora letter may shed light on the nature of James.

Characteristics of James as a Diaspora Letter

The fact that James addresses the "twelve tribes of the diaspora" lends support to the categorization of the work as a diaspora letter. Diaspora letters are didactic letters sent from authoritative leaders in the religious center (i.e., Jerusalem) to the communities in the Jewish diaspora. These kinds of letters are found in Jer 29 (36 LXX); Bar 6 (Letter of Jeremiah); 2 Macc 1:1–9; 1:10–2:18; 2 Bar. 78–87; 4 Bar. 6:16–25; b. Sanh. 11b; t. Sanh. 2:6; Tg. Jer. 10:11; and Elephantine Letters 21 (Passover Papyrus) and 30 (see esp. Tsuji 1997, 23–37; Niebuhr 1998; Verseput 2000; Kloppenborg 2007a; Doering 2009).

Dale C. Allison (2013, 74) lists ten common features that James shares with the diaspora letters:

1. Addressed to Jews in the diaspora (1:1; cf. 2 Bar. 78:1, "to the nine and a half tribes");
2. Claimed authorship by recognized authority (1:1; cf. 2 Macc 1:10–2:18; 2 Bar. 78–87);
3. Composition in Greek (cf. 2 Macc 1:1–9; 1:10–2:18; 4 Bar. 6:16–25);
4. Strong didactic/paraenetic elements (cf. Jer 29:5–28; Bar [Ep Jer] 6:2–73; 2 Bar. 83:1–86:1; 4 Bar. 6:20–25);
5. Strong prophetic features (4:13–5:6; cf. Bar [Ep Jer] 6:2–73; 2 Bar. 78–87; 4 Bar. 6:16–25);
6. Consolation/encouragement in difficult circumstances (1:2–4; 5:7–11; cf. 2 Bar. 78:2–7; 81:1–82:1; 85:3–9; 4 Bar. 6:20–21);
7. Appeal to torah/law (1:25; 2:8–12; cf. 2 Macc 1:4; 2:2–3; 2 Bar. 84:1–11; 4 Bar. 6:23–24);
8. Appeal to God's generous/merciful nature (1:5, 13, 17–18; cf. 2 Macc 1:2, 24–25; 2 Bar. 78:3; 81:4; 4 Bar. 6:21);
9. Hope for/promise of a divinely wrought salvation (1:12; 2:5; 5:7–9; cf. Jer 29:10–14; 2 Macc 1:27–29; 2:7–8, 18; 2 Bar. 78–85; 4 Bar. 6:24);

10. Judgment of the unrighteous (2:13; 3:6; 5:1–6; cf. Jer 29:21–23; 2 Bar. 82:1–83:23; 85:9–15; 4 Bar. 6:17).

One should not infer that diaspora letters must have all of these characteristics, but the list does show that James has much in common with the diaspora letters of that era.[6] The function of such letters is to provide guidance for diaspora communities living away from the land of Israel to be loyal to the Lord of the covenant and to strive for the unity of the community of God's people. There is little doubt that both are matters of significant concern in the letter of James.[7] Therefore, in terms of its function, James can be classified as a diaspora letter.

Nevertheless, the quest for James's genre does not end with affirming its epistolary nature. The letter form can be used to frame a wide variety of other genres (see Berger 1984a, 1338; Bauckham 1988, 473; Starr 2004, 85). David Aune (1987, 170) even claims that epistolary postscripts and prescripts could "frame almost any type of composition." For instance, a letter that contains paraenesis can be classified as a paraenetic letter (Stowers 1986, 94–97). Therefore, the letter features in James, most notably the letter opening, could provide framework for the body of the letter, which could represent another genre. Because of this, we must further investigate whether James exhibits features of other genres within its epistolary framework, in particular, if it can be seen that the composition shows characteristics in accord with Jewish wisdom writings.

James as Wisdom Instruction

In light of the flexibility of the letter form, there is no contradiction if one identifies James both as a letter and as wisdom instruction. In this section we will argue for such a dual categorization.

Paraenetic and Wisdom Literature

Dibelius's classification of James as paraenesis once found wide acceptance. He characterized paraenesis as "a text which strings together

---

6. For a detailed study of most of these letters, see Doering 2009, 215–26.

7. In the New Testament, 1 Peter can also be classified as a diaspora letter. See, e.g., Elliott 2000, 12; Jobes 2005, 54–55; and Doering 2009, 226–35.

admonitions of general ethical content" (Dibelius 1976, 3). He regards James as a paraenetic text that lacks continuity of thought, coherence, and design, with only *"repetition of identical motifs in different places within a writing"* (Dibelius 1976, 11; emphasis original).[8] However, later scholars have rightly criticized his form-critical analysis of paraenesis as too narrowly defined.[9] Lack of coherent structure and continuity of thought are simply not the characteristics of paraenesis (see below).

Even if one accepts Dibelius's definition of paraenesis, James can hardly fit that description. Many recent scholars argue that James is carefully structured and much more closely bound together than Dibelius allows (see Taylor 2004, 86–115). Many scholars now have even questioned the validity of regarding paraenesis as a literary genre. Some regard paraenesis as merely an umbrella term for moral instruction or a mode of persuasion (Popkes 1995, 543; 2004; Wachob 2000, 51–52). Still, however, a host of scholars see the benefit of classifying paraenesis with respect to formal features such as pattern, style, and character.

The most comprehensive analysis of the classification of paraenesis has been undertaken by John G. Gammie (1990). According to him, the two literary genres of paraenesis and wisdom instruction have great affinity. Both can be categorized in terms of their formal characteristics. Both are very similar in form and style. In addition, both assume that the author and the audience share a common worldview. The main difference between paraenesis and wisdom instruction is that the former looks to models in ancient Greece whereas the latter has roots in the ancient Near East (Gammie 1990, 50–51). In the following, we will consider how James fits in the genre of wisdom instruction from the perspectives of form, content, and social function.

The Formal Characteristics of Paraenetic Literature and Jewish Wisdom Instruction

Hellenistic paraenesis (see Malherbe 1986, 124–25; Stowers 1986, 95–96; Aune 1987, 191; Fiore 1992, 163–64; Cheung 2003, 15–21) and Jewish

---

8. Scholars in support of Dibelius's view include Kümmel (1975, 404), Schrage (1973, 1–8), and Popkes (1995).

9. Among the most influential critiques to Dibelius's view are the discussion of the social setting of paraenesis in Perdue (1981, 241–56) and the discussion of James's form and structure in Davids (1982, 22–28).

wisdom instruction (Cheung 2003, 21–36) share the following formal features:

1. Collection of vivid and memorable precepts and maxims for moral argumentation;
2. The use of imperatives in exhortation, often accompanied by motive clauses;
3. The use of *encomia* (praises of moral persons) or moral examples;
4. General applicability.

All four of these features are evident in James. First, James employs various types of precepts and maxims. Bauckham (1999, 35–60) has demonstrated in detail the different kinds of aphorisms James employs in his work, including beatitudes (1:12, 25); "whoever" or "the one who" sayings (2:10; 4:4); conditional sayings (1:5, 26); synonymous aphorisms (4:8b); antithetical and paradoxical aphorisms (1:9–10a; 3:7–8a); wisdom precepts (with motive clause; 1:19b–20; 5:9a, 12, 16a); aphoristic sentences (1:3–4; 2:5, 26; 3:16); statements of reciprocity (2:13a); debate-sayings (1:13); and diatribe (2:18–23). Second, the use of imperatives is prominent in James. In James's 108 verses one finds a total of fifty-five imperatives (forty-six in the second-person) plus four imperatival future forms. Indeed, James has the highest ratio of imperatives to total words among New Testament books (see the analysis in Varner 2010, 50–51). Third, the use of exemplars in James is prominent and has been the subject of a recent monograph (R. Foster 2014). These examples serve specific functions within their particular contexts in the work: Abraham and Rahab are exemplars of an active faith that is completed with deeds (2:21–25), Job is an exemplar of steadfast endurance (5:10–11), and Elijah is an exemplar of effective prayer (5:17–18). Fourth, all the above can have general applicability to a number of different communities.

From a form-critical perspective, what distinguishes Jewish wisdom instructions from Hellenistic paraenesis is that for almost all Jewish wisdom instruction (both before and during the Second Temple period), the interpretative framework is provided by the prologue and epilogue of the work (von Lips 1990, 413; Cheung 2003, 34–36). In addition, wisdom instruction in Second Temple Judaism has a tendency to use a single maxim, either to introduce a series of other maxims or to round off a section on a particular topic (Fontaine 1982, 154; Cheung 2003, 26). This is similar to Walter T. Wilson's (1991, 41, 84, 93–95) observation that the text often starts with a programmatic statement and may end with a program-matic or concluding statement that frames the section.

It is clear that James demonstrates these features of Jewish wisdom instruction. First, one can argue that Jas 1:2–4 and 1:26–27 provide the framework for the prologue (1:2–27), which introduces the main topics in the subsequent chapters. Also, if the epilogue starts at 5:7 (thus 5:7–20), then 5:19–20 can be taken as the conclusion to the final section as well as to the whole book. The epilogue recaptures the main concern of the letter, namely the importance of endurance in testing and the urgency of repen-tance from the ways of the world. Hence the prologue and the epilogue provide the interpretative framework for the whole book. Second, the use of maxims to frame individual sections within the book is also apparent. James 2:1–13 opens in 2:1 with a precept that states the main concern of the section, and 2:13 closes the section with two concise aphorisms linked by the words "mercy" and "judgment." The following section (2:14–26) opens in 2:14 with two rhetorical questions, and it concludes in 2:26 with a symmetrical comparison. Then, 3:1–12 opens in 3:1 with another precept and closes with two rhetorical questions (3:11–12a) and a short aphoristic statement (3:12b). Next, 4:1–6 again opens with two rhetorical questions in 4:1 (cf. 2:14), and 4:6 closes the section with the quotation of the maxim from Prov 3:34. One might argue that 4:6 also opens the next section (4:6–10) that closes in 4:10 with a contrastive parallelism (Bauckham 1999, 65). The following two sections (4:13–17; 5:1–6) are distinct but related. Both begin with "come now" (4:13; 5:1). The first of these sections concludes in 4:17 with a proverbial saying in the third-person (which contrasts with the second-person addresses of 4:13–16). If 5:6b is taken as a rhetorical ques-tion ("Would he not resist you?"), then it can be seen as rounding off not only the subsection from 5:1 but also the larger section from 4:6, repeating the word "resist."

This analysis of the structure of James indicates its framing technique, which is not found in Hellenistic paraenesis but is typical of Jewish wisdom writings. It places James firmly within Jewish wisdom instruction.

The Content of Paraenetic Literature and Jewish Wisdom Instruction

A further characteristic of paraenetic literature relevant to James is its use of traditional materials in order to remind the audience of a shared cultural heritage. It does not introduce a significant quantity of new information. Rather, it is concerned with traditional moral issues, that is, references to something known and accepted, now presented in such a way as to serve the author's special purpose (see, e.g., Wilson 1991, 53, 94).

One of the major concerns of James is the faithful obedience to the law as an expression of wisdom and true religion. Such obedience is foundational to ethics, thus the two are inseparable. This understanding of the law as the sole standard of living is fundamental to the ethical monotheism in Second Temple Judaism. Hence, the emphasis on obedience to the law indicates James's affinity to Jewish traditions. The close relationship between James and the Jewish faith is further demonstrated by James's use of examples and quotations from the Jewish Scriptures (2:8, citing Lev 19:18; 2:23, citing Gen 15:6; 4:6, citing Prov 3:34). Moreover, the common cultural traditions that the author shares with the audience can be seen in the numerous topics on traditional Jewish piety, including the importance of loving God (1:12; 2:5); the antithetical ways of life of the righteous and the wicked (3:13–18; 4:7–10); the importance of the study of the law (1:25); the transience of life (4:13–17); the necessity of guarding and controlling one's speech (3:2–12); admonitions about enduring suffering and temptations (1:3–4, 12–15; 4:7–8, 10–11); reminders of religious duties such as almsgiving and care for orphans and widows (1:27; 2:14–16); and reflections on theodicy (1:13–17). All these subjects are matters of serious concern both in preexilic and Second Temple Jewish wisdom instructions. As mentioned previously, what distinguishes paraenesis from wisdom instruction is that the former looks to a model in ancient Greece (such as the three treatises on ethics by Isocrates, namely, *To Demonicus, To Nicocles,* and *Nicocles or the Cyprians*) and the latter looks to instruction traditions from the ancient Near East (such as Proverbs). In terms of source of influence of the content matter, as we have shown above, James is modeled more on Jewish wisdom instructions than on Hellenistic paraenesis.[10]

It should be noted that some scholars argue that James's eschatological worldview disqualifies the book from being classified in the Jewish wisdom tradition. Todd C. Penner (1996, 222–23), for example, contends that wisdom elements in James "must be viewed within the larger horizon of the eschatological and prophetic framework which undergirds the

---

10. Since the Epistle of James is intended for Jewish Christians, those who have faith in Christ the Lord of glory (2:1), the use of Jesus traditions plays a very important role in James. The author paraphrases and reapplies the teachings of Jesus. For detailed discussion, see especially the critical survey article by P. Foster 2014 and Bauckham in this volume.

community instruction of the letter." On the contrary, Patrick J. Hartin (1991, 23–35, 42–43) argues that wisdom traditions should take preeminence over the prophetic and eschatological elements in the book. It is true that both wisdom elements and an eschatological worldview are prominent in James. However, studies on the Qumran text 4QInstruction (1Q26, 4Q415–418, 4Q423) have demonstrated that traditional wisdom elements can be well incorporated into an eschatological worldview in a single document (Macaskill 2007; Adams 2008; Goff 2007; 2013; see also Wold in this volume). Wisdom and eschatology are clearly not incompatible on a generic level. Indeed, Bauckham (1999, 34) asserts that "an eschatological orientation is not therefore anomalous; it is to be expected in wisdom paraenesis from the first century C.E." Therefore, the eschatological worldview of James should not be a barrier for classifying the work as wisdom instruction.

The Social Function of Paraenetic Literature

Paraenetic literature often requires some form of positive relationship between the author and the audience. The author's self-presentation as either a friend or the audience's moral superior often provides the relational framework for influence and exhortation (Stowers 1986, 95; Fiore 1986, 66–67; Aune 1987, 191). By such self-presentation the author seeks to persuade the audience to accept the instructions given in the work.

Some scholars (under the influence of Victor Turner's sociological model) argue that paraenesis is for beginners and aims to resocialize individuals to transition from one social structure or allegiance to another (Popkes 1995, 542–44).[11] In another words, it is intended to provide instruction for new converts. James Starr (2004, 110), however, rightly concludes on the basis of his study of various Greco-Roman and Christian writings that "while moral exhortation is present at every stage of a person's instruction, the training of beginners in moral behavior was a secondary concern." As such, paraenesis functions to provide confirmation rather

---

11. Turner (1969, 94–95) identifies three stages of rites of passage in individual as well as group developmental cycle: separation, margin (the liminal transition), and aggregation. Some regard paraenesis functions mainly in the second stage to help the participants pass through the liminal phase by forming a new social reality for the novices and instructing them on the roles and responsibilities they are to assume after aggregation.

than to promote conversion: The paraenetic instruction aims to help individuals form their moral character in accordance with the worldview of the social group in which they are incorporated. It involves socialization, legitimation of a new worldview, and the reinforcement of identity (Quinn 1990, 195–97). Paraenetic literature aims to bring the shared community worldview to progressively more mature expression. It is thus appropriate to any stage in the process.

A number of scholars consider paraenesis to be an insufficient description for James and instead classify James as protrepsis (Baasland 1988, 3650–52; Johnson 1995, 20–21; Hartin 2003, 13–14; Wachob 2000, 48; McCartney 2009, 42–43). Protrepsis is a discourse used to persuade an audience—through systematic deliberative argumentation and philosophical reasoning—to succumb to the enchantment of the philosophical life. The goal is to "encourage commitment to a certain specified lifestyle or profession," and this is communicated "with a certain urgency and conviction" (Johnson 1995, 20–21). Protrepsis and paraenesis are indeed two related genres. Some scholars regard protrepsis as one of the functions of paraenesis (Perdue, 1990, 19, 23–24); others regard protrepsis as a subgenre of paraenesis (Johnson, 1995, 20–21). One might argue that though protrepsis is a conversion literature, it is not so much a call to adopt a new way of life as a call to adopt a different lifestyle (McCartney 2009, 43). Since James can be read as a text calling the audience to repent, it can be regarded as serving the function of protrepsis. However, it would be more appropriate to say that while James contains protrepsis (4:1–5:6), classifying the entire work as protrepsis goes beyond the evidence.

Conclusion

James is not a collection of isolated moral maxims unrelated to either its literary or historical context. From the above analysis, we conclude that James exhibits features of both a Jewish diaspora letter and Jewish wisdom instruction.[12] From a form-critical perspective, the letter's opening fits the expected form for a diaspora letter, and both the opening and closing correspond respectively to the prologue and epilogue of Jewish wisdom instruction. Both diaspora letters and Jewish wisdom instruc-

---

12. Scholars who classify James as Jewish wisdom instruction include Bauckham 1999, 21–23, 29–34; Riesner 2001, 1255; Cheung 2003, 21–52; Watson 2007; Lockett 2008, 16 n. 52, 76–79; Dunn 2009, 1131–32.

tion operate with the assumption that the person named as the author is a figure of recognized authority who is addressing the work to a Jewish group that holds the author in esteem. The attribution to an authoritative author gives the text a certain privileged status that makes it worthy of the recipients' careful attention. Both genres are types of confirmation rather than conversion literature. Both are intended to promote concern with traditional Jewish teaching on ethical behavior and adherence to the torah as the guide for one's prescribed way of life. The genres have so much in common that there are no obstacles to combining their literary elements, structures, and functions.

The identification of James as both a diaspora letter and Jewish wisdom instruction helps us to see how the work is structured, what traditional resources our author depends upon, and how the author intended to achieve the communicative goal of his work.

The Rhetorical Composition of the Epistle of James

Duane F. Watson

At the beginning of the twentieth century, Adolf Deissmann (1927, 233–45) made a distinction (a false one) between literary epistles using formal rhetoric and nonliterary (documentary) letters that did not. He classified the Epistle of James as a literary letter (Deissmann 1927, 242–43; Davids 1988, 3627–28). Today scholars classify James as a paraenetic letter, which by nature has rhetorical intent (Stowers 1986, 97; White 1988, 101). The purpose of such a letter is to persuade and dissuade its audience regarding a course of action, and to emulate the behavior of others held up as examples of that action (Pseudo-Libanius in Malherbe 1988, 68–69; Stowers 1986, 94–107). Wesley Wachob (2000, 6–8) argues that James is similar to the encyclical form of the literary letter used for administrative and religious purposes, and more specifically, a Jewish encyclical letter. James's use of maxims and exhortations indicates it is public address with rhetorical purposes. Rhetoric plays a purposeful role in the composition of James.

While classifying James as a literary letter, Deissmann (1927, 242–43) understood it as popular literature without a sophisticated rhetoric. While meaning to persuade and containing many rhetorical features, the formal composition of James continues to elude interpreters (Baasland 1988, 3648–61; Cheung 2003; Allison 2013, 76–81). It was Martin Dibelius's assessment of James that *"the entire document lacks continuity in thought. There is not only a lack of continuity in thought between individual sayings and other smaller units, but also between larger treatises"* (1976, 2, emphasis original). He attributed this apparent absence of structure to the preponderance of paraenesis in James, with paraenesis being understood as short sequential units of teaching and exhortation with more minor literary features like catchwords controlling the order (6–7). He asserted that James shares with paraenesis a "pervasive eclecticism" and "lack of continuity" (5–7, esp. 5). Dibelius's assessment of James was widely disseminated and highly influential. For example, Stanley Stowers (1986, 97) can write half a century later: "James consists of a series of seemingly disjointed hortatory topoi without any apparent unifying model or models."

Recent interpreters have added to our knowledge of invention, arrangement, style, and overall rhetorical strategy of James (Watson 1997; 2007; Kot 2006). James blends rhetoric common to both the Jewish and Greco-Roman rhetorical traditions. It is the objective of this essay to examine the mixed rhetoric of James in part and in whole, the role that paraenesis and the diatribe play in this rhetoric, and the placement of James in ancient rhetorical traditions. I propose that James is a product of the rhetoric of hellenized Jewish wisdom and paraenesis akin to that found in the Wisdom of Solomon, and rhetoric derived from the schemes for the elaboration of topoi (topics), theses, and chreiae found in Greco-Roman rhetoric.

Greco-Roman Rhetoric in James

Discovering the rhetorical composition of James involves exploring its use of Greco-Roman rhetorical conventions of invention, arrangement, and style. These conventions were basic to the education of young men for public life, are evident in speeches and letters, and are found in abstracted and systematic form in the rhetorical handbooks of the period. In 1916, James Hardy Ropes (1916, 14) gave this evaluation of the role of Greco-Roman rhetoric in James: "As in the diatribes, there is a general controlling motive in the discussion, but no firm and logically disposed structure giving a strict unity to the whole, and no trace of the conventional arrangement recommended by the elegant rhetoricians." While he was correct about the structure of James as a whole, recent rhetorical analysis of this epistle demonstrates that James does employ Greco-Roman rhetorical conventions in subunits.

Greco-Roman Rhetoric of James as a Whole

We begin our discussion with recent studies of the rhetoric of James as a whole. There are many studies that focus on the thematic unity of James (Francis 1970; Taylor 2004; Taylor and Guthrie 2006; Jackson-McCabe 2014). While these studies do involve rhetoric, I will focus on studies that seek to identify James as a literary letter that uses rhetoric or as a speech in written form having the typical elements of invention and arrangement. These elements include: (1) *exordium* introducing main topics to be developed; (2) *narratio* rehearsing the circumstances to be addressed; (3) *partitio* enumerating the proposition(s) to be developed, often called the *propositio* if there is only one proposition; (4) *probatio* or *argumentatio*, the main arguments supporting the *partitio/propositio,* containing a *confirmatio* supporting the speaker's case and a *refutatio* disproving the opponent's case; and (5) *peroratio* or conclusion that both recapitulates the argumentation (*recapitulatio*) and provides further exhortation based upon it (*conquestio*).

Modern study of the rhetoric of James as a whole began with Wilhelm Wuellner's (1978) groundbreaking investigation. He analyzed James using the new rhetoric, semiotic, and communications theory. He argued that James is pragmatic and its purpose is recruiting, not teaching. He outlined James as epistolary prescript (1:1), *exordium* (1:2–4), *narratio* (1:5–11), *propositio* (1:12), *argumentatio* in six units (1:13–5:6), and *peroratio* (5:7–20) consisting of a *recapitulatio* (5:7–8) and a *peroratio* proper (5:9–20).

Refining two of his earlier rhetorical analyses of James (1982, 121–22; 1988, 3654–59), Ernst Baasland (1992, 177–78) classified James as deliberative rhetoric, as protreptic that tries to convince the audience to adhere to a way of life. He gives the outline of James as *exordium* (1:2–15), *propositio* (1:16–22) with amplification (1:23–27), *argumentatio* (2:1–3:12), second *propositio* (3:13–18) with amplification (4:1–6), *argumentatio* (4:7–5:6) and *peroratio* (5:7–20). In another study, Hubert Frankenmölle (1990, 161–97) understands the *exordium* to be 1:2–18 and the *peroratio* to be 5:7–20, with 1:19–5:6 developing themes found in the *exordium.*

Lauri Thurén (1995, 262–84) categorized James as epideictic rhetoric because the letter attempts to strengthen values already held by its audience rather than persuade it to accept new ones. He outlined the arrangement of James as the *exordium* (1:1–18) introducing the two main themes of perseverance in trials in the areas of wisdom and speech, and money and action; the *propositio* (1:19–27) urging the recipients to accept and live by the word; the *argumentatio* (2:1–5:6) developing the two themes of the *exordium* in three parts (2:1–26 on money and action, 3:1–4:12 on wisdom and speech, and 4:13–5:6 on both themes focusing on the rich man); and the *peroratio* (5:7–20) comprising the *recapitulatio* reiterating the themes of perseverance and speech (5:7–11) and the *conquestio* or final exhortation (5:12–20).

While the studies of Wuellner, Baasland, Frankenmölle, and Thurén are careful and creative, they are not completely convincing. They discover many elements of invention, arrangement, and style and rhetorical strategy in James, but the diversity of their proposals demonstrates that James does not conform to Greco-Roman standards of invention and arrangement in its overall structure.

Greco-Roman Rhetoric of James in Subunits

J. D. N. Van der Westhuizen (1991, 89–107) provided a pioneering work on the rhetoric of a subunit of James when he analyzed 2:14–26. He classified this passage as deliberative rhetoric because it tries to convince the audience to take action (add faith to works), uses examples for its argumentation (Abraham and Rahab), and clarifies that the prescribed course of action is advantageous (yields salvation and justification). He carefully analyzed invention, arrangement, and style in the passage. It employs all three proofs from invention: logos (logical argumentation), ethos (authority), and pathos (emotion). External and internal or artistic proofs, both inductive and deductive, are present. External proofs are from Scripture (2:21, 25). Inductive proofs are from examples from everyday life (2:15–16), Jewish tradition (2:21–25), and nature (2:26). The deductive proof is an enthymeme, a conclusion with one premise (2:26). Van den Westhuizen proposed the following arrangement: *proem* (v. 14), proposition (vv. 14, 17), possible *narratio* (vv. 15–16), proof (vv. 18–25), and epilogue (v. 26). He demonstrates that the pericope employs a host of stylistic techniques common to Jewish and Greco-Roman rhetoric that clarify and amplify the argumentation.

While making many important discoveries, this study mistakenly assumes that the elements of rhetorical arrangement that typically structure an entire letter or speech will be found in complete form in subunits of these works. Subunits of a work will have analogous outlines and functions as the work as a whole because arrangement involves opening, middle, and closing. However, discovering the rhetorical arrangement of the smaller units of James and contemporary works lies elsewhere.

Despite his observation mentioned above that James lacked continuity in thought, Dibelius noted that "Jas 2:1–3:12, the core of the writing, is composed of three expositions, each having characteristics of a treatise" (1976, 1; see also 124–25). The subjects of these three expositions are partiality is inconsistent with faith (2:1–13), faith without works is unprofitable (2:14–26), and few should become teachers (3:1–12). Dibelius considered these expositions to be expansions of paraenetic sayings in diatribal form. He claimed that in the first two "the structure and lines of thought were apparently shaped by the author himself" (1976, 5). He was right, and we can also add the third exposition to the list. These expositions employ the pattern for elaborating a complete argument, with paraenetic and diatribal features added for amplification (Watson 1993a; 1993b; 2007, 102–4).[1]

All of Jas 2:1–3:12 is deliberative rhetoric intended to persuade the audience to pursue or avoid certain courses of action. Chapter 2 dissuades the audience from partiality, and 3:1–12 dissuades it from teaching without fully considering the devastating power of speech. The argumentation and its topoi (topics) in 2:1–3:12 are typical of deliberative rhetoric. Argumentation is based on examples and their comparison, and the focus is on what is advantageous, honorable, and necessary (and their opposites). The treatment of the rich and poor men in an ecclesiastical court is an example of partiality (2:1–13), and Abraham and Rahab are examples of faith accompanied by works (2:14–16). Forming the argumentation in 3:1–12 are three comparisons of examples: (1) horses and their bits, and ships and their rudders with the body and its tongue (vv. 3–5); (2) tamed animals with the untamable tongue (vv. 7–8); and (3) the spring, fig tree, and grapevines with the duplicity of the tongue (vv. 11–12). In chapter 2, partiality is dishonorable (vv. 6–7) and makes one a transgressor of the law (vv. 9–10), but to be impartial and supplement faith with works is to do well (vv. 8, 19), profit (vv. 14, 16), and receive mercy rather than judgment (v. 13). In 3:1–11 becoming a teacher is not advantageous or expedient because of the tongue's potential for evil (Watson 1993a, 100–102; 1993b, 53–54).

These three sections (2:1–13, 14–26; and 3:1–12) each employ the Greco-Roman pattern of argumentation used to elaborate themes (topoi), complete arguments, and chreiae (sayings of famous people and/or accounts of their actions; Mack 1987; 1990, 41–47; Mack and Robbins 1989, 31–67). The elaboration of themes is discussed in the Rhetorica ad Herennium (4.43.56–44.58) and the elaboration of the complete argument is discussed in the Rhetorica ad Alexandrum (1.1422a.25–27); Rhetorica

---

1. Jean Noël Aletti (2014) replicates much of Watson's analysis (1993a and 1993b) but with an unwarranted narrow emphasis on chreia development versus development of an argument or thesis. There is no formal chreia being developed in Jas 2:1–3:12.

ad Herennium (2.18.28–2.29.46; 3.9.16); Hermogenes, *Elaboration of Arguments* (Rabe 1913, 148–50); and Hermogenes, *Progymnasmata* in the discussion of the elaboration exercise of the chreia (Rabe 1913, 1–27; Mack and O'Neil 1986, 153–77; Kennedy 2003, 73–88). The particular pattern guiding portions of James is the elaboration of a complete argument as found in the Rhetorica ad Herennium (2.18.28; 2.29.46). This pattern is:

Propositio	Proposition
Ratio	Supporting Reason for the *Propositio*
Confirmatio	Proof Supporting the *Ratio* by comparison, example, and amplification
Exornatio	Elaboration of the *Confirmatio*
	Simile Comparison
	Exemplum Example
	Amplificatio Amplification
	Iudicatio Authoritative Judgment
Conplexio	Conclusion

This pattern in James 2:1–13 is given below (Watson 1993a, 102–8):

Propositio (v. 1)
Ratio (Proof from *Exemplum*) (vv. 2–4)
Confirmatio (vv. 5–7)
Exornatio (vv. 8–11)
    Judgment (*iudicatio*) (v. 8)
    Further Confirmation (vv. 9–11)
    Enthymeme incorporating a judgment (vv. 9–10)
    Enthymeme (v. 11)
Conplexio (as Epicheireme) (vv. 12–13)

The *propositio* to be elaborated is found in verse 1: "My brothers and sisters, do you with your acts of favoritism really believe in our glorious Lord Jesus Christ?"[2] Put in declarative form, the proposition is: "Favoritism is inconsistent with belief in Jesus Christ." The proposition is followed in verses 2–4 by the *ratio*, which provides a reason for the proposition, here a proof from example, which is a standard feature of deliberative rhetoric:

---

2. All biblical quotations are from the NRSV unless otherwise noted.

For if a person with gold rings and in fine clothes comes into your assembly, and if a poor person in dirty clothes also comes in, and if you take notice of the one wearing the fine clothes and say, "Have a seat here, please," while to the one who is poor you say, "Stand there," or, "Sit at my feet," have you not made distinctions among yourselves, and become judges with evil thoughts?

The example is a church court in which the verdict will be swayed in favor of the one sitting in the seat of honor. The *ratio* demonstrates that exercising favoritism is to be an unjust judge, a role inconsistent with belief in Jesus Christ as stated in the proposition.

The *confirmatio* supporting the *ratio* follows in verses 5–7:

Listen, my beloved brothers and sisters. Has not God chosen the poor in the world to be rich in faith and to be heirs of the kingdom that he has promised to those who love him? But you have dishonored the poor. Is it not the rich who oppress you? Is it not they who drag you into court? Is it not they who blaspheme the excellent name that was invoked over you?

This confirmation is a series of three rhetorical questions expecting a positive answer. They encourage the audience to conclude that extending partially to the oppressive and blasphemous rich is inconsistent with God's choice of the poor (and good sense!).

The *exornatio* follows in verses 8–11 and provides further support of the argument using judgments and enthymemes. Verse 8 is a *iudicatio* or judgment made by "the gods or by men of repute or by judges or by our opponents" (Rhet. Alex. 1.1422a.25–28; see also [Cicero,] Rhet. Her. 2.29.46; Quintillian, *Inst.* 5.11.36–44). Here the judgment is from God, a quotation of Lev 19:18: "You do well if you really fulfill the royal law according to the scripture, 'You shall love your neighbor as yourself.'" The judgment shows that any form of partiality is inconsistent with the Judeo-Christian faith.

The judgment of the *exornatio* is followed by two enthymemes. An enthymeme is an incomplete syllogism in which one of the two premises is unstated; it is a proposition with a single reason (Aristotle, *Rhet.* 2.22.1395b.1–3; Quintilian, *Inst.* 5.10.1–3; 5.14.1–4).[3] The first enthymeme of verses 9–10 proves that partially breaking the law breaks the whole law:

---

3. There is a vast modern discussion of the nature of the enthymeme, but it need not concern us here in this demonstration. See Aune 2003, 150–57.

Premise: "For whoever keeps the whole law but fails in one point has become accountable for all of it." (v. 10)

Assumed Premise: Showing partiality is a failure to obey the law.

Conclusion: "But if you show partiality, you commit sin and are convicted by the law as transgressors." (v. 9)

The second enthymeme of verse 11 makes the same point as the first, but more broadly—any transgression of the law breaks the whole law.

Premise: "For the one who said, 'You shall not commit adultery,' also said, 'You shall not murder.'"

Assumed Premise: If you break any individual commandment of the law you become a transgressor of all the law.

Conclusion: "Now if you do not commit adultery but if you murder, you have become a transgressor of the law."

The *complexio* or conclusion follows in verses 12–13. It is composed of an epicheireme, a syllogism with the major premise, a minor premise supporting the major premise, and a conclusion (Quintilian, *Inst.* 5.14.5–23). The lesson is that the exercise of either love or partiality has implications for God's judgment.

Major Premise: "For judgment will be without mercy to anyone who has shown no mercy."

Minor Premise: "yet, mercy triumphs over judgment."

Conclusion: "So speak and so act as those who are to be judged by the law of liberty."

James 2:14–26 is another development of an argument, broadening the discussion from partiality in 2:1–13 to faith and works (Watson 1993a, 108–16).

Propositio (v. 14)
Ratio (Proof from Example) (vv. 15–16)
Confirmatio (vv. 17–19)
    Restatement of the Proposition (v. 17)
    Anticipation and Personification (v. 18a)
    Dilemma (v. 18b)
    Anticipation and Irony (v. 19)

Exornatio (vv. 20–25)
  Amplification (v. 20)
  Proof from Example (vv. 21–22)
  Judgment (supernatural oracle) (v. 23)
  Amplification (v. 24)
  Proof from Example (v. 25)
Conplexio (Similitude) (v. 26)

Verse 14 is the *propositio* consisting of two rhetorical questions expecting a negative answer: "What good is it, my brothers and sisters, if you say you have faith but do not have works? Can faith save you?" This question can be reworded as "Faith that has no works does not profit, that is, is not salvific." The *ratio* follows in verses 15–16, consisting of an example framed as a rhetorical question illustrating how faith without works is unprofitable: "If a brother or sister is naked and lacks daily food, and one of you says to them, 'Go in peace; keep warm and eat your fill,' and yet you do not supply their bodily needs, what is the good of that?"

The *confirmatio* of verses 17–19 consists of a restatement of the proposition in verse 17 ("So faith by itself, if it has no works, is dead") and by a rhetorical question, anticipation, and a dilemma in verses 18–19 ("But someone will say, 'You have faith and I have works.' Show me your faith apart from your works, and I by my works will show you my faith. You believe that God is one; you do well. Even the demons believe—and shudder"). These verses vividly show the impossibility of demonstrating Christian faith without works, for even demons can confess and they certainly have no works of faith!

The *exornatio* follows in verses 20–25, beginning in verse 20 with amplification in the form of a note of surprise that restates the proposition of verse 14: "Do you want to be shown, you senseless person, that faith apart from works is barren?" The amplification is followed in verses 21–22 by an example in the form of a rhetorical question using the Akedah, the binding of Isaac from Gen 22:1–19: "Was not our ancestor Abraham justified by works when he offered his son Isaac on the altar? You see that faith was active along with his works, and faith was brought to completion by the works." This was the last act of Abraham's many acts of hospitality and charity before God declared him righteous and one that illustrates the need for works to accompany faith. A judgment from a supernatural oracle of a God follows in verse 23, a quotation of Gen 15:6: "Thus the scripture was fulfilled that says, 'Abraham believed God, and it was reckoned to him as righteousness,' and he was called the friend of God." The judgment is succeeded by a restatement of the proposition in verse 24 ("You see that a person is justified by works and not by faith alone") and by another historical example in verse 25, that of Rahab ("Likewise, was not Rahab the prostitute also justified by works when she welcomed the messengers and sent them out by another road?"; Josh 2:1–21; 6:17, 22–25). The argument concludes in verse 26 with a summary: "For just as the body without the spirit is dead, so faith without works is also dead."

These studies have shown that there is rhetorical structure in smaller units of James, and it is partially derived from elaboration exercises espoused for a complete argument in Greco-Roman rhetoric.

Paraenesis and the Diatribe in the Rhetoric of James

Paraenesis and the diatribe are two modes of argumentation central to the rhetoric of James. Paraenesis provides the topoi (topics) and content of James's exhortation and argumentation while the diatribe provides a rhetorical vehicle for the presentation of this and other content. Paraenesis is moral exhortation that an audience accepts as generally true or even irrefutable. It is a subdivision of paraenetic literature (the other division being instructions), which in turn is a subdivision of wisdom literature (the other division being reflective essays). Paraenesis has many subgenres, including admonitions, chreiai, encomia, examples, and exhortations (Gammie 1990). Abraham Malherbe (1992, 278–93) has identified the following characteristics of paraenesis: (1) traditional and conventional; (2) applicable to a variety of life situations; (3) addressed to those familiar with the paraenesis and only need to be reminded of it and encouraged to live according to its wisdom; and (4) uses examples of those who do or do not embody virtues to motivate others to imitate or not imitate them.

Paraenesis in James exhibits these characteristics. It includes traditional material drawn from the Old Testament (Gen 15:2 in 2:23; Prov 3:34 in 4:6), the Jesus tradition (2:8; 5:12), and Jewish and Greek wisdom. The paraenesis is extensively applicable to daily life, like enduring temptation (1:12–17) and guarding speech (4:11–12). It directs the recipients about familiar subjects like hearing-forgetting and knowing-doing (1:19–27; 4:13–17) and control of speech (3:1–12). It champions other people for emulation including Abraham and Rahab for hospitality (2:14–26), the Hebrew prophets and Job for patience during tribulation (5:7–11), and

Elijah for the power of the prayer of a righteous man (5:13–20; Perdue 1981, 242–46).

Dibelius (1976, 1–11) classified James as paraenesis, but he assumed that it was not addressing any actual life situation. He claimed that as paraenesis, this letter is a "stringing together of admonitions of general ethical content" (3). He and many interpreters after him often ascribe the apparent lack of continuity and structure in James to its use of paraenesis (5–11). However, the characteristics of paraenesis just outlined and shown to be at work in James illustrate that paraenesis is rhetorically useful for addressing an audience and can have a vital rhetorical role in texts, including letters, as they address the situations of actual audiences.

Pseudo-Libanius outlined a letter style designated as *paraenetic* (Malherbe 1988, 68–69). He described this letter style this way: "The paraenetic style is that in which we exhort someone by urging him to pursue something or to avoid something. Paraenesis is divided into two parts, encouragement and dissuasion" (trans. Malherbe 1988, 69; see also Stowers 1986, 94–106). By nature, persuasion and dissuasion (deliberative rhetoric) require rhetorical invention of which paraenesis can be instrumental in argumentation as examples, judgments of the past, and authoritative premises for enthymemes.

As expected, paraenesis in James is part of a structured, sophisticated use of rhetoric (Cheung 2003). Rhetoricians adapted paraenesis for effective address of their audiences. Even though paraenesis is general and applicable to a wide variety of situations, the rhetor's selection of paraenesis for argumentation was guided by the nature of the audience and the needs of the rhetorical situation (Stower 1986, 95). James has chosen pertinent paraenesis and woven it into his argumentation. A good example is 3:1–12, where paraenesis is an integral part of the development of an argument that not all should become teachers. It is found as the *propositio* ("Not many should become teachers," v. 1a), *ratio* (because "those who teach will be judged with greater strictness," v. 1b), and *confirmatio* ("blessings and cursing should not come from the same mouth," v. 10; Watson 1993b, 54–64).

Despite the important role of paraenesis in the rhetorical strategy of James, the epistle does not exhibit the formal features of a paraenetic work. It does not contain exhortation to emulate a particular type of character by upholding a model person or god for imitation, with maxims on specific attributes and behaviors arranged antithetically that define that character (Malherbe 1992, 278–93; Gammie 1990, 51; Johnson 1995, 18–20). The paraenesis in James is not an organizing feature of the letter overall, but is incorporated into the rhetorical argumentation.

Turning to the diatribe, David E. Aune (2003, 127) defines it as "a modern literary term describing an informal rhetorical mode of argumentation principally characterized by a lively dialogical style including the use of imaginary discussion partners (often abruptly addressed), to whom are attributed hypothetical objections and false conclusions" (see also Stowers 1981, 79–174; 1988, 71–83; Berger 1984b, 1124–32). Several elements of the diatribe are found in the argumentation of James, especially in the more structured sections of 2:1–3:12 and 4:13–5:6. Among others, these elements include the introduction of an imaginary dialogue partner in the third person as "someone will say" (2:18); a shift from addressing the audience to a dialogue with an imaginary dialogue partner in the second person (2:14–26; 4:13; 5:1); objections and false conclusions from the imaginary dialogue partner (2:18a, 19); a series of questions and answers to the imaginary dialogue partner (2:20–23; 3:11–12; 4:14), some of which are intended to compel that partner to reject their content (3:11–12; cf. 2:20); and personification (2:13, 17, 26; 3:5–6, 8; 5:3–4; Ropes 1916, 10–18; Watson 1993a, 118–20). These features of the diatribe are also found in Jewish literature, but the use of many of them in combination makes the style diatribal (Allison 2013, 88).

James demonstrates just how malleable these diatribal elements are in creating argumentation. They serve within the pattern for the elaboration of a theme or entire argument, particularly to amplify the argument (2:1–3:12) and rebuke the lifestyle of the opposition (4:13–5:6; Watson 1993a, 102–16; see also Kustas 1976). Also, elements of the diatribe work in tandem with paraenesis. For example, in 2:5 a rhetorical question presents Jesus tradition that God has chosen the poor to be rich in faith and heirs of the kingdom (Jewish and Christian paraenesis), and in 2:13 judgment and mercy are personified in paraenesis about mercy triumphing over judgment. As with paraenesis, diatribe does not provide overall structure to James, but does help create its argumentation.

The Placement of James Within Rhetorical Traditions

With all of its rhetorical features, the question arises about the placement of James within ancient rhetorical traditions—Jewish and Greco-Roman—and their blend in the first century CE. Greco-Roman rhetoric had influenced Jewish rhetoric by the first century CE. Greco-Roman rhetorical conventions had been incorporated in some form by Jewish rhetorical education and practice during the Hellenistic period (Hengel 1974, 1:70–78). Also, many Jewish and Greco-Roman rhetorical conventions were shaped independently from one another by the needs of a predominantly oral culture, and these conventions are often rooted in general rhetoric of human communication. Most people were illiterate; rhetorical forms were developed to facilitate speaking and hearing, and retention and memorization. These forms included a multitude of figures of speech and thought, argumentation by examples and comparison of examples, and repetitive structures like parallelism and chiasm in all their forms.

James has elements of Jewish, Greco-Roman, and general rhetoric. The introduction of topics in its beginning (1:2–27), development of these in the middle (2:1–5:13), and their reiteration in its conclusion (5:14–18) is a common format in these primarily oral cultures. This format helped audiences follow and remember what was being said. Comparison of examples for moral imitation and use of paraenesis in argumentation are common to the rhetoric of both cultures, while the diatribe as a mode of argumentation and the pattern of elaboration for themes and complete arguments are characteristic of Greco-Roman rhetoric.

This blend of rhetorical traditions in James is partly rooted in hellenized Jewish wisdom discourse. It is well known that James relies heavily on Jewish wisdom tradition. In the older, pre-Hellenistic wisdom work of Proverbs, wisdom is presented as authoritative statements or aphorisms given by a wisdom teacher. In Prov 10–31, the proverbs of Solomon and others, wisdom sayings and commands are presented with assurance that the audience accepts and complies with what is being presented. Wisdom is primarily composed in parallelism without logical proof and development because there is no need to persuade the audience of its truth. For example, "A wise child makes a glad father, but a foolish child is a mother's grief" (10:1).

In chapters 1–9, the wisdom poems with roots in Egyptian and Mesopotamian wisdom that postdate chapters 10–31, the reasoning is more developed. Wisdom has more motive clauses and logical connectives such as "because" or "for" that help form enthymemes (a conclusion with one premise). Still the reasoning is often limited to giving positive and negative consequences as a motivational premise to do what is advised or commanded. For example, "My child, do not forget my teaching, but let your heart keep my commandments; for length of days and years of life and abundant welfare they will give you" (3:1–2). Besides wisdom encapsulated as an enthymeme, there is a movement toward grouping proverbs on the same topic, like fearing the Lord (3:1–12), or a more cohesive discussion of a topic composed of a collection of related proverbs, like the wisdom of a father's instruction (4:1–27), which contains an extended contrast between the two ways of the righteous and the wicked (vv. 10–19).

When we look at the later wisdom book of Sirach from the early second century BCE, the presentation of wisdom has changed significantly. Sirach is composed of units of wisdom that are ten to twenty-five lines long and develop the topic at hand more fully. Sometimes a proverb is used like a thesis to introduce other proverbs on that topic. For example, 15:11–20 is developed in a manner similar to a thesis in Greco-Roman rhetoric:

> *Propositio* with a reason stated twice: God leads no one into sin because it is against his nature (vv. 11–12)
> *Ratio*: God hates abomination (v. 13)
> *Confirmatio*: God gave humanity free choice, so people lead themselves into sin or remain faithful (vv. 14–17)
> *Exornatio*: God's wisdom is great and he knows all human action (vv. 18–19)
> *Conplexio*: Reiteration of the proposition with a different nuance: God commands no one to sin (v. 20)

While there is growing length and cohesion of topical units, there is still no formal development of a topic or thesis in a Greek fashion as is found in James and the *progymnasmata*. There is no reasoning connecting each proverb, only a loosely fitting arrangement of related proverbs whose order and content function like elements of a thesis elaboration. Also absent are examples of persons who exhibited the vices being railed or virtues being promoted as would be found in Greek rhetoric. If examples are used, they are general groups like "the righteous" or "the wicked." For example, "Therefore walk in the way of the good, and keep to the paths of the just. For the upright will abide in the land, and the innocent will remain in it; but the wicked will be cut off from the land, and the treacherous will be rooted out of it" (2:20–22).[4]

---

4. For other literary characteristic of Sirach as wisdom discourse, see Cheung 2013, 24–26.

The Wisdom of Solomon from the first century BCE also contains longer units that develop wisdom topics as characterized the earlier Sirach. However, the presentation of the wisdom has changed. Facets of the wisdom topics are now explained with an attempt to persuade the audience addressed to follow wisdom. Logical connectives like "for" and "because" are now abundant in chains of subordinate causality creating enthymemes. The opening provides a good example:

> Love righteousness, you rulers of the earth, think of the Lord in goodness and seek him with sincerity of heart; *because* he is found by those who do not put him to the test, and manifests himself to those who do not distrust him. *For* perverse thoughts separate people from God, and when his power is tested, it exposes the foolish; *because* wisdom will not enter a deceitful soul, or dwell in a body enslaved to sin. *For…*" (1:1–4, emphasis added).

Wisdom is presented as propositions that receive structured development, not simply as gathered sayings on the same topic. Also, examples and comparison of examples in proof abound. For example, the transitory nature of a life without virtue is compared to the passing of ships on the sea, birds in the air, and an arrow to its target (5:9–14). There is now development of a topic or proposition using enthymemes, examples, and comparison of examples in larger units.

James presents wisdom in longer units like wisdom in Sirach and the Wisdom of Solomon. James also presents wisdom as logical proof based on the development of topics and propositions that use enthymemes, examples, and comparison of examples; developments also found in the Wisdom of Solomon. Examples of this kind of reasoning are present in James from the start: "Consider trials as joy *because* the testing of faith produces endurance, and in turn let the endurance have full effect *so that* you may be mature" (1:2–4, my paraphrase). "Ask in faith *for* the doubter can expect nothing" (1:5–8, my paraphrase).

This use of logical proof is not because the audience of James does not deem the author or his wisdom as authoritative. Rather, there is a need to persuade the audience of the merits of adhering to the wisdom being presented. This logical development of arguments is very much influenced by Jewish wisdom of the period and Greco-Roman rhetoric, as seen in our discussion above. This early Christian author builds a text that introduces, elaborates, and reiterates topics in a Hellenistic manner. However, the Jewish wisdom tradition guides his arrangement. He moves from topic to topic in the manner of the wisdom tradition. Although he sometimes develops wisdom topics using a Greco-Roman argumentative scheme, he does not organize the entire letter with elements of arrangement as Greco-Roman rhetoric advises. This dynamic is the key to understanding the rhetorical composition of James. It is Jewish Christian wisdom influenced by Hellenistic rhetoric, but arranged in the topic-to-topic manner of Jewish wisdom that had not fully adapted the Greco-Roman elaboration pattern of arrangement. The Wisdom of Solomon provides a similar work of topical development and arrangement from a hellenized Jewish context.

My proposal is partially supported by Luke Cheung. He provides a careful analysis of the close relationship between paraenesis and wisdom and their roles in James. He writes, "On stylistic grounds, it seems that James modeled itself more on wisdom instruction such as Ben Sira than on Hellenistic paraenesis. In terms of source of influence, there is no doubt that Jewish wisdom instructions (often modeled after Egyptian instructions) have a dominant influence of James" (2003, 40). Cheung is right to highlight the predominance of the wisdom instruction in James. However, the Hellenistic rhetorical influence in James has a stronger parallel in the Wisdom of Solomon. Both works mold wisdom instruction rhetorically to address their audiences, including the use of diatribe and paraenesis. These similarities warrant further study.

Conclusion

While the Epistle of James is highly rhetorical, its overall rhetorical strategy and structure is not apparent to our modern perceptions. Fortunately recent scholarship enables us to see the rhetorical strategy of the epistle more clearly and how its rhetorical elements work within that strategy. We have made a radical turn in James studies by abandoning the assumptions of Deissmann, that James is a nonliterary letter, and Dibelius, that James lacks structure because it is paraenesis. Clearly there is literary intent and rhetorical structure in James, including portions that develop topics and complete arguments using argumentative strategies and incorporating paraenesis and diatribe (2:1–3:12).

James does not conform to Greco-Roman rhetorical convention in its overall invention and arrangement. While topical development is a major concern of the epistle, this development is structured more like wisdom literature with topic following topic than it is Greco-Roman oratory with a central thesis, list of topics that will develop the thesis, development of those topics, and their reiteration in a conclusion. Attempts to outline the epistle from *exordium* to *peroratio* are unconvincing. Rather, topics are developed in sequence as in Jewish wisdom literature of Sirach and especially the Wisdom of Solomon. Even so, within this topical development, Greco-Roman rhetoric is employed.

The rhetorical strategy of James informs us of how an early Christian leader used rhetoric to address his community using a mix of Jewish and Greco-Roman rhetoric that defies clean classification and structure. The author comes from a Jewish background influenced by Hellenistic rhetoric. He builds his letter using a variety of rhetorical tools, but seems to lack a conventional blueprint.

The Good God and the Reigning Lord:
Theology of the Epistle of James

Peter H. Davids

When one approaches the theology of James, by which one means theology proper (the teaching about God, including Jesus), one cannot avoid being aware of irony.[1] If one goes back and reads Martin Dibelius (1976, 1–7) on James, one discovers that for Dibelius there is no real theology in James, for the work is simply a string of pearls, a series of wisdom sayings or paraeneses.[2] However, in the same year that the German original of this edition of Dibelius's work appeared, Franz Mussner (1964) produced a commentary that viewed James as very much having a theology. Mussner's perspective has been increasingly the view of scholars since then. Still, it took a while for a letter that Martin Luther famously termed "a right strawy epistle" (German: *eyn rechte stroern Epistel*) to be accepted as a theological work with its own deposit of gold, silver, and precious stones.

What one does not find in James is a developed Trinitarian theology. There is no mention of the Holy Spirit, even if wisdom takes over some of the functions of the Spirit.[3] So, at best one has an expressed binitarian

---

1. One includes Jesus at least to the degree that he carries out divine functions of cosmic ruling and judging.

2. Of course, the German original is dated 1964 and the original version of the commentary (without Greeven's revisions) goes back to the 1930s.

3. Wisdom does occur in chs. 1 and 3 of James, but it is not as personified as in Prov 8, let alone as in Sirach or Wisdom. Given James's apparent contact with Sirach, it could be that, if pushed, the author would personify Wisdom; however, given that one only has the five-chapter letter from the author, it is impossible to prove this. Furthermore, personification does not mean that one is thinking of wisdom as a person.

theology.[4] There are seventeen references to God and several more to other terms that refer to God, so there is some material for theology. But where does Jesus fit into this picture? He is certainly exalted and fulfills divine functions, but the explicit language of 2 Pet 1:3 and John 1:1–4 will not be found in James. James is in fact not writing a theology, let alone what would today be considered a complete theology, even if he reveals some very interesting theology.

God the Father

The most prominent divine figure in James is God the Father. One can use the phrase "the Father" because James explicitly refers to God as creator with the phrase "Father of [the heavenly] lights" (Jas 1:17) and later indicates the divine standard of judgment by describing what is "pure and undefiled" religion "before God and the Father" (Jas 1:27 RSV).[5] This is indeed the God of the Hebrew Scriptures referred to as not only "God" but also as "Father," which was the way that Jesus often referred to him.

But what does one learn about this God besides the assumption that he is the creator? First, one learns that God gives to all and that he gives generously (the best meaning of *haplōs* in this context) and that he does not criticize the person for asking. The particular gift under discussion is wisdom, which is what is needed to stand in the test and to control the tongue (Jas 1:4–5 and 3:13–18, respectively). That is, in Jas 1:5 God is "the God giving to all generously" and the topic under discussion is the need for divine wisdom if one finds oneself lacking in the testing situation.

There is, however, a condition to this generosity, which is that one have single-minded allegiance to God. In other words, one must not be "two-hearted," or *leb waleb* in Hebrew, which refers to attempting allegiance to more than one deity. This is the same as saying that one must be *haplōs* in the sense of single- and sincere-hearted and not "double-souled" (*dipsuchos*, a term that James may have coined for its Hebrew equivalent *leb waleb*). That same requirement of single-minded allegiance comes up

---

4. It is wisest to say "expressed," for the work is not a treatise on theology and it is short, so one must work with the material present without implying that this is the fullness of the author's thought.

5. Since there is a single article governing both nouns, one might better translate the phrase "the God and Father" or "God, even the Father." In other words, the two terms form a hendiadys. Unless otherwise stated, all translations are by the author.

again in Jas 4:1–5, 8. In that passage the other deity, now pictured as a second spouse or lover, is "desire" or "pleasure" or, in contemporary language, "drives."[6] The people are pictured as "adulteresses," like unfaithful Israel (see esp. Hos 1–3) and God is pictured as jealous over the "spirit" that he caused to dwell in us human beings. God will not be "two-timed" and will not give to those who are two-timing him.

Yet he is also the forgiving God, for if the people repent, an action that is vividly described in language from the Hebrew Scriptures (Jas 4:6–10), then God will in turn "draw near" to them, presumably showing his generosity to them. (All the verbs and pronouns are plural, so, just as in the case of the collective "adulteresses," James is thinking of a whole people or group of people, not an individual.)

Having returned to the theme of God's generosity, a glance back to James's first chapter shows that James instructs his readers that God *only* gives good (Jas 1:16–18). This point is underlined by two factors: (1) while God is the creator of the heavenly bodies ("Father of Lights"), unlike them he does not change.[7] That is, he is not double, he does not give good at one time and evil at another; and (2) he gives life. Both factors need to be reflected upon in James's context to fully understand their import.

The underlying issue in this section of Jas 1, as in Jas 4, is that of what makes a test or trial problematic. The problem is introduced in Jas 1:13: "God is testing me, trying to make me fall" (*apo theou peirazomai*), which is a perennial issue for those who view God as both sovereign and of mixed character; it finds its basis in Gen 22:1: "God tested Abraham" (LXX *ho theos epeirazen ton Abraam*). James is quick to assert that this action of accusing God of testing one is in itself an act of putting God to

---

6. *Hēdonē* in this passage is the equivalent of *epithymia* in Jas 1:13–14, as the reader sees when he or she notices that the verbal form of the latter noun appears between the two occurrences of *hēdonē* in Jas 4:1–5.

7. The "shadow due to change" expression in Jas 1:17 is the subject of a lot of debate in the commentary literature: Is it talking about the changes in the patterns of the constellations, or is it talking about the changing places of the planets, or is it talking about the changing phases of the moon (which could easily be expressed by an observer as a shadow on the moon)? While commentators make informed guesses, this is a question that is unlikely to be settled, in part because it does not need settling. James's point is that astronomical phenomena change; it does not matter which one or ones James has in mind. In contrast to astronomical phenomena, God is unchanging, perhaps because he is creator, but certainly because he is not double.

the test, which ought not to be done by evil people (Davids 1978a; 2003).[8] Furthermore, he continues, God does not test anyone. How can James say this given that he uses a Greek text from what eventually developed into the Septuagint, which was already quoted above? The answer is that James reads every narrative in the Hebrew Scriptures through Second Temple period Jewish literature (Davids 2009; 2012). In that literature, the testing of Abraham was reread though Job so that it is Satan (*Mastēma*) who puts the honor challenge to God that results in the testing (and it is *Mastēma* who is shamed when Abraham passes the test). According to this telling of the Genesis narrative, God did not change character. This test was not a test God initiated, but an honor challenge that God could not honorably reject. Instead of attributing it to God, in James the origin of testing or trials is traced to human drives, desires, or emotions, which are quite unstable (thus human beings are "double-minded," which, as noted above, is a term James may have created and uses twice) and end up giving birth not only to sin but also to death.

The point that James is making is that the unchanging God gives life. He does not do this accidentally, but by a deliberate willing choice. In contrast to desire and sin that give birth to death, God, as if impregnated by the word of truth, gives birth to life.[9] It was not just any life, either, but

---

8. The works cited argues for the appropriate translation at some length, the latter article adding information from the *Thesaurus Linguae Graecae*, which was not in existence when the first article was written.

9. The Greek words for both "desire" and "sin" are feminine in grammatical gender. One must not confuse grammatical gender, a language convention, with the use of the term "gender" in the contemporary period for a social construct pertaining to people, and thus the roles and identities that human individuals take on within that social world. That "desire" and "sin" are both feminine in grammatical gender allows our author to construct a metaphor by analogy to human females that has them functioning as females in conceiving and giving birth. But it remains a metaphorical structure, in a sense a pun on grammatical gender, which makes the result of this chain vivid. God giving birth is a fascinating and even daring image in which the earlier metaphorical structure is now applied to God. The verb for giving birth is normally only used to describe a woman giving birth, but, as already noted, it was used in the earlier chain to describe the metaphorical action of (grammatically feminine) sin giving birth to death. Now it is used of a grammatically masculine subject (God) where the grammatical pun will not work, to make the contrast with desire and sin clear: desire and sin give birth to death, but God gives birth to life. (Perhaps the image of God as creator is enough to keep the grammatical pun from totally failing.) "The glory of God is a

one that makes the human being into the firstfruit of creation. This is the action of the unchanging God.

This means, of course, that God is associated with creation, life, and life-giving virtues. There is a "crown of life" which God has promised "to those who love him" (Jas 1:12 RSV). Likewise, "God [has] chosen those who are poor in the world to be rich in faith and heirs of the kingdom which he has promised to those who love him" (Jas 2:5 RSV). This is a life-giving activity. Finally, the "wisdom from above" (Jas 3:17 RSV), which is divine wisdom and thus associated with God, is life-giving or community-building. One has a consistent foreground image of God as creator and life-giver.

But, as noted, God is also single, not dual. And that means that those who are dual, who trust God and who also trust "the world," are in a state of enmity with God (Jas 4:4). There is, then, a "not the wisdom from above" (Jas 3:15), that is, a so-called wisdom that means that one lacks divine wisdom (Jas 3:15).[10] There is human anger, which does not produce divine righteousness (Jas 1:20) and, indeed, shows a need for the "implanted word" (Jas 1:21 RSV), that word which gives life. In fact, it is only when one gets rid of this duality and repents and "draws near" to God that God does, perhaps even that God *can*, "draw near" to one (Jas 4:8 RSV). The person of dual allegiance is separated from God.

God is jealous "over the spirit he made to dwell in us" (Jas 4:5; Davids 1982, 162–64).[11] The life-giver is jealous over the life, lest it have dual allegiances; the Creator is jealous over the essence of his creature. So God resists the proud, those who have chosen their way over against God, and God gives grace to the humble, those who have submitted singly to the One.

---

human being fully alive," a phrase that stems from Ignatius of Antioch but is repeated often in the classic Christian spiritual tradition, expresses this idea well.

10. James uses the awkward negative expression to call attention to the idea that this is not wisdom at all. The only wisdom in James is divine wisdom, and this is not that, so James does not dignify it with the term "wisdom."

11. The work cited argues that this is the nonphysical part of the human being, the human spirit, since James does not speak of the Holy Spirit living in the human being. Unfortunately, there is no "scripture" in either the standard Hebrew Scriptures (as translated into Greek) or in Second Temple Jewish literature that has these words. It could be a paraphrase of Gen 2:7, but if so it just paraphrases the general idea without using any of the words. Thus, the reader is left to one's own weighing of the options, even if the original audience was apparently expected to recognize the source.

One almost wonders if one has here the beginnings of the picture of God as being itself (*esse ipsum*), classically found in Thomas Aquinas, lurking in the background. Or perhaps one has the beginnings of Augustine's concept of sin as the absence of good rather than a thing in itself. Obviously, it would be anachronistic to read these developed theological concepts back into James, but one must remember that the Greek philosophers upon whom these later theologians built were not unknown in the first century (or the second century, if one chooses to date James then) and their ideas would have floated around in popularized forms. For the purposes of this chapter it is enough to note the analogy. The adulterous wife has a duality of allegiance that makes the husband jealous (Jas 4:4). Until she gets singleness, she is in danger in his presence, although, to push the metaphor further, she will be received the moment she repents and seeks only him. The philosophical analogy would be that nonbeing cannot exist in the presence of being.

It is necessary to play with such analogies because James tiptoes around God's having an active judging role. When he wants to describe such a role, he assigns it to Jesus.

Jesus

Now it is true that James does not have many explicit references to Christology. In fact, there are two explicit references in James to Jesus by name in, Jas 1:1, in which James styles himself a slave of God and of "the Lord Jesus the Anointed One" (*kuriou Iēsou Christou*) and Jas 2:1, often read as the beginning of the body middle of the letter, in which James questions their "commitment to our glorious Lord Jesus the Anointed One" or "our Lord Jesus the Anointed One who belongs to the glory" (alternate translations for *tēn pistin tou kuriou hēmōn Iēsou Christou tēs doxes*). These two references parallel each other: both use the same title for Jesus, both start the title with a Greek term for a ruler (the one preferred by Paul, among others), and both end the title with a Greek translation of "messiah," the Jewish term for God's anointed king.[12] This Jesus is Lord over James, who

---

12. The exact phrase "Lord Jesus Christ" occurs fourteen times in the Pauline letters, especially the Pauline *Hauptbriefe* (Romans, 1–2 Corinthians, and Galatians), and once in Acts 28:31. If one limits oneself to the first two words, they occur nineteen times in the Pauline letters as well as numerous times in Acts. This does not include the many times both Paul and Acts simply use "Lord" (*kurios*) by itself, as in

describes himself as this one's slave, much as Moses is described in relation to God in the Hebrew Scriptures. Furthermore, Jesus is presently "glorious" or belongs to "glory" (Jas 2:1), which indicates an exalted, living status. He receives commitment or allegiance (*pistis* with a personal object complement implied) from those addressed, but such allegiance, while perfectly compatible with his being Lord or Messiah, is incompatible with favoritism. Of course, this associates him with God, for multiple times in the Hebrew Scriptures as well as the New Testament, God is described as being without favoritism or commanding human judges to be without favoritism. What is incompatible with God is also incompatible with his designated and exalted ruler. In other words, it is clear that the two times Jesus is explicitly named he is depicted as a ruler, a ruler who acts in character with the divine ruler.

But there are other references to Jesus that do not use his name. In Jas 5:7, in response to suffering at the hands of "the rich," one is to "be patient … until the coming [*parousia*] of the Lord." The exact phrase is found in 2 Thess 2:1, but, more importantly, *parousia* occurs twenty-four times in the New Testament, six times in the sense of the coming or presence of a person (e.g., Paul or Titus), once in the sense of the coming of an anti-God ruler, and the rest of the times in the sense of the coming or presence of Jesus as ruler or judge. It is these latter usages that parallel the use in the Greco-Roman world for the coming of a great leader, king, or Caesar on a formal visit in which he will exercise state power. Since Jesus is mentioned explicitly in the non-Jacobean New Testament references to the *parousia* of a divine ruler, it is probable that "Lord" in Jas 5:7 and 5:8 refers to Jesus. Then in Jas 5:9 there is an admonition not to complain or grumble against others in the community, "for the Judge stands at the doors." Again, a reference to Jesus is probable, especially since it parallels the function of Jesus as Lord in Jas 5:7 and 8.[13]

Rom 10:9, 12, 13. While the term *Christos* ("anointed one") certainly did not of itself mean much in Greek, because it was used as part of a title it was surely explained to neophytes, especially non-Jewish neophytes, within the first century Jesus movement. Once the gospels started circulating, it, in a sense, self-explained, for it was paired with "Son of the Blessed/Living God" in the passion narrative (i.e., Mark 14:61 and parallels). Furthermore, it occurs in the LXX for an anointed king or an expected messiah/anointed one.

13. There are, of course, references to the coming of YHWH in the Hebrew Scriptures, but in the LXX the translators do not use *parousia*. The only appearance of the term in the LXX is in Jdt 10:18, where it refers to Judith's arrival in the Assyrian camp.

But lest one think that all references to "the Lord" in James refer to Jesus, Jas 5:10 refers to the prophets who "spoke in the name of the Lord" and then goes on to refer to the Job of the Testament of Job and the "purpose of the Lord." Patristic writers refer to Jesus as the Word who spoke through the prophets, but they do it significantly later than James on most datings of James.[14] The Testament of Job clearly references God ("God, the maker of heaven and earth" or "the Lord") with these phrases, so in Jas 5:10 James is using "Lord" to refer to God.

There are also more ambiguous usages in Jas 5. In Jas 5:14–15, one reads that the elders are to anoint the sick "in the name of the Lord" and then "the Lord will raise them up." In the Hebrew Scriptures "the name of the Lord" refers to God, as it does in the gospels when Jesus's coming is "in the name of the Lord" (a reference to Ps 118:26). Again, in the Hebrew Scriptures prophets spoke "in the name of the Lord" (and those who did so falsely were to suffer capital punishment according to Deut 13). But before concluding that the James passages also refer to God/the Father, one must also consider that in Mark 10:13, the only other reference to followers of Jesus anointing the sick with oil, the Twelve are substituting for Jesus and going at the command of Jesus. There is no reference to a commission by God. Likewise, in ministry contexts in the New Testament, "in the name of the Lord" refers to acting in the name of Jesus (e.g., three times in Acts and once in Col 3:17). Also, Acts 3:6 and 16:18 have instances of healing where the formula "in the name of Jesus" (RSV) is used (and other instances where proclamation is done "in the name of Jesus"). Thus, for Acts at least, "in the name of the Lord (Jesus)" and "in the name of Jesus" appear to be parallel expressions. The result is that the expression in James is not clear. Prayer "in the name of the Jesus [the Lord]" and Jesus's acting

---

Given the context of the whole narrative, she may be viewed as an ironic "royal" visitor, for she will bring judgment upon Holofernes, but she is not God and the irony is never made explicit.

14. If one dates James as late as 180 CE as Nienhuis does (2007), then one does have James contemporaneous with the earlier patristic writers stressing the Word being the revealer active in ancient Israel. This is especially true since (1) the date of 180 CE is somewhat arbitrary, for the reasoning could support James being written as late as 230 CE, and (2) Nienhuis also argues that James was deliberately written to look like a first century work, and therefore one would expect the revelation to be "in the name of the Lord" as in Deut 13, rather than the later "by the Word," i.e., one would think the author would employ the earlier, more archaic usage, not the later patristic expression.

as healer and raising the person up make sense. But then no reader of the Hebrew Scriptures would doubt that "the Lord [i.e., God] is compassionate and merciful," so that reading also makes sense. Could it be that James is deliberately ambiguous? Is he functionally equating "the Lord" of the Hebrew Scripture (usually YHWH) with "the Lord" of community worship (Jesus)?

There are other ambiguous contexts in James, some less so and some more so. (1) In Jas 3:9, "Lord" and "Father" are joined by "and" and governed by a single article. If they are viewed as proper nouns, that is, if "the Lord" has come to refer to Jesus, then there are two who are being blessed, Jesus and the Father, which would make sense in a Christian context. But if "the Lord" is equivalent to YHWH or a title of God, then in Jas 3:9 one is blessing one person with two titles, "the Lord-Father," which makes sense in that this is followed by human beings having been made "in the likeness of God." (2) In Jas 4:12 there is a reference to the "lawgiver and judge," which one would normally think of as referring to God, especially since the referent in Jas 4:12 is referred to as "one" and since "lawgiver" appears in the LXX in Ps 9:21 for God. But in Ps 84:7 LXX the term is plural, so it does not always refer to God in the LXX. Also, in the Hebrew Scriptures Moses functions as the lawgiver par excellence and also as a judge, so those are not exclusive or undelegatable functions of God. Furthermore, Jesus is the Judge in Jas 5:9, so at least the judging function would fit well with the role of Jesus. (3) Who is "the Lord" who wills in Jas 4:15? James 1:1 styles James as a slave of "God and the Lord Jesus Christ" (RSV), so either could give a command or express a will over such a slave. The reference is ambiguous. The point of this discussion for our present argument is that there is a certain ambiguity in James; there are passages in which one could argue with more or less cogency that *either* God or the exalted Jesus could be intended by "Lord." Perhaps they are so closely associated for James that he is not concerned about clear differentiation or simply does not notice the ambiguity.

What one has, then, is a description of Jesus as the reigning Lord, who is glorious. He is the one who is coming, and his coming is as eschatological Judge. This contrasts with the Father who is described more mildly. The Father is jealous, indeed, but ready to receive the repentant and always prepared to send good and only good to his people. This is not an absolute contrast, but it is a surprising reversal of what one might expect from typical readings of the Christian Scriptures.

The Holy Spirit?

When one comes to the Holy Spirit the question mark is necessary, for the term does not appear at all in James. The question is, "What takes over the functions other New Testament authors would assign to the Holy Spirit?"

The first question is, What are the functions various New Testament authors assign to the Holy Spirit? In Acts, for example, the Spirit empowers for mission, directs the mission, and within the mission empowers for healing. In James the first is not mentioned, the second is attributed to the will of "the Lord" (assuming that Jas 4:13–18 is referring to direction), and the third is attributed to Jesus in an unmediated sense (the presbyters pray, anoint "in the name of the Lord," and "the Lord will raise [the sick person] up"). In 1 Pet 1:10–12 and 2 Pet 1:19–21, the Holy Spirit (or in 1 Peter, "the Spirit of Christ") brings revelation to the prophets of old and enables the proclamation of the evangelists of the present. James does not mention evangelism (unless the summary in Jas 5:19–20 is deemed to be an example of such), nor does he talk about the source of the inspiration of the writers of the Hebrew Scriptures. New Testament writers also assign a sanctifying function to the Holy Spirit that James does mention; he assigns it to wisdom.

The connection of wisdom with the Holy Spirit has been made before (e.g., Kirk 1969), but the scholarly consensus is that wisdom is not just another name for the Holy Spirit as "the Word" is another name for (the preincarnate) Jesus in the Fourth Gospel and for Jesus as divine in patristic writings. However, there is scholarly consensus that James is strongly influenced by Jewish wisdom literature and thus was familiar with the figure of Wisdom found first in Proverbs (most strongly personified in Prov 8) and then later in Sirach and the Wisdom of Solomon (Davids 1982, 51–56). In this literature wisdom is personified, but James does not personify wisdom nearly so clearly. Still, wisdom does have a function in producing holiness, even if she is neither strongly personified nor a stand-in for the Holy Spirit.

In Jas 1:5, one may lack wisdom and therefore request it from God (if one does so in single-minded commitment to God rather than in an attitude of trust in other things as well as God). The function of wisdom is to enable one to stand firm in the situation of trial or testing described in Jas 1:2–4.[15] Apparently in James, wealth and poverty are two of the trials that

---

15. One thinks of Wis 9, in which Solomon prays for wisdom to be dispatched by God from his throne so that Solomon will have the ability to govern according to divine standards.

one can face (Jas 1:9–11). The importance of standing in trial is resumed in Jas 1:12 in a type of *inclusio*, and then James goes on to argue that God is not two-faced: he does not approve of one standing firm in trial and also send the trial, so one should not blame God for the trial. Rather, what makes the situation trying is desire (Jas 1:14): James is picking up an important issue with *epithymia* in Greek literature that finds its parallel in the evil influence in the human being, the *yētser*, in Second Temple Jewish and rabbinic thought.[16] This same negative influence in human life is picked up in a synonym to *epithymia*, *hēdonē*, in Jas 4:1, resumed by the verbal form of *epithymia* in Jas 4:2, as was observed above. Thus we have a (grammatically feminine) human desire that creates sin and conflict, and the solution to this negative force, a divinely given wisdom (*sophia*), which is also grammatically feminine. Here one has the close-to-personified parallel to the loose woman and Lady Wisdom of Proverbs.[17] In Jas 3, of course, there is something that masquerades as "the wisdom from above" (RSV), which James does not dignify with the term "wisdom" (it is "not the wisdom from above"), but rather with descriptors like "earthly," "soul-ish," and "demonic," which would fit desire rather well. When the "wisdom from above" shows up, she inspires community-promoting and preserving virtues, which were also known in Paul, Qumran, and Matthew (see the chart in Davids 1982, 54).

There is, then, no reference to the Holy Spirit in James (although there are two to the human spirit), which contrasts to some of the Pauline letters (although not all: Philemon has no references to the Spirit and Colossians only one), the Johannine Epistles, the Petrine Epistles (mainly in terms of revelation), and Jude (which has one clear reference). But when it comes to promoting and enabling virtue and opposing the evil cause by human desire, there is a type of stand-in for the Spirit, a divine gift that enables one to live virtuously, and that is wisdom, which appears to be something of a less personified presentation of the two women of Proverbs.[18]

---

16. There was, of course, significant Hellenistic influence in the Jewish centers of Mesopotamia, Palestine, and Egypt, so the both-and of the two types of linguistic terminology should be expected.

17. It is "close to" in that desire lures and entices, conceives, and gives birth in Jas 1:14–15, so there is some slight personification, but nothing like the level of that in Proverbs.

18. The issues in Proverbs are a bit different, for the foolish or loose woman in Proverbs is enticing one into sexual adventures, in particular, adulterous ones, which

Conclusion

The theology James expresses, then, is a type of binitarian theology, with God the Father functioning as creator and the giver of good gifts to those who find themselves in need. He is, however, also One and expects exclusive allegiance and worship. Jesus is the exalted Lord, who rules now, whose teaching is or should be the law of the community (as repeated allusions to the teaching of Jesus demonstrate), and who is the coming eschatological Judge, even now at the door. The Spirit's function is carried out by a divine gift, wisdom, which enables one to stand in the test and to oppose the influence of desire that would draw one away from single-minded allegiance to God. This is not the Apostles' Creed, much less Nicea, but it is a step on the way (minus the Spirit), with the difference in accent being that the function of Jesus is more that of sitting "at the right hand of the Father" and judging "the living and the dead" than any other creedal function attributed to him, while that of the Father is indeed the function of creator, but also the function of a *paterfamilias* of unchanging character who quickly meets the needs of those in the family.

---

are not an issue in James. However, Lady Wisdom is teaching "the fear of God" and various forms of self-control, which fit well into the concerns of James.

Salvation in James: Saved by Gift to Become Merciful

Mariam Kamell Kovalishyn

The Epistle of James is not a text that is usually cited in discussions of soteriology, except perhaps for it to be dismissed as one that needs to be rescued because it might be read as teaching a wrong theology of salvation by works (e.g., Adams 2006).[1] When we approach James expecting certain terminology and specific affirmations, we may find ourselves disappointed with the text. This is Martin Luther's infamous complaint, of course, because while Luther himself argued that true Christian faith must bear fruit, he could not bear the language of justification paired with language of works as found in Jas 2, and so he deemed the author insufficient to the task he set himself. On the other hand, if we approach James seeking to hear how the epistle itself is put together and how it formulates its teachings in its context, we may be surprised by the picture that emerges. Karl-Wilhelm Niebuhr (2004) has argued that an ongoing "new perspective" on James has brought greater diversity and depth to interpretation of the epistle. Indeed, as we dig deeper, we find a wholly canonical picture of salvation, one consistent with Jesus, the prophets, and Deuteronomic covenantal law and firmly grounded in the character of God. We simply need to pay attention to the epistle's underlying narrative to see this drama.

In James, the story of salvation unfolds in the midst of practical instructions for life as minority communities (cf. 1:1, "the twelve tribes in the diaspora"). The allusion to diaspora here is generally read as referring to a Jewish Christian community, for whom the term had special significance as an echo of prior diaspora letters the Jewish community had received that instructed them on faithful living in their context (cf. Coker 2014, 441–53). The audience of the epistle seems to be largely poor

---

1. It should be noted that authorship is not in view in this article, and the title *James* is used interchangeably with the author for simplicity's sake.

and possibly undergoing oppression (cf. 2:6; 5:1–6). While some of James's churches may have been significantly above sustenance level economically (4:13–17; Kamell 2009, 166–75), the community as a whole likely was in need of practical advice for how to live in challenging circumstances. But more than that, the audience needed a vision that made coherent sense of the story into which they were called to live, one that ran directly against the grain of human nature (1:13–16) and culture (2:1–4; ch. 4). In order to do this, James grounds his letter in God's character, which is the foundation of the community's salvation and hope. From that basis, James then builds out his theology of sanctification and its relationship to salvation, concisely summarized as "faith without works is dead."[2]

James writes this impassioned letter out of concern that false assumptions about God's character or the role of faith and works will lead some to face the judgment of God rather than receive his mercy. There are three areas that are of particular import for James's *theology*: first, that God is good and generous to his people; second, that God is the source of his people's regeneration, and third, that God alone is judge. Together, these three points make clear the divine side of James's soteriology. On the human side, however, is the expectation that the audience will receive *and act in accordance with* the work of God for salvation. If they do not, they face the just judgment for their failure to live in a way that reflects the new nature God has gifted to them. If they do, however, then they discover that the mercy of God is triumphant for their cause.

The Character of God

The crucial starting point for understanding the Epistle of James is the author's theology. In contrast to the pessimistic views of Martin Dibelius (1976, 21–22) and Sophie Laws (1980, 28) among others, the Epistle of James roots its vision of salvation and sanctification in the character of God.[3]

The epistle begins with the vision of how a believer's life should progress: the audience members should rejoice as they face trials because of what they know, which is that God is at work in perfecting them through these times. In order to gain this perspective, however, the believer is cau-

---

2. Biblical translations throughout are my own.

3. See also the pessimistic approach of Chester (1994, 44–45), who concludes that "James' theology is limited in many ways," with little to no development on any theme but that of works.

tioned to turn in faith to God, because God will give what is needed for one to have that correct perspective. Here James's utter trust in God's good and generous nature makes its first appearance: "ask of the giving God [*tou didontos theou*]" who gives "to all generously and without finding fault, and it will be given to him/her" (Jas 1:5). James places the present participle between the article and noun rather than after the pair, placing the emphasis on the participle ("giving") as God's nature, not merely an action that God does.[4] It becomes, as it were, almost a title describing God's character: "the giving God" rather than simply "the God who gives," although translationally the latter works better. It is God's character to give—and to give *to all* (*pasin*)—as James counters any preconceived notion that God gives only to those who have some special reason for receiving (Vlachos 2013, 25). To drive this point home, James then uses both a positive and negative description, "singly" or "generously" (*haplōs*) and "without finding fault" (*mē oneidizontos*); the repetition provides rhetorical emphasis. God's inherent nature as generous should not be questioned: he is unstinting in his very nature.[5] It is in doubting God's character that they block themselves from being the beneficiaries of his nature (1:6–8). Whereas God is unchangeably generous, those who doubt this reveal themselves to be double-minded, unwilling to commit singly to God as he commits singly to giving to his people. They thus reveal their instability, their refusal to conform to the character of God: to become "mature and whole [*teleioi kai holoklēroi*], lacking in nothing" (1:4).[6]

This contrast is fundamental to the epistle. On the one hand is God's nature as "the giving God," who gives to all "single-mindedly."[7] On the

---

4. See Vlachos, who cites Mayor (1897, 39) that this is an unusual word order. Vlachos comments that "prominence is given by way of the attrib. structure to the character of God—he is the *giving God*" (2013, 25, emphasis original)

5. Allison (2013, 174) summarizes the first half of v. 5 as "saying that one may have utter confidence in the God who unreservedly gives gifts."

6. The terms *teleioi kai holoklēroi* are rich, but I chose the above translations because *teleioi* often indicates a "perfection" derived from testing and growth, namely, "maturity." Likewise, for *holoklēroi* (often translated as "complete"), I chose "whole" as a contrast to the schism that double-mindedness creates in a person.

7. This term generally is translated as "generous," but its alternate meaning of simplicity or singleness provides a perfect contrast with the immediately subsequent double-minded human. Adam (2013, 7) observes, "In the context of James' concern about doublemindedness (1:8; 4:8), we may hear this [*haplōs*] as an implied contrast with humanity's half-hearted generosity."

other is "the one who doubts," the "double-minded person, unstable in all one's ways" (1:6, 8).[8] The problem with such people is not that they did not have *enough* faith, it is that they do not trust God's character enough to commit to the path of sanctification outlined in verse 4. They doubt God, and this doubt makes it impossible to receive wisdom from God.[9]

James emphasizes this warning when he cautions, "Do not be deceived [*mē planasthe*], my beloved brothers and sisters!" James 1:16 is a hinge, closing out the prior caution against blaming God for temptations in verses 13–15, but also leading to further clarification of God's character in 17–18.[10] Verse 16 (and its parallel in 5:19) implies a soteriological significance of self-deception, also described as wandering away. God, James informs his audience, is wholly the source of good gifts. Failure to understand God's nature as it is revealed in verses 17 and 18 by believing evil of him (as in 1:13–15) can lead to a complete failure to receive his gifts, of which salvation is paramount. James 1:17 doubly emphasizes, "every good giving and every perfect gift" (*pasa dosis agathē kai pan dōrēma teleion*) is from God. Rather than blaming God for their failures, the audience is to trust God's unchangingly good and generous nature, which is again contrasted with things that change, this time the planets that wander. The fact that James underscores this contrast of God's steadily good and generous nature versus any changeableness twice already within the first chapter reveals its importance to his theology.[11]

---

8. For James, the adjective "restless" or "unstable" (*akatastatos*, 1:8, 3:8; related noun *akatastasia* in 3:16) is unequivocally bad, regularly contrasting with images of unity or wholeness. In 1:8 the adjective qualifies the *anēr dipsuchos*, the "double-souled person," while in 3:8 it characterizes the active tension of the evil embodied in the tongue. This instability of path (*odois*) reminds the reader of two ways teaching prevalent in both secular and Jewish teaching.

9. Cf. Martin (1988, 18), who notes "God's nature ... is not to be questioned, and his giving is marked by a spirit of spontaneity and graciousness. The theme of James is that of the 'prodigality of God' (Vouga)."

10. Ellis (2015, 186) concludes that 1:13–16 "rejects divine agency in probation based on the ontological nature of divine character.... God's goodness is constant and unchanging (*haplōs* in 1:5; *parallagē* in 1:17), a constancy that serves as the exhortation to human constancy within the mature believer vis-à-via *imitatio Dei*."

11. Verseput (1997) makes the important argument that creation imagery of this sort was also creedal and would have been familiar to James's audience as part of their morning prayers. James's argument of God's beneficence is thus grounded in common theology.

The most important gift, however, is the new birth pronounced in 1:18. The grammar emphasizes that this is God's work alone, done by God's will: "Being willing, he gave us birth" (*boulētheis apekyēsen hēmas*). The participle is foregrounded to make clear that the birth under discussion was not brought about by anyone's choosing except God's.[12] While a few scholars argue that this birth as firstfruits of creation refers back to the original creation of humanity, the majority would understand it as a statement about the congregation being the firstfruits of the *new* creation, born by God's redemptive act in Christ.[13] The God who willed initial creation into being by his word, now acts again: "Divine creation (of the stars in their courses) is matched by the new creation…. The participle *boulētheis*, 'he willed,' emphasizes how God acted freely without external constraint…. The effective instrument of the divine fiat is said to be *logos alētheias*, the 'word of truth'" (Martin 1988, 39). The firstfruits language then serves as a reminder to the congregation that they are set apart for God, much as the firstfruits of the harvest were to be set apart and offered to the Lord (e.g., Deut 26:1–11, so also the nation of Israel, Jer 2:3). But the language of first-fruits also signifies that more is to come.[14] The believers may be a minority in their communities now, oppressed and struggling, but they are not the culmination of the work of God. Rather, their birth is a signal that God's work has begun and, like Israel, they are to be a distinctive community that witnesses to the redemption of God.

The birth language is significant as well, however, because by it James creates a visceral contrast between the death cycle of sin in 1:13–15 and the life cycle of God's gifts in 1:17–18. Once desire has gained control of a person, the situation is dire: "desire [*hē epithymia*], once it has conceived, brings forth sin [*hamartia*], and sin once grown [*apotelestheisa*] gives birth [*apokyei*] to death" (v. 15). The fulfillment of desire is sin, the fulfillment of sin is death. In contrast, however, God is said to have "given

---

12. Adam sees the participle as either "manner, expressing *how* God brought us forth: 'deliberately'; or perhaps temporal: 'after having deliberated'" (2013, 20, emphasis original). Martin notes: "the verb denotes the free, sovereign will to create based on his determination" (1988, 39).

13. E.g., Elliott-Binns (1956, 156) views this as a reference "to the original creation of which man was the crown and the promise; [James] knows nothing of any 'new' creation or rebirth." Others, such as Jackson-McCabe (2001, 154) and Laws (1980, 75–78), agree, although Jackson-McCabe tends towards a Stoic background while Laws allows for some fluidity in meaning with Christian conversion.

14. But not so far as universalism (cf. Palmer 1957, 1–2).

birth [*apekyēsen*] to us by the word of truth" (v. 18). Birth by the "word of truth" sets the believers free, as it were, from the control of desire, and they themselves are reborn as firstfruits, in sharp contrast to a world controlled by desire, sin, and death. This is crucial: James's concern about sanctification stems from his understanding that *his audience members are already reborn out of the control of the world and its values, no longer controlled by desire and death.*[15] So when their actions in fighting and competing and showing preference to wealth show them to be still living according to the world, it raises the question of whether they have indeed received God's gift of the "word of truth" or have let it lie fallow amid "every filthiness and rampant evil" (1:21). In James, the new birth is by God's choosing and gift, but it must be received with humility and anything contrary pruned, as 1:21 makes clear.[16] Thus, although the regenerative work is entirely God's, humans are expected to respond appropriately for the work to take effect.

Salvation and Sanctification

Whereas James's first warning against self-deception has to do with not doubting the good character of God, the second in 1:22 develops the personal responsibility to receive God's work. James calls the readers to "be doers of the word and not merely hearers who deceive themselves." When people fail to act in accordance with the word by which they have been reborn, a word that is further qualified as the "perfect law of freedom" in 1:25, James declares that they also deceive themselves. In contrast to engaging the freedom the word brings from the cycle of sin and death,

---

15. So, Baker (2009, 204–5): "A solution to 1:21 can be suggested by recognizing the positive birth allegory of 1:18 as intended both to mirror and replace the negative allegory of 1:14–15 ... the child born from the union of God via the word of truth with those who submit to the gospel carries the DNA of the word of God. The birthed believer who is the product of this union in this picture, then, does in fact have the word within their genetic makeup. It is 'innate' from birth as Hart correctly lobbies. Just as Sin fully realizes her affinity to her mother, Desire, and gives birth to Death, so the birthed believer as she grows into maturity not only recognizes how she is 'like her father' but accepts and acts on the natural impulses to be like her father, the Word of Truth."

16. I have argued elsewhere (Kamell 2011, 19–28) that 1:21 reflects the tradition from Jer 31, wherein the new covenant will be placed *within* the people and "implanted" language echoes the planting imagery from Jer 31. This connection also serves to connect James to the covenantal tradition.

these people reveal their rejection of the implanted word by refusing to live according to it. Obedience is a necessary part of the process of salvation; without obedience, people deceive themselves regarding their relationship with God. James 1:22–25 introduces the controversial argument of 2:14–26, here made through the contrast of hearing and doing. To hear the word but not obey it is a completely impractical choice, one that indicates that the person has not received the word nor allowed it to take root. James assumes that anyone who truly encounters the word will begin to live accordingly, as a seamless outcome of the new birth into life as God's people. Soon James makes explicit what is implicit here: to be "deluded about the nature of authentic religion" produces a faith that *cannot save* (2:14, 26).[17]

Protestants have historically taken issue with obedience to the law as a part of salvation. In James it is, however, the law "of freedom." As was noted above, rebirth happens by the word of truth, which sets people free from the sin and death of their own natures. Obedience to the law of God, therefore, is merely living in accordance with the freedom one has been given. James views the law of God as freeing from the bondage of our sin nature, the law that gives life in contrast to the natural desires that brought death. If there truly are two ways of being as James depicts in 1:13–18, then one obeys *either* the law of sin and death *or* the word of truth that gives freedom. Obedience is a given; James only questions what one obeys; and so, like a forgetful person who fails to realize her nature has been gifted a transformation but continues in her prior patterns, those who continue to act according to their natural desires deceive themselves about the law they obey, and thereby bring forth death in themselves.

In contrast, what we see in the rest of the epistle is that when a person begins to act in accordance with the law of freedom, her character mimics the character of God. Chapter two gives two examples. First, the person

---

17. One can hear echoes of Jesus's parable of the four soils (Matt 13) in Jas 1:21–25, wherein the seed can be choked out by weeds or poorly prepared ground. The seed may be sown, and it may even take root (i.e., implanted), but unless it bears fruit of obedience, it fails of its purpose. Allison, quoted above (2013, 326) notes: "Interpreters often think in terms of a deception that leads to losing salvation. The point seems rather to be that some people are deluded about the nature of authentic religion: they believe—or through their inactions appear to believe—that listening to religious instruction is itself meritorious." Unlike Allison here, however, I argue that James's point is that to be deluded as to the nature of true religion is to lose salvation, a point brought out by the parallel between 1:22–25 and 2:14–26.

who lives according to the law of freedom should cease to evaluate other people based on their wealth, for that is a worldly evaluation. James 2:1–11 is likely a sermonette on Lev 19:15 and the command there against favoritism (see the Septuagint, which translates the Hebrew language for favoritism literally as *lēmpsē prosōpon*, from which the New Testament word *prosōpolēmpsiais* is derived).[18] Repeatedly through the Hebrew Scriptures, God is said not to show partiality to the wealthy but to bring justice for everyone who comes (cf. Deut 1:17; 10:17; 16:19). Unlike the sinful, God's people are to mirror his justice in their interactions. For this reason, showing partiality is a sign to James that a person is not living according to the law of freedom.[19]

James then uses the Decalogue in 2:8–11 to highlight the unity of the law, that one cannot pick and choose one's way through. This is a return to his larger theme of God's unity versus humanity's double-mindedness. God's law is a whole by which believers are reborn into his people according to his nature. Therefore, God's people cannot choose to obey or not obey various laws, because God's nature is not divisible. The reborn people of God should grow into people who do not show favoritism if the word of truth has taken root in them.

A second test case for checking the growth of the word of truth is given in the much-debated "faith and works" passage of 2:14–26. In this passage, practical examples are again given: Is one willing to help an impoverished member of the community in useful ways (2:14–17)? Is one willing to place God ahead of every other loyalty, and willing to do so in concrete

---

18. The wording in Lev 19:15 LXX (*lēmpsē prosōpon*) is unusual, elsewhere occurring together for "favoritism" only in Ps 81:2 and Mal 2:9. The term translated as "partiality" or "favoritism" more often shows up as *epignōsē prosōpon* (Deut 1:17; cf. Deut 16:19) or *thaumazei prosōpon* (Deut 10:17; cf. 2 Chr 19:7; Job 13:10; etc.). James's use of *prosōpolēmpsiais* in 2:1, combined with the quotation of Lev 19:18 in 2:8, ties Jas 2:1–11 closely to Lev 19:15–18. Johnson (1982, 391, 393) assumes that Lev 19 provides the background of Jas 2 and argues for its presence in Jas 5 as well.

19. Gowler (2014, 152–60) gives poignant examples from South African, Latin American, and African American theologians who lament the church's willingness to show partiality both to wealth and to race. He quotes D. J. Smit: "In many South African churches one will find the same kind of problem to which James refers in his example, namely, that the church—in spite of the fact that they are poor, oppressed, powerless, 'black,' themselves—pay much more respect and honor to the rich and powerful, than to the poor, the women, the widows, the orphans, the children, among their own members" (154).

acts (2:20–26)?[20] James makes effective use of Rahab in this context. She tells the two spies that "our hearts melted" when the people of Jericho heard about God's provisions for the Hebrews, then she confesses that "the Lord your God is indeed God in heaven above and on earth below" (Josh 2:11). These comments neatly parallel James's observation, "You believe that God is one, you do well; but even the demons believe—and shudder" (Jas 2:19). Belief, no matter how orthodox, in and of itself cannot save. Rahab's actions, however, showed that she understood that believing in God required more than simply trembling; it requires action appropriate to the revelation of God's universal power. Likewise, after earlier doubting God's promises, late in his life Abraham showed he was willing to risk his very lineage. The Akedah (or binding of Isaac) is significant because in this act, Abraham revealed he had come to trust God fully to account for his promises, and Abraham would no longer act on his own to make them come true. Faith in God to fulfill his promises was now the defining characteristic of Abraham's life.

Chapter 2, however, is not the only place where James emphasizes the need for a transformed life as a response to the implanted word. In 3:1–12 the author highlights the problems humans have with duplicitous speech. Humans reveal their failure to be single-minded in their speech: "no one can tame the tongue—a restless evil, full of deadly poison. With it we bless the Lord and Father, and with it we curse those who are made in the likeness of God. From the same mouth come blessing and cursing. My brothers and sisters, this ought not to be so" (3:8–10, cf. Matt 12:34; Luke 6:45). Peoples' doubleness is revealed in their speech, no matter how they may try to deny it. James uses repeated nature imagery as well as creation language to drive home the bizarre contradiction in human failure to be single-minded in speech.[21] He assumes that the people of God should be moving toward their intended state, single-mindedness in speech and action. Any other way of living ought not to be so.

---

20. This has traditionally been interpreted as two further illustrations of hospitality (see, e.g., Ward 1968, 283–90), but I agree with R. Foster (2014, 200) that the exemplars show a willingness to place God's call first, rather than prioritizing descendants or national loyalty.

21. Note the echo of Gen 1:26 LXX (*poiēsōmen anthrōpon kat' eikona hēmeteron kai kath' homoiōsin*) in Jas 3:9 (*tous anthrōpous tous kath' homoiōsin theou gegonotas*). See also Kamell Kovalishyn 2018a, 177–88.

Similarly, 3:13–4:12 makes very clear that acting in accordance with the values of the world leads not only to fighting within the community but also to a dire conclusion: "Adultresses [*Moichilides*]! Do you not know that friendship [*hē filia*] with the world is enmity [*echthra*] with God? Therefore, whoever wishes to be friends [*hōs ... boulēthē filos*] with the world makes oneself an enemy [*echthros*] of God" (4:4). The first term *moichilides* ought to be translated "adulteresses" (in contrast to the NRSV, ESV, and NIV), as it indicates not the gender of the audience but alludes to the prophetic tirades against Israel's covenant unfaithfulness. By failing to be single-minded, but instead choosing—in contrast to God's choosing of them in 1:18—to be "friends with the world," the audience is in fact committing covenant infidelity.[22] They are to be the new people of God, the firstfruits, but instead they are choosing an alternate fidelity. Growth in single-minded dedication to God is essential to James's worldview. The alternative brings the audience into the same prophetic judgment that caused Israel to go into exile: a covenantal adulteress who communally needs to repent and return to God.

Ultimately the concluding passage of 5:12–20 makes the same point: just as Elijah's nature miracle served to bring healing to Israel by bringing her back to single-minded worship of YHWH (cf. 1 Kgs 17–18), so the Epistle of James concludes with the call to bring back any who wander (so also Edwards 2003, 143). Healing in a church community can be individual and physical, but it can also be corporate and spiritual. To wander from their allegiance to God alone makes them instead enemies of God. As the book concludes, therefore, the covenantal thread, initiated by God's gracious act of giving birth to these people as firstfruits of his new creation, is now in full view as a key to understanding their relationship with God.

God as Judge

As a consequence, James also takes seriously God's role as judge. God is the arbiter of the covenant, the one who initiated and rescued his people. He therefore is the only judge as well. There are two main passages that make this argument, first in 2:12–13 and again in 4:11–12, although the theme can also be seen elsewhere in the text. For instance, in 1:26–27, God

---

22. Regarding James's use of purity language, see particularly Lockett 2008, 174–83.

is the one before whom religion is either acceptable or not, a determination based on a person's ability to control the tongue (cf. 3:1–4:12) and care for impoverished neighbors (cf. 2:1–15). Both of these actions indicate the moral reality that the person has resisted the moral staining of the sinful world order (cf. 4:13–5:20). Merely claiming to worship God is not sufficient; God expects the person to conform to his new creation order.

Likewise, in 5:7–11 God's role as judge is brought out in relation to his people's suffering and God's nearness. They are to endure their situations well, "for the coming of the Lord is near" (5:8). This can be an encouragement if they are enduring patiently, but if they begin to speak sinfully (whether in complaint or slander), this God's nearness is also threatening: "the Judge is standing at the doors!" (5:9). James wants them to take their community life seriously: they are to encourage and support one another, and to encourage them in this he reminds them of God's covenantal character from Exod 34:6, "the Lord is compassionate and merciful" (Jas 5:11). As the redeemed people of God, they are to trust in God's presence and mercy, but not to presume upon it.

The caution regarding grumbling against one another in 5:9 has a deeper context in 4:11–12. James makes very clear that God is the only one with the right to judge the spiritual state of any in the congregation. When members of the community judge one another, they step out of their position in the community and instead attempt to usurp God's throne. This idea that partiality usurps God's role may have already been flagged if the command to "sit at my feet" in Jas 2:3 alludes to Ps 110:1, where it illustrates God's judgment of his enemies, thereby this scene enacts a humiliating judgment on the poor person (cf. Johnson 1995, 223; McKnight 2011, 188; Weaver 2011, 446).[23] When humans attempt to judge, they cannot help but do it incorrectly by granting too much weight to external signals.

God, as the lawgiver, is the only one who can judge whether his will is being kept correctly: the lawgiver and judge are one (*heis estin*, in what could be an echo of Deut 6:4).[24] The roles cannot be divided. God is the one who brought the community into covenant (1:19) and is therefore the

---

23. Allison (2013, 392 n. 142) realizes but discards the implication: "If one were to find an allusion to the oft-cited Ps 110:1, then one might think of the speaker as sufficiently pompous to speak ironically like God. But this seems far-fetched."

24. James 4:12 at the start: *heis estin ho nomothetēs kai kritēs*; Deut 6:4 at the end: *kyrios ho theos hēmōn kyrios heis estin*. Both are speaking of God's identity and character; this strengthens the echo as both phrases emphasize the unity of God's nature.

only one who can evaluate covenant fidelity. While humans can pretend to judge one another, the only end result is to speak against one another. God, on the other hand, has actual power behind him, as he is "able to save and to destroy" (*sōsai kai apolesai*, v. 12). While human judgments appear to lead to slander or prioritize people wrongly, God's judgment is quite literally for life or death.[25] Given the unity of his lawgiving and judgment, James makes a powerful statement about God's role as covenant maker and arbiter. When humans attempt to usurp that role, they bring themselves into judgment.

It should be noted that while the audience members are called to seek out those who stray to bring them back, James consistently rebukes those who "speak evil against one another" (4:11) and "grumble against one another" (5:9). Seeing another's faltering faith should not lead to judgment but to mercy, again in keeping with developing character like unto God's (5:11). This points back to one of the most important of the texts for this discussion, Jas 2:12–13.

These verses are perhaps the most elusive pericope in the entire epistle, and yet they are also the most crucial for the current discussion. In this passage, human actions of mercy in some mysterious way cooperate with God's verdict for judgment or mercy. The context is James's prohibition of partiality, for in showing partiality they fail to judge as God does, preferring the signs of worldly wealth to the true wealth of the kingdom. James then intensifies his argument by noting the unity of the law.[26] Obedience cannot be partial: either one conforms to the "law of freedom" wholly, by which one's entire value system is reworked and one is freed to be a friend of God, or one's partiality reveals ongoing allegiance to the world. Judgment "by [*dia*] the law of freedom" (2:12) evaluates how well the community embodies the freedom they were given, empowered by "the implanted word which is able to save your souls" (*ton dynamenon sōzai*

---

25. *Sōzō* ("I save") appears five times in James (1:21; 2:14; 4:12; 5:15; 5:20). Of these, all except one are clearly in context of eschatological salvation (5:15 is ambiguous). Twice the object is *psychē* ("soul" or "self") and once *autos* ("self"), and it appears three times following *dynamai* ("I am able," thus, "able to save"). The picture throughout the epistle is that *sōzō* concerns the eschatological salvation of the individual, within the context of the community. *Apollymi* ("I destroy") appears twice, in 1:11 and 4:12, both in judgment on those who have misunderstood God's values.

26. Just as the lawgiver is *one* (4:12), so is the law he has given as his single-minded will for how people are to live.

tas psychas hymōn, 1:21). By this interpretation, the law of freedom is both *prescriptive*, much like the Decalogue, which James alludes to in 2:11, but it is also *performative*, because it is the power that makes salvation possible. In allowing the implanted word to take root, obedience is made possible. Covering the gamut of human behavior, verse 12 cautions everyone to speak and act fully in alignment with the freedom from sin that they have been granted, for by this freedom they will be judged. Most scholars agree that this does, in fact, warn of the final eschatological judgment.[27]

The crux comes in verse 13, which cautions that "judgment will be merciless [*aneleos*] to the one not showing mercy [*mē poiēsanti eleos*]; mercy [*eleos*] triumphs over judgment." The first part is clear: as a person fails to show mercy, so also he or she will not be shown mercy. This is a classic *lex talionis*, seen all through Scripture.[28] The *lex talionis* limits liability to a proportional amount (i.e., retaliation may not escalate), but it also creates a responsibility on the actor to realize that justice entails one's own actions returning on him or her. As one acts, justice dictates reciprocity. So far, James is adding nothing new; he simply reaffirms Mosaic law and Jesus's teaching.[29] It is with verse 13b, however, that the ambiguity arises: mercy triumphs over judgment. But whose mercy, and what judgment? Since in verse 13a, the actor is the merciless human and the judgment is God's, presumably the "mercy" in verse 13b is also performed by humans, the opposite of "the one not showing mercy." In verse 13b, the person *has* shown mercy.[30] However, with the context of

---

27. Wall (1997, 128) calls it "God's eschatological courtroom," while Richardson (1997, 126) adds, "Failure to show mercy to those in need calls into question whether there has been any true act of repentance in face of God's mercy. Instead of liberation, the full force of the law's condemnation falls against those who break the law."

28. Cf. Exod 21:23–24; Lev 24:19–20; Matt 6:13–14; 7:1–5; 18:21–35; Mark 11:25. Sirach 28:1 makes the same statement as Jas 2:13a but uses the language of vengeance rather than mercilessness. Davies and Allison (1988–1997, 1:454) also note the rabbinic parallel, "As long as you are merciful, the Merciful One is merciful to you" (t. B. Qam. 9:30).

29. Smith (1914, 128–29) sees the tie to Jesus's teaching and warns, "We think at once of the Lord's Beatitude and the Lord's Prayer. We remember His warning, 'With what measure ye mete withal, it shall be measured to you again.' We remember the Parable of the Two Debtors, and may learn from it not only the perils of the unforgiving temper, but also the operation of God's righteous mercy."

30. See Moo (2000, 118): "The 'mercy' that James has been referring to in this context is human mercy, not God's (v. 12). We therefore think it more likely that he is

imminent eschatological judgment, the text has potentially broadened to include the possibility of divine mercy. As a result, God's mercy triumphs over God's judgment (cf. Popkes 2001, 182). Laws (1980, 117–18) finds this contradictory to verse 11, because "there the law must be kept in full or there is liability for the whole; here the consideration of mercy may apparently serve to waive judgment." What she fails to consider is that, for James, acting mercifully *is* evidence of the fulfillment of the law of freedom, thus it is not simply a "get out of jail free" card but reveals a disposition of obedience to God's will. A person *is* obeying God's will fully when one shows evidence of his character in becoming merciful.[31] As 2:14–26 will make quite clear, good intentions do not suffice, and a faith that does not act hospitably and charitably fails to save. This makes the contrasting statements of 2:13 even more critical. Mercy must, it appears, be enacted in order to be efficacious.

Human mercy triumphs over the precise justice of the impartiality advocated in 2:1–4 because the practice of mercy fulfills the covenant requirement and defines one as righteous. Divine mercy likewise triumphs in that, to those who have shown mercy, it rewards them for their mercy rather than punishing them for their sins, weighing the human mercy favorably at the time of the final judgment. To those who have shown mercy, at the judgment their mercy invokes the divine mercy, and one or both together are depicted as "triumphing over" the strict judgment that would be expected. Ultimately, then, human *actions* of mercy appear necessary to a favorable declaration in justice. In 2:13, "judgment" and "mercy" might well be said to parallel the "destroy" and "save" of 4:12. Both mercy and judgment come from God, but God responds to repentance and to human acts of mercy (and thus law-of-freedom obedience) with his own mercy.

---

making a point about the way in which the mercy we show toward others shows our desire to obey the law of the kingdom and, indirectly therefore, of a heart made right by the work of God's grace."

31. So, Flesher (2014, 184) can argue: "To fail to love your neighbor as yourself is to fail to follow the law, and this will lead to the same judgment that one would experience if s/he were an adulterer or murderer. In the end, James equates this with a lack of mercy and concludes that mercy triumphs over judgment. This, of course, is the essence of the gospel wrapped up in one simple phrase. If it had not been for the mercy of God we would all suffer God's judgment; similarly, we are to be merciful to our neighbor."

Conclusion

The Epistle of James presents us with the full story of salvation, from initial birth into the new creation, to the life lived in keeping with God's character and law, to the final judgment before God. The pattern is, on an individual scale, a parallel to the larger biblical story: a rescue by God's choice rather than through human achievement, followed by the giving of a law that will train the person or community into God's ways, and ultimately judgment based on how that has been engaged. When Israel walked away from her covenant, committing adultery by engaging in idolatry, the prophets begged her to return, to repent, and to learn to care about the people the way that God does.[32] Religion that God desires from his people has less to do with rituals—although those are not ruled out—and more to do with the development of his character. As his people show mercy and become single-mindedly dedicated to God, they find the truth of the phrase, "Draw near to God, and he will draw near to you" (4:8).

The picture of salvation that James presents is holistic. To start anywhere but with God choosing to give his people new birth and implant the word/law that empowers them for transformation is to begin at a false premise. The story of salvation begins entirely with God and his gracious action. But then the assumption is that, given this rebirth and empowerment, a person shall live wholeheartedly according to God's will. Sanctification is inseparable from salvation. When people instead choose the idols of worldly power and wealth, or even nation or family over God, they reveal their double-minded hesitation, and for that they receive judgment.[33] In this economy, judgment is not the shock. Rather, God's responsiveness to his people's attempts at single-minded worship, mercy, and repentance is astounding. Perfection is not expected, but the letter depicts deep frustration over the audience's willful lack of growth. Their covenant adultery has James upset and concerned, because the only

---

32. E.g., Isa 1:16–17 could easily be in the background of James's thoughts, particularly for 1:26–27 and 4:1–12: "Wash yourselves; make yourselves clean; remove the evil of your doings from before my eyes; cease to do evil, learn to do good; seek justice, rescue the oppressed, defend the orphan, plead for the widow."

33. This pattern is eminently like Jesus's parable of the unmerciful servant in Matt 18. Forgiveness was extended by the king's will, but when the servant refused to emulate him, the initial forgiveness is revoked and the just judgment is returned.

outcome for such duplicity is judgment and destruction. But praise be to God, mercy triumphs over judgment.

The Devil and Demons in the Epistle of James

Ryan E. Stokes

Readers of the Bible are often surprised when they learn that the devil in the Bible is not exactly the figure they have always imagined. While most are aware that the Bible does not portray the devil as a red cartoonish figure with horns, a pointed tail, and a pitchfork, many do assume that the devil of the Bible is a fallen angel named Lucifer. No biblical text actually says this.[1] This idea arose long after the Bible was written. In fact, this belief is one of many widespread notions about the devil and related figures (e.g., demons, evil spirits, and fallen angels) that have their origins not in the Bible, but in Christian theological reflection of a much later era. The Bible's portrayal of the devil is significantly different from the portrayals of later theologians.

Furthermore, one finds different portrayals of the devil within the Bible itself. The Bible, which consists of a number of distinct books that were composed over the course of several centuries and by various authors, preserves a wide range of perspectives on the devil, demons, and other evil figures. During the centuries in which the biblical literature was written, beliefs about evil superhuman beings arose and underwent a process of development. Accordingly, the literature of the Bible and early Judaism contains several different ideas pertaining to these figures. One may distinguish earlier notions of these figures from later ones. The literature of early Judaism and Christianity also shows that different understandings of the devil and demons existed at the same time. This is certainly true

---

1. The biblical texts that are normally cited in conjunction with this traditional understanding of the devil are Isa 14:3–21 and Ezek 28:1–19. Isaiah 14 speaks of the fall of the king of Babylon, addressing the king as "Day Star, son of the Dawn." Ezekiel 28 compares the prince of Tyre to Adam, who sinned and was cast from Eden. Neither of these passages refers to the devil.

during the period in which the New Testament was written. This chapter summarizes the history of the development of beliefs about the devil and demons and contextualizes what the Epistle of James has to say about these figures within that history. It also situates the teachings of James concerning these figures among the diverse perspectives on evil superhuman beings that were available near the end of the biblical period.[2]

Early Jewish Beliefs about the Devil and Demons: Trajectories and Diversity

This is not the appropriate place for a comprehensive survey of early Jewish thought about the devil and demons, so this chapter will focus on four trajectories in the development of thinking about harmful superhuman beings in early Judaism that are particularly pertinent to the interpretation of James: (1) the growing importance of the devil and related figures in the theology of early Judaism; (2) the gradual combination of originally distinct traditions about the devil, demons, evil spirits, and other harmful beings into more comprehensive, systematic understandings of the superhuman realm; (3) the expansion of the activities with which Jewish literature credits the devil and evil spirits from merely that of causing physical harm to include, as well, deception and temptation, giving these beings greater and greater responsibility for human sin; and (4) the portrayal of the devil and spirits decreasingly as agents of God who carry out the deity's commands and increasingly as the enemies of God and of God's people. Further, as we will see, not all Jewish theologians were entirely comfortable with some of these developments, and earlier views of the devil and demons continued to exist alongside of more recent ones. As a result, a variety of perspectives on these figures existed simultaneously during the New Testament period.

The Growing Importance of the Devil and Demons in Early Jewish Thought

The devil is undoubtedly an important figure in first-century Christian theology. The frequency with which he appears in the writings of the New Testament, as well as the significant actions that are attributed to him,

---

2. There is some disagreement among scholars regarding the identity of the author of the Epistle of James. For the sake of convenience, this essay will refer to this author simply as *James* without entering into the authorship discussion.

reveal the prominence (albeit a very negative one) that he held in the belief and practice of the early church. The devil, however, did not always have this special status. In fact, at the time that the New Testament was composed, the devil had only recently acquired this position in the thinking of many Jews.

The devil of the New Testament writings has a number of literary and theological antecedents in the earlier Hebrew Scriptures, such as the destroying angel of the Lord (e.g., Num 22:22) and the mythological serpent Leviathan (e.g., Isa 27:1). The foremost of these antecedents is the figure of "the Satan" (*hassatan*), who appears in Zech 3 and Job 1–2. The title "the devil" (*ho diabolos*) is actually a translation of the Hebrew *hassatan*. The New Testament frequently refers to this figure by both designations, as "the Satan" (transliterating the Hebrew with Greek characters) and as "the devil." More will be said below about the significance of these titles in the biblical literature.

Although early Christian authors no doubt presumed that the devil/Satan they described was the same figure as the Satan of the Jewish Scriptures, it is not the case that these Christian authors conceived of this figure in precisely the same way as the authors of the biblical texts they read. One notable difference in their views of the Satan is the important position that this figure came to hold in the thinking of many later Christian writers in comparison with the earlier authors of the Hebrew Bible. In the Jewish Scriptures, the Satan appears to be a rather minor character, appearing in only two books. The Satan troubles the righteous Job (Job 1–2) and intends to harm the high priest Joshua (Zech 3).[3] When one comes to the New Testament, in contrast, the devil/Satan is nearly ubiquitous, appearing in some nineteen of the New Testament's twenty-seven books.[4] One might compare the prominence of the devil in the New Testament writings with that of Belial (another name for the Satan) in the sectarian Dead

---

3. If the traditional translation of 1 Chr 21:1 is correct, then "Satan" appears in this book as well. It is more likely, however, that this figure is not "Satan" but simply an unnamed "attacker" (Stokes 2009).

4. These are Matthew, Mark, Luke, John, Acts, Romans, 1 and 2 Corinthians, Ephesians, 1 and 2 Thessalonians, 1 and 2 Timothy, Hebrews, James, 1 Peter, 1 John, Jude, and Revelation. Farrar and Williams (2016) count a total of 137 references to the Satan in the New Testament and twenty New Testament books that mention this figure. They arrive at this total by including the expression "power of darkness" in Col 1:13 among the probable references, albeit an implicit one.

Sea Scrolls (e.g., Damascus Document, War Scroll). Further, as we will see below, the New Testament demonstrates the importance of the devil in early Christian theology not simply by the frequency with which this figure appears in the New Testament writings, but also by the way that these writings portray this figure and the activities they attribute to him. Similarly, demons and evil spirits figure far more frequently and prominently in the New Testament and early Jewish texts than they do in the Hebrew Bible.

For many Jews, the Satan and other evil superhuman beings were quite important. Of course, not all Jews held this estimation of the Satan. For some Jews, the Satan and evil spirits would remain marginal figures at best. For example, the Epistle of Enoch (1 En. 92–105), which will be discussed below, diminishes the significance of these figures. Nevertheless, these beings were rapidly growing in importance in the theology of many early Jewish thinkers, and they occupied a prominent place in the thinking of the early followers of Jesus.

The Devil, Demons, Evil Spirits, and Fallen Angels Join Forces

Although beliefs about the devil and demons are integrally connected in popular twenty-first century religious thought, as well as in in many ancient Jewish texts, the concepts of the devil and demons have not always been associated with each other. These were originally distinct traditions that were brought into conversation with each other for the first time only in the second century BCE. What is more, while demons and evil spirits are now typically regarded as roughly synonymous categories—that is, a demon is the same thing as an evil spirit in modern English—these were also at one time, in fact, believed to be distinct types of superhuman beings. Demons and evil spirits only gradually came to be identified with each other in the literature of early Judaism. Likewise, the notion of rebellious or "fallen" angels had a life of its own prior to being combined with those of evil spirits, demons, and eventually the devil.

These four traditions (those concerning the devil, demons, evil spirits, and fallen angels) appear independently—but never together—in the Hebrew Scriptures. As noted above, the Satan appears in the Old Testament books of Job and Zechariah. Other texts speak of harmful spirits who create various sorts of problems for human beings. Most notably, an "evil spirit" from God afflicts King Saul (1 Sam 16:14–23; 18:10; 19:9). Another spirit, a "lying spirit," tricks King Ahab into engaging in a battle that results in the king's death (1 Kgs 22:19–23). "Demons" (Hebrew *shedim*) appear in two passages in the Hebrew Scriptures (Deut 32:17; Ps 106:37) and are identified with the gods worshiped idolatrously by the nations. Yet another text contains an enigmatic story about certain divine "sons of God," who have children with human women (Gen 6:1–4). Many Jews would derive their understanding of the fall of the angels from this story. While each of these four traditions is found in the Hebrew Scriptures, nowhere in these writings are they related to one another. Theologians of a later era, however, would unite them in an effort to makes sense of the superhuman realm and the invisible forces of evil.

The beginnings of this gradual combination of traditions can be discerned in the Book of the Watchers, a third-century BCE work that belongs to the collection of writings now known as 1 Enoch.[5] The Book of the Watchers is itself a composite work. Different portions of it were composed at different times by different authors. One portion of this book contains an expanded version of the sons of God story (cf. Gen 6:1–4). According to the Book of the Watchers, the sons of God are angelic beings called "watchers." Two hundred of these watchers sin by marrying human women and having children with them. These sinful angels also taught a number of illicit arts to humans, such as how to practice sorcery and how to manufacture weapons. Most pertinent to the present discussion, the children produced by the illicit marriages between the watchers and human women turn out to be "evil spirits" (1 En. 15:8–16:1). In this way, the story of the fall of the angels and the origin of evil spirits are connected. Evil spirits are said to exist as a result of angelic rebellion and are in fact the offspring of these rebellious angels.

A slightly later section of the Book of the Watchers (1 En. 17–36) further combines maleficent superhuman being traditions. In this portion of the book, Enoch, the famed patriarch from the era before the flood, is guided by an angel on a tour of the earth. One site that Enoch sees on his tour is a deep chasm in which the sinful angels have been imprisoned. Enoch's tour guide, the angel Uriel, informs Enoch, "There stand the angels who mingled with the women. And their spirits—having assumed many forms—bring destruction on men and lead them astray to sacrifice to

---

5. The Book of the Watchers constitutes chs. 1–36 of 1 Enoch.

demons as to gods until the day of the great judgment" (19:1).[6] According to this text, demons and spirits are associated types of evil beings. They are not, however, the same kind of being. Demons are false gods, whom some humans erroneously worship. They are probably to be identified with the angels who sinned by marrying human women (Stokes 2016, 264). Spirits, on the other hand, serve the imprisoned angels/demons by misleading humans so that they worship the demons.

Another stage in the combination of these traditions may be observed the second-century BCE book of Jubilees. Here the designations "spirit" and "demon" are used interchangeably with reference to the same kind of beings (e.g., Jub. 10:1–5). In other words, in this second-century text demons and evil spirits are regarded as the same thing.[7] These spirits/demons are the offspring of the watchers. Jubilees also marks a very important shift in thinking about harmful superhuman beings in that this book associates spirits/demons with the Satan, whom Jubilees refers to as the Prince of Mastema or simply Mastema (which means "hostility"). According to Jubilees, God grants the Prince of Mastema authority over the spirits/demons, who carry out the prince's bidding, deceiving and harming the nations of the world (10:7–13; 11:4–5).

The Book of Parables (1 En. 37–71), another work in the 1 Enoch collection, further elaborates on the interrelationship between these evil beings. This text, which was likely composed sometime between 40 BCE and 70 CE, associates the Satan with the sinful watchers. The watchers who sinned prior to the flood, according to 1 En. 54:6, carried out this rebellion in the service of the Satan.

By the late Second Temple era, one could speak of evil spirits and demons synonymously (e.g., Luke 9:39–42). Nevertheless, some authors would continue to distinguish demons and spirits (e.g., Songs of the Maskil [4Q510 1 5]). Interestingly, in the New Testament, demons—but never spirits—are said to be the objects of illicit worship, perhaps preserving some of the distinction between these classes of beings at least terminologically (1 Cor 10:20–21; Rev 19:20). It was also common for writers speak of the Satan as the leader of evil spirits (Mark 3:22–30) or of evil angels (Matt 25:41). Numerous texts also continue to speak of the

---

6. All translations of 1 Enoch are from Nickelsburg and VanderKam 2012.

7. "Spirits" and "demons" may also be equated in Tob 6:8.

Satan acting alone, apart from the agency of subordinate spirits or angels (e.g., Matt 4:1–11).

The Satan and Demons Become Proponents of Wickedness

As mentioned above, a small number of passages in the Hebrew Scriptures speak of a figure called "the Satan." Although the Satan would eventually be regarded as the principal superhuman proponent of sin and is depicted as such in early Christian and Jewish literature, this is not the way the earliest texts portray this figure. The two texts in the Hebrew Scriptures that refer to the Satan actually presume that this figure is one who would physically attack sinners, bringing harm on them on behalf of an offended God. *Satan* is not the name of a person in the Hebrew Scriptures but merely a noun that means something like "attacker" and, in some instances, "executioner" (Stokes 2014). In Job and Zechariah, "the Satan" (*hassatan*) is the title of a particular figure that serves God as "the Attacker" or "the Executioner."[8] In Zech 3, the Satan stands ready to put the high priest Joshua to death (Stokes 2017, 1256–59). In Job 1–2, he attacks Job in a variety of ways, including killing Job's children and afflicting Job's body with sores. The Satan, however, is not said to be a tempter or deceiver in the Hebrew Scriptures.

Although the Satan and spirits would continue to be portrayed as beings that would afflict humans physically in the literature of early Judaism and in the New Testament (e.g., Jub. 48:2–4; Luke 13:10–16), they came to be regarded also as those superhuman figures that would tempt and otherwise mislead unsuspecting humans into moral and theological error. Recall that the Book of the Watchers claims that evil spirits lead humans to worship demons (1 En. 19:1). In Jub. 10, the Prince of Mastema is given charge of deceptive spirits who would lead the nations to worship false gods and commit acts of violence against one another. In the Damascus Document, one of the Dead Sea Scrolls, Belial deceives Israel so that they violate the Law of Moses (CD IV, 12–18). Only by returning to the Law of Moses is one able to protect oneself from Belial (CD XVI, 4–5).

---

8. Although translators often render the noun *satan* as "accuser," there is in fact little evidence that Hebrew *satan* means this. Rather a *satan* is one who would harm or kill another person (e.g., Num 22:22, 32; 1 Sam 29:4). Correspondingly, it is in the capacity of "attacker" or "executioner" that the Satan serves God in the Hebrew Scriptures, rather than as "accuser."

According to a passage from another Dead Sea Scroll, the Treatise on the Two Spirits, the Angel of Darkness and his spirits mislead humans into all sorts of evil (1QS III, 20–23). Numerous New Testament passages also speak of the devil leading or attempting to lead humans into various kinds of error (e.g., Matt 4:1–11; Acts 5:3; 2 Tim 2:26).

Several early Jewish texts, nonetheless, object to the teaching that forces external to humans were somehow responsible for human sin. Ben Sira, for example, cautions his students, "Do not say, 'It was the Lord's doing that I fell away....' Do not say, 'It was he who led me astray'" (Sir 15:11–12).[9] The Epistle of Enoch asserts, "lawlessness was not sent upon the earth; but men created it by themselves" (1 En. 98:4), likely responding to the belief that sin has been sent among humankind through the agency of the Satan and deceptive spirits (cf. Jub. 11:5; CD IV, 12–18; Stokes 2019, 126–37). The Epistle of Enoch goes on to characterize idolatry as the worship of "phantoms and demons and abominations and evil spirits and all errors, not according to knowledge" (1 En. 99:7). Interestingly, although this passage describes idolatry as the worship of demons, similar to Book of the Watchers and Jubilees, in the Epistle of Enoch spirits are merely the passive recipients of this worship, not the instigators of it as in the other works. In the Epistle of Enoch, humans are not misled by deceptive spirits but are "led astray by the folly of their hearts" (1 En. 99:8).

Explanations of human sin that held the Satan and deceptive spirits responsible were growing in popularity in the centuries just prior to the composition of the Epistle of James and the other New Testament books, but some Jewish authors voiced disagreement with this theological trajectory. These authors averred that humans, rather than any force external to them, were to blame for their transgressions.

The Satan Becomes the Enemy

The few passages that speak of the Satan and harmful spirits in the Hebrew Scriptures describe these figures not as the rebellious enemies of God, as they are depicted in later tradition, but as functionaries or emissaries of God. The title "the Satan," which means "the Attacker" or "the Executioner,"

---

9. Unless otherwise specified, all translations of texts from the Bible and Apocrypha/Deuterocanonicals are from the NRSV.

indicates that this figure was one who would harm humans on behalf of God (Stokes 2014). The Satan seems to have been among those superhuman figures mentioned in the Hebrew Scriptures who would serve God as punishers of the wicked, such as the angel of the Lord in the Balaam story of Num 22:22–35. In fact, although English translations obscure this, the angel of the Lord in this story is actually called a *satan* (Num 22:22, 32). In Zech 3, the Satan threatens to kill the high priest Joshua for coming before God in a state of impurity. In a like manner, certain spirits in the Old Testament function as God's agents of judgment. In 1 Sam 16:14–23, an evil spirit from God torments the disobedient King Saul (see also 1 Sam 18:10–11; 19:9–10). The "lying spirit" of 1 Kgs 22:19–23 also serves as God's agent of punishment against the wicked King Ahab.

The story of Job marks an important moment in the development of ideas regarding the Satan and his relationship to God's faithful people. The narrative of Job presumes that the Satan is God's punisher of the wicked, who would surveil the earth ready to strike evildoers. The Satan of Job, nonetheless, appears to deviate from his usual business of harming sinners. Twice he secures permission from God to harm Job, despite the fact that Job is innocent. Hence Job presents the Satan as one who might on occasion bring trouble even on the righteous. The Satan is not the enemy of God in this text. Nor is his work of troubling the righteous even said to be a regular occurrence. Nevertheless, Job's novel idea that the Satan could at times create problems for the faithful prepared the way for later thinkers to regard the Satan as the enemy of God's people and, eventually, even the enemy of God.

The book of Jubilees, while preserving the earlier notion of the Satan as the punisher of sinners (Jub. 10:8–9), presents the Prince of Mastema as one who tried to thwart God's plan to bless Israel (Jub. 48). In the War Scroll, Belial leads the "sons of darkness" in a war against the "sons of light" and is destined to receive God's wrath (1QM IV, 1–2). Several New Testament passages also preserve the notion of the Satan as one who works for God as a chastiser of errant (or potentially errant) humans. See, for example, 1 Cor 5, where Paul instructs a church to hand an immoral member over to Satan so that his flesh may be destroyed but his spirit saved (see also 2 Cor 12:7; 1 Tim 1:20). More frequently, however, the New Testament authors depict the Satan as one who opposes the work of God or Christ. God and the Satan rule two opposing and competing kingdoms (e.g., Luke 11:18–21). The Satan is also said to be in opposition to Christ (e.g., Matt 13:37–39) and will eventually be judged (e.g., Heb 2:14; Rev 20:10).

By the time that the Epistle of James was written, the devil and demons, relatively minor figures in the Hebrew Scriptures, had come to hold a prominent place in early Jewish and Christian theology. The Satan, who was once regarded merely as God's agent of punishment, had become in the minds of many religious thinkers the chief enemy of God and of God's people. These theologians believed that the devil was in league with demons and that these evil figures were at work in the world leading the unsuspecting people into various sorts of sin.

The Epistle of James on the Devil and Demons

The author of the Epistle of James was certainly among those early Christian and Jewish writers in whose theology the devil and demons figured importantly. Three verses in James's epistle explicitly mention the devil or demons. Stressing that it is necessary for works to accompany one's faith, James cautions, "You believe that God is one; you do well. Even the demons [*daimonia*] believe—and shudder" (2:19). Similarly, James argues that the way one lives reveals the nature of the wisdom that one possesses. With respect to those who practice evil, the epistle warns, "Such wisdom does not come down from above, but is earthly, unspiritual, demonic [*daimoniōdēs*]" (3:15, adapted from NRSV).[10] Finally, the epistle instructs, "Submit yourselves therefore to God. Resist the devil [*ho diabolos*], and he will flee from you" (4:7).

The Epistle of James, of course, contains no extended discussion of the devil and demons. An explanation of the nature and activity of these nefarious beings is not among the epistle's primary objectives. Nevertheless, in the course of his discussion of the sorts of thinking and behavior that James wishes to promote, as well as the sorts that he wishes to discourage, he finds multiple opportunities to mention the devil and demons. For James, these evil entities exist and are active in the world in ways that pose a significant threat to "the twelve tribes in the dispersion" to whom he writes. Accordingly, the epistle informs its recipients of the nature of the opposition that they face and instructs them on how they must resist it.

---

10. The NRSV translates *daimoniōdēs* in this verse as "devilish."

The Nature of and Relationships among Evil Superhuman Beings in the Epistle of James

Though some early Jewish texts offered explanations for the existence of demonic beings and often subordinated these entities to the Satan in the superhuman hierarchy, James gives little indication of what he thought about such fundamental matters. His epistle does not explain where demons come from or whether they are to be identified as fallen angels and/or evil spirits. Nor does it comment on the relationship between demons and the devil. James appears to assume that those to whom he is writing already possess a basic knowledge of these evil beings and require no introduction to them. That he would assume this may indicate that his thinking concerning these figures, generally speaking, was typical among early Christians.

That his understanding of these beings for the most part resembled that of other early Christian theologians comports well with what he does happen to reveal about his understanding of the devil and demons. For example, the connection between the devil, demons, and sin in the Epistle of James (which will be discussed below) is typical of early Jewish and Christian thinking about these evil beings. The Epistle of James does not say, however, that the devil has authority over the demons and that they lead humans astray at his bidding. Nevertheless, given how widespread this belief was in early Judaism and Christianity, it is not unlikely that the author of the epistle also believed that the devil and demons worked together. Given that both the devil and demons attempt to lure humans into sin, according to the epistle (3:15; 4:7), it would certainly make sense for both parties to operate in conjunction.

Some of what the Epistle of James says about demons may further suggest that the demonology presumed by the epistle, more specifically, has much in common with that of the Book of the Watchers. The epistle's contention that all sorts of wickedness derive from a wisdom that "does not come from above but is earthly, unspiritual, demonic" resembles the Book of the Watchers' teaching that a group of rebellious angels revealed illicit knowledge to human beings, giving rise to various sins (1 En. 7:1–8:3; Ellis 2016, 266). Moreover, the sinful angels of the Book of the Watchers, apparently referred to as "demons" in 1 En. 19:1, would not be permitted to return to heaven, but would be imprisoned in the earth on account of their sin (1 En. 14:5). The belief that demonic beings were confined to the earth perhaps provides some context for comprehending James's characterization of demonic wisdom as "earthly."[11]

Additionally, the statement in Jas 2:19 that the demons "tremble" may also reflect the Book of the Watchers' depiction of the rebellious angels. When these transgressors learn of their impending judgment, the Book of Watchers says that the angels "were all afraid, and trembling and fear seized them" (1 En. 13:3). They then have Enoch appeal to God on their behalf with the hope that their sins would be forgiven. Despite their fearful response to the announcement of their judgment, their sentence would not be commuted. The watchers were to receive the punishment that their deeds merited, which would make the evil watchers/demons a fitting illustration of James's point that faith is insufficient apart from righteous deeds.[12]

The Devil, Demons, Sin, and Suffering in the Epistle of James

Like so many writings from its era, the Epistle of James depicts the superhuman realm as one that is active in the moral corruption of human beings. The devil and demons are behind human sin. Though the epistle is very careful not to exculpate humans of responsibility for their sinful choices (1:13–16), it also says that forces external to human beings contribute to the downfall of morally responsible humans.

It is possible that the epistle preserves as well the earlier notion of the devil or of evil spirits afflicting sinful humans with illness. Near the end of his epistle, James instructs, "Are any among you sick? They should call for the elders of the church and have them pray over them, anointing them with oil in the name of the Lord. The prayer of faith will save the sick, and the Lord will raise them up; and anyone who has committed sins will be

---

11. First Enoch 15:8–10, as well, may be relevant to the earthly nature of demonic wisdom. These verses distinguish those spirits who dwell in heaven from "evil spirits" who dwell on the earth. It is not certain, however, whether James equated "demons" and "evil spirits." See also Phil 3:19 for "earthly" in a negative moral sense.

12. Several commentators associate the "trembling" (*phrissō*) of the demons with the trembling (*phriktos*) mentioned in a handful of Greek papyri that pertain to exorcisms (e.g., Laws 1980, 126–27). While this is possible, in the LXX *phrissō/phriktos* typically refers to trembling and fear more generally (e.g., Job 4:14; Wis 8:15; Jdt 16:10). Given the association of the demons with sinful wisdom and the earthly realm in James, one should at least consider the possibility that demonic trembling relates to the fearful trembling of the watchers.

forgiven" (Jas 5:14–15). Although these verses do not explicitly identify the direct cause of the illness as a demon or evil spirit, it is plausible that they presume such a scenario. Elsewhere in the New Testament, demons/spirits are associated with illness, and prayer is prescribed as a means of relieving one's affliction (Mark 9:29; see also 2 Cor 12:8). Especially intriguing is the similar description of the healing and exorcism work of Jesus's followers in Mark 6:13: "They cast out many demons, and anointed with oil many who were sick and cured them." While it is not certain that Jas 5:14–15 addresses illness that is believed to be caused by demonic and/or satanic forces, it is very possible that the epistle's author has precisely such a situation in mind.[13]

What is certain is that the Epistle of James, like so many other early Jewish and Christian writings, attributes human sin to the deluding influence of demonic and/or satanic forces. One passage in the epistle explicitly associates demons with human wickedness. James 3:15 refers to a kind of wisdom that produces sin. This wisdom is said to be "demonic." Whether the author envisions demons that mislead humans (e.g., Jub. 10:1) or else demons that are imprisoned in the earth but influence humans through their spiritual agents (e.g., 1 En. 19:1) is not clear. Whatever their channels of influence, James identifies demons as the source of thinking that leads to sin.[14]

Another passage speaks of the devil as one who would tempt humans to sin. James encourages his epistle's recipients, however, to resist the devil, assuring them that the devil will flee from them if they resist (4:7). The idea that the devil will leave a person alone resembles the teaching of the Damascus Document that, "on the day when a man takes upon himself (an oath) to return to the Torah of Moses, the angel Mastema shall turn aside from after him, if he fulfills his words" (CD XVI, 4–5 [Baumgarten and Schwartz 1995]). Perhaps these teachings envision a Satan who ceases

---

13. Dibelius (1976, 252) overconfidently refers to the procedure prescribed in this passage as an exorcism. Other scholars (e.g., McCartney 2009, 254) equally overconfidently reject this possibility.

14. McCartney (2009, 201) argues that *daimoniōdēs* ("demonic") means "like that of demons" rather than "inspired by demons." James 3:15, however, is concerned with the origin and nature of the wisdom under consideration: "it does not come from above, but is earthly, unspiritual, demonic." Given this context, and given how widespread the notion of demonic seduction was in early Judaism and Christianity, it is likely that James has in mind wisdom that is *from* demons, not merely *like that of* demons.

to tempt a person who has successfully resisted him (cf. Matt 4:11). Alternatively, and perhaps more likely, these instructions may indicate that the angel Mastema/devil will not inflict harm on a person who has avoided or turned from sin (cf. Jas 5:14–16; 1 Pet 5:8–9).[15]

Despite this active role of the devil and demons in the propagation of sin, James insists that humans are responsible for their moral choices. They certainly cannot blame God for their misdeeds: "No one, when tempted, should say, 'I am being tempted by God….' But one is tempted by one's own desire, being lured and enticed by it" (1:13–14). The Epistle of James's teaching in these verses is often and appropriately compared with that of Ben Sira: "Do not say, 'It was the Lord's doing that I fell away'" (Sir 15:11). It also resembles the thinking expressed in the Epistle of Enoch: "lawlessness was not sent upon the earth; but men created it by themselves" (1 En. 98:4). Unlike the Epistle of Enoch, however, which appears to reject the idea of evil spirits or demons misleading humans, James is able to reconcile his understanding of God's justice and human moral responsibility with the belief that superhuman personal forces are at work in the world, luring humans into sin.

The Devil and Demons as God's Enemies in the Epistle of James

James is able to reconcile the belief that superhuman forces seek to lead humankind astray with his understanding of human responsibility, since, according to his epistle, humans possess the ability to resist these forces (4:7). Also, unlike the author of the Epistle of Enoch, James is able to reconcile his conception of seductive superhuman forces with the justice and goodness of God because the Satan and his demonic forces had already come to be regarded by many as God's enemies by the time that the Epistle of James was composed. For James, the devil and demons are not merely agents of God, but are evil and opposed to God. That James adduces demons as an example of faith apart from works presumes that demons are wicked beings (2:19). The contrast between wisdom that comes from above and produces righteousness, on the one hand, and earthly, demonic wisdom that leads to sin, on the other, also suggests that James does not regard demons as God's agents. For James, one is to resist the devil but to

---

15. See also the teaching that Beliar will flee from those who avoid sin in T. Iss. 7:7; T. Dan 5:1; T. Naph. 8:4.

draw near to God. While the devil and demons would lead a person astray, God is not the source of this evil. Only good comes from God (1:13–17).

Conclusion

While there is much that we cannot know about James's thinking on the devil and demons, the handful of references to these figures in his epistle indicate that James had a robust understanding of superhuman evil. What James says about the devil and demons also suggests that James's theology is to be understood within the context of developing notions of evil superhuman beings in early Judaism and Christianity. It is possible that James's thinking about demons resembled that of the Book of Watchers. James certainly regarded the devil and demons as proponents of sin, as did many Jewish and Christian thinkers of his day. The devil and demons, for James, were the enemies of God who were out to lead humankind into error, and it was the responsibility of humans to resist them.

Poverty, Riches, and God's Blessings:
James in the Context of the Biblical Story

Scot McKnight

Bible reading, regardless of the translation or cross-referencing system used, is an exercise in connections, intertextuality, and contextual sensitivity. When one examines the covenant established with Abram in Gen 15 and 22, its torah expansion of that covenant in Exod 19–24 or the Davidic promise in 2 Sam 7, the promise of the future new covenant in Jer 31, and its fulfillment in Mark 14 at the Last Supper, each passage makes best sense from a Christian perspective only in light of the others. To read any apart from the others misreads it. There are more than a few debates among scholars about the best articulations of the connections of two testaments, but reading the Bible as a story or narrative is common practice (Klink and Lockett 2012) and brings clarity to central topics like "gospel" (Wright 1992; McKnight 2016). A story approach to Bible reading wisely pays attention to historical context as well.

The Story before James

Following a sketch of the diverse voices about poverty and wealth in the biblical story, I offer a reading of James in the context of the Bible's story about justice, about wealth and poverty, about blessings and curses, and about the tensions within the narrative of the Bible about these themes (Maynard-Reid 1987; Weinfeld 1995; Tamez 1990; Brueggemann 2016). The following sketch of the Old Testament themes, however, is not a historical-critical reconstruction of how these themes developed but a synthesis of separable (but not necessarily disconnected) themes. This chapter is mostly concerned with what resources the author of the Letter of James had when he began to speak about poverty and wealth and hence a synthesis of available themes is required. What is perhaps most important is the reminder that most of today's concerns with social justice more or less derive from themes about justice in the Old Testament, where we are reminded time and again that faith and the material world are integrated (Baker 2009; Hiers 2009, 165–211).

Prior to our study of these themes (or traditions), I offer the recent summary of six major conclusions about money and possessions in the Old Testament (which are mirror themes to poverty and wealth) recently proposed by Walter Brueggemann (2016, 1–9) in nothing less than an "economeneutical" reading: (1) "Money and possessions are gifts from God"; (2) "money and possessions are received as reward for obedience"; (3) "money and possessions belong to God and are held in trust by human persons in community"; (4) "money and possessions are sources of social injustice"; (5) "money and possessions are to be shared in a neighborly way"; and (6) "money and possessions are seductions that lead to idolatry." There are clear tensions between Brueggemann's conclusions and these tensions will emerge in what follows as well.

The Deuteronomic Blessing Tradition

One of the most noticeable themes for any reader of the Old Testament is the seemingly ineluctable connection between faithful obedience to the covenant and God's material blessings and its mirror opposite, disobedience and God's material curses that find their way to exile as the ultimate punishment. The fundamental expression of this wealth-is-a-blessing and poverty-is-a-curse tradition is in the Deuteronomic tradition in the reform of Judah under Josiah. This theme is found in the Deuteronomic histories and especially in Deut 28, though it has a substantive parallel in the priestly tradition of Lev 26–27. Thus, the only essential requirement is "if you will only obey the LORD your God, by diligently observing all his commandments" (Deut 28:1). If Israel does this, "the LORD your God will set you high above all the nations of the earth" (28:1) and Israel will "abound in prosperity" (28:11; cf. 28:12–13).[1] All of this is the promise for covenant faithfulness.

The reverse is what happens if Israel turns from covenant faithfulness to disobedience, that is, each of the above instead becomes its opposite,

---

1. All translations are from the NRSV.

as in "The LORD will send upon you disaster, panic, and frustration in everything you attempt to do, until you are destroyed and perish quickly, on account of the evil of your deeds, because you have forsaken me" (28:20), and on and on in detailed wretchedness (28:15–68). One can cite in its favor Prov 13:18 ("poverty and disgrace are for the one who ignores instruction") or its more pragmatic version in 20:13 ("Do not love sleep, or else you will come to poverty").

This same book has a prophetic tone to it and so gives more than ample exhortation to care for the poor in Israel (Deut 15:11; 24:10–15, in a text with echoes in Jas 5:1–6). Those who care for the poor will receive a reward, which at times at least suggests that acts of mercy can be atoning (Downs 2016a, 27–56).

As the Bible's story continues, one is required to ask what social conditions gave rise to this correlation of obedience and blessing. That is, surely one must at least consider that the Israel summoned to obedience was in a social world where they could choose obedience and expect to be rewarded with material flourishing. Or is Deut 28 a rhetorical creation for presenting to Israelites their calling before YHWH, the God of Israel?

The Blessing Tradition Challenged

Brueggemann's (2001) stirring and provocative *The Prophetic Imagination* proposed a challenge within Israel's story. Brueggemann contended that the Mosaic vision of equality was broken by the Solomonic tradition of prosperity, the latter the result of rapacious exploitation and taxation. Moses offered to Israel a God of justice and a politics of equality, justice, and divine freedom (Exod 15:1–18), while Solomon countered Moses with a politics of affluence, oppression, and divine accessibility (Exod 16:18 with 1 Kgs 4:20–23; Lev 25:35–42 with 1 Kgs 5:13–18 and 9:15–22; Exod 33:16, 19–20 with 1 Kgs 8:12–13; see Brueggemann 2001, 31; also McConville 2006; Houston 2006). Later Solomon's splendor and sin revealed the connection of disobedience and what appears to be material flourishing. Though the population was at an all-time high (1 Kgs 4:20) and the borders expanded (4:21), Solomon's opulence exploited the people through taxation and mercenary employment (4:22–26). So we read in 1 Kgs 11 of Solomon's heart being turned from covenant faithfulness (11:1–13). His successors were even worse than he was on the matter of taxation and exploitation (12:6–11).

A new chapter has been opened in Israel's explanation of poverty because now poverty can be framed not as a sign of disobedience but as the result of oppression. Thus, "the field of the poor may yield much food"— and here is an echo of Deut 28—"but it is swept away through injustice" (Prov 13:23). The famous passage in Isa 58 teaches us that poverty and oppression may be the result of the oppression of Israel's own leaders (58:3, 6–9). Turning from oppression to economic distribution and justice will bring flourishing (58:9b–14; Mic 2:2). Nothing, I suspect, expresses the utopian ideal more than the Jubilee of Lev 25, and nothing more (I would add) gives shape to an alternative sociopolitical imagination than the Jubilee. Israel was to observe seven-year cycles in which it worked the land and soil for six years but not the seventh—and God promised a bountiful produce in the sixth year of each cycle so everyone would have enough in the seventh. The Jubilee year was the climax of seven of these sabbatical-year cycles, and it was to be marked by the return of all property, forgiveness of all debts, and resumption of one's property. A sabbatical indeed!

Blessing Tradition Reversed

Full reversal of the blessing tradition occurs when God identifies *especially with the poor*. This preferential option for the poor is grounded in the harsh realities of Israel's life and turns the blessing and curses tradition of Deuteronomy inside out. So Ps 140:12: "I know the LORD maintains the cause of the needy, and executes justice for the poor." Inherent to this divine identification is the criticism of the oppressors (e.g., Amos 3:9–12; 4:1–3), not as a class or an institution but as moral agents acting unjustly, and the protest is not a call for a social revolution. The protest comes from the voice of the privileged that are sympathetic (Houston 2006, 52–98).

The reality of the oppressed (and not disobedient) poor and their need for justice and support comes to expression in Deuteronomy and the prophets, and those texts lead eventually to a Jewish ethic of almsgiving that both counters the negative, arrogant, and uncompassionate attitude toward the poor in surrounding cultures (Joubert 2000; Longenecker 2010) and elevates the poor in status. In particular, charity or almsgiving (Anderson 2013) takes on a special theological and eschatological shape in Judaism. The phenomenology of lending to the poor undercuts the common theory of benefaction in the Greek and Roman world in which gifts to others were largely the actions of the wealthy toward those whom they wanted to support and from whom they could expect reciprocation or reciprocal benevolence (Barclay 2015). In that system of benefaction, the poor were not only neglected but largely despised. Israel's response to the poor was different and gave to the ancient world a completely different posture toward the poor and a new form of measuring genuine piety (Longenecker 2010; Downs 2016a; 2016b).

Inherent to the phenomenology of charity was a treasury of merits and even atonement for the charitable (Anderson 2013; Downs 2016a). The charitable knew the poor could not reciprocate, so a theology of divine pleasure and future reward reframed charity, the latter funded by the treasury of merits. We find this already at work in the Old Testament: "Treasures gained by wickedness do not profit, but righteousness [Hebrew *tsedeqah*, "almsgiving"] delivers from death" (Prov 10:2; cf. Sir 5:8); and "Riches do not profit in the day of wrath"—another echo of Deuteronomy— "but righteousness [as above] delivers from death" (Prov 11:4). Sirach 29 articulates this theology even more completely: pragmatically speaking, pay back your debts and lend to others (29:1–4). "Lose your silver for the sake of a brother or a friend" (29:10). Why? "Lay up your treasure according to the commandments of the Most High, and it will profit you more than gold. Store up almsgiving in your treasury and it will rescue you from every disaster; better than a stout shield and a sturdy spear, it will fight for you against the enemy" (29:11–13). There it is: almsgiving, like the blessing of Deuteronomy, yields reward from God. Wealth, he adds, is a source of great temptation and moral stumbling (31:1–11) rather than a necessary sign of God's blessing. Tobit says much the same. "Do not turn your face away from anyone who is poor, and the face of God will not be turned away from you" (Tob 4:7). Even more: "For almsgiving delivers from death and keeps you from going into the Darkness" (4:10). Even more: "Almsgiving saves from death and purges away every sin" (12:9). (Should one want a fuller explanation of how almsgiving and purging from sin worked, David Downs recently offered a full explanation of the theme of atoning almsgiving in earliest Christianity in Downs 2016a).

Poverty as a Test

One more tradition deserves attention even if it cannot be examined at length, namely, the tradition of poverty that sees it as a permitted test from God. I speak of course of the wisdom tradition's famous book about Job. The story of Job is of a "blameless [*tam*] and upright [*yashar*]" man who "feared God and turned away from evil" (Job 1:1). He had seven sons, three daughters, as well as an abundance of livestock and servants (1:2–3). If ever a man flourished in the Israelite sense of God's blessing for obedience it was Job. So pious was he that he offered sacrifices for his children just in case they sinned (1:5). Satan, a term that means "adversary" in Job but not yet the "devil" of later thought, wanted to bring Job down. What is amazing is that YHWH permits Satan to erase all of the signs of God's blessing in Job's life (1:6–19). Job's response? He "arose, tore his robe, shaved his head, and fell on the ground and worshiped. He said, 'Naked I came from my mother's womb, and naked shall I return there; the LORD gave, and the LORD has taken away; blessed be the name of the LORD.' In all this Job did not sin or charge God with wrong-doing" (1:20–22). The narrative's flow need not detain us except to say that Job's humility and confidence emerge from the text: if he could be convinced he had sinned, he would confess; since he could not, he retains his confidence in his covenant faithfulness. The correlations of the Deuteronomic blessing tradition here meets its match.

While the text of Job ends on the note of the inscrutability of God's ways—especially when it comes to the correlation of the blessing tradition—the poverty of Job now has an entirely different explanation. Job was not impoverished because of sin but because YHWH permitted him to be sifted. That the book of Job ends on a note of Job flourishing once again is a confirmation of the blessing tradition on a new level, even if the grief of losing one's family is given scant attention (42:12–17).

Jesus and the Poor

Before we turn to James, let me say a few brief words about Jesus and the poor (see Wheeler 1995 for a thorough discussion of this issue). It is common to connect Jesus to a poor mother and father (Luke 2:22–24; cf. Lev 12:6–8). When Jesus arises to speak in the synagogue at Nazareth, his gospel message was good news for the poor (Luke 4:16–30, esp. 18–19). Jesus saw two economies in the world: the economy of injustice and hoarding, and an economy of the kingdom characterized by generosity and economic justice, made most explicit in almsgiving (Luke 12:13–34, esp. 33). For Jesus, the pious are the poor (Luke 6:20). God is on their side, so the message of Jesus turns toward economic justice (e.g., 16:19–31). Accordingly, Jesus's followers are to develop a lack of anxiety about possessions (Luke 12:22–32). Jesus echoes the treasury of merits when he speaks of generosity to the poor, or charity: "But when you give a banquet, invite the poor, the crippled, the lame, and the blind. And you will be blessed, because they cannot repay you, for you will be repaid at the resurrection of the righteous" (Luke 14:13–14). Jesus, in prophetic fashion, warned of the dangers of wealth (Mark 10:23; Luke 12:15; cf. the same at 1 Tim 6:9–10).

How was this to be lived out? Jesus taught in a deep Old Testament tradition of embodying economic justice in the way his own followers were to live (see Deut 15:1–18; Lev 25:8–3; Exod 23:10–11; cf. Deut 14:28–29; 24:19–22; Lev 19:9–10; 23:22). Jesus's followers had a common purse, and the earliest Christians in Jerusalem took up an economic justice theme in the way they conducted themselves (Acts 2:42–47; 4:32–5:11). Paul carried on an economic justice theme in his collection for the poor (2 Cor 8–9; Longenecker 2010; Downs 2016b). Nothing startles more in Paul's own understanding of his collection than his use of *isotēs* in 2 Cor 8:13–14: "do not mean that there should be relief for others and pressure on you, but it is a question of a fair balance between your present abundance and their need, so that their abundance may be for your need, in order that there may be a fair balance." While "fair balance," the NRSV's translation of *isotēs*, strikes a helpful note for seeing here reciprocal benevolence, the social economic vision is blunted unless one boldly translates with either "equity" or "equality" (Joubert 2000; Longenecker 2010; Downs 2016b). The choice of the term *episkopos* ("bishop" or "overseer") for a leader in Paul's early churches borrows from the Greek and Roman tradition of the financial overseer of a community and carries on the deep Jewish tradition of alms as the fundamental act of the genuinely pious (Stewart 2014).

The connections in the earliest Christian sources are deep and enduring. When we turn to James we turn to a voice that joins a chorus of others in the story of Israel, not least Jesus and other apostles, but we dare not diminish the role of the Old Testament and the Jewish tradition that countered the system of benefaction in the Roman Empire with gift-giving and alms for the poor. James's letter to the twelve tribes is filled with instances where the poor are in focus. James belongs to the Israelite tradition of the identification of God with the poor as well as with the tradition of Job, who is an exemplum at Jas 5:7–11 and who brings poverty into the world of a test by God. Yet, James, too, echoes the blessing tradition in Jas 1:12. How so? Those who are obedient or who have "stood the test" will receive, even if only in the age to come, the "crown of life."

James in the Story

The theme of poverty runs through the entire letter of James, making potent appearances at 1:9–11; 2:1–4, 5–7, 14–17; 3:17–18; 4:3, 13–17; and 5:1–6. I offer a brief exegesis of each with a summary statement to conclude the essay. (All of this is rooted in McKnight 2011.)

James 1:9–11

The paragraph operates with a polarity of good and bad: the poor are good and the rich bad. Social context of course determines this and we can know that context only because it is the only thing that makes sense: the rich are oppressors (cf. 2:1–13; 5:1–6) and the poor the oppressed believers. The author of the letter identifies with the poor as the prophets did in the Old Testament. Everything is turned upside down in James 1:9–11: the "believer who is lowly" in Greek is *ho adelphos ho tapeinos* and evokes the poor, faithful follower of Jesus. The text does not actually use the term "believer" (NRSV) but "brother," yet the notion of believing is inherent to this term in James (1:2, 16, 19; 2:1, 5, 14; 3:1, 10, 12; 4:11; 5:7, 9, 12, 19). Translating *adelphos* as "believer" erases the siblinghood at work in this term and reshapes the meaning to a more individualistic turn.

   Most importantly, James promises a Deuteronomic-like blessing to the brother or sister who is "poor" (*tapeinos*; Maynard-Reid 1987, 24–37; Crotty 1995). What is such a person's status: Is it social poverty or is it a spiritual poverty (cf. Jas 4:6)? The evidence is clear: inasmuch as the poor is contrasted in this text with the rich (1:10), the term *tapeinos* is a near synonym to *ptōchos* ("poor"; cf. 2:2–6), and the connections of the poor in James with the Jewish *anawim* tradition, that is, to the pious and socially destitute (Luke 1:48, 52–53; Brown 1999, 350–65), the word refers to the economically destitute and oppressed. James knows the poor member of the Jewish messianic community will someday be exalted just as he knows the future for the rich oppressor is God's judgment. On this James taps into Jewish traditions, and in a later section he does so even more trenchantly (5:1–6; cf. Deut 24:14–16). Knowing he or she will be exalted can be a source of joy for the brothers and sisters (1:2–4), but there is no sign that James puts off this exaltation until the final resurrection: there is here a hope for earthly realization and reversal (cf. Rom 5:2–4). What then is in mind? I offer the suggestion that exaltation means being lifted up in moral "perfection" in the practices of justice (1:20), love (2:8–11), and peace (3:18).

The NRSV's translation "the rich" in 1:10 raises a question: Should "brother" be added as an interpretation as well to "rich" so that James is describing tension within the Christian messianic community where the rich brother is being warned (cf. Jer 9:23–24)? Or is "brother" omitted because the "rich" is not in fact a brother but an oppressor? If the former, being "brought low" would refer to self-denial, while if the latter it would refer to the judgment of God in a reversal of statuses of both the poor and the rich (again, Jas 5:1–6; Batten 2007, 6–26). We need to read James in light of James, so we ask how James uses the term "rich" and does he think they are brothers and sisters? The answer is "Yes" (2:2; 4:13–17) and even more firmly "No." Perhaps 2:2 describes a brother, but more particularly in 2:1–13 the rich man comes off as the oppressor; the rich treat the poor unjustly (2:6–7) and are warned, as in our passage here at 1:10–11, of final destruction (5:1–6). Most significantly, the rich will "wither away" (1:11) and be destroyed (5:5). James could well be describing the priestly establishment (McKnight 2011, 99–100, 102–3), who were connected to courts (2:1–13), who dressed opulently at times (2:2–4), who were known for traveling (4:13–17), and who were connected to the temple whose demise James predicts (5:7).

James 2:1–4, 5–7; 3:17–18

James 2 focuses on partiality against the poor by the rich. James writes here about the inconsistency of faith in the Lord Jesus with treating the poor with contempt (2:1–4), then he turns to interrogate his readers on the partiality at work in the community (2:5–7), and finally he turns to instruction (2:8–13). Our concern here is only verses 1–4 and 5–7, for they bring to the surface the themes of poverty and wealth.

First, in verses 1–4 James sketches how the community is favoring the rich and dishonoring the poor. He opens with a prohibition (2:1), though the NRSV turns it into a question: "My brothers and sisters, do you with your acts of favoritism really believe in our glorious Lord Jesus Christ?" The NIV has the better translation: "believers in our glorious Lord Jesus Christ *must not show* favoritism" (emphasis added). The opening term "my brothers" ties back to 1:9–11 and to the siblingship created in the kingdom communities of Jesus, and it is that sibling relation that creates a foundation for 2:1–4. The issue is "favoritism," a term that always connotes inappropriate favoritism, bias, or prejudice in early Christian literature. Behind the prohibition of partiality is God, who is himself impartial, and that means the people of God are to behave similarly (Acts 10:34; Rom 2:11; Gal 2:6; Eph 6:9; Col 3:25; see also Matt 22:16; 1 Tim 5:21; 1 Clem. 1:3; also notice Job 34:17–20; Ps 82:2; Mal 2:9; Sir 35:14; McKnight 2011, 176 n. 19). What makes partiality wrong for James is that it is contrary to love of neighbor (Jas 2:8).

In his wondrous section on wisdom (3:13–18), James reframes the section on partiality in 2:1–4: wisdom "from above" is "full of mercy and good fruits," terms evoking almsgiving to the poor, and is "without a trace of partiality" (3:17–18). There is no word here of Christology (as we are about to see in 2:1), but instead he adds that is also without "hypocrisy," which is a capsule summary of the comic scene sketched in 2:1–4.

What makes partiality wrong even more is that the Lord Jesus, who is rarely mentioned in this letter (1:1; 2:1), was himself poor, his mother was poor (Luke 2:24), and this same Jesus was exalted to the highest station of all, to the throne of God. To dishonor the poor, then, is to dishonor Jesus himself. Translation of 2:1 is not as clear as one might like: Is it (1) "faith in our Lord Jesus (glorious) Christ," (2) "faith in our glorious Lord, Jesus Christ," (3) "believe in our glorious Lord Jesus Christ" (NRSV, NIV), (4) "faith in our Lord Jesus Christ, the Glorious One," or (5) "faith in the Glorious One, the Lord Jesus Christ"? Word order alone is about all we have to determine this, and the suspension of "glory/glorious" (*doxēs*) to the end of the sentence leads me to think the fourth option is best.

Second, James creates a comic scene that ridicules the behavior of partiality (2:2–4). By using caricature James presses upon the messianic communities that this sort of behavior in their gatherings for fellowship, instruction, and worship (Greek *synagōgē*; McKnight 2011, 181–83) contradicts their faith in Jesus. The irony is obvious, but these sorts of ironies are both learned behavior by the poor in the presence of the rich and nearly impossible to subvert by those with no power. What stands out is how the rich man and the poor man dress. The terms used by James have one intent: to unmask the rich man's desire to flaunt his status. What we have here is a direct connection back to the prophetic and wisdom traditions on poverty: these people are poor because they are oppressed; they are not necessarily disobedient. Rather, they turn injustice into an opportunity to be tested (1:12–16).

Third, James's concern is found in verse 4: "have you not made distinctions among yourselves, and become judges with evil thoughts?" Those who believe in the exalted Lord Jesus, who know he was poor, who are treating the poor with contempt and the rich with sycophantic behaviors, are now guilty of being judges (4:10–12) and creating divisions in the gatherings. Segregation by way of partiality is not the implication of the Lord Jesus; unity is (though this is a favorite theme of Paul's). If we read this division into the rest of James's letter, as we ought to do, we will see that other divisions appear: speech that divides (1:19–21; 3:1–12; 4:11–12), mistreatment of the marginalized (1:26–27), and general divisive behaviors (3:14–16, 18; 4:1–3; 5:8–9). We might not carelessly pile these on top of each other, but it is at least a suggestion that the divisions are deeper than the haves and have-nots.

The connection of 2:1–4 to 2:5–7 is a matter of dispute: is the setting for the former the same as that for the latter? If so, why the absence of a judge in 2:1–4? Is then the setting of 2:5–7 different and, if so, how can one avoid resonances from the second finding their way back to the first? We attempt to answer this question in our fourth observation: the interrogation is by way of a crescendo of escalating questions with obvious answers (2:5–7). Here James comes to the support of the poor against the rich in a way that both contradicts the previous participation of the poor in partiality and its system of status (mis)classifications and at the same time gives word to what ought to be their own beliefs. We are again treading in the waters of the prophets, who interrogate audiences who are not listening to them—but do so in front of those who are—in order to bring matters into fuller disclosure.

James shows that their poverty is actually a kind of riches: "poor in the world to be rich in faith" as well as "heirs of the kingdom" (2:5). How is this so? God makes it so. Once again we encounter an alternative to the blessing tradition with its strict (or at least stricter) correlation of one's condition and one's obedience. God, in true prophet fashion, is on the side of the poor: "Has not God chosen the poor?" The combination of election and poor jars any and every Jewish reader: election is a central theme in the Hebrew Bible, and the poor (in many of their Scriptures) are cursed (Deut 28). Yet, within that same Bible is the preferential option for the poor (e.g., Deut 26:7; Isa 11:3–4) that reorients the possibility James here exploits for election (as does Paul in 1 Cor 11:27–28). The verse numbering system trips up the reader: James follows (not with a new verse but) with "but you have dishonored the poor." Unlike God but like the rich, the messianic community by its behaviors has located the poor at the lowest level of society. Apart from their own Christology, with Jesus as one who became poor and who was exalted to glory, their own Jewish tradition had pockets of mercy and compassion for the poor in their almsgiving tradition, which by this time had become the deed par excellence. Rejecting both platforms for a new kind of behavior, the community had dishonored the poor.

James turns up the heat with three more questions (2:6–7) that evoke the following condemnations. The rich are oppressors, and this defines "rich" in the letter of James as nonbelievers and works back into 2:1–4 to clarify who the richly dressed man was. The rich drag them into court to exploit their powerlessness and lack of status. Finally, the rich have in fact blasphemed the very name that marks them off, that is, the name of Jesus, the glorious one (2:1, 7). We may not know *why* the rich are dragging the poor into court, but we know the final end of it all: they despise the name of Jesus. We may infer then that the reason for the injustice shown to the poor is their faith in Jesus as Messiah; thus, the rich oppose Jesus as Messiah.

Our understanding of the poor in Jas 1:9–11 now comes into full view, and it is entirely appropriate to read back what we see in 2:1–7 into that verse: the poor are poor believers who for no other reason than their belief were experiencing financial oppression (we will find this in 5:1–6) and legal injustices at the hands of the rich oppressors. What James promised the poor and the rich in 1:9–11 obtains as well in 2:1–7: the rich will be judged by God, they will wilt, and they will meet the rough side of justice (cf. 5:5). Again, there is little reason in this book—and this book has sufficient clues for us to interpret nearly every line and word—to think the day of justice is beyond death. Rather, James expects the judgment of God in this world, against those rich oppressors and in favor of these poor (cf. 5:7–11). "Judgment," James is about to tell them all (even those not listening), "will be without mercy to anyone who has shown no mercy" (2:13). The vocabulary at work in "mercy" is connected to the word "almsgiving," and we are confident mercy to the poor is uppermost in James's mind: he has his eyes on the disgusting behaviors in the synagogue (2:1–4).

James 2:14–17

We have space here only for a brief discussion of the poor in 2:14–17. What does James mean by "works?" Protestants have naturally worked hard to discern what James means by works and the options are basically two: either he means "works of the torah (law)" as in Paul, which would bring James into substantive conflict with Paul, or he means generally good works, which means James and Paul could be harmonized. There can be no dispute that James does not speak of works of the torah as does Paul, for whom it often refers to boundary markers between Jews and gentiles and for whom works represented covenant fidelity, nor can there be dispute that James's essential angle is good works in general or that these general good works are mapped out in the torah and expressed in torah observance. This is what we find in texts like Jas 1:25 and 2:14–26. For some this seems to let James off the hook, but I am unconvinced it is as simple as an either-or. James is Jewish; he writes to a messianic Jewish community. It would be impossible for such a person or such a readership to hear the word "works" and not connect it to the Mosaic torah. In fact, I propose not only that James means "works of the torah" when he says "works," but he means a life of loving God and loving others, and loving others means deeds of compassion toward those in need (McKnight 2011, 228).

To define a term we must respect an author's contours, and that means reading 2:14–17 as a window into James and James as a window on 2:14–17. "Mercy" in 2:13—which is defined by loving one's neighbor (2:8), and that means how one treats the poor (2:1–4)—triggers James's awareness that some think one can believe and not do works. So when James asks in 2:14 his double-sworded question ("What good is it, my brothers and sisters, if you say you have faith but do not have works? Can faith save you?"), we are pressed to ask what he meant in more concrete social realities. He asks another double-sworded question: "If a brother or sister is naked and lacks daily food, and one of you says to them, 'Go in peace; keep warm and eat your fill,' and yet you do not supply their bodily needs, what is the good of that?"

So when we get down to the social realities of faith and works and faith that works for redemption in James, it is about *undoing the social realities we just encountered in 2:1–4*, where the rich wear their apparel as conspicuously as possible while the poor are left unclothed or poorly clothed. Though James uses "naked" and "lacks daily food," these are metonymy for the poor and suffering and oppressed (cf. Matt 25:36, 38, 43–44; Acts 6:1; 1 Tim 5:3–20). The reason (once again looping in the rest of James on this topic) this happens is because the rich who are exploiting them and blaspheming the name of Jesus are not paying the poor workers their wages (5:1–6). That is, the faith that works for James in 2:14–17 is a faith that provides shelter and food for the poor. Faith for James is almsgiving (Anderson 2013; Longenecker 2010; Downs 2016a).

James again returns to the prophetic tradition, the wisdom tradition, and probably also the Job tradition to show that poverty is not necessarily a sign of being cursed; it is instead the lot of the covenantly faithful, and tragically but joyously an opportunity for them to be tested unto perfection by the faithful protection of God. James is drawing not on the blessing tradition of Deuteronomy but instead on the prophetic tradition: this, like Isa 58, functions as a stinging indictment of the lack of mercy, and it is an exhortation to repent and to practice the faith in obedience and allegiance to King Jesus, the poor man who was glorified.

James 4:3, 13–17; 5:1–6

Our next two passages concern the rich, and these two passages define what is meant by "rich" in 1:10 ("and the rich in being brought low") while they also fill in with more concrete social details the world of the rich (Maynard-Reid 1987, 68–98). The conflicts simmering below 4:1–10 are generated by misdirected desires, and now riches come to the surface: "to spend what you get on your pleasures" (4:3). This does not describe the world of the poor but the rich, which is precisely what 4:13–17 details.

James focuses in 4:13–5:6 on two features of the rich besides their status and legal oppression (2:1–7): their presumptuous plans for financial profit (4:13–17) and their exploitation of the poor (5:1–6). Planning for business trips as well as working for profit are less the concern of James than their disposition. That disposition takes front stage when James explains that they are not praying and trusting the Lord. Thus, "Instead you ought to say, 'If the Lord wishes, we will live and do this or that'" (4:15). This is "boasting" and "arrogance" and "sin" (4:16–17). Once again, James taps into the prophetic tradition about wealth: it comes by way of arrogance.

Even more, it comes by way of exploitation. Every word about the rich in 5:1–6 is simultaneously a word about the poor. As the rich will "wilt away" (1:11), so here they are to "weep and wail for the miseries that are coming to you" (5:1). Again, this verse explains what is being said of the rich and poor in 1:9–11. Wilting away now means riches are rotting, clothes are being destroyed by moths, and their precious metals are rusting, and to ramp up the image into a metaphor blender, "their rust will … eat your flesh like fire" (5:3). The warning to them is good news for the poor: their cries—the language of the poor in both the legal and prophetic traditions—are heard by the Lord who will bring judgment on the rich. That day is nothing less than "a day of slaughter" (5:5). One possible suggestion remains: if the rich of 1:9–11 are the priestly establishment (as mentioned above), then it is not far off to suggest the travelers and exploiters of 4:13–5:6 are the priestly establishment. This is but a suggestion, but it is worthy of intertextual connection.

James and the Story

The letter of James arises to give its voice in nothing less than a chorus of biblical if also contrapuntal voices. The Deut 28 tradition's correlation of obedience with material flourishing and disobedience with material diminishment is complemented by at least two other voices: the identification of God with the oppressed poor and the permission God grants at times to test the blessed with material diminishment. Material prosperity may result from exploitation, and material diminishment may be a divinely disapproved injustice; hence, God at times is on the side of the poor. Blessing for obedience is complemented by a challenge to that tradition, to a tradition that identifies God with the poor and that knows sometimes poverty is a test. These various traditions swim in the same river.

Where does James fit? Over and over we see that James is more like the prophets, at times like Job and only occasionally with a hint of material blessing as the reward of obedience. But in James's context, the poor are the good guys and the rich the bad guys, and James offers a word to the former by castigating the injustices of the latter.

Reading James with the Social Sciences

Alicia J. Batten

Kinship, collectivism, purity, honor and shame, limited good ... these are a sample of some of the topics and concepts that those employing the social sciences in their study of antiquity have explored over the past few decades. Aspects of this approach to the Bible and related literature have become widespread within the field of biblical studies. Within this method, theories and models drawn from—but not limited to—sociology and anthropology are used in order to understand ancient Mediterranean culture, and subsequently to appreciate how specific texts might be conforming to or challenging that culture. A basic rationale for the method is that because Greco-Roman and Jewish literatures emerge from a time period and from geographic locations far different from the contemporary western world, the exegete must be attentive to contextual differences before she attempts to interpret the text. On the one hand, the interpreter must be self-aware, cognizant of his location and perspective on reality, while on the other, he must attempt to understand the complex cultures of the world from which the text emerges (Rohrbaugh 2007, 1–17). These can be daunting tasks, but ethnocentrism and eisegesis can easily ensue without efforts to develop this cultural awareness.

Social scientific criticism is generally perceived to be distinctive from what is sometimes referred to as social description. John H. Elliott (2008, 30), for example, adheres to John Gager's (1979) view that social-scientific or sociological criticism includes a hypothesis or model often but not exclusively drawn from the fields of anthropology or sociology that is then applied to a set of data, thus enabling the investigator to provide an explanation for a set of social experiences or phenomena. Social description, however, limits itself to the descriptive task, providing description but not explanation. Of course, the two approaches can overlap a good deal, but it is important to indicate that they are not one and the same.

Studying the Letter of James from a social-scientific vantage point has its challenges. Like many documents from antiquity, James is tricky because so many of the basic historical questions regarding its authorship, date, and provenance remain debated. However, we know that it was written in an ancient Mediterranean context sometime in the first or second century, and probably to an urban audience (Kloppenborg 2010; Batten 2014b, 83–90; Kaden 2014). We may not be able to determine exactly what city this audience lived in or many precise details about them, but we can examine the implied audience and form a description of who these people might have been and what challenges they faced based upon the contents of the letter (Popkes 1986). It has also become increasingly clear that the letter employs rhetorical strategies as it attempts to persuade the audience to particular ways of thinking and acting. No longer do scholars view James primarily as a loose jumble of ethical teachings without any continuity of thought as Martin Dibelius's (1976, 1–11) influential 1921 commentary contended (see Wachob 2000, 36–52), although certainly ethical exhortation dominates the letter. These teachings are structured into arguments that have been carefully constructed. The Letter of James attempts to persuade (Watson 2007). Understanding some of its social scripts will enable readers to comprehend more clearly the nature of this effort at persuasion.

This essay begins by examining some of the features of James's social context that are relevant for the interpretation of the letter. For example, it is important to appreciate features of ancient economic life, as well as how patronage and benefaction were pervasive phenomena throughout the Roman Empire. The deeply held values of honor and shame, as well as of gender roles, were decisive in influencing human behavior, and knowledge of them illuminates various verses in James. In light of these dimensions of the ancient Greco-Roman world, the essay then pays specific attention to the letter's characterization of the rich, of the poor, and of God. It is my aim to demonstrate that the use of the social sciences and social description enriches our understanding of such portrayals. In contrast to the greedy and dishonorable rich people who hoard treasure (Jas 5:1–6), God is depicted as a magnanimous and reliable benefactor in a world where everything is perceived to be in limited supply (Jas 1:5); and while they are vulnerable to humiliation, the poor (as we will see) bear the noble masculine quality of endurance that was so widely admired throughout the ancient world. The author of James accuses the audience of "dishonoring the poor man" if they demonstrate partiality to the rich (Jas 2:6), but it is the rich, depicted in part as effeminate degenerates, who are dishonorable in James.

The Mediterranean Context

Economics

Given that the emphasis here will be on the rich and poor in James, I begin by sketching a brief model of the ancient Mediterranean economy, then turn to some other relevant social features. Unlike the industrialized modern West, the first-century Mediterranean economy was largely agrarian (Lenski 1984), meaning that the basis for the economy was the land and farm production (Fiensy 2010, 195), as well as fishing. The plow had been invented and there were fairly sophisticated forms of agriculture and trade networks. Peasants made up the majority of the population of the Roman Empire; otherwise there was a smaller retainer class that served the interests of an even smaller super elite level of society that consisted of approximately 1 percent of the population (Fiensy 2010, 196). The latter owned the bulk of the land and enforced their will through the military and other, sometimes brutal, operations. Also, the super elites and retainer classes tended to live in urban centers unless they were staying at their country villas. The economy was extractive: any surplus from the harvests and fish hauls was for the benefit of the urban elites and not the peasants and artisans who engaged in the work (Hanson and Oakman 2008, 89). Moreover, the majority of people had no say in how economic practices were managed; this was a top-down type of administration.

In such an economic context there existed a notion of "limited good." The anthropologist George M. Foster first developed this model based upon his fieldwork in a variety of peasant communities. Limited good is the notion that all goods, both material and immaterial, are perceived by members of a given community to be both in finite supply and usually insufficient. This means that if one or more people within the group gain more, others will have less. Members thus attempt to avoid being the loser by taking on what Foster (1972, 58) calls an "egalitarian, shared poverty, equilibrium, status quo style of life." In such contexts, therefore, efforts to gain more are judged negatively because such efforts would threaten the equilibrium of shared goods. If one has a chance surplus, moreover, one is expected to help others, as has been observed in modern peasant economies (Scott 1976, 5). Biblical scholars and classicists have observed this phenomenon of limited good within ancient texts, such as when the Jewish historian Josephus says that another person envies his own gains (*Vita* 25.122–123; see Neyrey and Rohrbaugh 2001, 469). Envy (*phthonos*) was a commonly discussed vice in ancient literature (see Konstan 2006), and the first-century Greek writer Dio Chrysostom makes it abundantly clear that envy is likely to arise when someone of the same occupation comes to the community. There is obviously a limited amount of business, and thus envy rears its head when the competition for goods arises (*Invid.* 3). Such competition and resultant jostling also underscores the agonistic character of ancient Mediterranean cultures. People were constantly competing with one another for honor, land, water, loyalty, and other perceived limited resources. There is no assumption of a possible increase for everyone or that that economy could "grow" in the manner that people expect today.

In addition, economic practices in antiquity were not isolated from other social forces. Over fifty years ago the historian, anthropologist, sociologist, and social philosopher Karl Polanyi argued that ancient economies were not separate, distinct spheres that operated according to a set of principles or mathematical laws divorced from society and politics. Ancient economies were embedded, maintained Polanyi (1944, 1957), in that they were subject to a range of social phenomena including the family, religion, and politics.

Not all historians have adopted the language of "embedded economy," but they generally concur that in antiquity, society and economy were interrelated. Even the notion of something called an economy as a separate sphere of activity is relatively modern (Bigelow 2003, 3). In addition, the economies of ancient Mediterranean societies were primarily based upon "use value" as opposed to "exchange value," the latter being more characteristic of modern economies (Meikle 2002, 246–47). "Use value" means that the various types of exchanges taking place were for the purpose of satisfying basic needs. Peasants were not able to amass wealth or increase savings; their economic practices were focused upon the provision of food, shelter, and all of the needs a person would have. "Exchange value," in contrast, seeks to increase money or wealth as its own end. Those who did not siphon their energies into daily subsistence, namely the elites and those serving their interests, could engage in exchange value economic practices. Writers such as Aristotle disapprove of such activities; he thinks that engaging in exchange for the purpose of making a profit is immoral (*Pol.* 1.9.2–3).

All this is to say that economic practices within the ancient world had social, political, and moral meanings, as did perceptions of poverty and wealth. To be sure, poverty was not idealized; instead, the ideal for many philosophers was self-sufficiency (Balch 2004, 184). But if a person had more than he or she needed in order to satisfy basic wants, that person was expected to be generous and to perform acts of benefaction or *euerget-ism* toward others, as Cicero indicates (*Off.* 2.52–64). Most ancient writers themselves emerged from privileged contexts and do not demonstrate much sympathy for or interest in the truly poor who scrambled to survive each day. Yet these writers are quite willing to wage attacks on wealthy people for whom amassing riches was an end, and who lived luxurious lives. It is obviously difficult to determine what a poor person's perspective might have been, but even those who had means sometimes viewed the very rich as evil and greedy, for the rich were acquiring much more than they needed in a context in which everything was in limited supply. Bruce Malina (2001, 106) has gathered a variety of examples of negative attitudes towards the affluent, ranging from Plato (*Leg.* 12.743) to Menander (*Dysk.* 129K) to Jerome (*Epist.* 120). As he summarizes, wealth "is to be used with contentment and satisfaction … wealth is meant simply as another means for acquiring and maintaining honor. When the acquisition of wealth is an end, not a means, then the person dedicated to wealth acquisition is inherently demented, vicious, evil" (Malina 2001, 107). I will return to the topic of honor below, but suffice it to say that although many elites in the ancient world clearly did seek greater riches for their own sake, such activity was not generally condoned.

Patronage and Benefaction

Given the strong hierarchies between those who had wealth and power and those who had meager possessions, systems of exchange were also important throughout the ancient Mediterranean world. In the Greek East there had long been a practice of benefaction whereby a wealthy figure— the benefactor (*euergetēs*)—would provide for those who were in need and in turn receive the requisite honors and gratitude for his or her bestowal of funds. Key to this exchange was the fact that if the benefactor wished to uphold his or her honor to the group—perhaps to a city or an association—he or she had to continue providing benefits (*charis*). Failure to do so could result in being shamed by the potential beneficiaries, who themselves had upheld their end of the exchange by honoring the benefactor through an inscription or other means (Harland 2003, 100). Thus the recipients could exert a certain amount of pressure on their provider, even while they remained unequal to him or her in status and financial means (Batten 2010, 69).

Sometimes the deity was perceived as a benefactor. Inscriptions indicate that the divine benefactor would provide good things but could also inflict punishment upon those who did not abide by appropriate purity regulations (e.g., see *SIG* 985; Barton and Horsley 1981, 7–41). Father imagery appears in some of these materials together with the language of *euergetēs* (benefactor) and *sōtēr* (savior), and procreative power is attributed to the human or divine benefactor as well as a certain magnanimity and selfless and generous use of power (Stevenson 1996, 18). Hellenistic Jewish and Septuagint writers perceive God as a benefactor, and the term for benefit (*charis*, often translated as "grace") is regularly associated with benefactors both in the Hellenistic Jewish and Greek religious traditions. The recipients of this *charis* are those who trust in and remain loyal to their god (Batten 2010, 71; see also Crook 2004).

Patronage shared many features with benefaction, although it appears to be a specifically Roman phenomenon (Bowerstock 1965, 12). Both forms of reciprocal relationship existed between people of differing social levels, wealth, and power, and they consisted of a bestowal of goods such as money, land, or protection by the patron in exchange for honor, labor, or other forms of recognition and service from the client. But the notion that at certain moments during the Roman Empire clear distinctions were made in the roles of patrons versus benefactors is evident in some inscriptional evidence that identifies different people in each position (Eilers 2002, 91). This is not to say that the models of patronage and benefaction did not eventually merge, but at least in the first century they appear to have been perceived as different things among Greeks (see Joubert 2001).

Patronage, moreover, is not associated with the ideology of magnanimity and generosity that one finds in discussions of ideal benefaction (Eilers 2002, 101). In addition, what appears to have made a client a *cliens* was that he or she could not fully repay the benefit to the patron; this rendered the term *cliens* a somewhat degrading epithet, for it acknowledged that one was in the perpetual debt of another (Saller 2002, 8–11). As such, the client was vulnerable to exploitation by his or her patron, just as the client might act as a patron to someone beneath him or her and also engage in exploitative activities. Unlike benefaction, patronage "went beyond the elite" (Oakes 2010, 179).

Honor and Shame

Honor was one of the key goods that beneficiaries and clients would provide for their benefactors and patrons. This could be conveyed either through more official means, such as inscriptions and statues, or by means of daily activities, such as arriving at the patron's house in the morning to bow to him or her or else greeting the patron graciously in the street. Archaeological evidence indicates that in many Roman towns, people of different social levels regularly interacted, and neighborhoods were not necessarily divided by degrees of affluence (Oakes 2010, 182). There was ample opportunity for people to express honor for their local patron.

Honor consisted of one's recognized reputation in the public sphere. It was a core value in the ancient Mediterranean world, "the goal, the passion, the hope of all who aspired to excel" (Rohrbaugh 2010, 109). Honor could be ascribed, meaning that one who came from an honorable lineage automatically had a certain amount of honor, or it could be acquired through victories in competitions and conflicts. Like all goods, honor was in limited supply, and therefore if one gained honor, another person would lose it. Thus ancient people, especially men, were constantly competing to maintain or acquire more honor if they could.

Honor was an aspect of all dimensions of daily life, and it was expected to be upheld by how one dressed, walked, ate, spoke, and interacted with other people. There were assumptions about how honorable persons were to behave, and most people constantly faced the pressure of public scrutiny (see Lendon 1997). Moreover, the behavior of one's family and close associates could affect one's honor rating because these persons did not perceive themselves in the individualistic terms of the modern West, but as members of wider groups, especially the family, village, and people. If a son or daughter engaged in shocking and inappropriate activities, for example, a father could suffer a loss of honor in the community. If a husband was cuckolded by his wife, he would be humiliated or shamed.

"Being shamed" thus meant a loss of honor in the eyes of the larger community and could result in very serious consequences such as social ostracism and the loss of access to important social networks. Shame in this sense was very negative, but there was also a positive notion of shame. Having shame meant that one was concerned about how one was perceived by the community (Rohrbaugh 2010, 112). Women in particular were associated with having shame, and thus they were generally expected to conform to the stereotypes of wearing modest dress, obeying their male guardian or husband, managing the household, and not speaking too much (see Sir 26:13–16). We see these values reflected, for example, in some of the instructions within the New Testament (e.g., 1 Tim 2:8–15).

Gender

Constructions of gender in such a context were intimately bound up with honor and shame. As indicated above, men had to seek and uphold their honor through their comportment and by competing with other men (Osiek and Pouya 2010, 45). Women were expected to uphold, as mentioned above, the proper level of shame. These roles were sharply defined for both male and female, and thus any crossing over or blurring of the gender roles was scandalous and invited ridicule.

One of the primary characteristics of the ideal male was his ability to manifest self-control (*enkrateia*); this is a virtue that the apostle Paul, for example, values (1 Cor 7:9). This meant that the male was to practice mastery over his appetites such as sexual desire, eating and drinking, and spending money. Although it was important to be self-sufficient, as discussed above, it was equally necessary not to live a soft life of luxury in which one grew flabby and was unable to resist the urge to overindulge in sex or sumptuous food and drink. If a man did engage in such a lifestyle, he was not, in fact, truly a man and could be accused of effeminacy. And as Carolyn Osiek and Jennifer Pouya (2010, 46) point out, for Roman culture, "the next worse thing to effeminacy in male thinking was to be a woman." Men were often scrutinized for signs of effeminacy as evident in ancient handbooks (Gleason 1990). Particularly suspicious behavior included not only movement, voice, and dress, but reckless spending, dancing, and debauchery. Sometimes overeating was compared to financial greed, such as in Catullus's poetry (Richlin 1988, 361). Men who engaged in such antics were decried and complained about by writers such as Seneca the Younger, who found effeminate men who wore rings to be particularly offensive (*Nat.* 7.31.2), and Cicero, who deemed so-called girly men to be politically weak and thus dangerous because they lacked proper self-mastery (*Fam.* 16.27.1).

Wealthy males could therefore easily come under attack if they demonstrated signs of lacking in self-control. In contrast, men who labored and worked the land were often admired, even when they were in short supply of financial means. In their strength, fortitude, and simplicity of lifestyle they embodied the masculine ideal. Ancient writers such as

Horace think that the farmer, for example, is qualified to teach wisdom (*Sat.* 2.2.1–7). Juvenal laments the fact that Romans are no longer happy with simple food from their kitchen gardens and instead expresses admiration for shepherds and rural laborers who possess the central virtues of modesty and honesty, which he wishes the wealthy would manifest (*Sat.* 11). Columella laments that male city-dwellers have abandoned working on farms only to engage in licentiousness and debauchery, and they have grown fat and weak (*Rust.* 1.preface.15–17). Such characterizations are deeply unflattering and illustrate the level of dishonor to which these writers think that some well-to-do men have sunk.

Social-World Scholarship on James

To a certain extent, some of the phenomena discussed above have been used to illuminate dimensions of the Letter of James. Although a focus upon the social world of the New Testament, whether social-scientific or socially descriptive, has existed since the early 1970s (Elliott 2008, 26), social-scientific or socially descriptive work on James did not emerge until a decade later because this letter has tended to be overlooked in comparison to the gospels or letters of Paul. Among the earliest studies was that of Pedrito Maynard Reid (1987), who performed an exegesis of various passages in James dealing with the rich and poor after briefly presenting a model of first-century social stratification. Although he used somewhat anachronistic terminology (such as "capitalist" and "laissez-faire policy") to describe aspects of the ancient economy (1987, 13–23), he did try to situate the letter's teachings within the context of his understanding of economic and social relations. Others, such as Elsa Tamez (1990, 44), have attended to questions of rich and poor in James and pointed out that when the letter refers to the "poor man" (*ptōchos*, Jas 2:3), it means that the man is materially poor, and not a devout or pious man as other ancient literature sometimes indicates (see also Kloppenborg 2008) and as previous scholarship on James has often argued (such as Dibelius 1976, 39–45).[1] Although she did not perform a social-scientific study of James, Tamez tried to keep the ideas in the letter rooted in social and material realities. Matthias Ahrens (1995, 138) also produced a study of the social conditions of James's context, and like Tamez, he rejected the notion that *ptōchos*

---

1. See also the essay by Tamez in this volume.

refers to a pious poor man; instead, this is an indigent person bereft of any kind of material wealth.

More recently, Wesley Hiram Wachob (2000) has written a detailed rhetorical analysis of Jas 2:1–13. While the focus is upon the argument of this section of the letter, Wachob situates the passage within the context of a society characterized by limited good, patronage, and honor and shame. David Hutchinson Edgar (2001) has used communication theory in his examination of James, but again, he contextualizes his discussion of the letter in the reality of patronage and benefaction by the rich. Both of these scholars take the material reality of poverty seriously in their understanding of "the poor" in James. But they think that *ptōchos* is not purely socioeconomic; it also refers to "pious poor" and has to do with an orientation to "the world" and, at least in Hutchinson Edgar's (2001, 108) case, refers to itinerant charismatics who have chosen to become followers of Jesus.

Some scholars have engaged social-scientific models in their analyses of James (J. Elliott 1993; Lockett 2007; 2008), such as the insights of anthropologist Mary Douglas, who pioneered significant research into the social and symbolic functions of purity and pollution. Others have employed frameworks from post-colonial criticism together with a focus on Roman imperial politics for understanding the letter's context and aims (Coker 2015; Mongstad-Kvammen 2013). In addition, the notion that the author has in mind a situation in which a community is threatened by the potential influence of a wealthy patron in Jas 2:1–13 (an idea that at least goes back to the work of Nancy Vhymeister in 1995) has now become more widespread (Kloppenborg 1999; Wachob 2000; Batten 2010).

The Rich and Poor in James

Building upon the work of others, I have argued elsewhere that Jas 2:1–7 is likely depicting a scenario—whether real or imagined—in which a potential patron is threatening the welfare and moral fortitude of the community (Batten 2010, 180–81). The figure dressed in fine clothes and gold rings (Jas 2:2) enters the assembly, potentially causing others to scurry and offer him the best seat. They consequently order the poor man to sit at their feet (Jas 2:3). The suggestion that the rich man is dishonorable is present given the explicit mention of his expensive dress and gold ring. Is the author indicating that this is an effeminate? In any case, the letter indicates exasperation with the audience because such behavior or the potential for it can cause distinctions in the audience (Jas 2:4) and leads to the dishonoring of the poor man (*ptōchos*). Notice here that the poor man will be dishonored by the way in which he has been treated and not by virtue of the fact that he is poor. The author then elaborates more on the actions of the rich. They oppress people, drag persons into court, and blaspheme the holy name invoked over the community (Jas 2:7). Clearly these rich (*hoi plousioi*) are not honorable people.

The *hoi plousioi* reappear in Jas 5:1–6. Here the author wages a direct attack through the characterization of their lifestyle. He claims that they "cry out and howl" (Jas 5:1) because of encroaching miseries. A true man in Greco-Roman antiquity does not display such outbursts so explicitly. He may cry discretely, but overt expressions of emotion and distress were perceived as a lack of self-discipline (Batten 2014a, 52). Participating in such dramatic expressions of distress was the role of women, who would show up at funerals to ululate and wail (Erker 2009). The letter then states that the wealth of the rich has rotted and become moth-eaten, references to decaying food and garments that the rich have been able to stockpile. Their affluence extends well beyond self-sufficiency, and in Jas 5:3 the author reinforces his criticism of such greed by referring to their stores of treasure. In addition, in Jas 5:2, the gold and silver of the rich have rusted, and will "eat" (*phagetai*) their flesh (*sarkas*). I have noted elsewhere that since the metals will eat the flesh, James may well have in mind the rings of the wealthy man in Jas 2:1, which in Jas 5:3 will eat into the fingers of the rich (Batten 2014a, 54). The plural for *sarx*, namely, *sarkas*, arises in the book of Revelation, where it refers to that which is fed upon (Rev 17:16; 19:18, 21). It is thus not a simple reference to the body (*sarx*) but to the fatty consumable parts. One can easily imagine a gold or silver ring cutting into the fleshy fingers of a wealthy man.

James does not stop here with the negative characterization of the affluent, but continues on to describe how they cheat the laborers and how they have lived in luxury and pleasure (Jas 5:4–5). Clearly these are people who have lost control of their appetites. They are greedy such that not only do they store extra for themselves, but they also exploit those who work for them for their own gain such that they can live a life of debauchery. In Jas 5:5 the author uses the verb *etruphēsate*, which was often employed by classical writers to refer to effeminate men (Batten 2014a, 55). He reinforces their greed and lack of self-discipline with the reference to the fact that they have "fattened their hearts" (Jas 5:5). The latter is an unusual phrase (see Batten 2014a, 56), but it reinforces this negative description of them as degenerates who indulge in their own bodily appetites.

In contrast to the rich who are portrayed in the most insulting and dishonorable terms possible, the poor appear as noble figures in James. Although it is possible to dishonor such people as a consequence of showing partiality (Jas 2:5), the poor are chosen by God and are the heirs of the kingdom (Jas 2:5) because they are committed to God. Wachob (2000, 195) claims that the manner in which James argues in Jas 2:1–13 effectively seeks to persuade the audience to identify with these poor. These poor are those who must withstand trials and tests in order to receive the crown of life promised by God for those who love God (Jas 1:12). The poor are the loyal recipients of a beneficent God (Jas 4:6). There is an economic dimension to being poor here, but also a religious aspect.

In addition, James draws upon interesting examples of people who embody virtues such as endurance or steadfastness (*hypomonē*, Jas 1:3–4, 12) advocated by the letter, and who are committed to God. After the condemnation of the rich who defraud their laborers, James makes it clear that the laborers or harvesters cry out to God and that God hears them (Jas 5:4). The author supplies the example of the patient farmer who waits for early and late rains (Jas 5:7–8). Next we encounter the prophets (Jas 5:10) who manifest suffering and patience and who spoke in the Lord's name. The famous figure of Job is then supplied as a model of *hypomonē* (Jas 5:11). It is uncertain whether the letter writer is thinking of the figure in the canonical book of Job or the Job of the apocryphal Testament of Job, but in both texts he was a farmer. He is masculine, steadfast, and honorable. Finally, the figure of Elijah emerges in Jas 5:17 as an example of prayer and as someone who is similar to the audience (Jas 5:17). The reference to Elijah concerns the story in 1 Kgs 18:42 in which Elijah prays fervently for rain; after much waiting, heaven does provide rain, which in turn causes the earth to bring forth the fruit for which the farmer was waiting (Jas 5:7). Like the farmer, the laborers, and Job, Elijah not only has an affinity with the audience, but he is another example of someone in a rural context that serves as a positive and honorable model of how James's audience should behave (see Batten 2013, 16). These examples are consistent with the positive portrayal of laborers and farmers found in Greco-Roman literature—they embody a masculine ideal and reflect no hint of libertinism or effeminacy, whereas the latter characteristics were evident in portrayal and satires of wealthy degenerates.

God

Finally, when we consider the negative characterization of the wealthy potential patron in Jas 2:2, it is useful to recall some of the distinctions between the models of patronage and benefaction discussed earlier. Benefaction was a reciprocal relationship between people of unequal social levels in which the benefactor provided goods and services in exchange for honor. There was a notion of magnanimity associated with the ideal benefactor, although it is hard to say whether or not any human benefactors actually embodied such an ideal. Benefactors upheld their reputation as generous givers by continuing to provide; otherwise, their beneficiaries would not furnish the requisite honor and might seek benefactors elsewhere. Patronage, a particularly Roman institution that came to supersede benefaction by the late imperial period, involved an exchange between unequal persons as well, but it was not accompanied by an ideology of liberality as benefaction was. Moreover, the *cliens* was forever in the debt of the patron unless the more powerful party met disaster. The client was more vulnerable to exploitation. In addition, one could be both a patron and a client at the same time.

James 2:1–7, as has been argued by several scholars, depicts a situation in which the arrival of a potential patron risks causing distinctions in the community and the subsequent humiliation of the poor. The author is aware of the problems that patronage could create and warns his audience away from it. But what would be the alternative? Does it mean that God is the true patron and that those of more means in the audience should become patrons of the less fortunate among them, as has been suggested by Wachob (2000, 197)?

Certainly, the author exhorts his audience to care for the impoverished (Jas 2:14–17), but not as patrons given the understanding of the practice and ideology of patronage. I would suggest that rather than viewing God as the patron and advocating patronage among community members, the Letter of James presents us with a model of divine benefaction that should extend to benefaction among community members. This latter benefaction includes the sharing of wealth and resistance to the envy and jostling that was so pervasive in ancient Mediterranean society (Jas 4:1–10).

Throughout James, God is depicted as a divine benefactor. In Jas 1, the text indicates that God gives to all simply and without reproach (1:5). The use of *haplōs* ("simply") is an indicator that God does not give with concealed or hidden purposes. Interestingly, the author seeks to clarify that God does not tempt either (Jas 1:13). God provides good and perfect gifts (1:17–18), and the recipients of these gifts are expected to respond through their behavior and faithfulness to God (1:6; 1:27).

The portrayal of God as a benefactor continues in subsequent sections of the letter. For example, in Jas 4:3 the audience is chastised because they are not asking God for things properly. They must not ask in order to spend on their passions, and they are exhorted to draw near to God with cleansed hands and pure hearts (Jas 4:8). Thus it is clear that God is the sort of benefactor who demands that human beings use God's benefits appropriately. Faithfulness or loyalty to God, moreover, is not negotiable, and if such faithfulness is present, it can save the sick person, and if that sick person has sinned, he will be forgiven (Jas 5:15). Prayer, coming from a righteous person, is assured to be effective. God is a reliable benefactor, provided the beneficiaries uphold fidelity to God and proper behavior toward one another (Jas 5:16).

Conclusion

This essay has argued that when equipped with some of the ideas and models developed through social-scientific work, we can appreciate dimensions of James that might not otherwise be clear or obvious upon a surface reading of the letter. In particular, the degree to which the text characterizes the rich as dishonorable and the poor as honorable is clearer when we attend to how honor and shame functioned within the context of ancient understandings of limited good economies. Also, we can better perceive the role that gender played in characterizing people as honorable or shameful. When we appreciate the vital importance of honor and shame in ancient Mediterranean contexts, and how being shamed, for example, could lead to social disaster, then we better understand the power and daring of this letter. If the rich in James are part of the audience—and many commentators have argued that they are—then such rich people are the recipients of very harsh words from this letter writer. The author is not cowed by the rich but is willing to portray them in a deeply dishonorable fashion, while describing the poor as those who are truly honorable.

In addition, awareness of the models of patronage and benefaction assists in appreciating not only the letter's criticism and, indeed, rejection of patronage but also the characterization of God. God is a generous benefactor, and the audience is expected to honor God through their behavior and purity. Such a characterization would not be strange upon the ancient landscape, but instead it would be familiar to those who shared the values and culture of the ancient Mediterranean that social-science criticism enables us to elucidate.

Don't Conform Yourselves to the Values of the Empire

Elsa Tamez
Translated by Kevin Johnson

Postcolonial reading of the Bible has been more widespread in the United States than in Latin America, most notably in the work of R. S. Surgirtharaja, Fernando Segovia, and more recently in the work of Musa Dube. The reading of the Bible in Latin America known as popular or community reading began before postcolonial reading and accompanied the rise of liberation theology. This popular reading was not popular in the sense of "well-known" or "famous," but in the sense of being done from the perspective of the common people, especially the poor. Likewise, the idea of community reading of the Bible refers to pastoral reading.[1]

Popular and communal reading share many points with postcolonial reading, especially in the countercultural reading from the perspective of the marginalized and silenced in the search for social change. But one must say that postcolonial hermeneutics of the Bible enriched the popular reading of the Bible by considering as foundational cultural anthropology, asymmetric intercultural relationships, the presence of the other, and the criticism of the text itself when it is colonizing. Indeed, not every text is liberating, as was affirmed in the beginning; there are oppressive texts that cannot be accepted as normative (Tamez 2007).

The young Colombian biblical scholar Juan E. Londoño (2016), drawing principally on Segovia and Sugirtharajah in general, summarizes some points of postcolonial hermeneutics that today are also present in the popular reading of the Bible. The most important aspects include the recognition that postcolonial hermeneutics provides an alternative reading to traditional readings and that it rescues the silenced voices in the biblical

---

1. The terms *community* or *pastoral* replaced the term *popular*, because popular reading of the Bible was considered subversive and politicized in the Cold War era.

texts that dissent from the dominant voices (e.g., reading Gen 16:1–16; 21:9–21 from the perspective of Hagar). As such, it makes numerous contributions: (1) it makes oppressive voices in the texts visible; (2) it brings to light the colonial political ideology that texts and their interpretations promote; (3) it challenges the line of thought that dominates the classic academic world and that does not recognize the colonialism of the texts themselves or in their interpretations; (4) it opens itself to new voices of texts that have been colonized (such as indigenous peoples, African Americans, women, sexual minorities, and Palestinians); and (5) it proposes strategies of interpretation in the world of colonial relationships, encouraging new intercultural relationships and social change. To Londoño's list we could add the use of different exegetical-hermeneutical approaches and the relativization of the historical-critical methods when these are seen as the only way to discover the truth of the text.

This chapter's hermeneutical approach follows the popular reading of the Bible, whose perspective is liberative from the perspective of the economically oppressed. In this reading—which in effect is a rereading— three dimensions are taken into account: the text, the text's context, and the readers' context. Since we know that the economic-political context of the letter of James is difficult to pinpoint, we draw on the rhetorical situation and intratextuality, that is, we relate the texts among themselves with the goal of achieving a coherent content.[2] The emphasis will be on immigrants and on liberative spirituality. With the goal of taking greater advantage of intratextuality for our analysis of spirituality, we are guided by using the concentric structure of René Krüger (2005, 131–32).

James: A Circular Letter for Immigrants

The Context of the Readers (Both Ancient and Modern) as Starting Point

There have always been migratory movements: the Bible, from beginning to end, is full of stories of migrants. The current problem of migration and forced displacements, however—whether by hunger, threats of death, war, and violence, or simply to prosper—is in view. Globalization, for its part, magnifies the news since the means of communication (especially social

---

2. There is no consensus regarding the author, date, and place where the letter was written, therefore we will determine the context from the text itself.

networks) are present among almost all the peoples and corners of the earth. Rich countries have become more reluctant to accept immigrants. The Mediterranean Sea, a symbol of relaxation, has become a large mass grave for people who flee from violence or poverty; since May 2016, five thousand emigrants have died on their trip by sea to Europe (Tamayo 2017). Walls, so hated during the Cold War, have become fashionable to stop the arrival of the "wetbacks" of Mesoamerica or "terrorists" of the Near East. Immigrants, depending on the color of their skin, ethnicity, social class, gender, religion, or language, will have to bear the disdain of the dominant population, accept the conditions to which they are subject, and even become rivals among themselves for survival. So, it is not difficult to predict that immigrants in any country in the world experience problems external to themselves: discrimination and oppression on the part of the society in which they live, and internal problems among the immigrants themselves, such as competition, rivalry, and seeking to improve one's status at the cost of others.

The experience of living in a strange land is similar in every time and empire. In the Bible, there are several texts that speak of this reality. One of them is the Letter of James. It is an official circular letter of the encyclical type (Bauckham 1999, 13), addressed to migrant Jews who lived outside of Syria-Palestine. They could be in Asia Minor or in any province of the Roman Empire.[3] We know from the greeting that they are immigrants, since the letter is addressed to "the twelve tribes in the dispersion." The greeting already offers certain interesting indications regarding the recipients: (1) They are followers of Jesus, since a servant of God and of the Lord Jesus Christ writes to them; (2) they are Jews, since the phrase "the twelve tribes in the dispersion" alludes to the Jewish people; and (3) since they are immigrants, it is understood that they suffer certain hardships for not being part of the place's culture, for being different in their beliefs, and for not having the same political and social rights (Elliott 1981, 25; Tamez 2008, 12–13).

The attribution of the Letter to James alludes more to a figure than to a historical person. There are many debates regarding the identity of the author, whether he is the brother of the Lord or a pseudonymous author of a letter written later. But for our purpose it is more important

---

3. Areas in Asia Minor include Bithynia, Cappadocia, Pontus, Galatia, mentioned in 1 Pet 1:1, where the addressees are also called the tribes of the dispersion.

to emphasize the name of James as a figure, that of a leader of the church in Jerusalem who is concerned about the communities that followed Jesus that are located in the provinces of the empire. That is why he sends a circular letter with pertinent exhortations that have to do with the difficulties they face in their hostile environments and with the internal problems that wear them down. He proposes that they lead an integral and consistent life as faithful followers of the law of love, that they not let themselves be crushed by the hostility of their environment, and that they not conform themselves to the often-seductive values of the empire. In other words, he exhorts them to live out a genuine spirituality expressed in their lifestyle. Before looking at the proposal regarding spirituality, let us first see what the internal and external problems of these migrant communities were.

Situation of the Immigrants

On various occasions the author mentions economic difficulties of some members of the community. We read this clearly in 2:15–16, which does not necessarily deal with a hypothetical case (Krüger 2005, 208–9). It makes perfect sense that members of the congregation faced hunger and cold, and the example of a poor sister (*adelphē*) or brother (*adelphos*) enables the author to show what genuine faith is. On the other hand, we find the antithetical aphorism about the humble person and the rich person. The author does not include this aphorism by chance, but rather because he wants to express his solidarity with the humble in the congregation (he speaks of *adelphos*, "brother") and his quarrel with those rich people who are busy in their business (1:10). The humble person (*tapeinos*)—who appears in contrast to the rich person (1:10)—is a person without importance in the social stratification and who likewise is poor (but here not indigent; cf. the latter in 2:1–6). In 5:1–6, the author uses the force of the apocalyptic genre to attack the oppressive landowners who do not pay the peasants' wages. It is likely that day laborers belonged to the communities of followers of Jesus. Otherwise, one would have to think that some of the landowners were members of the community, which is not very likely.

Although it is not very clear, it could also be said that another difficulty that the communities faced was persecution for their faith in Jesus Christ (Laws 1980, 51). The first verses after the greeting (1:2–4) speak of strong and painful trials that occur and the importance of bearing these trials and not losing strength. In the end, they will come out stronger and more whole (*teleios*). In 5:7–11, the author again insists that they be patient and persevere (*hypomenō*) like the prophets who spoke in the name of the Lord. He reminds them that the Lord's coming is near. With Sophie Laws (1980), we think, then, that they could be experiencing both economic difficulties and persecution.

In addition to these difficulties, the recipients suffered discrimination for their ethnicity. Being monotheists and not following the Greco-Roman customs were reasons for the inhabitants of the place to marginalize them (cf. Acts 16:20–21). We know that Juvenal, in his satires of the Sabbath as a day of rest, made fun of the worship of the Jews and of circumcision (*Sat.* 14.96–106). Also, as we mentioned above, many foreigners suffered from a lack of civil rights.

The situations mentioned—such as difficulties related to economics, persecution, and discrimination—are problems that come from outside. Yet they not only faced *ad extra* problems, but problems also abounded *ad intra*, within the communities.

One of them was letting oneself go along with the values of the Roman imperial society, as with patronage and the discriminatory paradigm of honor and shame (Míguez 1998, 92; Krüger 2005, 211–12). This problem is clearly seen in 2:1–6. Honor is given to the one who has wealth and power, but the indigents (*ptōchos*) are discriminated against. The one who enters in the assembly is probably a person of the elite belonging to the class of the decurions, to whom one perhaps had to pay a certain favor. James's critique is sharp; for him the community, dazzled by the one who has wealth and power, does not realize that these are the kind of people who not only exploit them (*katadynasteuousin*), but also, when they do not receive payment for what was loaned, lead them by force (*helkousin*) to the courts.

The seductive values regarding obtaining profit are another evil that plagues some members of the communities. To do business on a large scale (Krüger 2005, 254), being absent for a year or going from city to city to accumulate profit (4:13–17), is harmful for the followers of Jesus. Accumulation and the desire to have more and more produce envy, rivalry, wars, and violence (4:1–3). These easily become idolatry, and for this reason one cannot be God's friend and a friend of the values of society (4:4). Theologically, James expresses this in the exhortation against falling into temptation (1:13). Here the author is not addressing trials, but rather temptations, although the same Greek work is used (*peirazō*). The admonition begins with greed (*epithymia*), which drags a person along, seduces him or her, and gives birth to sin and finally leads to death (1:14–15).

These seductive situations can make people insensitive to effective solidarity with their brothers and sisters of the community of faith (2:15–16), the defenseless in society (1:27), or anyone who needs pastoral accompaniment (5:20). Likewise, they can produce discriminatory behaviors without one being conscious of them, as in the case of the response to the indigent poor person who one day enters the assembly.

The other internal problem that is very serious for the author is the lack of control of one's words. It seems that this is not a simple commonplace of wisdom literature. The author devotes many verses to it: he introduces the problem in 1:26 and explains and expands on it in 3:1–12. He uses beautiful literary figures, but he also reveals human corruption when one does not control the tongue. The consequences can be disastrous.

Finally, for James, several things characterize those whose behavior is not consistent with that of someone who is a disciple of Jesus. They let themselves be seduced by and conform themselves to the values of a society that is not compatible with the values proclaimed by the royal law (that is, of the kingdom), the prophets, and Jesus; they neither enter into solidarity with the needy nor control their tongue. For James, their faith is empty and thus does not save them (2:14).

Proposal of a Genuine Spirituality as Lifestyle

Various commentators on James have given up on explaining the literary structure of James, and it is not easy to find one due to the form in which the discourse is constructed. But Krüger (2005, 130–36) offers an interesting concentric structure that is coherent. In his proposal we observe a carefully constructed structure, and with just one look we perceive what could be the original intent of the author. The thematic coherence of the letter is lost when it is read without an organizing thread like this, due to the proliferation of brief themes. Chapter 1, for example, presents a series of aphorisms.[4] This has traditionally been the obstacle to finding the structure. Instead, it seems that the whole first chapter is an introduction to the letter, so the themes that will be addressed later are briefly introduced, as

---

4. I.e., they are sentences or maxims in indicative mode that encapsulate general themes. E.g., 1:6: "the one who doubts is like a wave of the sea, driven and tossed by the wind" (NRSV), or 1:9–10a: "Let the believer who is lowly boast in being raised up, and the rich in being brought low" (NRSV). Unless otherwise indicated, all translations are mine.

Richard Bauckham (1999, 69–71) suggests. Luke Timothy Johnson (1995, 15), for his part, sees the first chapter as an epitome, that is, a compendium that summarizes the themes that will be developed later. He argues that this was a practice of ancient rhetoric. Krüger, drawing on a significant number of authors, also affirms that it is the introduction to the letter. Therefore, in his concentric structure the first chapter covers half of the thematic development.

Let us look at his structure:

Opening of the letter 1:1
A 1:2–8 Perseverance (patience); Request for wisdom
   B 1:9–11 Exaltation of the humble brother; Humiliation of the rich person
      C 1:12 Tested in temptation
         D 1:13–15 Origin of temptation
            E 1:16–18 The gift from on high
               F 1:19–25 Doers of the word
                  G 1:26 Restraining the tongue
                     H 1:27 Pure and spotless worship
                       X 2:1–13 Against partiality
                     H' 2:14–26 Faith and works of love
                  G' 3:1–12 The power of the tongue
               F' 3:13–16 Good conduct
            E' 3:17–18 The wisdom from on high
         D' 4:1–3 Origin of evil
      C' 4:4–12 Between the world (sin) and God (trial)
   B' 4:13–5:6 Humiliation of the rich
A' 5:7–20 Patience, petition for health; Responsibility toward the one who has wandered

In this kind of concentric structure, the center generally gains the greatest importance. We may observe that the center is in 2:1–13, which speaks against partiality. Here, in the center marked with the letter X, the central teaching is the integrity or consistency that there must be between calling oneself a Christian and one's behavior. The author offers an example of discrimination against the poor (2:1–4) and gives the theological basis for orienting one's practice toward nondiscrimination (2:5–11). This theme is framed by exhortations that point to consistency between faith and practice (2:1), whether in the affirmation "May faith not mix with favoritism," or in the variant with a question, "Are you Christians and you show favoritism?" The other frame is made up of the close of that section, "So speak and so do" (2:12–13).

We can visualize it in this way:

A 2:1 The believer does not discriminate.
    B 2:2–4: Practical example of favoritism: in detriment to the poor.
    B' 2:5–11: Theological basis: God does not discriminate; God elects the poor.
A' 2:12–13 The believer shows consistency between what one says and what one does. (This is the law of liberty.)

According to Krüger, this is the center of the whole epistle. This basic teaching points to genuine faith or religiosity: the consistency between calling oneself a Christian and demonstrating it in everyday practice.

Now let us see the points of the structure closer to the center, in ascending and descending manner. We will see how those themes line up with one another and reiterate the importance of an integral spirituality.

Spirituality and Solidarity

In the center of the structure we saw that the Christian is to be distinguished by integrity or consistency between what one says and does. If we note the nearby themes that are above and below, we see that there is a significant emphasis regarding the spiritual life of the believer, marked by the center of the structure. Remember that the statements above introduce each of the themes and those below (the prime letters) develop them.

The immediately preceding theme is pure and spotless worship (H, 1:27). At first sight, due to the terminology a modern reader might think that the perfection of worship is the correct praise of God through song and the sincerity of heart in dedicating worship to God, and perhaps we could also add the absence of evil thoughts, especially at the moral level. The author, however, sees that part as one side of the coin, an incomplete part that loses its significance without the other part: the concrete proof of love to the needier neighbor. To this theme of worship, introduced here, section H' (2:14–26) corresponds; here the author develops it at length, with examples and argumentation from Scripture.

Let us look at H (1:27) in greater detail, with the chiastic form better visualizing the content.

A Religion that is pure and undefiled before God, the Father is this:
  B to care for orphans and widows in their distress, and
A' to keep oneself unstained by the world. (NRSV)

Religion that is pure and without stain (A) and keeping oneself without stain from the world (A') form the frame of the central passage, which is B, to come to the aid of orphans and widows. As can be seen, it is not about Jewish ritual purity, nor about the perfection of piety through the rites of the official Roman religion of that time, but rather about ethical purity (McCartney 2009, 128), which separates oneself from the corrupt values of the world (Bauckham 1999, 146). Orphans and widows represent the neediest people. God appears as the father of the orphans and, it may be inferred, the husband of the widows. The sense is that God is the one who looks out for them through those who practice pure religion. For the author, authentic religiosity or spirituality is that in which purity of heart and honesty are shown in the practice of loving one's neighbor. Obviously in the texts we find echoes of the prophet Isaiah when he spoke of true fasting (Isa 58:5–8). The prophet alludes to a profound spiritual experience: doing justice in the path where we walk and feeling the glory of God as a rearguard, which is radiating the light of God like the dawn, and knowing that salvation, or every kind of healing, is near.

In H' (2:14–26), the author expands and clarifies with concrete examples and biblical arguments what has just been announced here. The question that the author asks his recipients is the following: Can faith, or that spiritual life that is not shown through good works, save? Since the question is rhetorical, it requires a negative response: "That faith does not save." After giving an example from daily life and two examples of model characters from Scripture, he again concludes by affirming that a faith of that kind cannot save, because it is dead. Now let us look at the details.

The argument is elaborated in three stages. Just as in section X at the center of the structure, the first stage (2:14–17) starts with an example from daily life among Christians. If in the congregation there are brothers or sisters who do not have clothing or food, and one desires their good but does not give them what they need, that person's faith or spirituality is useless. The forceful affirmation that such "faith" does not save appears framed at the beginning (2:14) and at the end of the example (2:17): it

is a dead faith. The same thing happens in the exhortation against discrimination against the poor (section X): those who act thusly believe in
Jesus and yet they do not show it through their works (2:1–13). Again, the
example leads us to H (1:27), which speaks about genuine religiosity, pure
and without blemish, focused on solidarity with orphans and widows.

The second stage (2:18–19) of the discourse's reasoning is introduced
through a dialogue with an imagined opponent (2:18), a common literary tactic in Greco-Roman diatribe. Verse 18 presents certain exegetical
problems, but the important thing here is to understand the movement
and reasoning of the discourse. In this stage, the point of James is to show
two mistaken types of faith or spirituality. The first of these is faith separated from works. It is impossible to show genuine faith if there are no
works involved to make it visible; instead, one can see faith through works,
because good works are the fruit of faith. The other kind of mistaken faith
is that which only consists of accepting a creed or a dogma in an intellectual manner (McCartney 2009, 155). The author, again using irony, makes
the opponent see that demons also believe in one God and tremble (2:19).
This type of faith is unproductive.

The third stage (2:20–25) presents the theological or scriptural basis
regarding the inseparable relationship between faith and works. The author
continues dialoguing with his imaginary opponent until 2:24, where he
changes from second-person singular to second-person plural to address
himself directly to his audience. He draws on the support of the Scriptures
through two characters of faith who were very well known within the rabbinic Jewish tradition, Abraham and Rahab; these figures are presented as
models that the congregation must follow. Speaking of the masculine and
feminine genders, it is interesting to observe the symmetry in the use. For
example, 1:27 speaks of orphans and widows, 2:15 of brother or sister, and
2:25 of Abraham and Rahab (Krüger 2005, 176).

Note how four rhetorical questions mark the movement of this stage
(2:20, 21, 22, 25). All the questions require an affirmative answer, which
suggests that the audience knows well the traditions about Abraham and
Rahab regarding their faith. Here faith must be understood as total trust in
God. The author emphasizes that Abraham's faith did not exist in isolation
from his works; rather, for the author Abraham's works were those that
strengthened and perfected his life of faith (2:22). In the center of this last
part of the section (2:23 and 24, if we consider 2:21 as introduction), the
author now addresses himself directly to his audience, leaving behind the
imaginary opponent. Here the well-known declaration of James appears,

that a person is justified by works and not only by faith (2:24). This declaration is based on the example of Abraham, who believed God and it was
counted to him as righteousness (2:23), and he was called God's friend.
In the case of Rahab, the other character who serves as a model of faith,
her good work alludes to her hospitality offered to Joshua's messengers.
Risking her life, she saved them from being destroyed (Josh 2:1, 5). For
that action Rahab, just like Abraham, was justified by God. Note how the
center of this last stage (2:23 and 24) divides two radically distinct characters, a man and a woman, a Hebrew and a Canaanite, a man of good
reputation and a woman who was a prostitute by trade. Both, without discrimination, are welcomed by God thanks to their good works that show
a genuine faith in God.

The section closes the discourse with an analogy between a body without spirit and a faith without works (2:26). For James, both are dead. The
whole section corresponds to the explanation of why pure and spotless
religion is solidarity with the most disadvantaged. People who act in that
way keep themselves separated from or uncontaminated by the values of
society, which, with their parameters based on patronage and the code of
honor and shame, discriminated against the least important.

Let us visualize the structure of the section:

First block: Example from daily life
A 2:14 Faith without works does not save.
   B 2:15–16 Example of false spirituality (wishing the needy well
      without helping).
A' 2:17 Faith without works is dead.

Second block: Debate with an imaginary interlocutor
A 2:18 Debate about faith separated from works.
   B 2:19 Example of false spirituality (the demons also believe and
      tremble).
A' 2:20 Faith without works is dead.

Third block: Support from the Scriptures: Examples from the biblical
   tradition
A 2:21 Abraham was justified by works.
   B 2:22 Works cooperated with and perfected faith.
      C 2:23 Abraham believed and was justified and was called
      God's friend.

B′ 2:24 People are justified by works and not only by faith.
A′ 2:25 Rahab was justified by works.
Closing 2:26: Just as the body without the spirit is dead, so also faith
    without works is dead.

We find two types of false spirituality: desiring the good without doing
it, and believing in God without demonstrating it through love for one's
neighbor. The case of Abraham is clarifying. He demonstrated his total
trust in God—that is, his faith—in an act of surrender of what he most
loved: his work perfected his faith. What does that mean? That he believed
and he demonstrated it with his acts. His faith, evidenced in his acts, was
counted to him as righteousness, and he became God's friend.

Let us now go to the themes that precede and follow the sections
marked with the letter H. That is, let us study the sections G and G′, which
deal with the theme of the control of words or of the tongue. For James, the
control of the tongue and solidarity are at the same level: both practices
show the true spiritual life.

Spirituality and Control of the Tongue

In everyday life it is not common to relate the use of words to spirituality. Generally, spirituality is rather reduced to the matter of not saying
bad words or swear words or mentioning the name of God in vain. For
James, the control of the tongue is foundational to spirituality. It is like a
thermometer that indicates the degree of the presence or absence of God
in the life of people and of the community. He introduces the theme in
1:26 and expands on it in 3:1–12. In 1:19 he also alludes to watching the
tongue: one must be "quick to listen and slow to speak." It stands out that
in such a small book the author dedicates fourteen verses to a theme that
for many is not foundational. This means that the author wants to call
attention to a problem within the community to which rightful importance is not given. Moreover, he places it as a foundational criterion to
indicate if one's spirituality in everyday life is false or true. We know that
the theme of the control of the tongue is common in wisdom literature,
both Hebrew and Hellenistic. However, the reiteration and extent of the
theme reveals a grave problem within the community that the recipients
must take very seriously.

James 1:26 presents a similar structure to 1:27.

A If any think they are religious,
    B and do not bridle their tongues but deceive their hearts,
A' their religion is worthless. (NRSV)

This verse, we said, is the introduction of what he will develop in G' (3:1–12). From this point on, it is clear that restraining the tongue is the criterion that indicates whether a person's religiosity is an empty spirituality or a genuine one. All the devotion that someone believes one has toward God is worth nothing if one is not in control of one's words, and one is self-deceived (*apataō*, 1:26) or, better, pleases only oneself. In the Septuagint the verb *apataō* sometimes appears as "enjoy," "entertain," or "give pleasure" (Johnson 1995, 211). The verse orients the interpretation that should be given to the theme developed extensively in 3:1–12.

Let us look at the structure to have a vision of the whole:

3:1 Introduction to the whole chapter
A 3:2 We all offend with words. The one who does not do so is perfect.
    B 3:3–4 Illustrations: horses and large ships are controlled by something small.
        C 3:5 The tongue, a small member, boasts of great things; like a small flame it sets a whole forest on fire.
        C' 3:6 The tongue has a great destructive power: it can put an end to the whole creation.
    B' 3:7–8 Every wild animal has been able to be controlled, but not the tongue. The tongue is a mortal evil that controls the body.
A' 3:9–12 Call to be integral, perfect, and to bless God and human beings.

In section G' (3:1–12), the author explains the importance, power, and danger of the tongue. The introduction in 3:1 seems strange and disconnected from the following verses. It speaks of the great responsibility of being a teacher, because such a one will be judged more severely than the rest. Therefore, the author of James recommends considering carefully whether one wants to be a teacher. The only connection that we find with the tongue is that teachers need to use it to teach, that is, they teach with their words. But that is not the only reason for 3:1. In fact, it could be the introduction to the whole chapter because the second part of the chapter will deal with the wise and wisdom. In any case, what interests us here are the verses that allude to the use of words. The structure of the discourse is the following.

The author begins by affirming that the perfect, mature, integral, complete person is the one who does not cause offense with words, because if one manages to restrain the tongue, one can restrain the whole body and thus has self-control. But the reality, the author indicates, is that in some way we all fail, and he includes himself. Then he begins to speak of the power of the tongue using three examples or illustrations, two positive and one negative. The horse is controlled by the bit that is placed in its mouth; only with that will the horse obey the rider. The great ships are also controlled by a small device, the rudder. It does not matter how big the storms and the winds are—the rudder directs the vessel to where one desires.

The negative illustration introduces the destructive power of the tongue. A spark, a match, or a cigarette butt can produce a great fire and put an end to a forest. The tongue, says the author, is the same. On the one hand, it boasts of great things, like the rudder of a ship. We would say that with a good rhetorical discourse it is possible to move masses of people and lead them to the point of view of the one who uses the tongue. But on the other hand, that same small member can put an end to many lives, like the spark puts an end to the forest. Verse 6 continues with the destructive power of the tongue. The author describes the maximum perversion to which the bad use of words can lead. In these circumstances the tongue is influenced by the principle of evil, that is, hell: it destroys the existence of everything created, beginning with the life of the person and of those nearby. "Body" can refer to the life of the person or to those who constitute the assembly. Verse 7 responds to the illustrations: Humanity has been able to tame every kind of animal, whether they live on land, in the seas, or in the air. Likewise, they have controlled horses with the bit, or the ship with the rudder. But they have not been able to control a small organ that is in their body. Verse 8 radicalizes the evil power of the tongue that, like serpents, injects mortal venom. The author is quite pessimistic regarding dominion or control of the tongue. That is why the person that does control it is perfect.

The author finishes the discourse on the theme alluding to the lack of integrity in the use of the tongue (3:9–12). He explicitly touches spirituality, but false spirituality, that which on the one hand blesses God but on the other curses people. People are like images of God here on the earth, therefore by cursing people one curses God. For the author it is imperfection to bless and to curse, since one uses the same means of communication. There are no perfect people in reality, but with this exhortation it is possible that people correct themselves permanently and meditate on what they are going to say. The goal is to be consistent and whole. The author gives three illustrations from nature: the spring, the fig tree, and the vine. The salty spring always produces salty water, the fig tree always produces figs, and the vine always produces grapes. The recipients of the letter who live in the hostile context of the Roman Empire must walk toward that perfection.

Conclusion

We have undertaken a rereading of James, emphasizing the condition of the recipients as communities of immigrant Jewish followers of Jesus, established in any province of the Roman Empire outside of Palestine. They are communities whose members suffer both economic problems and problems of discrimination for their ethnicity, for their faith, and for being foreigners. These communities also experience problems inside the community, such as the lack of solidarity of some with the poorest and rivalry among those who seek money and power. This happens because the context of the empire seduces them, and its values—which are contrary to those of the prophetic tradition and Jesus—have been introduced into the congregation. The desire to have and accumulate goods leads them to envy and a lack of sensitivity and solidarity with the neediest. As an antidote to that situation, James writes a circular letter exhorting them to assume a liberating spirituality, one visible in a lifestyle that is whole and consistent with their faith in Jesus Christ. This kind of spirituality goes beyond praises, fasting, and prayer since it is expressed in all the relationships among people and is marked by a consistency between what one says and what one does. It becomes especially visible in one's solidarity with the neediest and in one's self-control and maturity in the use of words.

Textual Criticism and the Editio Critica Maior of James

Peter J. Gurry and Tommy Wasserman

The task of textual criticism is to recover the earliest text of a work that no longer exists in its first form. In addition, textual criticism often asks further questions about how that text was read, received, and changed over time. The text of James has come down to us in at least 662 Greek manuscripts (Aland and Aland 1989, 79) as well as many more in Latin, Coptic, Syriac, Ethiopic, and other translations. Further witnesses to its text include citations by church fathers, although here James is not nearly so well endowed as are the Gospels or Paul, for example.

The earliest witnesses are fragmentary papyri. P20 and P23 date to the third century and contain text from Jas 2:19–3:9 and 1:10–12, 15–18, respectively. P100 is dated to the third/fourth century and contains text from Jas 3:13–4:4; 4:9–5:1. The first complete copy of James in Greek is found in the fourth century uncials, Codex Sinaiticus (‭א‬ 01) and Codex Vaticanus (B 03). Today these two remain the most important sources for reconstructing the initial text of James which, along with the rest of the New Testament, has suffered from the ravages of weather, war, religious persecution, and, above all, the wayward pen of copyists. In all, there are 2,724 textual variants in 820 places of textual variation in James according to the most extensive critical edition of James ever published, the Editio Critica Maior or ECM (Mink 2004, 18, 78 n. 14). Most of these variants, of course, are not significant for interpretation—over one quarter are nonsense readings.

This chapter will introduce this important edition and its relationship to its smaller siblings, the Nestle Aland (NA[28]) and United Bible Societies' (UBS[5]) editions of the Greek New Testament. Discussing the ECM also requires an introduction to a new computer-assisted method behind it known as the Coherence-Based Genealogical Method. Finally, an example variant from James is discussed to show how the ECM and Coherence-Based Genealogical Method can be used to resolve textual problems.

A New Edition of James: The ECM

The most important development in the textual criticism of James in the last century is the publication of the ECM. The first installment, covering James, was published in 1997 (Aland et al. 1997), with the remainder of the Catholic Letters following in 2000, 2003, and 2004 (Aland et al. 2000, 2003, 2004). The second, revised edition of the entire Catholic Letters was published in 2013 (Aland et al. 2013), and its text has since been adopted in the NA[28] and UBS[5]. The ECM has been widely praised for its clarity, accuracy, and extensive detail. In its more popular form of the NA[28] and UBS[5], the text of the ECM is now the starting point for scholars, students, and translators around the world, although many of these users have little or no firsthand knowledge of the much larger ECM.

Brief History

The origin of the ECM lies in the 1960s when Kurt Aland, Jean Duplacy, and Bonifatius Fischer first conceived of a new edition of the Greek New Testament that would be for their day what Constantin von Tischendorf's (1869–1872) eighth edition had been for his, namely, a comprehensive edition that provided an up-to-date, expansive, and reliable apparatus as well as a new, critically-reconstructed text (Aland 1970, esp. 163–64).[1] The driving force behind this edition was Aland himself, along with a small group of colleagues at the Institute for New Testament Textual Research in Münster, Germany. In 1983, Kurt Aland's leadership transferred to his wife, Barbara, who oversaw work on the ECM until 2004, when Holger Strutwolf succeeded her in the role of director of the institute. Today, work on the ECM continues; volumes on Acts appeared in 2017, and those on the Synoptic Gospels will follow. Concurrently, work

---

1. An apparatus (or critical apparatus) accompanies a text critical edition of an ancient text and displays the primary source material. In the case of NA[28]/UBS[5], the textual witnesses cited in the apparatus at the bottom of each page are Greek manuscripts, early translations (versions), and quotations of the New Testament by early Christian writers (church fathers). For details about the critical apparatus in NA[28], see that volume's introduction, 55–81*.

is being done on John and certain Pauline letters at the University of Bir-
mingham (UK), Thessalonians at the Aristotle University of Thessaloniki,
the Pastoral Letters at Shepherds Theological Seminary (US), and Revelation at the University of Wuppertal.

Purpose and Scope

The introduction to the ECM lays out clearly the goal of the edition to
provide "the full range of resources necessary for scholarly research in
establishing the text and reconstructing the history of the New Testament
text during its first thousand years" (Aland et al. 2013a, 21*). The nature of
"the text" that is established has been the source of some misunderstanding, not least because of the adoption of the term "initial text" (from the
German *Ausgangstext*) to refer to it (Epp 2014; Gurry 2017, 89–101). The
confusion is part of a larger debate among New Testament textual scholars
about the nature of the "original text" itself as a proper or even possible
goal for the discipline (Epp 1999; Holmes 2013). Despite the muddle, the
ECM itself is quite clear on the matter, explaining that the "initial text" is
"a hypothesis about the text from which the entire tradition originated"
(Aland et al. 2013a, 30*). It needs emphasizing that this point *from which*
the entire extant tradition started may not always take us back to the original authors. Sometimes it may take us close without quite getting us there.
In the case of James and the other Catholic Letters, however, the editors
believe that there is little reason to suppose any substantial gap between
the two. Thus, they claim that their initial text is "a hypothesis about the
text of the *authors*" (Aland et al. 2013a, 30*, emphasis added). This is not
to say they were always able to determine the initial text to their own satisfaction. On the contrary, they have used a diamond (♦) symbol in the
ECM (and the NA[28]/UBS[5]) to mark places where the editors "cannot assess
which variant [of two] has a higher claim to be the initial one" (Aland et al.
2013a, 34*). In total, there are forty-three diamonds used in the Catholic
Letters, eight of which are in James (1:22; 2:11; 3:4; 4:9, 12, 14; 5:4, 18).
In these places, the ECM prints a split main line whereas the NA[28]/UBS[5]
default to the reading from their previous editions in the main text, placing the alternate reading in the apparatus. (In future editions of the NA/
UBS, the alternative reading may be placed in the margin.)

In terms of scope, the edition includes the evidence from 183 Greek
manuscripts of the Catholic Letters (Aland et al. 2013a, 22*) along with
information from the three major translations (Latin, Syriac, and Coptic),

later translations (Armenian, Georgian, Old Church Slavonic, and Ethiopic), and Greek patristic citations up through the time of John of Damascus in the seventh/eighth century. In terms of the Greek evidence, all variants are recorded with the exception of the most common spelling differences. Even nonsense readings—those that made neither logical nor grammatical sense to the editors—are marked with an f (for the German *Fehler*) in the main apparatus and given in full in the supplementary volume (Aland et al. 2013b, §2.4). For patristic citations, the editors made a decision to be "restrictive in order to ensure their reliability" (Aland et al. 2013a, 23*). In practice, this means patristic sources are cited only where their text is identical with that found in Greek manuscripts with only rare exceptions. Fortunately, the supplementary volume includes full references to these citations, a major advantage over the nominal citations of the NA/UBS hand editions that leave readers to track references down themselves.

In terms of Greek manuscripts, the introduction explains that 183 of 522 Greek manuscripts were selected using ninety-eight test passages. From this, it is claimed that the ECM contains "all the known readings which have appeared in the history of the text from its earliest beginnings through the formation and final establishment of the Byzantine text" (Aland et al. 2013a, 22*). Certainly the scope of the edition has been admirably achieved. Even still, users of the ECM need to be aware that it remains a *major* edition (*editio maior*), not a *maximal* one (*editio maxima*). A comparison of the ECM with the exhaustive collation for Jude (Wasserman 2006), for example, shows that the four hundred or so witnesses excluded from the ECM still contain interesting and occasionally significant variants. In all, the ECM includes a little less than half the variants extant in all our Greek manuscripts of Jude.[2] Similar numbers would probably be found for James were the data available.

Layout of the Edition

The layout of the ECM can intimidate the first-time reader, but repeated use discloses the edition's remarkable clarity and efficiency so that, in time, it becomes quite natural to use. To illustrate the layout, a sample from James 2:1 is provided in figure 1.

---

2. Wasserman's edition of Jude records 1,694 variants compared to the ECM's 789, the 145 in NA[28], and the 47 in UBS[5] (cf. Gurry 2016b, 110).

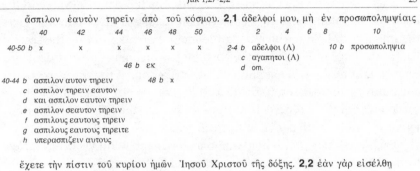

ἄσπιλον ἑαυτὸν τηρεῖν ἀπὸ τοῦ κόσμου. **2,1** ἀδελφοί μου, μὴ ἐν προσωπολημψίαις
        40   42   44   46   48   50   2   4   6   8   10

40-50 *b* x   x   x   x   x   x   2-4 *b* αδελφοι (Λ)   *10 b* προσωποληψια
                                 46 *b* εκ   *c* αγαπητοι (Λ)
                                                   d om.

40-44 *b* ασπιλον αυτον τηρειν   48 *b* x
     c ασπιλον τηρειν εαυτον
     d και ασπιλον εαυτον τηρειν
     e ασπιλον σεαυτον τηρειν
     f ασπιλους εαυτους τηρειν
     g ασπιλους εαυτους τηρειτε
     h υπερασπιζειν αυτους

ἔχετε τὴν πίστιν τοῦ κυρίου ἡμῶν Ἰησοῦ Χριστοῦ τῆς δόξης. **2,2** ἐὰν γὰρ εἰσέλθῃ
      12   14   16   18   20   22   24   26   28   30   2   4   6

12 *b* εχητε   18-30 *b* της δοξης του κυριου ημων ιησου χριστου   *7 b* τις
                       c του κυριου ημων ιησου χριστου
                       d του χριστου
                       e ιησου χριστου

Jak 2,1

2-4 *a* αδελφοι μου P74. 01. 02. 03. 04. 025. 044. 5. 33.
        69. 81. 88. 206. 218. 322. 323. 398. 400. 429. 436.
        522. 614. 621. 623. 629. 630. 631. 808. 915. 918.
        945. 996. 1067. 1127. 1175. 1241. 1243. 1270. 1292.
        1297. 1359. 1409. 1448. 1490. 1505. 1524. 1563.
        1598. 1609. 1611. 1661. 1678. 1718. 1735. 1739.
        1799. 1831. 1842. 1852. 1890. 2138. 2147. 2200.
        2298. 2344. 2412. 2464. 2492. 2495. 2523. 2541.
        2652. 2805. **Byz**. PsOec. **L:**FV. **S:**H

    b αδελφοι (Λ) 1251. 1751. 2243. L427. L590. L593.
        L596. L884. L921. L938. L1141. L1281. L1441. L2087.
        Antioch. Cyr

    c αγαπητοι (Λ) L422

    d om. L623

    ↔ a/b 2374. **K:**SB. **S:**P

    − P20. P23. P54. 048. 0166. 0173. 0246. 1066. 1846.
        L60. L156. L170. L1126. L1442

10 *a* προσωπολημψιαις 01. 02. 03*. 04. 1175. Antioch.
        Cyr. PsOec. **S:**H

    ao προσωπολημψιαις 03C2. 025. 044. 5. 33. 69. 81.
        88. 206. 218. 322. 323. 398. 400f2. 429. 436. 522.
        614. 621. 623. 629. 630. 631. 808. 915. 918. 945.
        996. 1067. 1127. 1241. 1243. 1270. 1292. 1297. 1359.
        1409. 1448. 1490. 1505. 1524. 1563. 1598. 1609.
        1611. 1661. 1678. 1718. 1735. 1739. 1751f3. 1799.
        1831. 1842. 1852. 1890. 2138. 2147. 2200. 2298.
        2344. 2374. 2412. 2464. 2492. 2495. 2523. 2541.
        2652. 2805. **Byz** [459(*f1). 2243(*f2). L2087f4]

    b προσωποληψια 442. L884. **K:**SBA^V. **A**^{mss}

    ↔ a/ao/b P74

    ↔ a/b **L:**FV. **S:**P

    ↔ ao/b 2423

    − P20. P23. P54. 048. 0166. 0173. 0246. 1066. 1846.
        L60. L156. L170. L1126. L1442

12 *a* εχετε ... 38f. Antioch. Cyr. PsOec

    b εχητε 61. 94. 459. 642. 808. 996. 1127. 1661

    ↔ a/b **L:**FV. **K:**SB. **S:**PH

    − P20. P23. P54. 048. 0166. 0173. 0246. 1066. 1846.
        L60. L156. L170. L1126. L1442

18-30 *a* του κυριου ημων ιησου χριστου της δοξης 01.
        02. 03. 04. 025. 044. 5. 69. 81. 88. 218. 322. 323. 398.
        400. 621. 623. 629. 808. 915. 918. 945. 996. 1127.
        1175. 1241. 1243f. 1270. 1297. 1359. 1524. 1563.
        1598. 1609. 1661. 1678. 1718. 1735. 1739. 1751.
        1842. 1852. 2298. 2374. 2464. 2492. 2523. 2805.
        Byz. Cyr. PsOec. **L:**FV

    b της δοξης του κυριου ημων ιησου χριστου
        206. 429. 436. 522. 614. 630. 1067. 1292. 1367. 1409.
        1448. 1490. 1505. 1611. 1799. 1831. 1890. 2080.
        2138. 2147. 2200. 2412. 2495. 2541. 2652. **K:**S^{mss}B.
        S:PH

    c του κυριου ημων ιησου χριστου 33. 631.
        Antioch

    d του χριστου 2344

    e ιησου χριστου **K:**S^{ms}

    ? **K:**S^{ms}

    ↔ a/b **Ā**

    − P20. P23. P54. P74. 048. 0166. 0173. 0246. 1066.
        1846. L60. L156. L170. L1126. L1442

Jak 2,2

2 *a* εαν ...

    ao αν 442

7 *a* om. ... Antioch. PsOec. **L:**FV. **S:**PH

    b τις 398. Cyr. **G:**B

    ↔ a/b **K:**SBA

    − P20. P23. P54. P74. 048. 0166. 0173. 0246. 1066.
        1846. L60. L156. L170. L1126. L1442

Fig. 1. A sample from Aland et al. 2013a for Jas 2:1

Each page is divided into two sections. The top half is devoted to the editorial text along with the main variant readings. The main line gives the initial text, below which hang the main variants from it. The second half of the page is devoted to the apparatus, which gives greater detail for each variant reading. What immediately strikes one is the sheer size of the apparatus in comparison to the text. Whereas the NA[28] lists only a single variation with three different readings for Jas 2:1, the ECM gives four different variations with a total of thirteen readings.

Each verse starts with bold numbers for chapter and verse (**2,1**). New to the ECM are further numbers referencing the words and spaces for each verse. These are assigned anew for each verse, with words assigned even numbers and the spaces between them odd numbers. Within these, each individual reading is assigned a letter of the alphabet. In this way, the ECM allows for precise references not only to verses, but also to variation units, and even to specific variant readings within them. For example, the first variation unit in Jas 2:1 can be referenced with "Jas 2:1/2–4." If we want to refer to the first variant (*my brothers* = ἀδελφοί μου, *adelphoi mou*) we can do so using "Jas 2:1/2–4a." At the bottom of the page we see this variant listed under "2–4," which is, in turn, listed under the bold heading "Jak 2,1."[3]

The editors' initial text (or *Ausgangstext*) is always the first reading and hence designated *a*. At Jas 2:1/2–4, there are four readings: (*a*) *my brothers* (ἀδελφοί μου, *adelphoi mou*), (*b*) *brothers* (ἀδελφοί, *adelphoi*), (*c*) *beloved* (ἀγαπητοί, *agapētoi*), and (*d*) an omission. Whenever a reading is considered as an orthographic difference or a nonsense reading, an *o* or an *f* is appended to mark them as such (cf. reading *ao* at Jas 2:1/10).[4] Following these variant letter addresses, we find two more notations. The first is a bidirectional arrow (↔) followed by "a/b" to indicate that the editors could not decide whether the witnesses cited have reading *a* or reading *b*. Last, a dash (–) marks witnesses with lacunae or another defect at this point.

For each variant reading, the evidence is cited in the order of Greek manuscripts (in the order of papyri, majuscules, minuscules, and lectionaries)

---

3. The book references here and at the top of each page are one place where the ECM is not bilingual but instead follows German abbreviations. "Jak" is short for *Jakubus*, i.e., James. Likewise, German often uses commas where English uses periods and vice versa.

4. As noted above, the *f* is for the German *Fehler*, which means "error."

followed in turn by church fathers and the versions.[5] Each witness is separated by a period, and we should note that the majuscules are always cited by their Gregory-Aland numbers rather than their alphabetic designations (thus, e.g., 03 and not B for Codex Vaticanus). However, the supplementary volume does offer both (Aland et al. 2013b, §2). The abbreviation "Byz" is used to represent a group of manuscripts that preserve the Byzantine text in James.[6] All ninety-seven of these manuscripts are listed in the supplement along with the sixty-one places in James where they differ from the initial text. The versions are listed with a bold letter to designate the versional language (e.g., **S** = Syriac). A colon separates the general language from its specific translations (e.g., **S:PH** = the Syriac Peshitta and Harklean Syriac). Readers will note that these designations follow the German rather than English so that "**K**" is for *Koptisch* (Coptic) and "**Ä**" for *Äthiopisch* (Ethiopic).

At Jas 2:1/2–4 the overwhelming external evidence supports the editors' preferred reading (*a*). The alternatives all bear the marks of either lectionary influence (in the case of *b* and *c*) or an accidental omission in the case of *d*, triggered by the repetition of -μου (*-mou*) in τοῦ κόσμου ἀδελφοί μου (*tou kosmou adelphoi mou*).[7]

A New Method for Editing James:
The Coherence-Based Genealogical Method

Along with the extensive scope of its apparatus, the ECM's other defining characteristic is the use of a new method to establish the initial text. This method is known as the Coherence-Based Genealogical Method, which is

---

5. The Greek manuscripts are divided into four classes: (1) Papyri—often the earliest manuscripts of the New Testament, these are written on papyrus in capital letters (uncial script); (2) Majuscules (or "uncials")—manuscripts written in capital letters on parchment; (3) Minuscules (or "cursives")—manuscripts written in minuscule script on parchment or paper (the letters developed into modern lower case Greek letters); (4) Lectionaries—manuscripts which contain church lessons in the order that they are read (written in uncial or minuscule script on parchment or paper). Note that there is an overlap between these classes in terms of dates, e.g., there are a few early majuscules that are older than many papyri, and some minuscules that are older than late majuscules.

6. The new siglum "Byz" to represent the Byzantine text will successively replace the 𝔐 (Majority Text) in future editions of Nestle-Aland; the change has been implemented in the Catholic Letters of NA[28].

7. Lectionary influence is marked in the ECM by the use of *lambda* (Λ).

a computer-based tool for relating manuscript texts and using these witness relationships to study the most likely relationships of their variants. The method's larger goal is to identify the initial text and trace its development. In this section, we briefly introduce the method, explain how it works, and describe some of the changes it has brought with it.[8]

A Brief History

The Coherence-Based Genealogical Method's origins reach back to the 1970s, when researchers at the Institute for New Testament Textual Research were busy applying computers to textual criticism (Ott 1973; Aland 1979). As part of this effort, Gerd Mink began to work on a way to find new manuscript groups using computer databases. His attempts very quickly moved beyond this into an effort to relate manuscript texts into a stemma or "family tree" (Mink 1982), a goal that has long eluded those who study the New Testament text (see Colwell 1969). In the beginning, Mink was limited to a tiny selection of data, but this changed dramatically with the publication of the ECM of James in 1997 (see Aland et al. 1997a). Although not used in this first installment, the ECM's publication provided the major catalyst for his method in terms of the amount of available data. Whereas James had previously provided only 25 places to compare texts, the new ECM offered 761. Over the next ten years, Mink's method grew and developed in step with the first edition of the ECM of the Catholic Letters so that by its completion in 2005 it had become "indispensable" for the editors (Aland et al. 2004a, 37*). A second edition, this one applying the Coherence-Based Genealogical Method consistently and throughout, was published in 2013 and today the data and tools used to produce it can all be explored online.[9] In less than a decade, Mink's method went from being unused on the ECM to being one of its characteristic features (Aland et al. 2003a, preface), one predicted to be "equal to any past advance" in its significance (Parker 2008, 178). This is a rather swift development for a discipline whose advances are often measured in centuries.

---

8. More extensive introductions can be found—listed here in order of detail and complexity—in Wasserman and Gurry 2017; Gurry 2016a; Wasserman 2015a; Wasserman 2015b; Mink 2011; 2004; 2009.

9. http://intf.uni-muenster.de/cbgm/index_en.html.

How It Works

The Coherence-Based Genealogical Method works in three main steps. In the first step, the editors relate as many variant readings as they can at specific variation units. These variants are related in what are known as "local stemmata." These are essentially family trees applied to variants (see fig. 2).

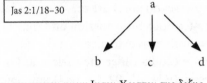

a. του κυριου ημων Ιησου Χριστου της δοξης
b. της δοξης του κυριου ημων ιησου χριστου
c. της κυριου ημων ιησου χριστου
d. του χριστου

Fig. 2. The local stemma for Jas 2:1/18–30

What is novel here is that at each of these local stemmata the computer tracks all the witnesses that attest each reading. In this way, as more and more local stemmata are drawn up, the computer is provided with more and more information about how to relate witnesses. The basic principle is that *the relationships of witnesses can be determined using the relationship of their variants*. At each place of variation, these relationships can be either one of agreement ($a = b$) or disagreement ($a \to b$ or $a \leftarrow b$), or the relationship may be uncertain (a–?–b). Combining this information across a book like James yields what is known in the Coherence-Based Genealogical Method as genealogical coherence. This describes the relationship between two or more witnesses. Comparing 01 and 03 in James, for example, we find that they agree 90 percent of the time (677 of 747 places of comparison). From the seventy places where they disagree, 03 has the prior reading forty-three times ($03 \to 01$), 01 has the prior reading twenty times ($03 \leftarrow 01$), and in seven there is no clear or direct relationship (03–?–01). In this, 03 is said to be a *potential* ancestor of 01 in the Coherence-Based Genealogical Method because it has the greater portion of prior readings.[10]

---

10. Note that in this context "ancestor" does not refer to a physical ancestor of a manuscript, as if 01, e.g., was copied directly from 03, but rather it refers to the differ-

Where this information becomes particularly potent within the Coherence-Based Genealogical Method is when it is applied to a group of witnesses in the form of "textual flow diagrams." These diagrams are drawn at specific points of variation and connect each witness with its closest ancestor by agreement, within the parameters set by the user. In this way, the most likely relationships between witnesses are used to study the relationships of their variants. Where the coherence is generally bad, that is, where the witnesses do not share the same reading with their closest ancestors, this indicates poor transmission and may be taken, depending on the variation in question, as evidence that the reading is secondary.

As an example, we can consider the variant at Jas 1:12/31 where our oldest Greek witnesses (P74, 01, 02, 03, 044) and some others read that those who endure suffering will receive "the crown of life, which *he* promises [ἐπηγγείλατο, *epēngeilato*] to those who love him." The awkwardness of not specifying who gives the crown must have been felt by scribes since we find the following readings:

(*a*) omit
(*b*) "Lord" (κύριος, *kyrios*)
(*c*) "the Lord" (ὁ κύριος, *ho kyrios*)
(*d*) "God" (ὁ θεός, *ho theos*)
(*e*) "the true God" (ὁ ἀψευδὴς θεός, *ho apseudēs theos*)

To see the coherence between the witnesses that attest each of these readings, the computer can display only those cases where a witness disagrees with one of its ten closest ancestors. In this, we are asking to see where coherence is at its *worst*. The resulting textual flow diagram is shown in figure 3.

The arrows show us where witnesses disagree with their closest ancestors. Each witness is bounded by a box grouping witnesses with the same reading at this point. From this, we can see evidence for multiple witnesses dropping the article from reading *c* to produce reading *b* (e.g., 104 → 459) and the reverse is never attested. Reading *a* produces all the other readings except for *e* (A → 04; A → 025; 02 → 1735). Finally, there is one case where reading *a* develops from reading *c* (2423 → 996). This entails the phrase "the Lord" being lost, which is not hard to imagine happening by acci-

---

ent stage of the texts in these two witnesses, i.e., 03 contains a higher proportion of prior readings.

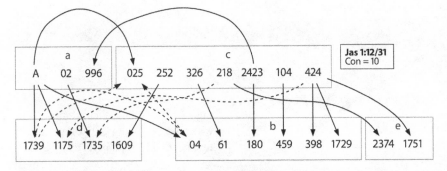

Fig. 3. The textual flow diagram for Jas 1:12/31 showing those relationships where a witness disagrees with its ten closest potential ancestors at this point. The solid lines connect witnesses with their closest potential ancestor and the dashed lines with their second or third closest.

dent at least once. Overall, the diagram reinforces our initial explanation, namely, that the absence of an explicit subject was a vacuum that scribes abhorred and so filled repeatedly.

Using textual flow diagrams like this one, the editors check their work against their own earlier decisions. These diagrams sometimes confirm their earlier decisions but sometimes challenge them. Once the editors have reviewed enough of their own decisions in this way, the second major step of the Coherence-Based Genealogical Method is to reduce the number of potential ancestors for each witness. This process produces what are known as "optimal substemmata," as shown for witness 35 in figure 4.

These substemmata provide a map of the most likely influences for each witness. Once enough are constructed, they can be combined into a "global stemma" in the third and final step of the Coherence-Based Genealogical Method. This final stemma is global in that it encompasses all the editors' decisions in the local stemmata; ideally, none are left out. The global stemma can then be used to investigate further historical questions about how the text developed over time (cf. Wachtel 2015, 5–6; Gurry 2017, 145–79). The very top of the global stemma for the Catholic Letters is shown in figure 5.

Unfortunately, no complete global stemma for the Catholic Letters yet exists, in part because its current construction requires significant manual input from the editor. Hopefully in the future more automated approaches can be used to speed up the process.[11]

---

11. For one way to do this, see Gurry 2017, 167.

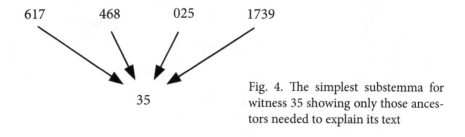

Fig. 4. The simplest substemma for witness 35 showing only those ancestors needed to explain its text

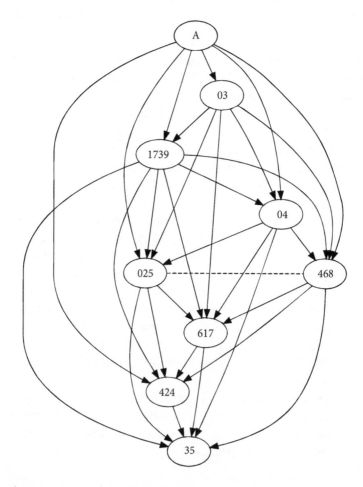

Fig. 5. The top portion of the global stemma for the Catholic Letters

The Effect on Textual Criticism

Along with the new data provided by genealogical coherence, the Coherence-Based Genealogical Method has brought with it a number of other important changes to the discipline of textual criticism including (1) a slight shift in goal; (2) changes to the text of the Catholic Letters; (3) newly valued witnesses including the Byzantine text; and (4) the rejection of most text-types as useful to the editors.

Starting with the first of these, we have already noted that the Coherence-Based Genealogical Method and the ECM are aimed at the initial text rather than an unqualified original text. This initial text may be the text of the author but may not be. In the case of James and the other Catholic Letters, the editors think that their hypothetical initial text is a close approximation to it. However, the qualification "hypothetical" here is meant to convey that this text is open to revision. In cases where the diamond is used, the editors have signaled their inability to decide on the initial text.

This leads to the second change, which is the most obvious, namely, changes to the text of NA and UBS. For the Catholic Letters as a whole, there were thirty-three changes (see NA[28], 50*–51*), five of which are found in James (1:20; 2:3, 4, 15; 4:10). Most of these do not carry great exegetical weight, but we will discuss the textual change in Jas 2:3 in detail below, which does affect the meaning somewhat. However, we should include here changes where the editors recorded their own uncertainty about the text. In earlier editions of the NA, the editors used square brackets to mark where they were "not completely convinced" of the authenticity of text (NA[27], 49*). In the NA[28], they have abandoned the brackets for the diamond, which instead marks places where they have left their decision "open" (NA[28], 51*). Whereas the NA[27] marked only two places in James with brackets (4:12, 5:14), the NA[28] marks eight places with the diamond (1:20; 2:11; 3:4; 4:9, 12, 14; 5:4, 18). In this, the editors are less certain about the text of this epistle more often. If we compare both editions of the ECM to the NA[27], we find a total of twenty places in James where they differ either in terms of what the editorial text is or about whether they are uncertain about it (Gurry 2017, 223–24).

A third change introduced by the Coherence-Based Genealogical Method is the importance ascribed to certain witnesses. The editors now evaluate manuscripts partly based on how closely the texts of these manuscripts are to the editors' initial text. This has led to a new appreciation for the Byzantine text as a whole. This can be seen in two ways. First, five of the thirteen witnesses included in the list of consistently cited witnesses for James are Byzantine: 307, 442, 642, 1243, 2492 (NA[27], 62*; NA[28], 65*; cf. Aland et al. 2013b, 10). Second, because Byzantine witnesses were found so close to their own initial text from the ECM1, the editors revisited all the places where the unified Byzantine text disagreed with their own text (Aland et al. 2013a, 34*). As a result, ten of twelve changes between their first use of the Coherence-Based Genealogical Method on the Catholic Letters and their second use are in favor of the Byzantine readings over against readings found in witnesses from the third to fifth centuries such as P72, Sinaiticus (01), Alexandrinus (02), Vaticanus (03), and Ephraemi Rescriptus (04).[12] In the editors' own words, the Byzantine text is "an important witness to the early text," agreeing with their initial text of James in 700 of 761 places (Aland et al. 2013b, 10–11).

Finally, and most importantly, the use of the Coherence-Based Genealogical Method has led the editors of the NA[28]/UBS[5] to reject most text-types. For over a century, New Testament scholars have spoken about the "Alexandrian," "Western," "Byzantine" (or "Syrian"), and sometimes "Caesarean" text-types.[13] The main benefit of these groupings is that they have often been related to each other and then assigned relative values. Traditionally, the Alexandrian has been thought to be best and the Byzantine the worst. For reconstructing the text of the New Testament, they are seemingly indispensable.[14] For many, New Testament textual criticism can hardly be conceived of without these comfortable categories. But this is precisely what the editors using the Coherence-Based Genealogical Method have done, the only exception being the retention of the Byzantine text, which they still recognize as a historically identifiable "text," though not one created as a concerted recension in the fourth century (Wasserman and Gurry 2017, 9; Gurry 2018). Aside from the Byzantine text, however, they have largely replaced appeals to text-types and their relative value with appeals to over one hundred *individual* witnesses and their relationships within the Coherence-Based Genealogical Method.[15] The computer's ability to keep track of these numerous relationships

---

12. Jas 1:20; 2:4, 15; 4:10; 1 Pet 5:1; 2 Pet 2:18, 20; 2 John 5, 12; 3 John 4.

13. Not all of these are equally relevant to all parts of the New Testament, of course.

14. As a thought experiment, one might consider how much of Bruce Metzger's (1994) textual commentary would need to be rewritten in light of this shift.

15. It should be noted that this rejection was presaged in the Alands' adoption of

makes text-types unnecessary in practice. More importantly, by focusing on individual witnesses instead of text-types, the editors have completely bypassed the knotty problem of defining where one text-type ends and another begins. Instead, the individual manuscript texts become the locus of the investigation. Whether other scholars will accept or reject this conclusion about text-types remains to be seen (contrast Parker 2008, 171–74 with Epp 2013, 556–71). What is certain is that no one working on textual criticism can afford to ignore the seismic shift represented in the ECM and, by implication, the NA[28] and UBS[5], too.

Example: A Change to the Text of James 2:3

In Jas 2:3–4, the author warns his readers not to make distinctions between the rich and the poor:

> and if you take notice of the one wearing the fine clothes and say, "Have a seat here, please," while to the one who is poor you say, "Stand there," or, "Sit at my feet," have you not made distinctions among yourselves, and become judges with evil thoughts? (NRSV)

The textual problem in this example has traditionally concerned the placement of the adverb "there" (ἐκεῖ, *ekei*) in the address to the poor person. The NRSV reflects the Greek text in NA[27], σὺ στῆθι ἐκεῖ ἢ κάθου ὑπὸ τὸ ὑποπόδιόν μου, " 'Stand **there**,' or 'Sit at my feet,' " which has now been changed in the ECM (and NA[28]) to σὺ στῆθι ἢ κάθου ἐκεῖ ὑπὸ τὸ ὑποπόδιόν μου, " 'Stand,' or 'Sit **there** at my feet.' " The ECM gives us the following readings and attesting witnesses at Jas 2:3/44–48:

(a) η καθου εκει 03. 945. 1175. 1241. 1243. 1739. 1852. 2298. 2492. **L**:F. **K**:S^mss

(b) εκει η καθου 02. 044. 33. 81. 206. 218. 429. 522. 614. 630. 996. 1292. 1359. 1448T. 1505. 1611. 1661. 1718. 1799. 1890. 2138. 2200. 2412. 2495. Cyr. **L**:V. **K**:S^ms. **S**:H. **Ä**

(c) εκει και καθου 04*

(d) εκει η καθου ωδε 01. 025. 5. 69f2. 88. 322. 323. 398. 400. 436. 621. 623. 629. 631. 808. 915. 918. 1067. 1127. 1270. 1297. 1409. 1448Z.

---

manuscript "categories" in place of the traditional text-types (Aland and Aland 1989, 332–37).

1490. 1524. 1598. 1609. 1678. 1735. 1751. 1831. 1842. 2147. 2344.
2374. 2464. 2523. 2541. 2652. 2805. **Byz** [252(*f1)]. PsOec. **K**:B.
S:P. **G**:G-D. **SI**:ChDMSi

(*e*) εχει και καθου ωδε 04C2. **K**:S[ms]

(*f*) εχει 1563

(*g*) ωδε η καθου εχει 365

↔ *d*/*e* P74 (the papyrus is damaged but supports either reading *d* or *e*)

The main choice here is between readings *a*, *b*, or *d*. In previous editions
of NA/UBS, reading *b* was adopted. On behalf of the UBS editorial committee, Bruce M. Metzger explained that the long reading *d* is secondary:
ὧδε, "here," was added to create "a better parallelism," corresponding to the
previous address to the rich ("'Have a seat *here*, please'" ... "'Stand there'
or 'sit *here* at my feet'"). Further, the adverb clarifies that the place "at my
feet" (literally "by my footstool") is near to the speaker.[16] Metzger rightly
points out that this reading nevertheless supports the position of ἐκεῖ,
"there," immediately after στῆθι, "stand" (as in reading *b*). The committee further proposed that reading *a*, attested by Codex Vaticanus (B 03),
1739, and some other witnesses, transposed ἐκεῖ so that the passage refers
to two places rather than three: the rich person is to sit *here* (ὧδε) whereas
the poor is asked either to stand or sit *there* (ἐκεῖ) by my footstool.[17] This
scenario presupposes the stemma shown in figure 6.

James H. Ropes, however, defended the reading of Codex Vaticanus as
the initial, and more difficult reading (*lectio difficilior*), which led to various emendations. He explained that

> the reading of B ff makes the rough words an invitation to stand or to
> take a poor seat.... The readings of A *al* and ℵ *al* seem to be different
> emendations, both due to the wish to make στῆθι explicit and so to create
> a better parallelism ... the effect is to lessen rather than intensify the
> rudeness of στῆθι, and the product is a weaker text than that of B ff (sah).
> The text of B ff is thus on both external ... and internal grounds to be
> preferred. (1916, 191)

---

16. Metzger 1994, 609–10. Interestingly, the rating expressing the confidence
of the committee was upgraded from "C" to "B" between UBS[3] and UBS[4] to reflect
increased confidence, before the text was changed in UBS[5].

17. Most commentators who discuss the passage adopt reading *b* on similar
grounds, e.g., Dibelius 1976, 131; Davids 1982, 109; Johnson 1995, 223. Ropes (1916,
191) is an exception.

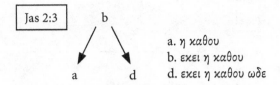

Fig. 6. The stemma previously assumed by the UBS committee in Jas 2:3

In a comment on this change in the ECM1, one of the editors, B. Aland, suggested that readings *a* and *b* were "almost of equal value" but nevertheless suggested that the reader (an ancient scribe) would have expected the adverb ἐκεῖ, "there," to follow immediately after στῆθι, "sit" (as it does in readings *b–e*), in parallel with the previous address to the rich (Aland 1998, 11). In regard to reading *d*, she added, "In addition to putting ἐκεῖ after σὺ στῆθι, the Byzantine reading *d* augments ἢ κάθου with the adverb ὧδε" (Aland 1998, 11).

By this time, the Coherence-Based Genealogical Method had not yet been applied to the text of James. The decision was made on purely philological grounds, and reading *a* with the simple στῆθι was considered slightly better than reading *b*. The latter was, however, marked with a bold dot to indicate a passage "of equal status" (Aland et al. 1997a, 11*; cf. Aland et al. 2000a, 24*).[18] In the ECM2 (Aland et al. 2013a), the adopted variant was retained, apparently confirmed by the application of the Coherence-Based Genealogical Method. However, the editors changed their mind about reading *d*, which is not restricted to the Byzantine tradition; it is attested by Codex Sinaiticus and a number of other significant textual witnesses that have largely been unknown in the past but have turned out to be close to the reconstructed initial text.[19] On the basis of thousands of other textual decisions in the Catholic Letters, the accumulated genealogical data suggest that reading *b* originated from reading *d* and not the reverse, as earlier commentators had presumed.

---

18. In effect, this decision marked a return to Westcott and Hort (1881, 1:319), who adopted reading *a* but noted reading *b* in the margin as an alternative reading.

19. In addition to Codex Sinaiticus, there are six other witnesses to reading *d* that are even closer to the reconstructed initial text (A) in the Catholic Letters: 323 (91.5%), 025 (91.4%), 623 (90.7%), 808 (90.6%), 5 (90.4%), 1735 (90.3%), 01 (90.0%). See "Potential Ancestors and Descendants" at http://intf.uni-muenster.de/cbgm2/PotAnc5.html.

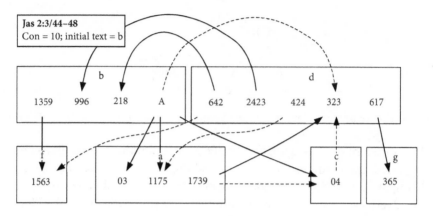

Fig. 7. Coherence at Jas 2:3/44–48 if reading b is designated the initial text

Figure 7 illustrates the genealogical coherence in the variation unit if we presume that reading *b* is the initial text. Here we see that in 218 and 996, in particular, reading *b* more likely originates from witnesses with reading *d* and not the initial text. The same is true for 323, which is an important witness—its closest potential ancestor (1739) actually attests reading *a*. In this scenario we have to posit that the initial text was created several times by scribes independently.

Figure 8, on the other hand, shows that reading *a* has better coherence in light of the genealogical data in the Catholic Letters; it is not derived from any reading (therefore the box is placed on the top). The textual flow diagram in this case is more consistent with the overall textual flow in the Catholic Letters.

The choice in terms of genealogical coherence rather stands between readings *a* and *d* since reading *d* also shows good coherence when set as the initial text. As we have seen, however, transcriptional evidence strongly suggests that ὧδε, "here," was added to create a parallelism with the previous address to the rich (σὺ κάθου ὧδε, "you sit here").[20] When reading *a* is weighed against reading *d*, Metzger's note that ὧδε, "here," clarifies that the place "by my footstool" is near the speaker, becomes all the more important—the alternative reading *a* with ἐκεῖ, "there by my footstool," is clearly a harder reading. Moreover, it has stronger attestation

---

20. Dibelius and Greeven (Dibelius 1976, 131) state, "The first reading [*d*] can quite certainly be traced back to the unwarranted insertion of ὧδε ('here') by analogy with the preceding words spoken in v 3 to the rich man."

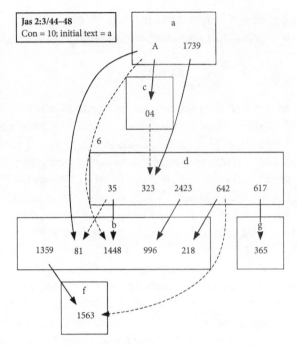

Fig. 8. Coherence at Jas 2:3/44–48 if reading *a* is designated the initial text

from witnesses closer to the initial text than reading *d*, in particular Codex Vaticanus and 1739.[21] In conclusion, the editors chose reading *a* for the ECM2 (and NA[28]/UBS[5]), notably without a diamond.[22] From an exegetical standpoint, the poor person's choice, according to the new text of Jas 2:3, is not so much between two different places in the room as between two

---

21. There are seven witnesses to reading *a* (including Vaticanus and 1739) that agree with the initial text at more than 90% of places of comparison: 03 (96.0%), 1739 (93.0%), 945 (91.4%), 2492 (90.5%), 1175 (90.4%), 1243 (90.4%), 1852 (90.4%). See "Potential Ancestors and Descendants" at http://intf.uni-muenster.de/cbgm2/PotAnc5.html.

22. The bold dot in the ECM1 was not governed by any precise definition; sometimes, but not always, it signaled that an alternative reading was of equal value. In the ECM2, the use of the bold dot was therefore abandoned as the editors admitted that "its definition was inconsistent and too vague" (ECM2, 34*). Now, the diamond symbol is used in passages where the editors could not reach a decision about which text to adopt; i.e., it marks variants that "are both candidates for the initial text" (ECM2, 34*).

unattractive options, either to stand up or to sit down at somebody's feet, in contrast to the attractive seat offered to the rich person.[23]

Conclusion

In this chapter we have introduced the new critical edition, the ECM of James, which is unsurpassed in its scope, including the evidence from 183 Greek manuscripts plus early translations and Greek patristic writers yielding 2,724 variants in 820 places of textual variation. Further, we have introduced the method behind the ECM known as the Coherence-Based Genealogical Method, and how it is used to reconstruct the initial text of New Testament writings. We have considered the main steps of the method: (1) working out local stemmata at specific variation units providing the computer with more and more information about how to relate witnesses; (2) reducing the number of potential ancestors for each witness by creating optimal substemmata (maps of the most likely influences for each witness); and (3) combining all the data into a "global stemma," which encompasses all the editors' decisions in the local stemmata.

The application of the Coherence-Based Genealogical Method has brought about thirty-four textual changes in the Catholic Letters including five in James. Further, there are forty-three variation-units where the editors cannot decide between two competing readings; these passages are marked with diamonds, and there are eight in James. The Coherence-Based Genealogical Method has also brought to light new important witnesses and led to a higher appreciation of the Byzantine text, whereas the traditional scheme of text-types has largely been abandoned.

Finally, we have discussed an example of a textual change in NA[28] as a result of the Coherence-Based Genealogical Method, where Jas 2:3 now reads, σὺ στῆθι ἢ κάθου ἐκεῖ ὑπὸ τὸ ὑποπόδιόν μου, " 'Stand,' or 'Sit there at my feet,' " which is the harder reading. It is important, in this connection, to note that the traditionally accepted criteria of textual criticism, for example, to prefer the harder reading (*lectio difficilior*), still play an important role when evaluating readings.[24] The Coherence-Based Genea-

---

23. Adamson (1976, 107) comments on James's word "footstool" (ὑποπόδιόν, *hypopodion*) here: "To come under or to lick the shoe for the Jew meant slavish subjection and even conquest."

24. For a larger discussion of criteria for evaluating textual variants and the Coherence-Based Genealogical Method, see Wasserman 2013.

logical Method, nevertheless, helps the critic to make decisions that are coherent with the genealogical relationship between witnesses—data that is accumulated successively as a result of the critic's decision-making in thousands of local stemmata. Further, the Coherence-Based Genealogical Method has revealed witnesses that are very close to the editors' initial text of the Catholic Letters. In the case of Jas 2:3, seven witnesses including Codex Vaticanus (03) and 1739 agree with the initial text more than 90 percent.

In all, the ECM and the Coherence-Based Genealogical Method with it are ushering in a new era of textual criticism, one in which the power of the computer is combined with the best of human text-critical practice to reconstruct the initial text of the New Testament and to help us trace its subsequent development.

James "the Brother of the Lord" and the Epistle of James

John Painter

My title brings into sharp focus a number of matters that were contentious in the fourth-century struggle toward the establishment of the New Testament canon.[1] These have become contentious in new ways in recent times. In the fourth century, the authenticity of the epistle as the work of James of Jerusalem, known as James the Just and as "the brother of the Lord," was disputed because it lacked early attestation.[2] Although the role of James as an important early Christian leader is evident in the literary remains of the second century, there is no reference to an epistle from him.[3] In the third century, the epistle was known to Origen (writing ca. 230–251), who quoted it more than thirty times, and when quoting Jas 5:20 he indicated that he believed he was quoting Scripture (*Hom. Lev.* 2.3). He was also aware that this view did not enjoy universal support (*Comm. Jo.*, frag. 6; see Brooke 1896, 2:216; and Painter 2012, 14). By the early fourth century, the Epistle of James appears at the head of the Catholic Epistles, a collection of seven writings which, apart from 1 Peter and 1 John, were not initially received as canonical letters.

By this time, the brothers (including James) and sisters of Jesus (see, e.g., Mark 6:3; Matt 13:55–56; and the discussion below) were widely viewed as older stepbrothers and stepsisters rather than younger siblings of Jesus. This view persisted in the East, but by the end of fourth century they were considered to be cousins via Cleopas and Mary's sister

---

1. For the evidence of the early struggle to establish a canon, see Eusebius, *Hist. eccl.* 2.23.24–25; 3.25; and the discussions in Painter 2004, 142, 234–39; 2012, 10–16.

2. As in my title, I use *James* to refer to the person and *Epistle of James* to refer to the biblical book.

3. For the identification and discussion of the sources, see Painter 2004, 105–58, and the brief summary below.

in the West. The process of distancing James and his siblings from Jesus contributed to the minimization of the leading role of James and Jewish Christianity in the period following the death of Jesus until at least 135 CE. This occurred despite the fact that historical research suggests that James was a/the dominant figure in Jewish Christianity until his death in 62 CE. Even then, the Jewish leadership of the Jewish Jerusalem Chuch survived his death and continued beyond the destruction of Jerusalem until 135 CE. Reading the collection of literary sources preserved by Eusebius of Caesarea in his *Ecclesiastical History* (ca. 320 CE) allows the reader to discern this. But the removal of the Jewish Jerusalem church in 135 CE—in the aftermath of the disastrous second Jewish revolt against Rome and the resulting ban of Jews from the city—made the transition to the gentile church of all nations in Jerusalem more straightforward than it otherwise would have been. As a consequence, even Eusebius in early fourth-century Caesarea seems to be unaware of the implications of the early sources he preserves as he pursues his advocacy of the church of all nations in the Roman Empire. The transition was reinforced by the alliance of the church with the Roman Empire, first through Constantine in the time of Eusebius, and then via subsequent emperors. The consequence of minimizing the significance of James of Jerusalem was not intended by Jerome, who in his *Lives of Illustrious Men* placed James second, following only Peter. Though he placed James second, Jerome devoted almost twice as much space to him as he gave to Peter (Painter 2004, 221–22). Nevertheless, his argument that the siblings of Jesus were actually cousins distanced James from Jesus, and the role of James in the Jewish Jerusalem church is not in focus for Jerome.

In due course, this James, who was known by Paul and in early tradition as "the brother of the Lord," became known as "the Lesser James," and James the brother of John was "the Greater" (see Hintlian 1989, 52–53). The Armenian Cathedral of Saint James in Jerusalem boasts the resting place of the head of James the apostle, brother of John, and the body of James, "the brother of the Lord" and "the first bishop of Jerusalem." While the cathedral also features the latter's throne, the primary focus of devotion in the cathedral is James the apostle, because James of Jerusalem is perceived as "the lesser" (see also Painter 2004, 129, 154, 322). Indeed, this was the position of the Western church and continued to be so beyond the Reformation. None of this might have happened had there not been a transition from the Jewish Jesus movement in Jerusalem after 135 to the gentile Jerusalem church of all nations, a movement that was strengthened by the later partnership of the church with the Roman Empire.

In what follows several matters are discussed in more detail, including those identified as siblings of Jesus in the canonical gospels and other New Testament evidence and the alternative interpretations that arise in subsequent centuries. Discussion of the disputed authorship of the epistle that bears the name of James follows, leading to the observation that the letter bears some marks of Jamesian tradition, even if the brother of Jesus was not its actual author.

Some of the major sources for information about the historical James of Jerusalem have been referenced already, and others will also be addressed below. The Greek name for this James is *Iakōbos*, which would normally be translated as "Jacob" though the name is also spelled *Iakōb* in the New Testament, but never for the followers of Jesus.[4] This James is identified as one of the brothers of Jesus in Mark 6:3 and Matt 13:55. Similarly, he is "the brother of the Lord" in Gal 1:19 according to Paul, who also names James among the three pillar apostles in Jerusalem (Gal 2:1–14, esp. 9, 12) and as one of the witnesses to the risen Jesus (1 Cor 15:7). Acts 12:17 and 21:17 imply his status as leader of the Jerusalem church, confirming his role in 15:13, 19 where he presides at the so-called Jerusalem Conference/Council (cf. Gal 2:1–10). The late first-century CE Jewish historian Josephus calls James "the brother of Jesus the so-called Christ" and reports his martyrdom (*A.J.* 20.197–203), as does the fourth-century Christian chronicler Eusebius (*Hist. eccl.* 2.1.2–5; 2.23.1; 3.5.2; 3.11.1; 4.5.1–4; 4.22.4; 7.19.1), who emphasizes James's reputation for piety and his role as the first bishop of Jerusalem, often drawing on earlier traditions attributed to Hegesippus (ca. 110–180), Clement of Alexandria (ca. 160–215), and Origen (ca. 185–251).[5]

---

4. In the New Testament, the transliterated form (*Iakōb*) was used only for the patriarch Jacob and for the father of Joseph in the Mathaean genealogy (3:15–16). All references to followers of Jesus by this name use the Hellenistic translated form (*Iakōbos*). By the time Josephus wrote (and Eusebius later) only the translated form was used, whether of the patriarch or of a follower of Jesus. But the difference in the text of the New Testament was the basis for using James of Jesus's followers and Jacob of the patriarch and other Jews in English translations. This practice presupposes a connection between the two names in English. See Painter 2004, 2–3.

5. See Painter 2013; and especially the extensive discussion in Painter 2004 for additional analyses of these texts and use of James in other early Christian and gnostic texts.

Concerning the Family of Jesus

The New Testament provides no evidence to challenge the view that Jesus was one of a family of brothers and sisters whose parents were Joseph and Mary. It is true that Matthew and Luke portray Mary as mother of Jesus via divine intervention, but no other writing in the New Testament refers to "the virginal conception," and there is no suggestion that the brothers and sisters of Jesus were not children of both Joseph and Mary. This was publicly assumed of Jesus as well (Mark 6:1–3; and esp. Matt 13:54–56; Luke 3:23; 4:22). Thus, those called his brothers and sisters are portrayed as *at least* his younger half-brothers and half-sisters. This brief summary is accurate, as far as it goes, but it hides complexity that has been used to undermine the relationship of James to Jesus and to weaken the evidence of the importance of his role.

The Status of the Birth Stories in Matthew and Luke

Although each of the Gospels of Matthew (1:18–25) and Luke (2:26–38) provides an account of the virginal conception of Jesus by Mary, Matthew does so from the perspective of Joseph and Luke from the perspective of Mary. Nevertheless, each provides a genealogy from the line of Joseph (Matt 1:1–16; Luke 3:23–38). Matthew, with a strong Jewish perspective, first announces the "book of the genealogy of Jesus Christ, son of David, son of Abraham" (1:1) before beginning the genealogy, "Abraham was the father of [or 'begat'] Isaac" and so on through to "Matthan begat Jacob and Jacob begat Joseph the husband of Mary, of whom Jesus was born."[6] This formulation avoids any statement concerning the paternity of Jesus although, without 1:18–25, a reader would assume that the husband of Mary was the father.

Luke begins with Jesus and works back to an earlier beginning, to Adam, whom he calls "son of God." Whereas Matthew traces Jesus's lineage back to Abraham, in an appeal to Jewish origins, Luke goes back to Adam, as the father of all humans. But this is not the only difference. Matthew avoids stating that Joseph begat Jesus, saying only that he was "the husband of Mary"; Luke describes Jesus as "being the son, as it was supposed [*hos enomizeto*], of Joseph, the son of Eli," clearly implying that it

---

6. Unless otherwise noted, all translations are by the author.

was commonly assumed that Joseph was the father of Jesus. While Luke's genealogy overlaps Matthew's, the two genealogies are more marked by difference than agreement. Luke identifies Joseph as the son of Eli, while Mathew names Matthan as the father of Joseph. For some interpreters, these (and other differences) raise questions about the origin and accuracy of these genealogies. The lack of any reference to the virginal conception of Jesus by Mary in the New Testament outside the infancy stories of Matthew and Luke might suggest that these stories have been designed to undergird the conviction of the messianic vocation of Jesus. The *use* of Isa 7:14 in Matt 1:23 as a messianic prediction, on the assumption that the reference to "the young woman" (Hebrew *ha'almah*) was to a "virgin," might have given rise to the tradition of the virginal conception, especially in the light of the translation in the LXX of Isa 7:14 as *parthenos* ("virgin"). In Isaiah the text probably refers either to the wife of the king (Ahaz) or to the wife of the prophet himself. Further, the genealogies in Matthew and Luke trace Jesus's ancestry via Joseph to establish the line of messiahship, despite their independent accounts of the virginal conception. At this time, Jewish descent was taken to be by paternity, but this is awkward because each gospel narrates the virginal conception, clearly implying that Joseph was *not* the father of Jesus.

The genealogies and infancy stories are not known independently of Matthew and Luke, each of which probably was not written earlier than 80 CE. Given that James died in 62 CE, these traditions were unlikely to be known to him, who clearly *was known* as "the brother of the Lord" (as Paul identifies him in Gal 1:19). And although James was one of four brothers (Mark 6:3 et al.; see above), he is referred to as "*the* brother of the Lord," establishing his unique place in the earliest church. But at least two factors led to the underestimation of the role of James and the family of Jesus: the distancing of James and his siblings from Jesus by denying their relationship to him as brothers and sisters, and the modern interpretation of the family in an unsympathetic role during Jesus's mission.[7]

---

7. For a fuller discussion of the New Testament evidence concerning the family, see Painter 2004, 11–102.

Protevangelium of James and Jerome

The Protevangelium of James, a text that narrates the circumstances of the birth of Jesus, but gives more attention to the background and character of Mary, is first known to us in the early third century (see Painter 2004, 198–200, 299–304). It was used widely in the East, and was also read in the West with the support of Origen (185–251 CE), the greatest and most influential biblical scholar/theologian of that period. It provides the earliest surviving evidence of a challenge to the New Testament traditions concerning the family of Jesus.[8] For this, it developed an alternative story that filled some of the many gaps left by the sparse nativity stories of Matthew and Luke. Apart from the genealogies, those two gospels tell us nothing about the earlier lives of Mary and Joseph, thus they provide the Protevangelium with a blank canvas. Its author works in the gaps left by the nativity stories of the canonical gospels with a view to asserting the continuing virginity of Mary. While the Protoevangelium avoids outright contradictions, it can hardly be said to provide a story that is a good fit with Matthew and Luke.

In the New Testament gospels, the brothers and sisters of Jesus simply appear at the beginning of Jesus's Galilean mission and are identified as his siblings and as children of Joseph (the carpenter) and Mary (Mark 6:3; Matt 13:55–56; Luke 4:22). Only Luke 2:41–52 fills a small gap between the nativity scenes and the beginning of Jesus's mission, describing the customary family visit to Jerusalem at Passover when Jesus was twelve. Here there is no mention of brothers or sisters. This is as much a problem for Protevangelium as it is for the canonical gospels. Nevertheless, the latter portray Jesus's brothers and sisters with the family at the beginning and during his mission, even if they allow room for Protevangelium to provide an alternative story.

In Protevangelium, James, identified as the stepbrother of Jesus, narrates the story of Mary and of the birth of Jesus. His narrative makes clear that those known as brothers and sisters of Jesus were the children of Joseph, understood as an older widower who fathered them in his earlier

---

8. One should also note the Gospel of Peter in this regard. It is first attested ca. 200 CE by Bishop Serapion of Antioch. According to Origen, it appears to support the view that Jesus's brothers were sons of Joseph by a previous wife, but this is not attested in the fragments of the book that have survived. The work was treated as pseudepigraphal by Eusebius. It comes from a period roughly the same as Protevangelium, on which it might be dependent.

marriage and before his betrothal to Mary. It also makes clear that Mary remained a virgin throughout the process of conceiving and giving birth to Jesus. The understanding of the family relations of Jesus expressed in Protevangelium remains the view of the Eastern church.[9]

Although Protevangelium was used initially by Ambrose (339–397) and Augustine (354–430), Jerome (347–419/20) persuaded them to reject it because it was not a "received" book but was instead deemed a pseudepigraphic apocryphal book. Jerome's criticism of Protevangelium and other apocryphal writings was scathing. He referred to their views as raving (see Painter 2004, 300–301). Instead, he promoted the idea that the "brothers and sisters" were actually "cousins" of Jesus, and in his defense of his position he also argued against the understanding of Helvidius (fl. 380s), who insisted that the brothers and sisters were children of Joseph and Mary and blood relatives of Jesus. Jerome inadvertently preserved that view by describing it in his refutation titled *Against Helvidius*. His refutation was aided by his appeal to second century evidence defending the virginity of Mary, but a closer reading of the second century sources suggests that the virginal conception as narrated by Matthew and Luke is what they defended (see Painter 2004, 213–20, esp. 215).

Because the view of Protevangelium became pervasive in the East, as did that of Jerome in the West, the view of the New Testament was obscured. On the whole, the argument of Helvidius remains persuasive, although Jerome successfully refuted it for the Western church because his view, like that of Protevangelium, maintained the continuing virginity of Mary. Indeed, on Jerome's view both Mary and Joseph were models of virginity for the growing monastic movement. Thus, with the support of Ambrose and Augustine, Jerome's view became the Western view, ousting both the Helvidian view and that of Protevangelium.

Obviously Jerome did not oppose Protevangelium because it described the continuing virginity of Mary. His objection was its apocryphal, pseudepigraphic, nonscriptural, alternative story. His own approach was to search the text of the canonical gospels to find evidence for the continuing virginity of Mary. The virginal conception of Jesus by Mary already has a basis in Matthew and Luke. But there is no suggestion in the New Testament that the brothers and sisters of Jesus were

---

9. For a fuller discussion of the Protevangelium of James, see Painter 2004, 198–213, 297–308. For the text of Protevangelium, see J. K. Elliott 1993, 48–67.

not children of Joseph and Mary. This was publicly assumed of Jesus as well (Mark 6:1–3; and esp. Matt 13:54–56; Luke 3:23; 4:22). But Jerome found ways of identifying people of the same name in such a way as to argue that those called brothers and sisters were actually cousins, being children of Clopas (the brother of Joseph) and another Mary, who was the sister of the mother of Jesus. John 19:25 is a crux text for his view. It describes four women standing by the cross of Jesus (Jesus's mother, his mother's sister, Mary the wife of Clopas, and Mary Magdalene; see Painter 2004, 221–22). The first two are identified by their relationship to each other and to Jesus; the latter two are named in a way that identifies and distinguishes them, though each is named Mary. The mother of Jesus is not named anywhere in John, but is referred to as "the mother of Jesus" (John 2:1, 3, 5, 12; 19:25, 26, 27), and her sister is identified simply as "the sister of his mother." If the reader knows independently that the mother is named Mary, it is unlikely that her sister was also, and thus there is no reason why she should be identified with another named person (as Jerome does by equating the sister with Mary the wife of Clopas, thereby reducing the group at the cross to three). Given that Mark 15:40 identifies an unspecified number of women among whom three are named, there actually is no implied need to reduce the four identified in John to match the three named in Mark (Mary Magdalene, Mary the mother of James the younger and of Joses, and Salome), especially when the motivation is to make Jerome's novel hypothesis work.

Tal Ilan (2002) has shown, although from a limited sample of Jewish names from Palestine between 330 BCE and 200 CE and a relatively small number of Jewish women's names, that the two most common names (by a very large margin and in this order) were Mary and Salome.[10] These references are important for the use of the names Mary and Salome and also for an awareness of the fragility of the status of the evidence. Ilan gathered the names over a long period of time (ranging 530 years) in a broad and complex region (Palestine), and they constitute a fragmentary sample.[11] In spite of the limited evidence, it remains likely that there were very many Marys at the time of Jesus and that there is no reason to think that either of the latter two in John 19:25 was a sister of the mother of Jesus.

---

10. For a discussion of the significance of this evidence, see Painter 2004, 280–85, 288, 308.

11. Though *Palestine* is a post-135 CE term, it is widely used of the broader region, encompassing the Roman province of Judea and other territories.

J. B. Lightfoot (1865) asserts that Jerome's argument was novel, without precedent before his own suggestion (ca. 380). The evidence preserved by Eusebius also notes that James, the first bishop of Jerusalem, was "the brother of the Lord," while the second, Symeon, was a cousin of Jesus. The tradition recorded makes a clear distinction between James as brother and Symeon as cousin (see Eusebius, *Hist. eccl.* 4.5.1–4; 4:22.4; and Painter 2004, 151–58).

Although Lightfoot's critique of Jerome's view was compelling and has continued to be found so by recent scholars, his critique of the Eastern (or Epiphanian) view was less rigorous (see Lightfoot 1865; Painter 2001, 12–24; 2004, 2, 153, 213–23, 279–80, 295–308). Lightfoot uses the names of the three fourth-century advocates to describe the three views: Helvidian, Epiphanian, and Hieronymian (i.e., the view of Jerome). Only the view of Jerome had no precedent. Following Lightfoot, some scholars from the Western tradition have forsaken Jerome's view and turned to affirm the Epiphanian view based on Protevangelium. In so doing, they have ignored Jerome's critique of Protevangelium as a pseudepigraphic apocryphal text, not based on Scripture but on wild imagination. While Jerome's view was without precedent, he sought to reconstruct it from Scripture. But, as Lightfoot showed, this construction was not only novel, it was contrived. Likewise, although the story of Protevangelium might not directly contradict any of the sparse details concerning the birth of Jesus in Matthew and Luke, its account does not emerge spontaneously or naturally from the biblical gospels, where there is no suggestion that Joseph was an older man with an existing family. Nor, contrary to Lightfoot and those who follow him, does the lack of any mention of Joseph in the later period show that he was dead because of his old age. Even if he was dead, that does not demand that he was old by our standards when he became betrothed to Mary. After all, more than thirty years had passed since the birth of Jesus to the beginning of his mission. Further, the sisters are not mentioned in Acts 1:14 either, despite the statement there that Mary and Jesus's brothers were present with the eleven disciples after Jesus's ascension. Do we suppose the sisters were dead also?

Given the sparse treatment of the family in the gospels and Acts, the prominence of James in Acts and the letters of Paul is all the more notable and exceptional. Stephen Barton (1994, 23–56) argues that the gospels have minimized the role of the family in the interest of universalizing the Jesus movement. In contrast, that James was notable is confirmed by the tradition concerning "the brother of the Lord" preserved in Acts, the letters of Paul, and later tradition preserved by Eusebius.

From the perspective of this critique, I consider the most likely conclusion to be that James was a younger brother of Jesus, a child of Joseph
and Mary but older than his other siblings, as seems implied by the prominence of James and by the order of listing the names of the brothers in the
gospels. The treatment of James in the evidence gathered by Eusebius from
the first two centuries attests his special relation to Jesus. This includes
Paul's address of James as "*the* brother of the Lord" and other evidence
from Paul's letters and the role of James according to Acts (see Painter
2004, 42–57, 105–58). The biblical evidence reveals a tense relationship
between Paul and James, because of the focus of James on the Jewish
mission in Jerusalem and Paul's concern for the mission to the nations.
Because of this conflict of interests, the priorities of the one tended to be
in tension with the other. Even so, Paul was constrained to refer to James
as "the brother of the Lord" and to acknowledge his leadership role in the
Jerusalem church and beyond (see Painter 2004, 42–82).

The Contemporary Negative View of "the Family" during Jesus's Mission

The literary evidence from the second century, much of it preserved
by Eusebius, provides a clear view of the leading role of James and the
Jerusalem church. The later view of that leadership was weakened by the
dispersal of the Jewish Jerusalem church in 135 and the transition to the
gentile Jerusalem church that, although it honored James, did not honor
or perpetuate his Jewish perspective. With this transition, the early movement entered a path that led to the church of all nations standing over
against Judaism. Consequently, although not intended, the distancing of
the family by Protevangelium and Jerome aided the church of all nations
to let go of Jewish influences and priorities. Here I raise the question as to
whether Protevangelium reflects an early *Jewish* Christian origin. I suspect not, but against this background—regardless of how this question is
answered—we may understand a little better how in contemporary interpretation the family could be portrayed as antagonistic to Jesus. Recent
interpretation of two passages in the gospels has fueled this view of the
family during Jesus's mission as discussed in Mark 3:20–35 and John 7:1–9.

Mark 3:20–35

Many scholars now identify the family as *hoi par autou* who go out to
restrain Jesus because they (or others) consider that Jesus is "beside him-

self" (*exeste*; Mark 3:21). However, although Matthew and Luke have parallel accounts of Mark 3:22–30 (in Matt 12:22–37 and Luke 11:14–23), each of them omits Mark 3:20–21. Considering that only about thirty verses of Mark are not used by either Matthew or Luke, and that Mark 3:20–21 contain a complete subincident introducing Mark 3:22–30, why would Matthew and Luke omit this connected subevent? In particular, Matthew omits only fifty-five verses of Mark. Why omit Mark 3:20–21? While the omission of most of what is peculiar to Mark is readily explicable (see Mark 3:7–12; 4:26–29; 7:31–37; 8:22–27; 14:51–52), what explains the omission of 3:20–21 as a subevent in 3:20–35? It is part of a distinctively Markan treatment of tradition.

In Mark, this subevent follows immediately after the account of the calling of the Twelve *to be with Jesus* as disciples and that he might send them out, in due course, as apostles to preach (3:13–19, and note 3:14). While the calling and naming of the Twelve happens in 3:13–19, they are not sent out until 6:7–12. In the meantime, they are to be with Jesus as disciples preparing for mission. Consequently, if they were not with Jesus when he went into a house in 3:20, their absence is surprising and unexpected. It is more likely that their presence is implied and that *hoi par autou* in 3:21 is a reference to them, rather than a reference to the *as yet unmentioned* family, who are first cited in Mark 3:31. It is not as if *hoi par autou* is a specific reference to the family. It could just as easily be a reference to the disciples, who are "his associates" and are expected in the scene. My interpretation is not novel, except in current interpretation.

The argument that *hoi par autoui* in 3:21 is a reference to the family seems contrived. Is it really confirmed because the family arrive outside the door of the place where Jesus was with his followers in 3:31, apparently the house mentioned in 3:20? This makes no sense, unless 3:21 is an obscure reference to them leaving their home in Nazareth, arriving only in 3:31. Did the rumor of the disturbing events of 3:20–21 somehow reach them there? That is an unlikely reading. Further, 3:21 appears to describe an immediate intervention, an attempt to restrain Jesus at that point, thus more likely a reference to an attempted intervention by the disciples. In the turmoil of the pressure of the crowd, possibly the disciples heard murmuring and went out, perhaps to rescue or even to restrain Jesus. Whichever, the action reveals a misunderstanding of Jesus. But then, in Mark the disciples are certainly fallible followers, and this incident shows them to be fallible from the beginning. That this Markan motif was unacceptable to Matthew and Luke would explain their omission of it. So then, there is no evidence of the opposition of the family here; they arrive unheralded only in Mark 3:31 (Painter 1999, 498–513; see also Painter 1997, 66–76, 97–103; 2004, 11–41).

John 7:1–9

John 7:1–9 portrays the brothers of Jesus as "not yet" believing in Jesus (7:5). This implies that they subsequently came to believe. While their unbelief is singled out here, it is not clear that they were in a different position than the disciples, who are not featured in this scene. What the brothers seem to want is a showdown with the Jewish authorities in Jerusalem and, although Jesus declines, that is what eventually happens in what follows. The narrator's evaluation—that they do *not yet* believe—is given from the perspective of authentic Johannine belief. This evaluation certainly applies to the disciples also. See Jesus's response to the disciples' affirmation of belief: "Do you now believe? Behold the hour comes, and it has come when you will each be scattered to his own place and you will leave me alone" (16:31–32). This certainly undermines their affirmation of belief. Disciples and siblings manifest a failure of nerve and belief arising from a misunderstanding of Jesus. Nevertheless, despite their failings, these two groups continued as followers of Jesus.

Contrary to the modern undermining of the role of the family during the mission of Jesus and the earliest period following his death, the evidence attests their presence in John (2:1, 3, 5, 12; 7:1–8; 19:25, 26, 27). Acts 1:14 depicts the mother of Jesus and his brothers among the believers from the beginning of the movement in Jerusalem following the death of Jesus. James emerges as the leader of the believing community alongside Peter, who led the Jerusalem mission (Gal 2:6–10). In Acts 12:17, after his release from prison, Peter, the leader of the mission, reports to James the leader of the community.[12] Nowhere does Peter emerge as community leader; rather, he prominently led the mission from the beginning (Acts 2:14–36; 3:1–26; 10:1–48). Though it almost certainly uses anachronistic language, the early tradition chronicled by Eusebius that names James as the first bishop of the Jerusalem church nevertheless portrays the reality of James's leadership (Painter 2004, 151–58).

---

12. See Painter 2004, 42–44, 48–73, 106, 112–15, 122–24, 142–43, 151–52, 154–58, 162, 308–9, 323–24, 325, 329–30.

James the Brother of the Lord and the Disputed Status of the Epistle

In the New Testament, relevant Nag Hammadi texts, and other so-called apocryphal writings, the status of James was built on recognition of his relationship to Jesus as "the brother of the Lord" (Gal 1:19; see Painter 2004, 159–226). Acts 1:14 specifically notes the presence of the mother and brothers of Jesus along with the eleven disciples, establishing a basis for James's leadership of the Jerusalem church as depicted in Acts. The presence of James from the original foundation of the Jerusalem community is also supported by the historical records concerning him preserved by Eusebius (Painter 2004, 105–58). Nevertheless, evidence of the disputed status of the Epistle of James continued well into the fourth century, as Eusebius notes in his *Ecclesiastical History* written circa 320 (*Hist. eccl.* 2.23.24–25; cf. 3.25, where Eusebius discusses "recognized, disputed, and spurious" works and there again classifies the Epistle of James as "disputed"). Eusebius specifies that the lack of early attestation of the epistle is the primary impediment to the recognition of its authenticity. In addition, the absence of any reference to it in three books from the Nag Hammadi library of gnostic texts, the Apocryphon of James or either of two books titled Apocalypse of James, also adds weight to this silence noted by Eusebius. Though not mentioned by Eusebius, even the evidence of the epistle itself also raises questions concerning direct authorship by James. Given that Eusebius also lacked an awareness of the Jewish Jerusalem of James, it is not surprising that he failed to notice its absence from the epistle.

Had the Epistle of James been written and circulated during James's lifetime, it is almost unthinkable that it would be unattested in patristic texts of the second and third centuries. Yet that is the state of affairs noted by Eusebius. There is no early reference to the epistle. When it is noted by Eusebius, it is among a collection of seven short epistles classified as "Catholic Epistles." That classification apparently implies that these seven epistles have no specific addressees, but are addressed instead to the church of all nations generally. But if the Epistle of James is from "the brother of the Lord," directly or indirectly, the address to "the twelve tribes of the diaspora" is not a symbolic reference to the church of all nations scattered throughout the Roman Empire and beyond. Rather, it almost certainly means exactly what it says, to "the twelve tribes of the diaspora." What is more, all seven epistles in this collection seem to have Jewish connections. But the church of the third and fourth centuries had become predominantly non-Jewish, and so had the reading of the Epistle of James.

In contrast, the evidence of Acts and the letters of Paul portray James as committed to the Jerusalem church and its mission to his own people in Jerusalem. The Epistle of James, however, conveys no sense or impression of coming from Jerusalem, the mother church. Rather, it is addressed "to the twelve tribes in the diaspora" as if *all* were in the diaspora, and it focuses on that situation. Such a form of address is more appropriate for the period following 135 CE, when a new enforced diaspora for all "Jews" began when the Roman forces crushed the Bar Kokhba revolt. The word *Jews* is not used in the Epistle of James, which is addressed to "the twelve tribes of the diaspora"; instead, the author uses language appropriate for one who was writing from a modified nationalistic perspective and seeking the renewal of "Israel." Though the epistle does not use the word *Israel* either, it is implied by the use of "the twelve tribes." More important is the emphasis on diaspora, the new reality after 135. The absence from the epistle of any sense of Jerusalem or the temple puts in question its straightforward authorship by James, who died in 62 CE and whose focus was that city and its holy sanctuary. After the destruction of Jerusalem (including the temple) in 70 CE, and even more so after the disastrous second revolt of 132–135 CE, enforced exile became the new reality for all Jews who now were all in diaspora. The language and style of the epistle is appropriate for this purpose and suggests the hand of a Greek-speaking diaspora Jew. The lack of any early attestation of the epistle makes publication in the lifetime of James unlikely.

Views of Authorship

Although many men were named James (*Iakōbos*) in the early centuries of the church (see Eusebius, *Hist. eccl.* 2.23.4), there is no serious dispute that James the brother of the Lord was *intended* to be identified in the opening address. This leaves open various possibilities, ranging from the genuine self-identification of the author to pseudonymous composition. In between is attribution to James because genuine Jamesian tradition is embodied in the letter. I adopt this third possibility as best complying with all available evidence. It involves the recognition of three things: the diaspora orientation and the character of the Greek language of the letter (see Dibelius 1976, where the case is made, not only in the introduction in 26–38 but in the notes on the text throughout the commentary), Jesus tradition shaped by Jamesian transmission, and the nature and purpose of the letter or encyclical.

A "Quasi-encyclical" Addressed "to the Twelve Tribes in the Diaspora"

The epistle opens with these words: "Jacob [*Iakōbos*], servant of God and of the Lord Jesus Christ, to the twelve tribes in the diaspora, Greeting [*chairein*]." It is significant that the name "Jacob" should be joined with "the twelve tribes" that took their names from the twelve sons of Jacob/Israel (see Painter 2012, 16–18). This language has a broader reach than something like "exiles from Judea," and it is inclusively consistent with the reality that all "Israelites" were in diaspora after 135 CE. Reference to "the twelve tribes" is suggestive of a renewal mission to all scattered Israelites, and Jas 1:1 is rooted in the renewal vision of Jesus to regather all Israel. It is unlikely to be a reappropriation of these traditional words to become a symbolic reference to the church of all nations, which apparently was assumed when James came to be considered a Catholic Epistle. The address "to the twelve tribes in the diaspora" captures the scattered nature of the settlement of those tribes, not only in the western Roman Empire but also in the East. Yet, the form of the greeting is not the Hebrew *shalom*—not even its Greek form as used by Jesus to his disciples in John 20:19, 21, 26 (*eirēnē hymin*)—but the thoroughly Greek *chairein*. This small touch betrays the hand of a Greek-speaking diaspora Jew (see Painter 2012, 39–42).

Seeing the Epistle of James as a quasi-encyclical letter to Jews was not new when I proposed that in the first edition of my book *Just James* in 1997 (see now Painter 2004, 244–45) and later utilized it in my commentary on the text (Painter 2012, 42–45). Nevertheless, I was glad to see that Richard Bauckham advocated this view in his 1999 book on the epistle (Bauckham 1999, 11–28, in a chapter titled "An Encyclical from James to the Diaspora"). Bauckham further defines the letter as a "paranetic encyclical" (13). Of course, there are important differences between our positions, but I find it helpful to begin with the agreements. We each see the encyclical addressed to the Jews of the diaspora and not as a symbolic address to all Christians. We each recognize that the letter embodies unacknowledged Jesus tradition which the author of the epistle uses as if his own. We differ in that I take seriously that the letter does not specifically limit readers to *believing* Jewish exiles, though I acknowledge that such people were more often likely to be the actual readers and/or hearers. But this was not the intent of the more open address.

By James or in the Name of James?

Bauckham and I also differ in that he treats the letter as straightforwardly from James as the actual author. He affirms that James was capable of writing a Greek letter *of this character.* He argues that those who attribute the letter to a diaspora Greek-speaking Jew have lost sight of the widely-known studies of Martin Hengel (1974, 1989), who argued that Palestine, like the lands of the diaspora, was hellenized.

This, of course, is true (Painter 2012, 21–22). Herod the Great built Jerusalem as a great Hellenistic city architecturally. It was cosmopolitan, and Herod's temple was a wonder of Hellenistic architecture. Bauckham is aware that it would be simplistic to infer uniform hellenization, and, I would add, especially in the case of Judea and Galilee. It is no accident that the thoroughly Jewish Dead Sea Scrolls were found in the Judean desert, or that the amorphous movement known as Zealots should thrive in Palestine rather than the diaspora. The continuing use of Hebrew and Aramaic in the Judea of the time of Jesus is now commonly known. Nor is it surprising that the philosophically inclined Philo was an Alexandrian Jew, not a Judean. I suspect that the evidence of the survival of his writings attests a much wider group of like minds in the diaspora than Bauckham allows, as does the evidence concerning the Hellenistic character of Alexandria. Bauckham also fails to ask specifically about what we know of the Judaism of James, with his focus on the continuing mission to the Jews of Jerusalem. During the life of James, the presence of the temple made Jerusalem the focus of Jewish festival pilgrimage, ensuring a Jewish character not possible in the diaspora. There is also the difference between "the land," where Jews were in the majority, compared to their minority (though sometimes significant) status in the diaspora. In the land, "Jews" was not their chosen self-description. Instead, this was the name applied to them by the Romans, based on the Roman provincial term "Judea."

James was determinedly fixed in Jerusalem, the center for the continuing Jesus movement, of which he was leader. Jerusalem was the focus of his mission to the circumcision (Jews), and he maintained a law-observant ethos, intent on winning other law-observant Jews (see Acts 21:17–26; Painter 2004, 54–57; 2012, 27–31, 40–43). This James is unlikely to have either the Hellenistic learning to write the epistle or the inclination and/or intent to expand the Jerusalem mission to the diaspora. His preoccupation was to ensure that the mission to his own people in the land did not fail. The focus on the diaspora was the work of others, Peter (i.e., Cephas) to the circumcision, Paul to the nations (Gal 2:6–10). In spite of the best efforts of James, his mission failed, the twelve tribes were not renewed, and the Jesus movement became the gentile Christian church. His early death (perhaps by execution or assassination) in 62 meant that he did not live to see the first stage of failure in 70.

Lack of Early Attestation of the Epistle and the Jerusalem-Centered Mission

As noted already, there are strong reasons for thinking that the Epistle of James was not written in the lifetime of James. The most compelling evidence is actually the *lack* of it—the lack of any early attestation of the epistle. Had the book been written in the lifetime of James, such lack of early attestation seems unlikely. When it does appear, it is treated as a General (or Catholic) Epistle for all Christians. Had it been written before the death of James in 62, that reading would not have occurred because of the strong association of James with the Jerusalem church.

A number of studies have argued for a two-stage hypothesis in the composition of the epistle. The biographical information we have about James implies that he breathed the air of Jerusalem and, as far as we know, he did not leave it from the day Jesus entered the city for the last time. This view is supported by Acts, and it is assumed and asserted by the author of the Pseudo-Clementines (see Painter 2004, 42–57, 187–97). The portrayal of James in his total devotion to the mission to his own people in Jerusalem is assumed as a noncontroversial element of his life and work. James was committed to the mission of his brother Jesus to renew Israel (see Painter 2016, 218–37). From this perspective, Jerusalem remained the crucial center of the vision of James. In 135, with the Roman suppression of the second rebellion, *all* of Israel became scattered and thus, with the already existing diaspora, may be called the twelve tribes in the diaspora.

Jamesian Tradition and Its Character

Although there is no early reference to the epistle, it is not too much to believe that James left a tradition that endured, not only after the Jewish war of 66–74, but also well beyond that time—a tradition that was cherished by the continuing Jewish leadership in Jerusalem, first in the person of his cousin Simeon, and then in a succession of other Jewish leaders until 135. Eusebius refers to the "throne of James" that his successors in Jerusalem treasured, not only the Jewish leaders until 135, but also the leaders of the gentile Jerusalem church that succeeded them (*Hist. eccl.* 2.1.2–5; 2.23.1; 3.5.2–3; 3.2.7–12; 3.11.1; 4.5.1–5; 7.19.1; and see the discussion in Painter 2004, 110–13, 118, 142–48, 154–58, 196, 209–12, 308–14, 325). The Jewish succession up to 135 would also have treasured the teaching tradition of James. However, the subsequent expulsion of Jews from Jerusalem and the land involved transition to a gentile Jerusalem church insensitive to its Jewish roots.

Four observations combine to make it unlikely that the Epistle of James comes directly from James of Jerusalem. First, it lacks any sign of the reality of Jerusalem *for the author*. Second, the focus on the Jewish diaspora is uncharacteristic of James. Third, the character of the epistle is more consistent as a composition by a diaspora Jew. Fourth, undergirding all else is the evidence that in the first quarter of the fourth century, the authenticity of the epistle was contested because it lacked early attestation (Painter 2012, 7–16). Any attempt to argue for direct authorship by James faces that considerable hurdle. The repute and status of James of Jerusalem in the earliest church would have guaranteed reception of any genuine letter by him in his lifetime. That it emerges later supports what is implied by what we observe in the epistle itself, that it comes from a later time. But if the epistle comes from a later time, what is there to connect it with James?

The Epistle of James and the Jesus Tradition

The most important evidence of the use of Jamesian tradition in the Epistle of James is the presence of unannounced early Jesus tradition. The classic commentary of Joseph B. Mayor (1897) notes over sixty allusions to the Jesus tradition of the Synoptics. A decade later, G. Currie Martin (1907, 174–84) argued that an allusion to Jesus tradition is signaled whenever the author of the epistle addresses the audience as "brothers." The plural "brothers" (*adelphoi*) is used fifteen times to address the audience (1:2, 16, 19; 2:1, 5, 14; 3:1, 10, 12; 4:11; 5:7, 9, 10, 12, 19). Of these, twelve times it appears in the phrase "my brothers" (1:2, 16, 19; 2:1, 5, 14; 3:1, 10, 12; 4:11; 5:12, 19), including three occurrences of the phrase "my beloved [*agapētoi*] brothers" (1:16, 19; 2:5). On three occasions (four uses) the epistle refers to a member of the audience's community as a "brother" (1:9; 2:15; 4:11 [2x]). In 2:15 the reference to "a brother or a sister" alerts the reader to the flaw in the address "brothers." The reality was "brothers and sisters." In 4:11, in addition to the plural address, there are two singular references to a brother.

The argument about the presence of such Jesus tradition in James is not dependent on the acceptance of the identifying role of the author's address of his readers as "brothers." This is only an alert for the reader to look out for the *influence* of Jesus tradition that is pervasive in the epistle. Such influence of the Jesus tradition is also argued by Bauckham (1999, 85–108, 111; see also his chapter in this volume) and many others (e.g., Mayor 1897; Painter 2012, 34–39).

The earliest signal of Jesus tradition using "my (beloved) brothers" is found in 1:2, immediately following the opening address of 1:1. The second is in 1:16. Both introduce allusions to Jesus traditions that are rooted in Galilee; these reveal the benevolence of God in creation and link with his teaching about asking and receiving, seeking and finding (see Freyne 2004, 24–28). The Jesus tradition identified with the theme of the generosity of God is foundational for Jesus and the argument of the epistle. The goodness (*tob*) of the creation (Gen 1:4, 10, 12, 18, 25) is rooted in the goodness or generosity of God (Pss 106:1; 107:1; 136:1). Both Jesus and James grew up in Galilee. Thus it is not surprising that an epistle attributed to James the brother of the Lord shares the distinctive Galilean creation theology also attributed to Jesus. This is not restricted to an act of creation in the past, but includes the continuing presence and creative activity of God in loving care (Matt 6:25–34 // Luke 12:22–31; Matt 7:7–11 // Luke 11:9–13). In these Q passages Jesus responds to the anxiety of the disciples about the uncertainty of life by appealing to the beauty and bounty of the creation and God's care of it. Beauty is an aspect of the goodness (*tob*) of God in creation, which underlies the assurance of God's care for humans. James 1:17 is a strong affirmation of God's role in creation and continuing care: "Every good [or generous] act of giving and every perfect gift is from above, coming down from the Father of Lights, with whom there is no shadow caused by turning." (On the phrase *pasa dosis agathē kai pan dōrēma teleion* see Painter 2012, 73–76.) These sentiments come close to Lam 3:22–23, "The steadfast love of the Lord never ceases, they are new every morning, great is your faithfulness." But James, aware of the mystery of God and the enigma of the world in which we humans have to make our way, characterizes "the gift-giving God" who freely gives wisdom to everyone who sincerely asks in faith (Jas 1:5–6, 17; Painter 2012, 3–6, 34–35, 73–76). Wisdom is necessary in a world that, though graced by the generosity of God, is fraught by trials and temptations.

The author of the Epistle of James also makes use of Jesus's interpretation of the torah in the tradition found only in traditions unique to

Matthew (M) or sometimes traditions overlapping Luke (thus corresponding to the Matthean form of Q, i.e., Q^{Matt}). Here it seems that Matthew's use
of Q has been shaped by M materials. It is possible that James was associated with the transmission of the M tradition and for the interpretation
of Q as it came to be used in Matthew (Q^{Matt}). But Matthew is, at a later
stage, a Petrine gospel, reflecting the circumcision mission to the nations
(28:19–20) that essentially overrides the earlier mission of James that was
restricted to Israel (10:5–6; see the discussion in ch. 4 of Painter 2004). For
me, this evidence supports the hypothesis that this second-century diaspora epistle embodies tradition from James the brother of the Lord (on the
date of the epistle, see Painter 2012, 25). It now maintains his commitment
and mission to his own people, although they are all now in the diaspora.
There is no room to do justice to this theme here. For support, I appeal
to others who have dealt with the role of the wisdom of Jesus in James in
much more detail than is possible here. My task has been to show that the
wisdom of Jesus via the wisdom of James comes *indirectly* from him to the
twelve tribes in the diaspora sometime after 135.

Conclusion

The major part of my essay has been devoted to the evidence that has led
me to the view that the epistle does not come from the hand of James the
brother of the Lord. The most important evidence is the lack of any early
attestation of the epistle and consequently its disputed status early in the
fourth century. Had the epistle been sent in the lifetime of James, this situation would not have occurred. The character of the epistle also supports
the view that it belongs to a later period and speaks from the diaspora to
the diaspora. The author gives no sense of speaking from Jerusalem and
writes Greek more like a diaspora Jew than the brother of the Lord, who
was devoted to the mission to his own people in Jerusalem. The turn to
the twelve tribes of the diaspora reflects the reality of the new state of diaspora for all Jews after 135. At the same time, it is generally agreed that the
author, who identifies himself as "James," intends readers to understand
the letter as from the brother of the Lord. No other serious contenders
have emerged. But because there is no evidence of the epistle in the lifetime of James, it seems likely that it is pseudepigraphical, or at least a later
sending of Jamesian tradition adapted to a later time. I have argued that
the epistle embodies early Galilean creation tradition, shared by Jesus and

James, and that this is embodied in the epistle now addressed to the twelve tribes of the diaspora.

In the epistle we meet the wisdom of Jesus via the wisdom of James the brother of the Lord, adapted and transmitted by a second century diaspora editor in a quasi-encyclical to the twelve tribes of Israel in the diaspora. Foundational for an adequate understanding of the epistle is the portrayal of the generous giving God (Jas 1:2–5, 16–17). At the same time, the epistle has a perceptive evaluation of the propensity of human desire to become a destructive and deceitful force, leading to conflict and strife (Jas 1:12–15). It is an enigma that in a world that expresses the abundance of the gracious giving of God, human desire acts in self-interest, failing to care for those in need, and behaves carelessly in ways destructive of life. The Epistle of James, like the Synoptic Jesus, sets out to unmask the strategies of those who claim to be religious and yet act out of narrow self-interest (Jas 1:26–27). In so doing, the author exposes the exploitive strategies of the rich and powerful and reveals the plight of the poor. The world, now as then, is divided sharply into rich and poor nations, and all nations are also divided into rich and poor. In the poor nations, the poverty is pitiful, and in the struggle for survival the poor, wherever they are, cannot win. Meanwhile the rich live in wasteful luxury, obscuring reality while justifying the inequality into which people are born and from which they cannot escape. In this situation the James of the epistle says, "My brothers and sisters, it ought not to be so!"

Use, Authority, and Canonical Status of James in the Earliest Church

Darian R. Lockett

The early reception history of James is a difficult story to tell. One of the most influential twentieth-century interpreters of James, Luke Timothy Johnson (1995, 124), noted in his Anchor Bible commentary that an "adequate account of how James was first received and subsequently interpreted has yet to be written." Though a decade later Johnson (2004) offered a fuller account, to which now David Nienhuis (2007) has given further supplement, Johnson's words from 1995 still remain largely true.

There are two primary reasons that especially the early reception history of James is a difficult tale to tell. The first is the prevailing dominance of the historical-critical model of interpretation that generally results in viewing the reception of New Testament documents as deriving from a "precritical" time and thus of less importance for their accurate interpretation. That is, according to the methodology of historical-critical interpretation the early reception history of James is not viewed as important for understanding the meaning of the letter. This view, though once dominant, has now been somewhat tempered. The perspective that concludes the history of interpretation only exerts an optional influence on the objective historical exegesis of the text has come under closer scrutiny, and this has fostered a growing awareness of the importance of the intervening reception of James. Markus Bockmuehl (2006, 64–65) reflects on the importance of reception history (or history of influence), arguing that "New Testament scholars explicitly adopt the history of influence of the New Testament as an integral and indeed inescapable part of the exercise in which they are engaged." Focusing on the history of influence, according to Bockmuehl, will provide a "more historically embedded understanding of not just the background but also the foreground ... of the New Testament."

It thus seems like an opportune time to reconsider the reception history of James in order to offer a "more historically embedded understanding" of the letter.

A second reason the early reception history of James has been difficult story to tell is that there is very little direct reference to or citation of the letter before the time of Origen (184–254 CE). David Gowler (2016, 6) notes: "The most striking thing about the reception of James in the early church is the paucity of references to James—especially in the West." This so-called *silence* among the patristic authors has been interpreted in different ways by modern scholars. For example, Nienhuis (2007, 101), after surveying recent attempts to date the letter within the mid-first century, argues that "it is my opinion that none of them offer a convincing explanation for the complete lack of attestation before ... Origen in the early third century." On the other hand, Johnson (1995, 126), while acknowledging that "*explicit* recognition of James before the time of Origen is inarguably sparse," nonetheless goes on to assert that there is enough evidence to suggest James was received and used before Origen and that such evidence "takes the form of allusion and appropriation rather than that of direct citation" (127). Adding to the impasse of scholarly opinion regarding the early use of James is the fact that such use (or lack thereof) has been key in determining whether to date the composition of James early (for example, 40 CE and within the lifetime of James, the brother of Jesus) or late (180 CE in the case of Nienhuis's hypothesis that James is a canon-conscious pseudepigraph). Indeed, one of the strongest arguments put forward for an early (first-century) date for James is that the letter was known and used by 1 Clement and the Shepherd of Hermas (see Nienhuis 2007, 118)—something I will consider in the first section below. The situation is neatly summed up by Nienhuis (2007, 100): "If anything like a scholarly consensus does exist, it is that the letter appears to resist easy historical assessment"—not the least because there is sparse early and explicit use of the letter.

In this chapter I will consider the early reception history of the Epistle of James through the end of the fourth century, by which time the letter had been received as part of the canonical New Testament. First, though the evidence for James's circulation prior to Origen is slight, I will begin by considering the epistle's literary relationship with 1 Peter, 1 Clement, and the Shepherd of Hermas, because (as noted above) these texts serve as key indicators (or not) of the early reception of James. Second, I will weigh evidence of early knowledge and use of James in patristic citation and its presence (or absence) in early canon lists. Third, because the presence or absence from canon lists or early citation is by no means the only criterion for determining early use of our letter, I will also consider the manuscript tradition and what such early Christian artifacts might suggest about the use and authority of James. Then, in conclusion, I will briefly reflect on what this evidence might indicate regarding the journey James took as it was finally included in the New Testament canon.

James's Reception in 1 Peter, 1 Clement, and the Shepherd of Hermas

In this section I briefly survey the evidence for reception of James in 1 Peter, 1 Clement, and the Shepherd of Hermas. As the opening paragraphs suggest, this is highly contentious territory: very few scholars agree on the dates of composition for 1 Peter and James, let alone the nature and direction of influence between these early Christian texts. Assessments of the literary relationships among James and 1 Peter, 1 Clement, and the Shepherd of Hermas (whether the latter texts borrowed from James, James borrowed from them, or if there is evidence of any borrowing at all) largely depends on other decisions such as the date of writing and historical authorship of each text. Though I will not draw any conclusions regarding date or direction of influence, I will present some of the evidence suggesting a degree of literary connection between these texts, which some scholars have taken as indication of James's early reception.

James and 1 Peter

Likely the earliest text with which James bears striking literary resemblance is 1 Peter. In his recent commentary on James, Dale Allison (2013) notes the extensive similarities in theme and vocabulary between James and 1 Peter. These include: the address to the diaspora (Jas 1:1; 1 Pet 1:1), rejoicing in suffering (Jas 1:2; 1 Pet 1:6–9), proving of faith and perfection (Jas 1:3–4; 1 Pet 1:7–9), use of Isa 40:6–8 (allusion in Jas 1:10–11; quotation in 1 Pet 1:24), birth through the divine word (Jas 1:18; 1 Pet 1:23), call to rid the self of evil (Jas 1:21; 1 Pet 2:1), call to good conduct (Jas 3:13; 1 Pet 2:12), warning about desires at war within the self (Jas 4:1–2; 1 Pet 2:11), quotation of Prov 3:34 from the Greek version of the Old Testament (Jas 4:6; 1 Pet 5:5), command to resist the devil (Jas 4:7; 1 Pet 5:8–9), promise that God will exalt those who humble themselves (Jas 4:10; 1 Pet 5:6), and quotation of Prov 10:12 (Jas 5:20; 1 Pet 4:8). In addition to these striking similarities, Allison notes that the "agreement in the order of the parallels … is arresting" (68). "If the relevant verses from James are numbered 1–12," he notes, "the order in 1 Peter is this: 1, 2, 3, 5, 4, 6, 7, 8, 9, 11, 10, 12" (68). The only sequential deviation occurs between 4 and 5 then between 10 and 11. Furthermore, he notes that whereas resemblances among ancient catechism or collections of moral imperatives might be expected because of genre and content, both James and 1 Peter are clearly letters addressed to the diaspora (Jas 1:1; 1 Pet 1:1) and both cite the same three Old Testament texts (Isa 40:6–7; Prov 3:34; 10:12), which are nowhere else quoted together in the same New Testament text. A further connection Allison fails to notice is the extensive use both James and 1 Peter make of Lev 19. James 2:1–13 quotes Lev 19:18b (Jas 2:8) and alludes to the theme of partiality (Jas 2:1, 9), which appears in Lev 19:15. Likewise, 1 Peter quotes Lev 19:2 (in 1:16) and alludes to impartiality (1 Pet 1:17), which may be influenced by Lev 19:15, and finally calls his readers to mutual love in 1 Pet 1:22 (which may be an allusion to Lev 19:18b). The extensive similarities between James and 1 Peter may suggest that there is a direct literary relationship between the two letters (see Lockett, forthcoming).

In general, scholars have come to different conclusions regarding these parallels between James and 1 Peter. Some have argued for 1 Peter's dependence upon James or, more commonly, James's dependence upon 1 Peter, while still others have argued the parallels between James and 1 Peter are the result of shared traditional material used independently by both authors for their own rhetorical purposes.[1] In the end it is difficult to come to a confident conclusion regarding the relationship between James and 1 Peter. The shared vocabulary and sequence of ideas is very suggestive; whereas some scholars have argued that 1 Peter is one of the earliest texts (if not the first) that use James, most who argue for literary dependence between the two letters determine instead that James made use of 1 Peter.

---

1. First Peter's dependence upon James was the common view of scholarship in the nineteenth-century (see bibliography in Allison 2013, 68 n. 355). More recent was the position that James was dependent upon 1 Peter. Not only was this Martin Luther's view (Luther, *LW* 35:396) but many scholars from the early twentieth-century also held this view (see Allison 2013, 68 n. 355 for bibliography). Interestingly, two recent scholars (Nienhuis 2007, 169–231; Allison 2013, 67–71) have offered more recent support for this position. The de facto current scholarly consensus now is that where the two letters overlap this is evidence of common tradition used independently (again, see Allison 2013, 68 n. 355 for bibliography).

Whatever conclusions one draws from this evidence, it is important to assess the many parallels between James and 1 Peter and to consider what these striking connections suggest regarding their literary relationship.[2]

James and 1 Clement

As with the relationship between James and 1 Peter, there too has been much disagreement regarding the relationship between James and the early Christian writing known as 1 Clement (which could date between 70 and 140 CE, but more likely between 95 and 97 CE). Because of the "striking points of similarity," Johnson (1995, 75, see 72–75) argues that 1 Clement knew and used James, though he concedes that the case is not conclusive. On the other hand, Allison (2013, 17) argues that, although "1 Clement and James are linked in manifold and very interesting ways, no literary dependence can be established. The Oxford committee that produced *The New Testament in the Apostolic Fathers* did not even bother to discuss the issue, and the standard commentary on 1 Clement comes to a negative conclusion." Once again, the presentation of the evidence will be my focus.

If direct citation is the primary evidence of reception and use, then there are no clear references to James in 1 Clement. However, in this period authors often used and alluded to other texts without direct citation, thus Johnson (1995, 127) argues for "allusion and appropriation rather than … direct citation" as a means to discern the relationship between James and 1 Clement. Drawing a conclusion on this matter is complicated by two key factors. First, because James is written in the genre of wisdom or paraenetic literature, its language is not clearly distinctive and easily recognizable (that is, it shares a stock vocabulary of moral exhortation). Second, some of the material similarities between 1 Clement and James at the same time resemble material from other Christian texts, such as Hebrews and 1 Peter, making it more difficult to reach a confident conclusion regarding a connection between 1 Clement and James (Johnson 2004, 53).

One of the striking similarities between 1 Peter and James noted above is that both letters cite three particular Old Testament texts (Isa

---

2. In my opinion, failing to consider the relationship between James and 1 Peter results in scholars dating James quite late. There seems to be ample evidence that suggests a literary relationship between the two letters and, moreover, that 1 Peter has used James (see Lockett, forthcoming).

40:6–7; Prov 3:34; 10:12) that are cited together nowhere else in the New Testament. Interestingly, 1 Clement cites Prov 3:34 (1 Clem. 30:1–2) and Prov 10:12 (1 Clem. 49:5). First Clement does not directly cite Isa 40:6–7, but Isa 40:10 is quoted in 1 Clem. 34:3. Again, what seems interesting is that nowhere else in the New Testament are these three texts cited, yet here in 1 Clement two of the three are cited once again. This is not direct evidence of literary dependence, but its appearance alongside other shared vocabulary and topics reinforces the general similarity between 1 Clement and James.

Johnson notes several points of thematic similarity between 1 Clement and James. These include: the care of orphans and widows as a sign of repentance (1 Clem. 8:4; Jas 1:27), the use of the very rare term "double-minded" (*dipsychos*, 1 Clem. 23:2–3; Jas 1:8; 4:8), the comment that humans are created in the image of God (1 Clem. 33:5; Jas 3:9), the opposition between arrogance and humility (1 Clem. 2:1; 13:1; 61:3, and esp. 59:3; Jas 1:10–11; 4:5–12), the question of where divisions and war among people comes from (1 Clem. 46:5; Jas 4:1), and the demonstration of wisdom in good deeds (1 Clem. 38:2; Jas 3:13). Johnson (1995, 73) concludes, "taken separately, any one of these points can be dismissed; yet their cumulative effect becomes intriguing."

Beyond these key—but isolated—parallels, there are two striking examples of the "manifold and very interesting" connections between James and 1 Clement (Johnson 1995, 73). There is a cluster of shared language and concepts between 1 Clem. 10:1–7 and Jas 2:21–25 and between 1 Clem. 29:1; 30:1–3 and Jas 4:6–8. First Clement 10:1–7 is part of a group of ancient examples of obedience given by the author to encourage his audience to live ethical lives. After briefly considering Enoch and Noah, the author focuses on Abraham in chapter 10. The similarities with James include the phrase "Abraham, who was called 'the friend [*philos*]'" (1 Clem. 10:1; see also 17:2, "Abraham … was called 'the friend [*philos*] of God'"; cf. the similar phrase in Jas 2:23).[3] First Clement cites Gen 15:6 ("Abraham believed God, and it was reckoned to him as righteousness," 1 Clem. 10:6); this appears verbatim in Jas 2:23 and alludes to the sacrifice of Isaac in Gen 22 (1 Clem. 10:7; Jas 2:21). Finally, 1 Clement draws the examples of Abraham, Lot, and Rahab together by emphasizing that all three should

---

3. All translations of texts from the Apostolic Fathers (1 Clement and the Shepherd of Hermas) follow Holmes 2007.

be praised for the "faith and hospitality" of each (the reference to Rahab appears in 1 Clem. 12:1; Jas 2:25 also specifically highlights Rahab's faith demonstrated in hospitality). Allison (2013) considers why James has related the patriarch Abraham with the prostitute Rahab; he notes that the "closest parallel to James's juxtaposition is 1 Clem. 10–12, which offers short synopses of 'the faith and hospitality' of both Abraham (chap. 10) and Rahab (chap. 12)" (501). Yet, Allison goes on to note that the two accounts are separated by a description of Lot and, in the end, he is not at all convinced that this passage demonstrates that 1 Clement knew or used James. The similarities could be at least in part due to the common Jewish traditions regarding Abraham's faith and obedience, though the pairing of Abraham and Rahab does stand out as unique to James and 1 Clement.

Johnson draws attention to another set of dense parallels between 1 Clem. 29:1; 30:1–3 and Jas 4:1–10. Here the author of 1 Clement commands his audience to a life of holiness before God, "lifting up to him pure and undefiled hands" (1 Clem. 29:1; cf. Jas 4:8, "cleanse your hands, you sinners, and purify your hearts, you double-minded"). After this the author issues a call to forsake slander (1 Clem. 30:1; cf. Jas 4:11), cites Prov 3:34 (1 Clem. 30:2; cf. Jas 4:6), references humility and self-control (1 Clem. 30:3; cf. Jas 3:13, 17), discusses "being justified by works and not by words" (1 Clem. 30:3; cf. Jas 2:24), and concludes with a condemnation of arrogance (1 Clem. 30:8; cf. Jas 4:16). In Johnson's estimation, these parallels offer the highest degree of thematic and verbal similarity between James and 1 Clement. He concludes (2004, 55): "Some doubt may remain, but the probability is that Clement knew and used James" because the clusters along with the scattered verbal echoes indicate a strong similarity in theme and concept. Whether these similarities are enough to establish the fact that the author of 1 Clement knew and used James is difficult to tell with certainty. Some argue that it is just as plausible that these parallels are due to shared tradition and the similar genre of moral exhortation employed by both texts (e.g., Allison 2013, 29; Nienhuis 2007). However, like the similarities between James and 1 Peter, these parallels must be considered when discussing the date and early reception of James.

James and the Shepherd of Hermas

The resemblance between James and the Shepherd of Hermas (composed in either the late first or mid-second century) is even stronger than that between James and 1 Clement. This situation leads Johnson (1995, 79;

2004, 56) to conclude that the relationship is "unmistakable" and "virtually certain." While noting the correspondences are striking and that perhaps the Shepherd of Hermas represents the best possible case of early reception of James, others nevertheless argue that the evidence for a literary relationship between the two texts is inconclusive (e.g., Dibelius 1976, 32; Allison 2013, 23).

One of the more striking similarities between James and the Shepherd of Hermas is the shared use of the rare term "double-minded" (*dipsychos*). Whereas James uses the term twice (1:8; 4:8), the Shepherd of Hermas uses the noun or verbal form of the term some fifty-five times, with especially Mand. 9 comprising a full discussion on the need to rid oneself of "double-mindedness" (see more below). Nienhuis (2007, 120) observes that the "word and its cognates are repeated so frequently that the concept develops into a major sub-theme of the book." Likewise, in the Shepherd of Hermas the opposite of "double-mindedness" is "simplicity" (*haplotēs*), a term that appears throughout the text. Whereas James only uses this term once, in his description of God's generous giving (1:5), Johnson (1995, 76) notes correctly that the concept "matches perfectly what James understands by being *adiakritos* (3:17) and 'pure of heart' (4:8)." These concepts, "simplicity" and "pureness of heart," are interchangeable in the Shepherd of Hermas too. For example, "You, therefore, cleanse your heart of all the vanities of this life" (Herm. Mand. 9.4) is equivalent to "keep this commandment … in order that your repentance … may prove to be sincere and pure and innocent and unstained" (Herm. Mand. 2.7). Johnson notes that this is parallel to the idea in James that cleansing the heart demonstrates repentance (Jas 4:8), which is also a major theme of the Shepherd of Hermas (Herm. Vis. 4.2.5). Further similarities include the cosmological dualism represented in the conflict between God and the devil (Jas 3:13–18; 4:7; Herm. Mand. 3.1; 9.9; 12.4, 7), the problem of wealth and poverty for the Christian community (Jas 1:9–11; 2:5–7; 5:1–6; Herm. Sim. 2.5; 4.4, 5; 9.20; Vis. 3.9.6), concern for speech ethics (Jas 3:3–8; Herm. Mand. 2.2, 3; Sim. 8.7, 27), and patient endurance (Jas 1:2–4; 5:7–10; Herm. Mand. 5.1–3; 9.10).[4]

---

4. Allison (2013, 20–21) offers a somewhat comprehensive list of the parallels between James and the Shepherd of Hermas: Jas 1:1 (Herm. Sim. 9.17.1); Jas 1:5 (Herm. Mand. 2.4; 9.4; Sim. 5.4.3); Jas 1:6–8 (Herm. Mand. 9.1–12); Jas 1:12 (Herm. Vis. 2.2.7); Jas 1:17 (Herm. Mand. 9.11; 11.5); Jas 1:21 and Jas 2:14 (Herm. Sim. 6.1.1); Jas 1:27 (Herm. Mand. 2.7; 8.10; Sim. 1.8); Jas 2:7 (Herm. Sim. 8.6.4); Jas 2:19 (Herm.

The most extensive set of parallels between the two texts occurs in Jas 1:5–8 and Shepherd of Hermas, Mand. 9. Both passages address the danger of double-mindedness, especially in the context of asking something of God (Jas 1:6; Herm. Mand. 9.1–2, 4–6). Though no phrases are repeated verbatim, the two passages share a density of terms and concepts, all of which are organized in a similar way. Allison (2013, 167–68) lists the similarities: both passages focus on asking God for something in the context of trial; they both refer to the eventual outcome (one either receives or does not receive); both passages stress the character of God's giving (he is good and gives without rebuke or grudge); and both insist that such asking must be done in faith not doubting or with double-mindedness. So striking are these similarities that even Dibelius (1976, 31), who denied any literary relationship between the two texts, observes that "*Herm. mand.* 9 is the best interpretation of Jas 1:5–8 imaginable," to which Johnson (2004, 95) quips, "But isn't the best explanation of such an 'interpretation' the use of James by *Hermas*?" On the other hand, Allison (2013, 23) argues that because the dating of the two texts is unclear and the content in the Shepherd of Hermas, Mand. 9 cannot be explained by comparison to James, in the end it is best to conclude that both documents are dependent upon a common source that has not survived. He conjectures the common source could be the fragmentary text called Eldad and Modad (168–69). Here, once again, we see how the same evidence can been evaluated by scholars in strikingly different ways.

Are these examples of the early reception of James in 1 Peter, 1 Clement, and the Shepherd of Hermas, or do these suggestive literary similarities indicate that the Epistle of James was written later and instead was dependent upon these sources? A third option acknowledges that the literary similarities are somewhat striking but credits them to the use of shared themes in early Christian tradition. Not only is the literary relationship between these texts important for understanding the early reception history of James, but they have played a central role in the discussion of dating the Epistle of James as well. Perhaps what is most

---

Mand. 1:1); Jas 3:8 (Herm. Sim. 9.26.7; Mand. 2.3); Jas 3:15 (Herm. Mand. 9.11; 11.5–6); Jas 3:17 (Herm. Mand. 11.8); Jas 3:18 (Herm. Sim. 9.19.2); Jas 4:3 (Herm. Mand. 9.4; Sim. 5.4.3); Jas 4:5 (Herm. Mand. 3.1; Sim. 5.6.5); Jas 4:7 (Herm. Mand. 12.2.4; 12.5.2); Jas 4:11 (Herm. Mand. 2.2); Jas 4:12 (Herm. Mand. 12.6.3; Sim. 9.23.4); Jas 5:4 (Herm. Vis. 3.9.6); Jas 5:11 (Herm. Mand. 4.3.5; Sim. 5.4.4; 5.7.4).

clear—even from this brief discussion—is that scholars who have access to the same textual evidence remain divided in their assessments, and this likely is due to their other historical and theological commitments about these early Christian writings.

James in Patristic Sources and Early Canon Lists

It is difficult to discuss patristic use of James because, as noted above, explicit citation of the letter before Origen is sparse. Also, patristic authors often did not directly quote their sources when making allusions to texts and traditions, so this renders the identification of the quotations or allusions quite difficult and presents an additional challenge for this investigation. Furthermore, again there is a range of scholarly opinion regarding what the evidence indicates. Johnson (1995, 129), noting the slender and disputed evidence for knowledge of James before Origen, observes that the evidence for James is not "significantly worse than for some other New Testament writings," while Allison (2013, 20) concludes that there are "no sure traces of James in literature from the first or first half of the second century." In the following I will survey some of the possible allusions to James in the patristic material.

Irenaeus (130–200 CE)

Many scholars have pointed out that Irenaeus writes in his *Against Heresies* that Abraham "believed God, and it was imputed unto him for righteousness; and he was called the friend of God" (*Haer.* 4.16.2 [*ANF* 1:481]). This of course bears resemblance to James's description of Abraham as the "friend of God" (2:23). However, Nienhuis (2007, 36–37) has argued convincingly that because this phrase was known in earlier Jewish writings, it is just as plausible that both Irenaeus and James appeal to earlier literature for this description.

Clement of Alexandria (150–215 CE)

Eusebius preserves a suggestive passage in which he indicates that Clement of Alexandria provided commentary on all the "canonical scriptures," which includes the Catholic Epistles. But is this evidence that Clement knew James? According to Eusebius, Clement had written in his *Hypotyposeis* "concise explanations of all the Canonical Scriptures, not passing over even the disputed writings [*antilegomenas*], I mean the Epistle of Jude and the remaining Catholic Epistles" (*Hist. eccl.* 6.14.1).[5] Though Jude is mentioned, it is unclear which of the "remaining" Catholic Epistles he is referring to in particular; yet, this might suggest that Clement in fact did know of James. Though Eusebius does not enumerate the contents of the collection, it is plausible that he is referring to "the remaining Catholic Epistles" as a discrete collection that eventually included James. As we will see below, by the time of Eusebius such a collection including James was known, but how much earlier than Eusebius such a collection was in circulation it is very difficult to tell.

Nienhuis points out another witness to Clement's now lost *Hypotyposeis*. Though quite late, the ninth-century Byzantine Patriarch Photius commented on the *Hypotyposeis* in his work called *Bibliotheca*. He claimed that Clement's work "is supposedly an interpretation of Genesis, Exodus, the Psalms, St. Paul's epistles, the Catholic Epistles, and Ecclesiastes" (translation from Nienhuis 2007, 49). Though Nienhuis expresses little trust in the document as a source for the precise contents of the *Hypotyposeis*, this later witness uses the phrase "Catholic Epistles," which may refer to a discrete collection of texts because it stands in the list beside "St. Paul's epistles." Again, because Clement refers to a group of "Catholic Epistles," one might understand this as an indirect reference to James as a member of that collection.

Finally, Johnson (1995, 129) argues that "Eusebius' testimony would seem to support the notion that Clement had devoted some commentary to James." He continues, "Eusebius himself quoted extensively from Clement's traditions concerning James the Just in *Hypotyposes* Books 6 and 7. It would seem logical that these reminiscences would have been attached to Clement's concise explication of the letter itself" (129). Furthermore, Johnson (2004, 45) notes, "Since both Clement and Origen were sensitive to the differences between what was traditionally received and what was not, the Alexandrian sponsorship of James would seem to argue for some prior period of acceptance, at least in their church" (but see the strenuous disagreement in Nienhuis 2007, 56). Though Nienhuis wisely stresses caution, Johnson is much more confident that Clement knew and perhaps used James. The paucity of evidence precludes one from drawing definite

---

5. All translations of texts from Eusebius's *Ecclesiastical History* are from the LCL edition by Kirsopp Lake and John E. L. Oulton.

conclusions, but it is possible that Clement was aware of a collection of New Testament letters known as the Catholic Epistles, and if this collection bore a resemblance to its later canonized form, it is possible that the Epistle of James was included in it.

Origen (185–253 CE)

Whereas it is uncertain whether Clement knew of James, his successor at the catechetical school in Alexandria "listed James in his canon and cited him frequently" (Johnson 2004, 69). In several places Origen refers to the Epistle of James (*Sel. Ps.* 30.6; 118.153; *Fr. Jo.* 126; and in Latin, *Hom. Exod.* 3.3; *Hom. Lev.* 2.4; 13.2) and understood the epistle to be authoritative and written by James (*Hom. Exod.* 8.4, "the apostle James says"; *Sel. Ps.* 30.6, "according to James"). However, some insist that Origen nevertheless was hesitant about accepting James. While commenting on the Gospel of John, Origen makes a passing reference to something "in the letter of James that is current" (*Comm. Jo.* 19.23.152).[6] In Allison's estimation, this phrase echoes the comments of Eusebius, namely, that some in the early church doubted James's authenticity because "few ancients quote it" (*Hist. eccl.* 2.23.24; see further below).

Both Nienhuis (2007, 56) and Allison (2013, 19) argue that this phrase should not be taken as Origen's expression of doubt toward the letter because of what we know otherwise about Origen's use of James. Rather, it likely registers the doubts of others. Yet, it is curious that Nienhuis (2007, 56) nevertheless concludes, "This is an important point, because it recognizes that in Origen's day the letter was still in its early use and was not fully authoritative even to those in Origen's audience.... Indeed, his appeal to the letter is that of a document recently arrived." Though Origen's comment might suggest that some in his audience did not receive James as fully authoritative, it does not follow that the Epistle of James was therefore a newly composed text, as Nienhuis seems to suggest. This judgment could owe more to Nienhuis's overall historical reconstruction of a late date of

---

6. The translation is from Dibelius 1975. Allison (2013, 19) instead renders it as "the epistle current by the name of James," and Johnson (1995, 130) translates, "the letter that circulates under the name of James." Nienhuis (2007, 55) provides the translation "the so-called epistle of James," though he notes the term "current" or "so-called" (*pheromenos*) need not carry the idea of doubt because Origen used the same term to refer to the other apostolic letters (*Comm. Jo.* 1.15).

composition for James than to an assessment of Origen's attitude toward the letter. For Allison (2003, 14), it is suspicious that whereas Origen knew of and used James, his "Latin contemporary, Cyprian (d. 258), Bishop of Carthage … shows no knowledge of James." That Cyprian passes over James is further evidence for Allison that the letter was sparsely used even after the time of Origen.

Eusebius (260–340 CE, writing ca. 324–325)

In Eusebius we find what some consider the first reference to the Catholic Epistles as a technical designation for the collection of letters that included James through Jude. Two passages in Eusebius may suggest that James was included in the Catholic Epistles collection. Following an elaborate record of the martyrdom of James, the Lord's brother, Eusebius notes:

> Such is the story of James, whose is said to be the first of the Epistles called Catholic. It is to be observed that its authenticity is denied [*noth-euetai*], since few of the ancients quote it, as is also the case with the Epistle called Jude's, which is itself one of the seven called Catholic; nevertheless we know that these letters have been used publicly with the rest in most churches. (*Hist. eccl.* 2.23.24–25)

Eusebius notes that James and Jude are included in a larger collection of letters, "the seven called Catholic." Furthermore, though he indicates James's authenticity was disputed due to lack of attestation by the "ancients," both James and Jude are nevertheless "used publicly with the rest in most churches." Though Eusebius notes lack of use of James by the ancients, Joseph Mayor's (1897) caution against any hasty conclusion that Eusebius was therefore suspicious of James is worth repeating. "His own practice," Mayor noted of Eusebius, "betrays no suspicion of its genuineness, as he not only recognizes it as an authority … but in one passage quotes James iv.11 as Scripture (*Comm. In Psalm.* P. 648 Motnf.), in another quotes James v.13 as spoken by the holy Apostle" (xlix).

Despite Eusebius's comment regarding lack of attestation, he reports that James and Jude "have been used publicly … in most churches." It was the practice of a wide scope of churches to use these particular letters, and their use throughout the church was along "with the rest" or perhaps "with the remaining [letters]," that is, either the rest of the Catholic Epistles or perhaps the rest of the letters included in the canonical New Testament. Eusebius notes elsewhere: "I mean the Epistle of Jude and the remaining

Catholic Epistles" (*Hist. eccl.* 6.14.1), where "remaining" clearly refers to the rest of the Catholic Epistles. The phrase "with the rest" or "with the remaining [letters]" in *Hist. eccl.* 2.23.24–25 must rather refer to the rest of the received or apostolic letters. If this is correct, the passage above suggests that Eusebius not only received a tradition of using these letters ("as in most churches"), but also that this tradition affirmed that James and Jude were received along with the rest of the apostolic letters.

In one of the most famous passages in *Ecclesiastical History*, where he focuses on the New Testament canon, Eusebius distinguishes between "recognized writings" (*homologoumenoi*, namely, the gospels and letters of Paul) and "disputed writings" (*antilegomenoi*, specifically James, Jude, 2 Peter, 2 and 3 John). Eusebius writes:

> At this point it seems reasonable to summarize the writings of the New Testament which have been quoted. In the first place should be put the holy tetrad of the Gospels. To them follows the writing of the Acts of the Apostles. After this should be reckoned the Epistles of Paul. Following them the Epistle of John called the first, and in the same way should be recognized the Epistle of Peter. In addition to these should be put, if it seem desirable, the Revelation of John, the arguments concerning which we will expound at the proper time. These belong to the Recognized Books [*homologoumenois*].[7] Of the Disputed Books [*antilegomenoi*] which are nevertheless known to most are the Epistle called James, that of Jude, the second Epistle of Peter, and the so-called second and third Epistles of John which may be the work of the evangelist or of some other with the same name. (*Hist. eccl.* 3.25.1–5)

The passage continues with a third and final group of texts that Eusebius distinguishes from the first two groups, namely, those that are not *genuine* (including the Acts of Paul, Shepherd of Hermas, the Apocalypse of Peter, Barnabas, and the "Teaching of the Apostles" or the Didache). Johnson (1995) summarizes Eusebius's logic for excluding texts from the New Testament canon: (1) "lack of recognition by earlier ecclesiastical writers," (2) "language different from that of the 'apostolic style,'" and (3) "heretical content and perspective" (127, citing Eusebius). From this Johnson concludes

---

7. Dungan (2007, 71) notes that *homologoumenoi* is "a shorthand expression that has a very precise meaning for Eusebius.… Its full meaning [is] unanimously *acknowledged* by all orthodox bishops in apostolic succession churches throughout the empire, all the way back to the beginning" (emphasis original).

that "by his own criteria, Eusebius includes James in the canonical category *because* it is 'recognized by many,' has the 'apostolic style,' and is orthodox in its teaching" (127). Furthermore, Johnson notes, Eusebius does not hesitate to use James as authoritative, even calling it "Scripture" (*Comm. Ps.* 100.5). Eusebius, writing sometime around 325, was recording traditions that had been passed on from previous generations. From these passages it seems that Eusebius received and recorded the tradition of using James as an authoritative text that was both part of a growing New Testament canon in general and a specific subgroup of New Testament letters called the Catholic Epistles specifically. Therefore we might confidently say that by the time of Eusebius not only was James received along with "the rest" of the apostolic letters, but further, it was placed within a specific canonical subcollection of New Testament letters called the Catholic Epistles.

Early Canon Lists

From Eusebius onward, the Catholic Epistles are limited to seven in number, with the ordering of the texts usually being James, Peter, John, and Jude. This reinforces the general conclusion that James was both known and listed among the canonized Catholic Epistles by this time. About fifty years after Eusebius, Cyril of Jerusalem (ca. 350 CE) records a canon list which, in part, states: "Receive also the Acts of the Twelve Apostles; and in addition to these the seven Catholic Epistles of James, Peter, John, and Jude; then as a seal upon them all, and the last work of disciples, the fourteen Epistles of Paul" (*Catechesis* 4.36 [McCauley and Stephenson 1969, 137]). In canon 60 of the Synod of Laodicea (363 CE), the seven Catholic Epistles are counted by name after the four gospels and Acts and before the Pauline letters. Athanasius's Easter letter (367 CE) lists the "Acts of the Apostles and seven letters, called catholic, by the apostles, namely: one by James; two by Peter; then three by John; and after these, one by Jude. After these there are fourteen letters by the apostle Paul" (*Ep. fest.* 39.18 [Gallagher and Meade 2017, 123–24]). Both Apostolic Canons 85 (ca. 375–80 CE) and Gregory of Nazianzus (ca. 381–90 CE) list all seven of the Catholic Epistles without dispute, yet the Apostolic Canons gives them in the order James, 1–3 John, Jude, and 1–2 Peter. It is worth noting that whereas Eusebius famously labels James, 2–3 John, and Jude as disputed, all the Catholic Epistles, including James, are listed by Cyril, canon 60 of the Synod of Laodicea, Athanasius, and Apostolic Canons 85 without any question regarding their authority or status as canon. However, roughly thirteen years after Athanasius, Amphilochius (ca. 380 CE) once again notes a degree of caution. After listing the epistles of Paul, Amphilochius notes: "So far so good, what is the rest? Of the catholic epistles / Some say seven; but others only three / It is necessary to accept: the one of James, / And one of Peter, and those of John, / But some receive three [of John], and in addition to them the two / Of Peter, and that of Jude a seventh" (*Iambi ad Seleucum* 310–15 [Gallagher and Meade 2017, 154]). Though Amphilochius registers some variation in number—the "others" may represent the Syrian churches—he is clearly working within a tradition that received the seven Catholic Epistles including James. This terminology was also introduced in the Latin West by Jerome (ca. 347–419 CE; *Vir. ill.* 1–2).[8]

The Muratorian fragment, which likely originated in Rome before 200 CE, could be the oldest surviving canon list and thus constitutes valuable early information regarding the formation of the New Testament canon.[9] Whereas many have lamented the quality of its Latin (some have noted the copyist was stunningly careless), the fragment was most likely copied from an original Greek canon list. The fragment, of course, is not complete, yet even considering that not all of the text has survived the contents we do have are unusual (as will be seen below).

The fragment begins in mid sentence enumerating two of the four canonical gospels (Luke and John). Then, after mentioning the book of Acts and the epistles of Paul (omitting Hebrews), the fragment names only Jude and two epistles of John from the books of the Catholic Epistles. One finds in lines 68–69: "the Epistle of Jude and two of the above-mentioned (or, bearing the name of) John are counted (or, used) [*habentur*] in the catholic [Church]" (in Gallagher and Meade 2017, 181). The meaning of *in catholica*, which may refer either to the "catholic church" (as most suppose) or perhaps to a collection of the Catholic Epistles, is uncertain. If *in catholica* refers to "in the catholic epistles," what is the significance? On one hand, this vague reference in the fragment could merely refer to 1 John as a letter with a general (catholic) address, as it was understood by Origen. However, if, as for Origen, 1 John is *the* "catholic epistle," then

---

8. It must be said that James and Jude (and Hebrews) are missing from the Cheltenham Canon (360 CE); see Allison, 2013, 18. Johnson (1995, 135) notes a connection between the James omission from the Cheltenham canon and the "dramatic … absence of any acquaintance with James among the first Latin theologians in Africa."

9. For discussion regarding the controversy over the dating of the Muratorian Fragment, see Hahneman 2002, 405–15; Gallagher and Meade 2017, 175–78.

the author would be connecting Jude and two other letters of John (2 and 3 John?) to 1 John. Though very slight, this possibility could suggest a partial collection of the Catholic Epistles.

At any rate, the selection of only Jude and two of the Johannine letters is unique among the canon lists. This is idiosyncratic in terms of both contents and order. Hahneman notes:

> The absence of 1 Peter (and James) is extraordinary, and most probably implies omissions in the Fragment. The letters found in the Fragment, namely 2 (and 3?) John and Jude, are elsewhere found only in larger collections of the catholic epistles.... Jude, which is listed before the letters of John in the Fragment, was usually listed last among the catholic epistles both in the East, where the order James, Peter, John, Jude was standard, and in the West, where the order varied. (1992, 181)

Though it does not definitively clarify what was contained in the fragment, Hahneman's comments are confirmed both in early attestation and in the manuscript evidence. This strongly suggests that the fragment has for some reason omitted reference to at least 1 Peter and 1 John and perhaps James as well.

Manuscript Evidence of Early Reception

The presence or absence of James in canon lists or early citation is by no means the only criterion for determining the early use and authority of a New Testament text. The manuscript tradition must be taken together with the above evidence for a composite picture of the early reception James. Whereas the manuscript evidence strongly suggests that the four gospels and the Pauline letters were collected together and circulating by 200 CE at the latest, it is harder to determine when the same happened for the Catholic Epistles (see Porter 2004, 95–127; 2013, 110). Manuscripts provide another means of assessing the early reception of James, but the extant evidence for the letter is extremely fragmentary. Here I consider the role manuscript evidence plays in the journey James took into the canon of the New Testament.

There are three early papyri manuscripts containing fragments of James, all of which likely date to the third century: P20 (containing Jas 2:19–3:2, 4–9), P23 (containing Jas 1:10–12, 15–16), and P100 (containing Jas 3:13–4:4; 4:9–5:1). All three of these fragments were discovered in the ancient trash heaps outside Oxyrhynchus, Egypt, and Lincoln Blummell and Thomas Wayment (2015, 180) conclude that these fragments constitute "examples of Christian codices from Oxyrhynchus that began with the Epistle of James." P20 (P.Oxy. 9.1171) consists of a "small scrap of papyrus" (85) containing a few lines from James, none of which are complete. The scribe incorporated reading aids, namely, diaereses (the use of pronunciation marks above vowels), the use of apostrophe noting the end of proper names, and *nomina sacra* (the practice of abbreviating certain divine names in early Christian manuscripts).

P23 (P.Oxy. 10.1229) originally was dated by scholars to the third century but "has more recently been dated to the second century by P. W. Comfort and D. P. Barrett" based upon handwriting comparison (Blummell and Waymet 2015, 88). The text contains some punctuation and page numbers, but there are no indications of *nomina sacra* (the surviving passages do not contain any of the relevant names).

P100 (P.Oxy. 65.4449) has large line spaces that may signal paragraph divisions, and the scribe used *nomina sacra* as was the norm in early manuscripts. Furthermore, P100 consists of a single page from a codex. It has twenty-six "fragmentary lines of text on both the front and reverse sides. Pagination from both the front and reverse are preserved in the upper margin, and the pages are numbered sequentially ... [6 and 7]. This would indicate a codex that began with James and that could have included other texts following James" (Blummell and Wayment 2015, 134). Porter agrees: "The page numbers ... indicate ... that page 1 was the beginning of the Epistle of James." Therefore, Porter (2013, 123) concludes, "it is possible either that both P23 and P100 were manuscripts of just the Epistle of James or that they were the first book in a collection of the Catholic (or General) Epistles."[10] The presence of pagination cannot, on its own, indicate conclusively that either of these codices contained some or all of the Catholic Epistles besides James. However, within the context of the eventual development of the Catholic Epistles, Porter (2013, 124) concludes that if the latter is "the case, there is evidence of the Catholic Epistles being gathered together possibly by the second century and almost assuredly by the third."

Finally, we should consider Uncial 0173, a nearly complete leaf from a fifth-century parchment codex that contains Jas 1:25–27.[11] Interestingly,

---

10. Blummell and Wayment note that if this is evidence of such a collection, "it would be the earliest witness to a codex of the Catholic Epistles" (2015, 134).

11. Uncials are manuscripts written completely in capital letters, and a codex is a manuscript with pages bound on one side (like a modern book) as opposed to a scroll.

the pagination (17–18) suggests that this miniature codex began with the Epistle of James. As noted above, these manuscripts were all discovered in Egypt, and the fact that P20, P23, and P100 likely date to the third century supports the conclusion above that Origen had access to James in Alexandria. Furthermore, some of these manuscripts suggest that James was collected along with other texts from the Catholic Epistles, which might suggest a growing awareness that James was received and read along with other authoritative Christian texts.

Elsewhere, the text of James is represented in the major Greek codices of the fourth and fifth century. These uncial codices regularly present Acts with the Catholic Epistles and place them either before (Vaticanus and Alexandrinus) or after (Sinaiticus) the Pauline corpus. Codices Sinaiticus (ℵ 01) and Vaticanus (B 03) both date to circa 350 CE, with Vaticanus perhaps slightly earlier than 350 due to the absence of ornamentation (which suggests a later development). Alexandrinus (A 02) dates to the beginning of the fifth century (ca. 400 CE) and may have been copied in Egypt. James is included along with the other Catholic Epistles in each of these codices, thereby reinforcing what seems to be the common judgment of the early canonical lists surveyed above.

Conclusion

As noted at the beginning of this chapter, the reception of a text is not incidental or irrelevant to its interpretation. It is important for interpreters to become more aware of how early Christian texts were read and used in subsequent Christian worship and theological debate. In particular, it is necessary to investigate the early reception history of the Epistle of James in order to understand it well.

Though the early reception history of James has been a difficult (and neglected) story, there has been a growing appreciation of the epistle's reception and how this reception is relevant to understanding the meaning of the text. Knowledge and use of the Epistle of James was perhaps sparse in the early church, but this so-called *silence* was not, in the end, a reason to exclude the text from the New Testament canon, nor did it deter Origen and others from receiving it as an authority. Rather, the somewhat patchwork story of James's early reception reveals that the text was finally accepted not only as an authoritative Christian text, but also as one associated with the subgroup of canonical New Testament texts called the Catholic Epistles.

Salvation, the Church, and Social Teaching:
The Epistle of James in Exegesis of the Reformation Era

Stephen J. Chester

Like so many other biblical books, the Reformation era saw the Epistle of James enter a new, much more controversial phase in the history of its reception. Whether in relation to teaching about salvation, about the nature and composition of the church, or about ethical concerns in social life, sixteenth-century interpreters viewed James through the lens of contemporary conflicts. Their concerns were those of their own time and place, but the influence of their conflicts endures in that it has shaped the expectations held and the questions asked about James by interpreters in diverse subsequent contexts right down to the present day.

The Epistle of Straw: Luther on James

Of all the sentences penned about the Epistle of James in the Reformation era, only one has dominated subsequent perceptions and is well-known even today. In 1522, Martin Luther (*LW* 35:355–411) wrote prefaces to accompany the different books of his translation of the New Testament into German. His guidance was intended to assist readers in the unfamiliar experience of reading and interpreting the Bible in the vernacular rather than in Latin. In particular, he sought to encourage them to interpret the texts according to the new theology that Luther himself had developed through extended engagement with the New Testament, especially the Pauline letters. The stakes were high because Luther had been excommunicated by the pope the previous year. To read in Luther's way was to choose his side in a dispute now in the process of dividing the Western church. In a general passage designed to help readers identify the most essential New Testament books that should guide their interpretation of the rest (John's Gospel, Paul's letters, 1 Peter), Luther (*LW* 35:362) wrote that compared to these central texts, "St. James' epistle is really an epistle of straw … for it has nothing of the nature of the gospel about it." He also moved James from its traditional position and placed it at the end of the New Testament, together with Hebrews, Jude, and Revelation, other books about which he had doubts.

Normally Luther's ability to coin a memorable phrase served him well, but this proved an exception, and this passage was omitted from later editions of the German Bible (Gowler 2014, 11). His characterization of James as "an epistle of straw" had proved a significant tactical mistake that handed ammunition to his opponents. Luther was a theologian intent on indicting the church of his day for what he regarded as its unbiblical teaching, yet he now found himself describing a portion of the word of God in an apparently derogatory way. In later centuries, this description of James would both encourage those Protestants who wished to set aside elements of Scripture they found theologically uncongenial and puzzle those desiring to maintain the authority of the whole canon.[1] The latter asked how Luther could adopt such a position, especially when he himself frequently quoted passages from James with approval and preached on texts from the epistle on several occasions? In fact, Luther's comments in the preface dealing with the content of James clarify his position considerably and provide a consistent basis for his future practice. Yet they do this within the content of his new theology and his accompanying hermeneutic of law and gospel. To understand his comments requires a grasp both of the new theology that Luther was proposing (Chester 2017, 175–217) and of that against which he was reacting (Chester 2017, 63–103). Before evaluating Luther's specific comments about James, it is therefore necessary to summarize these competing theological perspectives.

The breach between Luther and the Catholic Church revolved around incompatible interpretations of New Testament texts concerning justification by faith. Since Augustine's dispute with Pelagius in the early fifth

---

1. Thus, e.g., Watson (1994, 231–36) employs Luther's hermeneutic of law and gospel to argue that the authority of the gospel is greater than that of the text and therefore interpreters ought to resist the literal meanings of biblical texts when they discern them to be oppressive. In contrast, Thompson (2004, 285) argues that Luther "was willing to identify the text of Scripture as the Word of God repeatedly and without qualification" (but he does admit that Luther's comments about James represent a "genuine tension point in his approach to Holy Scripture" [136]).

century concerning the parts played in salvation by divine grace and human free will, it had been recognized by all Catholic interpreters that salvation begins with divine initiative. The impact of sin means that fallen human beings can only act justly as a result of the gift of God's grace given in initial justification. No one can make oneself righteous apart from this gift, which is available only because of the person and work of Christ. Nevertheless, the medieval church taught that once this initial gift of grace is received in baptism it is the Christian's responsibility to cooperate with the gift by performing good works in love of God and neighbor. There is not only initial justification but also justification as a lifetime process in which individuals gradually became more Christlike. Within this process their sins result in a loss of grace, but the merits of their good works and their access to the grace made available through the sacraments of the church result in its increase. There are mortal sins (e.g., murder) that might endanger the whole process, but otherwise works such as fasting, almsgiving, and prayer are sufficient to address a whole host of less serious venial sins. When the baptized person still experiences desire for things contrary to God's will, this is not in itself sin and does not in itself lead to a loss of grace and justice unless these desires are assented to and acted upon.

According to medieval Catholic thought, no one can know with certainty where he or she has reached in one's journey of justification or whether and how much time in purgatory might be necessary to complete the process of becoming fit for heaven. As such, while hope can be strong, complete assurance is possible only in relation to God's desire to forgive and not in relation to whether a person has attained salvation. Faith plays an important but carefully defined role in this process. It is from faith that good works flow, and yet faith by itself is not capable of such works. Faced by the need to coordinate Pauline texts that assert that faith is the instrument through which God justifies (e.g., Gal 2:16) with James's denial that justification is by faith alone (Jas 2:24), medieval theologians understood Gal 5:6, where Paul asserts that in Christ what counts is faith working through love, to indicate that faith works only when it is formed by love. Apart from love, faith (typically translated from the Greek noun *pistis* using the Latin noun *fides*) is intellectual assent to the truth of the gospel that needs love to make it alive. Under the impact of vivifying love, faith is no longer primarily cognitive but becomes active and transforming. Christians progress in righteousness and begin to fulfill God's law when they have this faith formed by love.

To his own surprise and to that of his contemporaries, Luther comes to regard all of this as a travesty of New Testament teaching. He reacts particularly strongly against the part played by the merit of human works as an efficient cause of justification. Where the medieval church saw consistency with Augustine's insistence on the priority of divine grace, Luther instead saw its contradiction. He came to view grace not as something infused by God into the person who believes, but instead as God's undeserved favor toward sinners in Christ. The gift received is that of faith, in which Christ is present and by means of which the person who believes is united with Christ and his righteousness. Those who receive Christ's righteousness in union with him and are declared righteous by God are therefore justified wholly and completely. Their subsequent works play no part in causing justification; they can be sure that they are indeed saved because this certainty is based not upon their own merit or transformation but solely upon the perfect person and work of Christ. It is sin when the baptized person still experiences desire for things contrary to God's will, but such sin is forgiven through Christ's saving work.

For Luther, the faith from which assurance of salvation springs is not intellectual assent to the truth of the gospel alone but instead it is trust in divine promises after the pattern of Abraham (Rom 4:18–22). It is inherently living and active, or else it is not faith, and the medieval doctrine of faith formed by love is to be utterly rejected. Luther hears in Gal 5:6 not a statement of faith's inability to work until it is made alive by love but rather the assertion of faith's own effectiveness in empowering deeds of love. Therefore, although the transformation of the believer is not a *cause* of justification, it is an inevitable *consequence* of justification. Faith will produce good works by its very nature, just as the sun will shine or a good tree will produce good fruit (Matt 7:17–18); the persistent absence of such works would indicate that faith is not genuine. Although justification is caused by faith alone, justifying faith never comes alone—it is always accompanied by works of faith that express in love of God and neighbor one's gratitude for the gift of Christ. Rather than pursuing a lifelong journey toward a final righteousness that can only be obtained at its end, the Christian is called to live in growing conformity to a righteousness that is nevertheless already complete in Christ.

These two competing theological perspectives, that of the Catholic Church and of Luther's own new theology, form the context of Luther's comments about James. Luther, of course, is convinced that his new theology reflects what the New Testament truly teaches, and he hears in James some significant contradictions of that teaching:

In the first place it is flatly against St. Paul and all the rest of Scripture in ascribing justification to works [2:24]. It says that Abraham was justified by his works when he offered his son Isaac [2:21]; though in Romans 4[:2–22] St. Paul teaches to the contrary that Abraham was justified apart from works, by his faith alone, before he had offered his son, and proves it by Moses in Genesis 15[:6]. (*LW* 35:396)

Whatever else there is in the Epistle of James that he can wholeheartedly approve, Luther hears in chapter 2 a contradiction of Paul. This is startling because it was axiomatic for others in the sixteenth century that there could be no contradiction between these different biblical texts: James *must* have intended to say something compatible with Paul (and vice versa) and thus any differences in interpretation really concern the way in which harmonization is to take place. One must read both biblical writers either in a manner consistent with Luther's understanding of justification, in which case James cannot intend to deny that justification is through faith alone, or else one must read them in a way compatible with the teaching of the medieval church, in which case Paul cannot intend to say that justification does come through faith alone.

An inevitable question therefore arises: why should Luther be so different in his attitude towards the harmonization of James and Paul? The answer is twofold. First, Luther has doubts concerning the apostolic authorship of James, doubts fueled by awareness that its acceptance into the canon by the early church was hesitant and late precisely because of questions about authorship (Eusebius, *Hist. eccl.* 2.23.25). Yet, one suspects, Luther's suspicions about authorship might not have been aroused had James not appeared so problematic to him in some of its contents.

Second, and much more significant in leading Luther to hear James as contradicting Paul, is the epistle's lack of christological content. It contains a wealth of ethical advice about how its readers should live but "does not once mention the Passion, the resurrection, or the Spirit of Christ. He names Christ several times; however he teaches nothing about him, but only speaks of general faith in God" (*LW* 35:396). From Luther's perspective, James lacks precisely what authentic apostles should provide: it lacks a proclamation of the gospel. It is this omission that indicates that James occupies a lesser place within the canon than Paul's epistles and some other New Testament books. For Luther had not only developed a new theology, but he was also in the process of developing a new principle of biblical interpretation with which to guide the reading of Scripture and in which the gospel is one of two main categories. He formally states this new hermeneutic for the first time in a sermon preached in Advent 1522, only months after the publication of his German New Testament (traditionally known as *The September Testament* for its month of publication):

> Therefore, hold to this distinction, and no matter what books you have before you, whether of the Old or of the New Testament, read them with this distinction so that you observe that when promises are made in a book, it is a Gospel book; when commandments are given, it is a Law book. But because in the New Testament the promises are found so abundantly, and in the Old Testament so many laws are found, the former is called "Gospel" and the latter, "the Book of the Law." (*LW* 75:146)

The distinction between law and gospel had been understood by medieval interpreters primarily in terms of two eras, one before the incarnation of Christ, which was the time of the law, and one after his coming, which is the time of the gospel. Luther instead assigns the distinction a primary significance based on how the contents of biblical books function in relation to readers. Books like James, full of instructions for behavior, can highlight for readers their sins and their need of Christ and/or provide positive guidance for living. But they cannot be gospel for readers, proclaiming to them the good news of Christ's death and resurrection and kindling faith in God's promises of salvation. As opposed to what he appears to say in sometimes intemperate phrases like "epistle of straw," what Luther actually does with James coheres with his hermeneutic of law and gospel. Luther treats James as of subsidiary value compared to other texts, but he still values its ethical instruction and still preaches from it and quotes from it.[2] Luther can conclude that James is wrong about justification and that James fails to proclaim the gospel without completely rejecting the letter.

Easy of Exposition, Difficult in Performance: Erasmus on James

If Luther stands alone in his hermeneutical approach to James, the same is not true in relation to his interpretation of its contents. Luther and

---

2. The Epistle of James traditionally appeared in the lectionary in the post-Easter season, and for Luther this compounded the epistle's christological deficit. The church should in this season especially be proclaiming Christ's death and resurrection. Luther nevertheless did still preach from James when it was appointed. See *LW* 57:190–98; 77:216–23.

Desiderius Erasmus differ little in the content of what they hear James say. The two are far apart, however, in terms of how they evaluate the theological value of this content. As a humanist, Erasmus believed in the power of returning to the sources (*ad fontes*). In culture this meant returning to classical Greek and Latin texts; in religion it meant returning to the Greek and Hebrew of the biblical texts themselves. The latter was controversial, because for centuries the prevailing practice within scholastic medieval theology was to use the Latin Vulgate translation of the Bible (Rummel 1995). In 1516 Erasmus published his *Novum Instrumentum*, which provided a carefully researched text of the Greek New Testament, a corrected Vulgate translation conformed to this new text, and explanatory annotations. Multiple editions followed over nearly twenty years, and Erasmus also produced paraphrases of the New Testament texts, with the volume on James appearing in 1520 (see *CWE* 44). Erasmus always remained loyal to the Catholic Church, and with the publication of *The Freedom of the Will* in 1524 he become embroiled in public and acrimonious debate with Luther. Yet, like Erasmus, the Reformers claimed that they were returning to the authentic teaching of Scripture, based on intensive study of the texts in their original languages. Once Luther burst upon the European scene, Luther's quarrel with the church could all too easily be regarded by Erasmus's critics as a new chapter in the existing dispute between scholastics and humanists. Erasmus fell under suspicion of doing Luther's work for him and promoting heresy, and criticism of Erasmus's work by important scholastic theologians only intensified (Jenkins and Preston 2007, 3–80; Rummel 1986, 123–80).

What Erasmus wrote about James was only a small part of this larger controversy, but it did not help. For Erasmus, the center of the gospel is found in the deeds of ordinary Christians rather than in the rites and ceremonies of the church, so the emphasis of James on practical piety (where faith in God is expressed in good works) fitted perfectly. In this context, it was difficult for Erasmus to express what James says about faith in terms consistent with the doctrine of faith formed by love. Erasmus certainly insisted that love "is the inseparable companion of saving faith" (*CWE* 44:151), but he also asserted that if faith is just words "it should no more be called faith than a human corpse merits the name of human being" (*CWE* 44:151). To his critics, this seemed to say with Luther that either faith is active in works or it is not faith, rather than to say with scholastic theology that faith that merely believes may be real and a genuine gift from God, but still lacks the love that is needed to form it into good deeds. Erasmus also several times translates faith not as *fides* (belief) but *fiducia* (trust), appearing to imply that steadfast hope in divine promises is as much part of the nature of faith as assent to the historical truths proclaimed in the gospel. His defense against his critics is to say that neither he nor James is discussing the doctrine of faith formed by love. Instead, they are discussing faith that justifies, and justifying faith both trusts God and either exists or does not exist (for, as his opponents agreed, faith not yet formed by love is not justifying faith). Yet he also cannot resist reiterating his original point that calls into question the whole distinction between two kinds of faith: "the apostle James gave me the occasion to speak in this way when he said that faith which does not work through love is dead.... What he calls dead I call an empty name. And what is empty and dead I say is not worthy to be called by the name so magnificently preached by Christ and his apostles" (*CWE* 82:71).

Erasmus's understanding of the nature of faith in the Epistle of James therefore does seem close to that of Luther. Their understanding of what James says about justification is close, but, whereas Luther is horrified, Erasmus is approving. Erasmus holds that Abraham's deeds "originated from faith," but it is precisely such deeds that exhibit trust in God and, as in Abraham's willingness to sacrifice Isaac (Jas 2:21), merit "the praise of righteousness from deeds" (*CWE* 44:152). The deeds of Abraham number among the causes of his justification. The text from Genesis quoted by James to prove his point, "Abraham believed God and it was reckoned to him as righteousness" (Jas 2:23 NRSV, quoting Gen 15:6), does come earlier in Abraham's story than does the episode of Isaac's near sacrifice, but God "knew that the active and living faith of the old man would refuse nothing if the occasion offered itself" (*CWE* 44:152). Scripture would not record the declaration of Abraham's justification had God not foreknown his deeds.

For Erasmus, this is not a contradiction of Paul's teaching but instead an expression of the same theology. When Erasmus discusses Paul's use of the example of Abraham in Rom 4, he insists that there too faith is trust (*fiducia*) but that it is also a work by which Abraham merited justification (*CWE* 77:678–80). For Erasmus, James is of a piece with the rest of the New Testament, and while Erasmus is doubtful about the epistle's apostolic authorship, this does not cause him to question its canonical status (*LB* 6:1038C–D). He is also not disturbed by the apparent lack of focus in James on the person and work of Christ, but instead he sees the teaching of James as representing the teaching of Christ to the reader. Here Erasmus makes explicit what the text leaves at most implicit by introducing numerous references to Christ into his paraphrase of James. For Erasmus, the true challenge of James lies in its instructions for Christlike living. On the whole, the epistle's teachings "cannot present very much difficulty in the exposition, though they are most difficult in the performance" (*CWE* 44:133).

The Devils and the Antichrist:
The Catholic and Reformed Traditions on James

Erasmus's position—closer to that of Luther on the issue of what James understands to be the nature of faith but closer to previous medieval interpretations on what James means by justification—proved unpersuasive to most fellow Catholics over subsequent decades as the divisions of the Reformation hardened. The period of the Council of Trent (1545–1563), which formulated an official Catholic response to early Protestant teaching, saw a hardening of Catholic feeling against Erasmus:

> As division deepened through the 1550s and into the last period of the council's life (1562–3), Erasmus was left for Catholics more and more on the far side of the gulf. The history of the Index makes the point. The Index of Paul IV (1559) placed Erasmus in the first class of heretics whose whole output was condemned.... If this frantic judgment was an aberration, the revised Index of Pius IV (the 'Council Index,' 1564) still revealed a profound suspicion of him. (Mansfield 1979, 26–27)[3]

In this atmosphere, Catholic interpretation of James became completely committed to maintaining the apostolic authorship of the epistle and traditional medieval interpretations of what it says about both faith and justification. By the time that Robert Bellarmine, one of the great Catholic controversialists against Protestant teaching, wrote about James in his *Controversies of the Christian Faith* (1581–1593), the boundaries of what was considered acceptable opinion had tightened so considerably that

---

3. The *Index Librorum Prohibitorum* (List of Forbidden Books) was a catalog of publications deemed heretical or contrary to morality and therefore not to be read by Catholics. It went through twenty editions from 1559 to 1948 and was abolished in 1966.

most of his reflections on the epistle were devoted to correcting the doubts of Erasmus concerning apostolic authorship (Bellarmine 2013, 61–67).[4] In the decree of the Council of Trent on justification (1546), Jas 2 is quoted to support the necessity for hope and charity to be added to faith (Schroeder 1941, 34) and to support the idea of the Christian's growth in justice through good works (Schroeder 1941, 36). In the *Rhemes New Testament* (1582), the first approved Catholic translation of the New Testament into English, all elements of James relevant to the confessional division are treated as opportunities for stating opposition to heresy in the marginal notes intended to guide the interpretation of the reader. For example, Jas 2:26, where faith apart from works is said to be dead just as the body apart from the soul is dead, is held to indicate not only that faith and works are joint causes of justification, but even that James "makes works the more principal cause, when he resembles faith to the body, and works to the spirit or life of man" (*Rhemes New Testament*, 646).[5] Faith is like a lifeless body until love breathes life into it and works are possible. This is harmonized with Paul by insisting that James here speaks specifically about the process of justification that comes after baptism. In this process "nothing gives more hope of mercy in the next life, than the works of alms, charity, and mercy" (*Rhemes New Testament*, 645). If Paul makes statements that say that justification is not by works, he is not contradicting this but excluding from the causes of justification only works performed prior to baptism: "there is a difference between the first justification, whereof St. Paul specially speaks: and the second justification, whereof St. James does more specially treat" (*Rhemes New Testament*, 646). Bellarmine appeals to Augustine (354–430) to support precisely this distinction (Bellarmine 2013, 64; Augustine 2000, 364–65).

This coordination of the two apostles clears the way for other notes to resist further aspects of Protestant teaching. James 1:5, which stresses the importance of bringing requests to God in prayer with faith and without doubting, is held not to require assurance of salvation but only the absence of any doubts about God's intention to be merciful or God's power to grant requests (*Rhemes New Testament*, 643). James 1:15, which speaks of desire

---

4. The tightening of boundaries is so extensive that Bellarmine corrects not only Erasmus on this issue of the authorship of James, but also Cardinal Cajetan, who had been the papal examiner of Luther's orthodoxy at Augsburg in 1518.

5. I have modernized the spelling in all quotations from sixteenth-century English sources.

conceiving and giving birth to sin that when full grown leads to death, indicates that desire "of itself is not sin ... but when by any content of the mind we do obey or yield to it, then is sin engendered and formed in us" (*Rhemes New Testament*, 643). James 5:14, which speaks of the anointing of the sick and the confessing of sins to one another, is taken to support the sacrament of extreme unction (*Rhemes New Testament*, 651). James is even perceived himself to enter the debate directly on the Catholic side. When James says that even demons believe (Jas 2:19) and rhetorically asks whether someone wants to be shown that faith without works is useless (Jas 2:20), the notes to the reader assert that James "speaks to all heretics that say, faith only without works does justify, calling them vain men and comparing them to devils" (*Rhemes New Testament*, 645).

The "devils" referred to now included not only followers of Luther, but also all in the Reformed tradition that had emerged in the context of cities like Zurich (under the leadership of Huldrych Zwingli) and Geneva (under the leadership of John Calvin). From the very outset, the Reformed had a different, less tense, relationship with the epistle of James than Luther. Preaching in the 1520s, Zwingli seems to have no doubts about apostolic authorship (George 2000, 24–25), and the same is true of Calvin, who published a commentary on James in 1550. Calvin writes that James "is a rich source of varied instruction, of abundant benefit in all aspects of the Christian life" (*CNTC* 3:259). Nor is he perturbed by the epistle's lack of christological content: "we must remember not to expect everyone to go over the same ground" (*CNTC* 3:259). This more positive attitude toward James reflects Calvin's hermeneutical approach to interpreting Scripture, which is not determined by Luther's dialectic between law and gospel. Calvin does hear a contrast between the two in Paul's statements connecting the law with sin and condemnation (e.g., Rom 3:20; 1 Cor 15:56). One of the law's God-given purposes is to reveal to human beings the extent of their bondage to sin and to highlight their need of Christ. Yet in such texts Paul speaks only of what distinguishes the law from the rest of Scripture and may uniquely be said of it. An appropriate wider understanding of the law emphasizes its nature as a divine gift and expression of grace, for the law has abiding validity as the expression of God's will for human behavior and instructs believers how to live. The focus of James on practical ethical instruction can therefore be embraced without reservation.

As part of this instruction, Calvin hears the major emphasis of Jas 4 as the avoidance of quarrels and factions within the church and aversion to judging one's neighbor. He has also earlier told his readers that "God expressly commends to us both the alien and the enemy" (*CNTC* 3:279). Yet there is one exception to this avoidance of judgment: "Some people would have us speak more softly, if we call the pope Antichrist, when he exercises tyranny upon souls, making himself a legislator on a par with God.... I call it prevaricatory obedience—the devil's goods—to accept any other than God as Legislator for the government of souls" (*CNTC* 3:302). On each side of the Protestant/Catholic divide in the sixteenth century the other came to seem so arrogant that mutual vituperation was the only possibility. Perhaps unsurprisingly in this context, Reformed opinion concerning questions of faith and justification in James is almost a mirror image of Catholic interpretation. Calvin rejects the doctrine of faith formed by love, commenting on Jas 2:14 that "he calls faith lifeless if it is empty of good works. Thus we deduce that it is not in fact faith at all, for being dead it can hardly keep the name" (*CNTC* 3:283). James is to be harmonized with Paul by recognizing that they use the vocabulary of justification differently. Paul speaks of the causes of justification before God, whereas James speaks of the demonstration that justification is real by its impact on the behavior of the believer. This approach was applied very fully in the notes for readers contained in *The Geneva Bible* (1560), a translation produced by English Protestants propelled into exile in Geneva during the reign of the Catholic Mary I (1553–1558). According to the annotator, Jas 2:14 asserts that

> Paul shows the causes of our justification, James the effects: there it is declared how we are justified: here how we are known to be justified: there works are excluded as not the cause of our justification: here they are approved as effects proceeding thereof: there they are denied to go before them that shall be justified: and here they are said to follow them that are justified. (*Geneva Bible*, 107b)

The Necessity of New Birth: The Radicals on James

A final significant group of readers of James in the Reformation era are the Protestant radicals, largely Anabaptists opposed to infant baptism, who reject the Catholic Church but are also unable to accept either of the emerging Lutheran or Reformed traditions. Often in the face of severe persecution both from other Protestants and from Catholics, these radical groups held that the church must include only believers who demonstrated their faith by undergoing adult baptism and by living in purity.

There was great appeal for the radicals in the teaching of Jas 1:18 that God "gave us birth by the word of truth, so that we would become a kind of first fruits of his creatures" (NRSV). From their perspective, James here provides a concise summary of the need for rebirth, which comes through responding with faith to the preaching of the gospel and which results in holiness of life. Here there is little substantive tension with Luther, for Jas 1:18 is the text in the epistle he appeals to most often and for similar reasons (McNutt 2014, 172). The disagreement is ecclesiological: "the radical view of Jas 1:18 was inextricably linked to an ecclesiology grounded in a visible, true church" (McNutt 2014, 173). Luther might argue that genuine justifying faith is always expressed in deeds, but the lives of the (infant) baptized masses within his churches, or indeed within Reformed churches, appeared to the radicals merely as so much unripe fruit.

In his tract *True Christian Faith* (1541), Menno Simons, the Dutch radical who was to give his name to the Mennonite tradition, complains that

> The Lutherans teach and believe that faith alone saves, without any assistance by works. They emphasize this doctrine so as to make it appear as though works were not even necessary; yes, that faith is of such a nature that it cannot tolerate any works alongside of it. And therefore the important and earnest epistle of James (because he reproves such a frivolous, vain doctrine and faith) is esteemed and treated as a "strawy epistle." (Simons 1984, 333)

Lutherans would certainly have found this an unfair caricature of their position, but from the radicals' perspective there was a huge difference between those who now had a secure place in an emerging Protestant order in various territories in Europe and their own willingness to risk losing everything through persecution. It is unsurprising that radicals found it necessary when reading Jas 2 to insist that while faith alone justifies, only those who follow in the obedient footsteps of Abraham have his faith. In their view, there were few who had this faith in sixteenth-century Europe.

James is thus very important for the radicals because it insists on the necessity of rebirth and spells out what it means to be obedient in the new life. To be doers of the word and not merely hearers (Jas 1:22–25) required correct application of James's practical advice. For example, the radicals "frequently quoted Jas 5:12 ('Do not swear') as a warrant for their eschewal of all oaths" (George 2000, 28). The teaching of Jas 5:12 and several other texts in James could plausibly be coordinated with the teaching of Jesus in the Sermon on the Mount in Matthew's Gospel (Batten 2017, 543–46, 550). The emphasis in James on simplicity of life and the substantial critiques of wealth and status (Jas 2:1–9; 5:1–6; offered with the assumption that the epistle's readers do not enjoy either) were also congenial to groups marginalized and persecuted in their own contexts: "James, in addition to many other biblical texts, appears to have contributed meaningfully to making sense of these ordeals" (Batten 2017, 539). Their interpretation of James and their social location were mutually reinforcing.

Weeping and Wailing: James and Wealth

James anticipates only deep misery in store for the rich, who are addicted to the economic exploitation of others (Jas 5:4) and are destined for divine judgment (Jas 5:3). Weeping and wailing would be the only fitting response to what lies before them (Jas 5:1). For twenty-first-century readers, this message of judgment inevitably raises questions about how society is ordered and the fair distribution of resources (Gowler 2014, 23–25). Yet, as our survey has suggested, interpreters in the Reformation era were focused largely on the relevance of James for controversies concerning salvation and the nature of the church. Groups at the radical end of the spectrum provide something of an exception because their positions in those debates predisposed them to social critique. Yet, precisely because James's assault on the rich fitted their own context and experiences as persecuted and marginalized groups, the radicals were scarcely in any position to shape wider society. They had little choice other than to heed the advice to "be patient, therefore, beloved, until the coming of the Lord" (Jas 5:7 NRSV). At the Catholic end of the spectrum there is a conviction that the existing social order reflects divine intentions and that James cannot intend to undermine it. The annotator of the *Rhemes New Testament* does acknowledge that defrauding laborers of their wages (Jas 5:4; *Rhemes New Testament*, 580) is a great sin that God will punish, but this is clearly an individual failing rather a generic issue with wealth itself. The injunction in 2:1–9 against offering preferential treatment to the rich has already prompted the response that, although there is no distinction to be made between rich and poor in spiritual matters,

> the Apostle means not, as the Anabaptists and other seditious persons sometimes gather hereof, that there should be no difference in com-

monweals or assemblies, between the magistrate and the subject, the free man and the bond, the rich and the poor, between one degree and another. For God and nature, and the necessity of man, have made such distinctions, and men are bound to observe them. (*Rhemes New Testament*, 645)

An interesting contrast to this is offered by Calvin, who does not domesticate James's message about riches and the poor to the same extent as many other commentators (Gowler 2014, 268–69). Calvin was no social revolutionary in any modern sense, and he too thinks it legitimate to show respect to those of high rank in the world (*CNTC* 3: 276). Yet this must not be exclusive, for "sin is bestowing honor *only* upon the rich" (Allison 2013, 368), and honor to the rich must be shown in a way that does not shame the poor or move the focus of the church from Christ to the rich (*CNTC* 3:276–77). Calvin acknowledges that God's election is first of the poor (*CNTC* 3:277–78), and he hears Jas 5:1–6 not as an invitation for the rich to repent but as a pronouncement of judgment on sins that are ingrained. A genuinely holy rich person is possible, but such an individual is also clearly unusual: "there are some rich folk of equity and moderation, men who keep clear of any foul play, but there are not many to be found like this" (*CNTC* 3:278). Calvin's judgment is strikingly opposite to that of English preacher Richard Turnbull, who argues that "there are many rich who use their riches to God's glory and the comfort of their poor brethren, who are to be exempted from this threat of the apostle" (Rittgers 2017, 254). Calvin is of the view that riches tend to corrupt and that great riches tend to corrupt greatly, always to the detriment of the poor. This is connected for Calvin to his reflection on the poverty of Christ, God's call upon believers to imitate it, and "the thesis that the kingdom of God on earth is marked by poverty and affliction, not splendor and glory" (Pattison 2006, 226). It is through "physical and outward afflictions and impoverishment of the church, that God restores the Church's inward and spiritual health" (Pattison 2006, 231).

Then and Now: Reformation Era Interpretations of James in Contemporary Perspective

The most obvious difference between Reformation era and contemporary interpretations of James is that the deep divisions of the sixteenth century over issues of salvation and the nature of the church no longer determine exegesis of the epistle. As Dale Allison (2013, 106) observes, "most of the implicit theology in recent commentaries is generic; that is, it seems aimed at Christians in general, not Christians of this stripe or that denomination." Further, the work of historical scholars in ancient primary resources has produced "appreciation of the degree to which James is indebted to the Jewish tradition" (Allison 2013, 107). Negative stereotypes of Judaism are happily now much less frequent than in all previous eras, including that of the Reformation. In some instances, the more irenic approaches typical of commentary on James today reflect the settling of exegetical questions. It seems unlikely, for example, that the view that James speaks of the doctrine of faith formed by love, with its insistence that faith can be dead but somehow still genuinely count as true faith awaiting animation by love, is due for imminent revival even in Roman Catholic interpretation. As sixteenth-century Protestant interpreters pointed out, if the dead faith of which James speaks (Jas 2:26) is genuine but unformed faith that awaits love's animating touch, then James's statement that even the demons believe (Jas 2:19) implies the unlikely conclusion that the forces of hell in some sense possess genuine faith: "the devil likewise has a true and real faith" (Morgan 1588, s.v. Jas 2:26). Yet this in no way lessens the validity of the impulse that lay behind the doctrine, which is the continuing necessity for interpreters to explicate James's message that faith must find expression in action, nor does it guarantee unanimity in how this is understood.

The question of the relationship between James and the Pauline letters and how their teaching about justification either coheres with or contradicts each other also persists. Following the rise in the late 1970s and early 1980s of the New Perspective on Paul, which rejects trajectories of interpretation of Paul stemming from Luther and other Reformers, some have wished to attempt to hear James completely independently of Paul and his interpretation (e.g., Johnson 1995, 111–12). Others wish simply for the significance of James not to be restricted to or dominated by its relationship with the Pauline letters (e.g., Bauckham 1999, 112–13; McCartney 2009, 272). Yet Allison—perhaps the most distinguished recent commentator on James—espouses the view that James represents Christian Jews who wished to demonstrate their genuine Jewish credentials and to remain on good terms with fellow Jews who did not believe in Jesus. As such, James deliberately responds to and corrects Pauline teaching in order to counter suspicion in the wider Jewish community that those who believe in Jesus as Messiah wish to separate faith and works (Allison 2013, 43–44, 425–57). Another recent study argues that James was canonized by the ancient church (despite earlier hesitations) and placed at the head of the collection of the Catholic Epistles to act as a counter-balance to Paul's letters and his emphasis on "faith alone," which "had become the somewhat troubling hallmark of the Pauline tradition" (Nienhuis and Wall 2013, 45).

This points us back to where we began, with the abiding interest of Luther's startling refusal to harmonize James and Paul. It is difficult to fault him for this in purely exegetical terms. While it is relatively easy to make a case that James and Paul in fact understand the nature of faith in similar ways, it is difficult to place Jas 2 alongside Rom 4 and Gal 3, with their profoundly different uses of the example of Abraham, and hear them as teaching identically about justification. Luther is here able to hear James's distinctive voice clearly in a way that others were not. Luther does not make James sound like Paul on justification or vice versa, and neither does he import explicitly christological content into James where it is absent. Oda Wischmeyer argues that it is Luther's recognition of what he judges to be James's christological deficit, his realization that James is largely law and not gospel, that allows him to read James's statements according to their normal grammatical sense. Nobody else was able again to read James with this level of philological accuracy before the twentieth century (Wischmeyer 2017, 2). However, Luther is more vulnerable to criticism on hermeneutical grounds. He complained against his critics that all he had done in relation to James was to "interpret it according to the sense of the rest of the Scriptures" (*LW* 34:317). The problem is that he did this by decisively subordinating James to Paul and marginalizing James within the canon. A more fruitful approach is to recognize that an important function of James, along with the other general epistles, is positively and helpfully to close the door on crudely antinomian readings of Paul's letters (Nienhuis and Wall 2013, 52–53). James forbids any view of salvation, of the church, and of the Christian life that minimizes the significance of how faith is embodied in deeds.

Bibliography

Adam, A. K. M. 2013. *James: A Handbook on the Greek Text*. BHGNT. Waco, TX: Baylor University Press.

Adams, Marilyn McCord. 2006. "Faith and Works, or, How James Is a Lutheran!" *ExpTim* 117:462–64.

Adams, Samuel L. 2008. *Wisdom in Transition: Act and Consequence in Second Temple Instructions*. JSJSup 125. Leiden: Brill.

Adamson, James B. 1976. *The Epistle of James*. NICNT. Grand Rapids: Eerdmans.

———. 1989. *James: The Man and His Message*. Grand Rapids: Eerdmans.

Ahrens, Matthias. 1995. *Der Realitäten Widerschein oder Arm und Reich im Jakobusbrief: Eine sozialgeschichtliche Untersuchung*. Berlin: Alektor.

Aland, Barbara. 1998. "Novum Testamentum Graecum Editio Critica Maior: Presentation of the First Part: The Letter of James." *TC* 3: https://tinyurl.com/sbl0397a.

Aland, Barbara, Kurt Aland, Gerd Mink, Holger Strutwolf, and Klaus Wachtel, eds. 2004a. *Novum Testamentum Graecum: Editio Critica Maior IV: Catholic Letters: Part 1: Text: Installment 4: The Second and Third Letter of John, the Letter of Jude*. Stuttgart: Deutsche Bibelgesellschaft.

———. 2004b. *Novum Testamentum Graecum: Editio Critica Maior IV: Catholic Letters: Part 2: Supplementary Material*. Stuttgart: Deutsche Bibelgesellschaft.

———. 2013a. *Novum Testamentum Graecum: Editio Critica Maior IV: Catholic Letters: Part 1: Text*. 2nd ed. Stuttgart: Deutsche Bibelgesellschaft.

———. 2013b. *Novum Testamentum Graecum: Editio Critica Maior IV: Catholic Letters: Part 2: Supplementary Material*. 2nd ed. Stuttgart: Deutsche Bibelgesellschaft.

Aland, Barbara, Kurt Aland, Gerd Mink, and Klaus Wachtel, eds. 1997a. *Novum Testamentum Graecum: Editio Critica Maior IV: Catholic Letters: Part 1: Text: Installment 1: James.* Stuttgart: Deutsche Bibelgesellschaft.

———. 1997b. *Novum Testamentum Graecum: Editio Critica Maior IV: Catholic Letters: Part 2: Supplementary Material.* Stuttgart: Deutsche Bibelgesellschaft.

———. 2000a. *Novum Testamentum Graecum: Editio Critica Maior IV: Catholic Letters: Part 1: Text: Installment 2: The Letters of Peter.* Stuttgart: Deutsche Bibelgesellschaft.

———. 2000b. *Novum Testamentum Graecum: Editio Critica Maior IV: Catholic Letters: Part 2: Supplementary Material.* Stuttgart: Deutsche Bibelgesellschaft.

———. 2003a. *Novum Testamentum Graecum: Editio Critica Maior IV: Catholic Letters: Part 1: Text: Installment 3: The First Letter of John.* Stuttgart: Deutsche Bibelgesellschaft.

———. 2003b. *Novum Testamentum Graecum: Editio Critica Maior IV: Catholic Letters: Part 2: Supplementary Material.* Stuttgart: Deutsche Bibelgesellschaft.

Aland, Kurt. 1970. "Novi Testamenti Graeci Editio Maior Critica: Der gegenwärtige Stand der Arbeit an einer neuen grossen kritischen Ausgabe des Neuen Testamentes." *NTS* 16:163–77.

———. 1979. "Neutestamentliche Textforschung und elektronische Datenverarbeitung." Pages 64–84 in *Bericht der Hermann Kunst-Stiftung zur Förderung der neutestamentlichen Textforschung für die Jahre 1977 bis 1979.* Münster: Kunst-Stiftung zur Förderung der neutestamentlichen Textforschung.

Aland, Kurt, and Barbara Aland. 1989. *The Text of the New Testament: An Introduction to the Critical Editions and to the Theory and Practice of Modern Textual Criticism.* 2nd ed. Translated by Erroll F. Rhodes. Grand Rapids: Eerdmans.

Aletti, Jean Noël. 2014. "James 2,14–26: The Arrangement and Its Meaning." *Bib* 95:88–101.

Allison, Dale C., Jr. 2013. *A Critical and Exegetical Commentary on the Epistle of James.* ICC. London: Bloomsbury.

———. 2014. "The Audience of James and the Sayings of Jesus." Pages 58–77 in *James, 1 and 2 Peter, and Early Jesus Traditions.* Edited by Alicia J. Batten and John S. Kloppenborg. LNTS 478. London: Bloomsbury T&T Clark.

Amphilochius of Iconium. 1969. *Iambi ad seleucum*. Translated by Eberhard Oberg. PTS 9. Berlin: de Gruyter.

Anderson, Gary. 2013. *Charity: The Place of the Poor in the Biblical Tradition*. New Haven: Yale University Press.

Augustine, 2000. *Psalms 1–32*. Vol. 1 of *Expositions of the Psalms*. Part 3.15 of *The Works of St. Augustine: A Translation for the Twenty-First Century*. Translated by Maria Boulding. New York: New City.

Aune, David E. 1987. *The New Testament in Its Literary Environment*. LEC 8. Philadelphia: Westminster.

———. 2003. *The Westminster Dictionary of New Testament and Early Christian Literature and Rhetoric*. Louisville: Westminster John Knox.

Baasland, Ernst. 1982. "Der Jakobusbrief als neutestamentliche Weisheitsschrift." *ST* 36:119–39.

———. 1988. "Literarische Form, Thematik und geschichtliche Einordnung des Jakobusbriefes." *ANRW* 25.5:3646–84.

———. 1992. *Jakobsbrevet*. Kommentar till nya Testamentet. Uppsala: EFS.

Baker, David L. 2009. *Tight Fists or Open Hands? Wealth and Poverty in Old Testament Law*. Grand Rapids: Eerdmans.

Baker, William R. 1995. *Personal Speech-Ethics in the Epistle of James*. WUNT 2/68. Tübingen: Mohr.

Balch, David L. 2004. "Philodemus, 'On Wealth' and 'On Household Management': Naturally Wealthy Epicureans against Poor Cynics." Pages 177–96 in *Philodemus and the New Testament World*. Edited by John T. Fitzgerald, Dirk Obbink, and Glenn S. Holland. NovTSup 111. Leiden: Brill.

Barclay, John G. M. 2015. *Paul and the Gift*. Grand Rapids: Eerdmans.

Barton, Stephen C. 1994. *Discipleship and Family Ties in Mark and Matthew*. SNTSMS 80. Cambridge: Cambridge University Press.

Barton, Stephen C., and G. H. R. Horsley. 1981. "A Hellenistic Cult Group and the New Testament Churches." *JAC* 24:7–41.

Batten, Alicia J. 2007. "Ideological Strategies in the Letter of James." Pages 6–26 in *Reading James with New Eyes: Methodological Reassessments of the Letter of James*. Edited by Robert L. Webb and James S. Kloppenborg. LNTS 342. London: T&T Clark.

———. 2009. *What Are They Saying about the Letter of James?* New York: Paulist.

———. 2010. *Friendship and Benefaction in James*. ESEC 15. Dorset: Deo.

———. 2013. "The Urban and the Agrarian in the Letter of James." *Journal of Early Christian History* 3:4–20.

———. 2014a. "The Characterization of the Rich in James 5." Pages 45–61 in *To Set at Liberty: Essays on Early Christianity and Its Social World in Honor of John H. Elliott*. Edited by Stephen K. Black. SWBA 2/11. Sheffield: Sheffield Phoenix.

———. 2014b. "The Urbanization of Jesus Traditions in James." Pages 78–96 in *James, 1 and 2 Peter and Early Jesus Traditions*. Edited by Alicia J. Batten and John S. Kloppenborg. LNTS 478. London: Bloomsbury T&T Clark.

———. 2017. "Early Anabaptist Interpretation of the Letter of James." *Annali di storia dell'esegesi* 34:537–51.

Bauckham, Richard. 1988. "James, 1 and 2 Peter, Jude." Pages 303–17 in *It Is Written: Scripture Citing Scripture: Essays in Honour of Barnabas Lindars*. Edited by D. A. Carson and H. G. M. Williamson. Cambridge: Cambridge University Press.

———. 1999. *James: Wisdom of James, Disciple of Jesus the Sage*. NTR. London: Routledge.

———. 2001. "James and Jesus." Pages 100–137 in *The Brother of Jesus: James the Just and His Mission*. Edited by Bruce Chilton and Jacob Neusner. Louisville: Westminster John Knox.

———. 2004. "The Wisdom of James and the Wisdom of Jesus." Pages 75–92 in *The Catholic Epistles and the Tradition*. Edited by Jacques Schlosser. BETL 176. Leuven: Peeters.

Baumgarten, Joseph M., and Daniel R. Schwartz. 1995. "Damascus Document (CD)." Pages 4–57 in *Damascus Document, War Scroll, and Related Documents*. Vol. 2 of *The Dead Sea Scrolls: Hebrew, Aramaic, and Greek Texts with English Translations*. Edited by James H. Charlesworth. Tübingen: Mohr; Louisville: Westminster John Knox.

Bellarmine, Robert. 2013. *Disputations about Controversies of the Christian Faith against the Heretics of this Age*. Translated by Peter L. P. Simpson. https://tinyurl.com/sbl0397b.

Berger, Klaus. 1984a. *Formgeschichte des Neuen Testaments*. Heidelberg: Quelle & Meyer.

———. 1984b. "Hellenistische Gattungen in Neuen Testament." *ANRW* 25.2:1031–1432.

Bernays, Jacob. 1856. *Ueber das Phokylideische Gedicht: Ein Beitrag zur hellenistischen Litteratur*. Berlin: Hertz.

Betz, Hans Dieter, ed. 1992. *Texts*. Vol. 1 of *The Greek Magical Papyri in Translation Including the Demotic Spells*. 2nd ed. Chicago: University of Chicago Press.

Bigelow, Gordon. 2003. *Fiction, Famine, and the Rise of Economics in Victorian Britain and Ireland*. Cambridge Studies in Nineteenth Century Literature and Culture 40. Cambridge: Cambridge University Press.

Blenkinsopp, Joseph. 2015. *Abraham: The Story of a Life*. Grand Rapids: Eerdmans.

Blummell, Lincoln, and Thomas Wayment, eds. 2015. *Christian Oxyrhynchus: Texts, Documents, and Sources*. Waco, TX: Baylor University Press.

Bockmuehl, Markus. 2006. *Seeing the Word: Refocusing New Testament Study*. Studies in Theological Interpretation. Grand Rapids: Baker Academic.

Boismard, M. E. 1957. "Une liturgie baptismale dans la Prima Petri: II— Son Influence sur l'Épître de Jacques." *RB* 64:161–83.

Bowerstock, G. W. 1965. *Augustus and the Greek World*. Oxford: Oxford University Press.

Boyle, Marjorie O'Rourke. 1985. "The Stoic Paradox of James 2.10." *NTS* 31:611–17.

Brooke, A. E., ed. 1896. *The Commentary of Origen on St. John's Gospel*. 2 vols. Cambridge: Cambridge University Press.

Brooke, George J. 2005. "The Wisdom of Matthew's Beatitudes." Pages 217–34 in *The Dead Sea Scrolls and the New Testament*. Minneapolis: Fortress.

Brouwer, René. 2014. *The Stoic Sage: The Early Stoics on Wisdom, Sagehood and Socrates*. Cambridge: Cambridge University Press.

Brown, Raymond E. 1999. *The Birth of the Messiah: A Commentary on the Infancy Narratives in the Gospels of Matthew and Luke*. 2nd ed. ABRL. New York: Doubleday.

Brueggemann, Walter. 2001. *The Prophetic Imagination*. 2nd ed. Minneapolis: Fortress.

———. 2016. *Money and Possessions*. Interpretation: Resources for the Use of Scripture in the Church. Louisville: Westminster John Knox.

Burkes, Shannon. 2002. "Wisdom and Apocalypticism in the Wisdom of Solomon." *HTR* 95:21–44.

Carlson, Donald H. 2013. *Jewish-Christian Interpretation of the Pentateuch in the Pseudo-Clementine Homilies*. Minneapolis: Fortress.

Carlston, Charles E. 1980. "Proverbs, Maxims, and the Historical Jesus." *JBL* 99:87–105.

Carson, D. A. 2007. "James." Pages 997–1013 in *Commentary on the New Testament Use of the Old Testament*. Edited by G. K. Beale and D. A. Carson. Grand Rapids: Baker Academic.

Chester, Andrew. 1994. "The Theology of James." Pages 1–62 in *The Theology of the Letters of James, Peter, and Jude*. By Andrew Chester and Ralph P. Martin. NTT. Cambridge: Cambridge University Press.

Chester, Stephen J. 2017. *Reading Paul with the Reformers: Reconciling Old and New Perspectives*. Grand Rapids: Eerdmans.

Cheung, Luke L. 2003. *The Genre, Composition and Hermeneutics of James*. PBTM. Carlisle: Paternoster.

Coker, K. Jason. 2014. "Calling on the Diaspora: Nativism and Diaspora Identity in the Letter of James." Pages 441–53 in *T&T Clark Handbook to Social Identity Formation in the New Testament*. Edited by J. Brian Tucker and Coleman A. Baker. London: Bloomsbury T&T Clark.

———. 2015. *James in Postcolonial Perspective: The Letter as Nativist Discourse*. Minneapolis: Fortress.

Collins, John J. 1997. *Jewish Wisdom in the Hellenistic Age*. OTL. Louisville: Westminster John Knox.

———. 2000. *Between Athens and Jerusalem: Jewish Identity in the Hellenistic Diaspora*. 2nd ed. BRS. Grand Rapids: Eerdmans.

———. 2017. *The Invention of Judaism: Torah and Jewish Identity from Deuteronomy to Paul*. Taubman Lectures in Jewish Studies 7. Oakland: University of California Press.

Colwell, E. C. 1969. "Genealogical Method: Its Achievements and Its Limitations." Pages 63–83 in *Studies in Methodology in Textual Criticism of the New Testament*. NTTS 9. Leiden: Brill.

Cribiore, Raffaella. 2001. *Gymnastics of the Mind: Greek Education in Hellenistic and Roman Egypt*. Princeton: Princeton University Press.

Crook, Zeba A. 2004. *Reconceptualising Conversion: Patronage, Loyalty, and Conversion in the Religions of the Ancient Mediterranean*. BZNW 130. Berlin: de Gruyter.

Crotty, R. B. 1995. "Identifying the Poor in the Letter of James." *Colloquium* 27:11–21.

Davids, Peter H. 1978a. "The Meaning of *Apeirastos* in James i.13." *NTS* 24:386–92.

———. 1978b. "Tradition and Citation in the Epistle of James." Pages 113–26 in *Scripture, Tradition, and Interpretation: Essays Presented to Everett F. Harrison by His Students and Colleagues in Honor of His Seventy-Fifth Birthday*. Edited by W. Ward Gasque and William Sanford LaSor. Grand Rapids: Eedrmans.

———. 1982. *The Epistle of James: A Commentary on the Greek Text*. NIGTC. Grand Rapids: Eerdmans.

———. 1988. "The Epistle of James in Modern Discussion." *ANRW* 25.5:3621–45.

———. 1993. "The Pseudepigrapha in the Catholic Epistles." Pages 228–45 in *The Pseudepigrapha and Early Biblical Interpretation*. Edited by James H. Charlesworth and Craig A. Evans. JSPSup 14. SSEJC 2. Sheffield: JSOT Press.

———. 2003. "The Meaning of Ἀπείραστος Revisited." Pages 225–40 in *New Testament Greek and Exegesis: Essays in Honor of Gerald F. Hawthorne*. Edited by Amy M. Donaldson and Timothy B. Sailors. Grand Rapids: Eerdmans.

———. 2009. "The Catholic Epistles as a Canonical Janus." *BBR* 19:403–16.

———. 2012. "What Glasses Are You Wearing? Reading Hebrew Narratives through Second Temple Lenses." *JETS* 55:763–71.

Davies, W. D., and Dale C. Allison. 1988–1997. *A Critical and Exegetical Commentary on the Gospel According to Saint Matthew*. 3 vols. ICC. Edinburgh: T&T Clark.

Deissmann, Adolf. 1901. *Bible Studies: Contributions Chiefly from Papyri and Inscriptions to the History of the Language, the Literature, and the Religion of Hellenistic Judaism and Primitive Christianity*. Translated by Alexander Grieve. Edinburgh: T&T Clark.

———. 1927. *Light from the Ancient East: The New Testament Illustrated by Recently Discovered Texts of the Graeco-Roman World*. Translated by Lionel Strachan. London: Hodder & Stoughton.

Deppe, Dean B. 1989. *The Sayings of Jesus in the Epistle of James*. Chelsea, MI: Bookcrafters.

Derron, Pascale. 2010. "Phocylides, Pseudo-." *EDEJ*, 1080–82.

DeSilva, David A. 2012. *The Jewish Teachers of Jesus, James, and Jude: What Earliest Christianity Learned from the Apocrypha and Pseudepigrapha*. Oxford: Oxford University Press.

Dibelius, Martin. 1976. *James: A Commentary on the Epistle of James*. Revised by Heinrich Greeven. Translated by Michael A. Williams. Hermeneia. Philadelphia: Fortress.

Doering, Lutz. 2009. "First Peter as Early Christian Diaspora Letter." Pages 215–36 in *The Catholic Epistles and the Apostolic Tradition*. Edited by Karl-Wilhelm Niebuhr and Robert W. Wall. Waco, TX: Baylor University Press.

Downs, David J. 2016a. *Alms: Charity, Reward, and Atonement in Early Christianity*. Waco, TX: Baylor University Press.

——. 2016b. *The Offering of the Gentiles: Paul's Collection for Jerusalem in Its Chronological, Cultural, and Cultic Contexts*. Grand Rapids: Eerdmans.

Dubrow, Heather. 2005. *Genre*. London: Methuen.

Dungan, David L. 2007. *Constantine's Bible: Politics and the Making of the New Testament*. Minneapolis: Fortress.

Dunn, James D. G. 1983. "The New Perspective on Paul." *BJRL* 65:95–122.

——. 2009. *Beginning from Jerusalem*. Christianity in the Making 2. Grand Rapids: Eerdmans.

Edwards, Dennis R. 2003. "Reviving Faith: An Eschatological Understanding of James 5:13–20." PhD diss., Catholic University of America.

Ehrman, Bart D. 2003. *The Apostolic Fathers*. 2 vols. LCL. Cambridge: Harvard University Press.

Eilers, Claude. 2002. *Roman Patrons of Greek Cities*. OCM. Oxford: Oxford University Press.

Elliott, J. K., ed. 1993. *The Apocryphal New Testament: A Collection of Apocryphal Christian Literature in an English Translation*. Oxford: Clarendon.

Elliott, John H. 1981. *A Home for the Homeless: A Social Scientific Criticism of 1 Peter, Its Situation and Strategy*. Philadelphia: Fortress.

——. 1993. "The Epistle of James in Rhetorical and Social Scientific Perspective: Holiness-Wholeness and Patterns of Replication." *BTB* 23:71–81.

——. 2000. *I Peter: A New Translation with Introduction and Commentary*. AB 37B. New York: Doubleday.

——. 2008. "From Social Description to Social-Scientific Criticism: The History of a Society of Biblical Literature Section 1973–2005." *BTB* 38:26–36.

Elliott-Binns, L. E. 1956. "James i.18: Creation or Redemption?" *NTS* 3:148–61.

Ellis, Nicholas J. 2015. *The Hermeneutics of Divine Testing: Cosmic Trials and Biblical Interpretation in the Epistle of James and Other Jewish Literature*. WUNT 2/396. Tübingen: Mohr Siebeck.

——. 2016. "A Theology of Evil in the Epistle of James: Cosmic Trials and the *Dramatis Personae* of Evil." Pages 262–81 in *Evil in Second Temple Judaism and Early Christianity*. Edited by Chris Keith and Loren T. Stuckenbruck. WUNT 2/417. Tübingen: Mohr Siebeck.

Epp, Eldon J. 1999. "The Multivalence of the Term 'Original Text' in New Testament Textual Criticism." *HTR* 92:245–81.

———. 2013. "Textual Clusters: Their Past and Future in New Testament Textual Criticism." Pages 519–77 in *The Text of the New Testament in Contemporary Research: Essays on the Status Quaestionis*. Edited by Bart D. Ehrman and Michael W. Holmes. 2nd ed. NTTSD 42. Leiden: Brill.

———. 2014. "In the Beginning Was the New Testament Text, but Which Text? A Consideration of 'Ausgangstext' and 'Initial Text.'" Pages 35–70 in *Texts and Traditions: Essays in Honour of J. Keith Elliott*. Edited by Peter Doble and Jeffrey Kloha. NTTSD 47. Leiden: Brill.

Erker, Darja Šterbenc. 2009. "Women's Tears in Ancient Roman Ritual." Pages 135–60 in *Tears in the Graeco-Roman World*. Edited by Thorsten Fögen. Berlin: de Gruyter.

Eshel, Esther, Hanan Eshel, and Armin Lange. 2010. "'Hear, O Israel' in Gold: An Ancient Amulet from Halbturn." *JAJ* 1:43–64.

Eusebius. *Ecclesiastical History*. 1926–1932. Translated by Kirsopp Lake and John E. L. Oulton. 2 vols. LCL. Cambridge: Harvard University Press.

Exler, Francis Xavier J. 1923. *The Form of the Ancient Greek Letter*. Washington, DC: Catholic University of America.

Farrar, Thomas J., and Guy J. Williams. 2016. "Diabolical Data: A Critical Inventory of New Testament Satanology." *JSNT* 39:40–71.

Fiensy, David A. 2010. "Ancient Economy and the New Testament." Pages 194–206 in *Understanding the Social World of the New Testament*. Edited by Dietmar Neufeld and Richard E. DeMaris. New York: Routledge.

Fiore, Benjamin. 1986. *The Function of Personal Example in Socratic and Pastoral Epistles*. AnBib 105. Rome: Biblical Institute Press.

———. 1992. "Parenesis and Protreptic." *ABD* 5:162–65.

Flesher, LeAnn Snow. 2014. "Mercy Triumphs Over Judgment: James as Social Gospel." *RevExp* 111:180–86.

Fontaine, Carole R. 1982. *Traditional Sayings in the Old Testament: A Contextual Study*. Bible and Literature 5. Sheffield: Almond Press.

Foster, George M. 1972. "A Second Look at Limited Good." *Anthropological Quarterly* 45:57–64.

Foster, Paul. 2014. "Q and James: A Source-Critical Conundrum." Pages 3–34 in *James, 1 and 2 Peter, and Early Jesus Traditions*. Edited by Alicia J. Batten and John S. Kloppenborg. LNTS 478. London: Bloomsbury T&T Clark.

Foster, Robert J. 2014. *The Significance of Exemplars for the Interpretation of the Letter of James*. WUNT 2/376. Tübingen: Mohr Siebeck.

Francis, Fred O. 1970. "The Form and Function of the Opening and Closing Paragraphs of James and 1 John." *ZNW* 61:110–26.

Frankenmölle, Hubert. 1990. "Das semantische Netz des Jakobusbriefes:
Zur Einheit eines umstrittenen Briefes." *BZ* 34:161–97.

Freyne, Sean 2004. *Jesus, a Jewish Galilean: A New Reading of the Jesus-
Story.* London: T&T Clark.

Gager, John C. 1979. "Social Description and Sociological Explanation in
the Study of Early Christianity. A Review Essay." *RelSRev* 5:174–80.

Gallagher, Edmon L., and John D. Meade. 2017. *The Biblical Canon Lists
from Early Christianity: Texts and Analysis.* Oxford: Oxford University
Press.

Gammie, John G. 1990. "Paraenetic Literature: Toward the Morphology of
a Secondary Genre." *Semeia* 50:41–77.

Geneva Bible: A Facsimile of the 1560 Edition. 2007. Peabody, MA: Hendrickson.

George, Timothy. 2000. "'A Right Strawy Epistle': Reformation Perspectives on James." *SBJT* 4.3:20–31.

Gleason, Maud. 1990. "The Semiotics of Gender: Physiognomy and Self-
Fashioning in the Second Century C.E." Pages 389–415 in *Before Sexu-
ality: The Construction of Erotic Experience in the Ancient Greek World.*
Edited by David M. Halperin, John J. Winkler, and Froma I. Zeitlin.
Princeton: Princeton University Press.

Goff, Matthew J. 2007. *Discerning Wisdom: The Sapiential Literature of the
Dead Sea Scrolls.* VTSup 116. Leiden: Brill.

———. 2013. *4QInstruction.* WLAW 2. Atlanta: Society of Biblical Literature.

Goodspeed, Edgar J. 1960. *Index Patristicus sive Clavis Patrum Apostolico-
rum Operum.* Naperville, IL: Allenson.

Gowler, David B. 2014. *James through the Centuries.* Wiley-Blackwell Bible
Commentaries. Chichester: Wiley-Blackwell.

Gurry, Peter J. 2016a. "How Your Greek NT Is Changing: A Simple Introduction to the Coherence-Based Genealogical Method (CBGM)."
JETS 59:675–89.

———. 2016b. "The Number of Variants in the Greek New Testament: A
Proposed Estimate." *NTS* 62:97–121.

———. 2017. *A Critical Examination of the Coherence-Based Genealogical
Method in New Testament Textual Criticism.* NTTSD 55. Leiden: Brill.

———. 2018. "The Harklean Syriac and the Development of the Byzantine Text: A Historical Test for the Coherence-Based Genealogical Method (CBGM)." *NovT* 60:183–200.

Hahneman, Geoffrey Mark. 1992. *The Muratorian Fragment and the Development of the Canon*. OTM. Oxford: Clarendon.

———. 2002. "The Muratorian Fragment and the Origins of the New Testament Canon." Pages 405–15 in *The Canon Debate*. Edited by Lee M. McDonald and James A. Sanders. Peabody, MA: Hendrickson.

Hall, Jonathan M. 2002. *Hellenicity: Between Ethnicity and Culture*. Chicago: University of Chicago Press.

Hansen, G. Walter. 1989. *Abraham in Galatians: Epistolary and Rhetorical Contexts*. JSNTSup 29. Sheffield: JSOT Press.

Hanson, K. C., and Douglas E. Oakman. 2008. *Palestine in the Time of Jesus: Social Structures and Social Conflicts*. 2nd ed. Minneapolis: Fortress.

Harland, Philip A. 2003. *Associations, Synagogues, and Congregations: Claiming a Place in Ancient Mediterranean Society*. Minneapolis: Fortress.

Hartin, Patrick J. 1991. *James and the Q Sayings of Jesus*. JSNTSup 47. Sheffield: JSOT Press.

———. 2003. *James*. SP 14. Collegeville, MN: Liturgical Press.

———. 2005. "'Who Is Wise and Understanding among You?' (James 3:13): An Analysis of Wisdom, Eschatology, and Apocalypticism in the Letter of James." Pages 149–68 in *Conflicted Boundaries in Wisdom and Apocalypticism*. Edited by Benjamin G. Wright III and Lawrence M. Wills. SymS 35. Atlanta: Society of Biblical Literature.

———. 2009. "James and the Jesus Tradition: Some Theological Reflections and Implications." Pages 55–70 in *The Catholic Epistles and the Apostolic Tradition*. Edited by Karl-Wilhelm Niebuhr and Robert W. Wall. Waco, TX: Baylor University Press.

———. 2014. "Wholeness in James and the Q Source." Pages 35–57 in *James, 1 and 2 Peter, and Early Jesus Traditions*. Edited by Alicia J. Batten and John S. Kloppenborg. LNTS 478. London: Bloomsbury T&T Clark.

Hengel, Martin. 1974. *Judaism and Hellenism: Studies in Their Encounter in Palestine during the Early Hellenistic Period*. Translated by John Bowden. 2 vols. Philadelphia: Fortress.

———. 1989. *The "Hellenization" of Judaea in the First Century after Christ*. Translated by John Bowden. Philadelphia: Trinity Press International.

Hiers, Richard H. 2009. *Justice and Compassion in Biblical Law*. New York: Continuum.

Hintlian, Kevork. 1989. *History of the Armenians in the Holy Land*. 2nd ed. Jerusalem: Armenian Patriarchate Press.

Hirsch, Eric D. 1967. *Validity in Interpretation*. New Haven: Yale University Press.

Holmes, Michael W., ed. 2007. *The Apostolic Fathers: Greek Texts and English Translations*. 3rd edition. Grand Rapids: Baker Academic.

———. 2013. "From 'Original Text' to 'Initial Text': The Traditional Goal of New Testament Textual Criticism in Contemporary Discussion." Pages 637–88 in *The Text of the New Testament in Contemporary Research: Essays on the Status Quaestionis*. Edited by Bart D. Ehrman and Michael W. Holmes. 2nd ed. NTTSD 42. Leiden: Brill.

Horst, Pieter W. van der. 1985. "Pseudo-Phocylides: A New Translation and Introduction." *OTP* 2:565–82.

Hort, F. J. A. 1909. *The Epistle of St. James: The Greek Text with Introduction, Commentary as Far as Chapter IV, Verse 7, and Additional Notes*. London: MacMillan.

Houston, Walter J. 2006. *Contending for Justice: Ideologies and Theologies of Social Justice in the Old Testament*. LHBOTS 428. London: T&T Clark.

Hutchinson Edgar, David. 2001. *Has God Not Chosen the Poor? The Social Setting of the Epistle of James*. JSNTSup 206. Sheffield: Sheffield Academic.

Ilan, Tal. 2002. *Lexicon of Jewish Names in Late Antiquity. Part One: Palestine 330 BCE—200 CE*. TSAJ 91. Tübingen: Mohr Siebeck.

Inwood, Brad. 1985. *Ethics and Human Action in Early Stoicism*. Oxford: Clarendon.

Jackson-McCabe, Matt A. 1996. "A Letter to the Twelve Tribes in the Diaspora: Wisdom and 'Apocalyptic' Eschatology in the Letter of James." Pages 504–17 in *Society of Biblical Literature 1996 Seminar Papers*. Atlanta: Society of Biblical Literature.

———. 2001. *Logos and Law in the Letter of James: The Law of Nature, the Law of Moses and the Law of Freedom*. NovTSup 100. Leiden: Brill.

———. 2009. "The Politics of Pseudepigraphy and the Letter of James." Pages 599–623 in *Pseudepigraphie und Verfasserfiktion in frühchristlichen Briefen/Pseudepigraphy and Author Fiction in Early Christian Letters*. Edited by Jörg Frey, Jens Herzer, Martina Janssen, and Clare K. Rothschild. WUNT 246. Tübingen: Mohr Siebeck.

———. 2014. "Enduring Temptation: The Structure and Coherence of the Letter of James." *JSNT* 37:161–84.

Jenkins, Allan K., and Patrick Preston. 2007. *Biblical Scholarship and the Church: A Sixteenth Century Crisis of Authority*. Aldershot: Ashgate.

Jobes, Karen H. 2005. *1 Peter*. BECNT. Grand Rapids: Baker Academic.

Johnson, Luke Timothy. 1982. "The Use of Leviticus 19 in the Letter of James." *JBL* 101:391–401.

———. 1983. "James 3:13–4:10 and the *Topos περὶ φθόνου*." *NovT* 25:327–47.

———. 1995. *The Letter of James: A New Translation with Introduction and Commentary*. AB 37A. New York: Doubleday.

———. 1998. "James." *NIB* 12:177–225.

———. 2004. *Brother of Jesus, Friend of God: Studies in the Letter of James*. Grand Rapids: Eerdmans.

Josephus. 1926–1965. Translated by Henry St. J. Thackeray et al. 10 vols. LCL. Cambridge: Harvard University Press.

Joubert, Stephan. 2000. *Paul as Benefactor: Reciprocity, Strategy and Theological Reflection in Paul's Collection*. WUNT 2/124. Tübingen: Mohr Siebeck.

———. 2001. "One Form of Social Exchange or Two? 'Euergetism,' Patronage, and New Testament Studies: Roman and Greek Ideas of Patronage." *BTB* 31:17–25.

Kaden, David A. 2014. "Stoicism, Social Stratification, and the Q Tradition in James: A Suggestion about James' Audience." Pages 97–120 in *James, 1 and 2 Peter and Early Jesus Traditions*. Edited by Alicia J. Batten and John S. Kloppenborg. LNTS 478. London: Bloomsbury T&T Clark.

Kamell, Mariam J. 2009. "The Economics of Humility: The Rich and the Humble in James." Pages 157–75 in *Engaging Economics: New Testament Scenarios and Early Christian Reception*. Edited by Bruce W. Longenecker and Kelly Leibengood. Grand Rapids: Eerdmans.

———. 2011. "Incarnating Jeremiah's Promised New Covenant in the 'Law' of James: A Short Study." *EvQ* 83:19–28.

Kamell Kovalishyn, Mariam. 2018a. "Life as Image Bearers in the New Creation: The Anthropology of James." Pages 177–88 in *Anthropology and New Testament Theology*. Edited by Jason Maston and Benjamin Reynolds. LNTS 529. London: T&T Clark.

———. 2018b. "The Prayer of Elijah in James 5: An Example of Intertextuality." *JBL* 137:1027–45.

Kennedy, George. 2003. *Progymnasmata: Greek Textbooks of Prose Composition and Rhetoric*. WGRW 10. Atlanta: Society of Biblical Literature.

Kirk, J. A. 1969. "The Meaning of Wisdom in James: Examination of a Hypothesis." *NTS* 16:24–38.

Klein, Martin. 1995. *"Ein vollkommenes Werk": Vollkommenheit, Gesetz und Gericht als theologische Themen des Jakobusbriefes.* BWANT 139. Stuttgart: Kohlhammer.

Klink, Edward III, and Darian R. Lockett. 2012. *Understanding Biblical Theology: A Comparison of Theory and Practice.* Grand Rapids: Zondervan.

Kloppenborg, John S. 1999. "Patronage Avoidance in James." *HvTSt* 55:755–94.

———. 2005. "*Didache* 1.1–6:1, James, Matthew, and the Torah." Pages 193–221 in *Trajectories through the New Testament and the Apostolic Fathers.* Edited by Andrew F. Gregory and C. M. Tuckett. Oxford: Oxford University Press.

———. 2007a. "Diaspora Discourse: The Construction of *Ethos* in James." *NTS* 53:242–70.

———. 2007b. "The Emulation of the Jesus Tradition in the Letter of James." Pages 121–50 in *Reading James with New Eyes: Methodological Reassessments of the Letter of James.* Edited by Robert L. Webb and John S. Kloppenborg. LNTS 342. London: T&T Clark.

———. 2008. "Poverty and Piety in Matthew, James, and the Didache." Pages 201–32 in *Matthew, James and the Didache: Three Related Documents in Their Jewish and Christian Settings.* Edited by Huub van de Sandt and Jürgen K. Zangenberg. SymS 45. Atlanta: Society of Biblical Literature.

———. 2009. "The Reception of the Jesus Tradition in James." Pages 71–100 in *The Catholic Epistles and Apostolic Tradition: A New Perspective on James to Jude.* Edited by Karl-Wilhelm Niebuhr and Robert W. Wall. Waco, TX: Baylor University Press.

———. 2010. "James 1:2–15 and Hellenistic Psychagogy." *NovT* 52:37–71.

Koester, Helmut. 1974. "φύσις κτλ." *TDNT* 9:251–77.

Konradt, Matthias. 1998. *Christliche Existenz nach dem Jakobusbrief: Eine Studie zu seiner soteriologischen und ethischen Konzeption.* SUNT 22. Göttingen: Vandenhoeck & Ruprecht.

———. 2003. Review of *A Spirituality of Perfection: Faith in Action in the Letter of James,* by Patrick J. Hartin; *Has God Not Chosen the Poor? The Social Setting of the Epistle of James,* by David Hutchinson Edgar; and *Logos and Law in the Letter of James: The Law of Nature, the Law of Moses, and the Law of Freedom*, by Matt A. Jackson-McCabe. *JBL* 122:182–89.

Konstan, David. 2006. *The Emotions of the Ancient Greeks: Studies in Aristotle and Classical Literature*. Robson Classical Lectures. Toronto: University of Toronto Press.

Kot, Tomasz. 2006. *La Lettre de Jacques: La foi, chemin de vie*. Rhétorique sémitique 2. Paris: Lethielleux.

Krüger, René. 2005. *Pobres y ricos en la epístola de Santiago: El desafío de un cristianismo profético*. Buenos Aires: Lumen.

Kugel, James L. 1997. *The Bible as It Was*. Cambridge: Belknap.

Kugler, Robert A. 2010. "Testaments." *EDEJ*, 1295–97.

Kümmel, Werner G. 1975. *Introduction to the New Testament*. Translated by Howard C. Kee. 17th ed. London: SCM.

Kustas, G. L. 1976. *Diatribe in Ancient Rhetorical Theory*. Edited by W. Wuellner. Protocol Series of the Colloquies of the Center for Hermeneutical Studies in Hellenistic and Modern Culture 22. Berkeley: Center for Hermeneutical Studies.

Laws, Sophie. 1980. *A Commentary on the Epistle of James*. BNTC. London: Black.

Lendon, J. E. 1997. *Empire of Honor: The Art of Government in the Roman World*. Oxford: Oxford University Press.

Lenski, Gerhard E. 1984. *Power and Privilege: A Theory of Social Stratification*. 2nd ed. Chapel Hill: University of North Carolina Press.

Lichtenberger, Hermann. 2003. "Makarismen in den Qumrantexten und im Neuen Testament." Pages 395–411 in *Wisdom and Apocalypticism in the Dead Sea Scrolls and Biblical Tradition*. Edited by Florentino García Martínez. BETL 168. Leuven: Peeters.

Lieu, Judith. 2002. *Neither Jew Nor Greek? Constructing Early Christianity*. London: T&T Clark.

Lightfoot, J. B. 1865. "The Brethren of the Lord." In *Saint Paul's Epistle to the Galatians: A Revised Text with Introduction, Notes, and Dissertations*. London: Macmillan.

Lips, Hermann von. 1990. *Weisheitliche Traditionen im Neuen Testament*. WMANT 64. Neukirchen-Vluyn: Neukirchener Verlag.

Llewelyn, Stephen R. 1997. "The Prescript of James." *NovT* 39:385–93.

Lockett, Darian R. 2005. "The Spectrum of Wisdom and Eschatology in the Epistle of James and 4QInstruction." *TynBul* 56:131–48.

———. 2007. "'Unstained by the World': Purity and Pollution as an Indicator of Cultural Interaction in the Letter of James." Pages 49–74 in

Reading James with New Eyes: Methodological Reassessments of the Letter of James. Edited by Robert L. Webb and John S. Kloppenborg. LNTS 342. London: T&T Clark.

———. 2008. *Purity and Worldview in the Epistle of James.* LNTS 366. London: T&T Clark.

———. Forthcoming. "The Use of Leviticus 19 in James and 1 Peter: A Neglected Parallel." *CBQ.*

Londoño, Juan Esteban. 2016. "Hermenéuticas postcoloniales." *Alternativas: Revista de análisis y reflexión teológica* 49:147–64.

Long, Anthony A., and David N. Sedley. 1988. *The Hellenistic Philosophers.* 2 vols. Cambridge: Cambridge University Press.

Longenecker, Bruce W. 2010. *Remember the Poor: Paul, Poverty, and the Greco-Roman World.* Grand Rapids: Eerdmans.

Longus and Xenophon of Ephesus. 2009. *Daphnis and Chloe; Anthia and Habrocomes.* Edited and translated by Jeffrey Henderson. LCL. Cambridge: Harvard University Press.

Macaskill, Grant. 2007. *Revealed Wisdom and Inaugurated Eschatology in Ancient Judaism and Early Christianity.* JSJSup 115. Leiden: Brill.

Mack, Burton. 1987. *Anecdotes and Arguments: The Chreia in Antiquity and Early Christianity.* Occasional Papers 10. Claremont: Institute for Antiquity and Christianity.

———. 1990. *Rhetoric and the New Testament.* GBS. Minneapolis: Fortress.

Mack, Burton L., and Edward N. O'Neil. 1986. "The Chreia Discussion of Hermogenes of Tarsus: Introduction, Translation, and Comments." Pages 153–81 in *The Progymnasmata.* Vol. 1 of *The Chreia in Ancient Rhetoric.* Edited by Ronald F. Hock and Edward N. O'Neil. Texts and Translations 27. Atlanta: Scholars Press.

Mack, Burton, and Vernon K. Robbins. 1989. *Patterns of Persuasion in the Gospels.* Sonoma, CA: Polebridge.

Malherbe, Abraham J. 1986. *Moral Exhortation: A Greco–Roman Source Book.* LEC 4. Philadelphia: Westminster.

———. 1988. *Ancient Epistolary Theorists.* SBLSBS 19. Atlanta: Scholars Press.

———. 1992. "Hellenistic Moralists and the New Testament." *ANRW* 26.1:267–333.

Malina, Bruce J. 2001. *The Social Gospel of Jesus: The Kingdom of God in Mediterranean Perspective.* Minneapolis: Fortress.

Mansfield, Bruce. 1979. *Phoenix of His Age: Interpretations of Erasmus c. 1550–1750.* Erasmus Studies 4. Toronto: University of Toronto Press.

Marcus, Joel. 1982. "The Evil Inclination in the Epistle of James." *CBQ* 44:606–21.

———. 2002. Review of *Logos and Law in the Letter of James: The Law of Nature, the Law of Moses and the Law of Freedom*, by Matt A. Jackson-McCabe. *CBQ* 64:577–79.

Martin, G. Currie. 1907. "The Epistle of James as a Storehouse of the Sayings of Jesus." *The Expositor* 7/3:174–84.

Martin, Ralph P. 1988. *James*. WBC 48. Waco, TX: Word.

Massebieau, Louis. 1895. "L'Épître de Jacques est-elle l'oeuvre d'un chrétien?" *RHR* 32:249–83.

Maynard-Reid, Pedrito U. 1987. *Poverty and Wealth in James*. Maryknoll, NY: Orbis Books.

Mayor, Joseph B. 1897. *The Epistle of St. James: The Greek Text with Introduction, Notes, and Comments*. 2nd ed. London: Macmillan.

———. 1913. *The Epistle of St James: The Greek Text with Introduction, Notes, and Comments*. 3rd ed. London: Macmillan.

McCartney, Dan G. 2009. *James*. BECNT. Grand Rapids: Baker Academic.

McCauley, Leo P., and Anthony A. Stephenson. 1969. *The Works of Saint Cyril of Jerusalem*. Vol. 1. FC 61. Washington, DC: Catholic University of America Press.

McConville, J. Gordon. 2006. *God and Earthly Power: An Old Testament Political Theology*. LHBOTS 454. London: T&T Clark.

McKnight, Scot. 2011. *The Letter of James*. NICNT. Grand Rapids: Eerdmans.

———. 2016. *The King Jesus Gospel: The Good News Revisited*. 2nd ed. Grand Rapids: Zondervan.

McNutt, Jennifer P. 2014. "James, 'The Book of Straw,' in Reformation Biblical Exegesis: A Comparison of Luther and the Radicals." Pages 157–76 in *Reconsidering the Relationship between Biblical and Systematic Theology in the New Testament: Essays by Theologians and New Testament Scholars*. Edited by Benjamin E. Reynolds, Brian Lugioyo, and Kevin J. Vanhoozer. WUNT 2/369. Tübingen: Mohr Siebeck.

Meikle, Scott. 2002. "Modernism, Economics and the Ancient Economy." Pages 233–50 in *The Ancient Economy*. Edited by Walter Scheidel and Sitta Von Reden. New York: Routledge.

Metzger, Bruce M. 1994. *A Textual Commentary on the Greek New Testament: A Companion Volume to the United Bible Societies' Greek New Testament (Fourth Revised Ed.)*. 2nd ed. New York: United Bible Societies.

Meyer, Arnold. 1930. *Das Rätsel des Jacobusbriefes*. BZNW 10. Giessen: Töpelmann.

Míguez, Néstor. 1998. "Ricos y Pobres: Relaciones clientelares en la Carta de Santiago." *RIBLA* 31:86–98.

Minear, Paul S. 1972. *Commands of Christ*. Edinburgh: Saint Andrew Press.

Mink, Gerd. 1982. "Zur Stemmatisierung neutestamentlicher Handschriften." Pages 100–114 in *Bericht der Hermann Kunst-Stiftung zur Förderung der neutestamentlichen Textforschung für die Jahre 1979 bis 1981*. Münster: Kunst-Stiftung zur Förderung der neutestamentlichen Textforschung.

———. 2004. "Problems of a Highly Contaminated Tradition: The New Testament: Stemmata of Variants as a Source of a Genealogy for Witnesses." Pages 13–85 in *Studies in Stemmatology II*. Edited by Pieter van Reenen, August den Hollander, and Margot van Mulken. Philadelphia: Benjamins.

———. 2009. "The Coherence-Based Genealogical Method, CBGM: Introductory Presentation." Slide presentation. http://www.uni-muenster. de/INTF/cbgm_presentation/download.html.

———. 2011. "Contamination, Coherence, and Coincidence in Textual Transmission: The Coherence-Based Genealogical Method (CBGM) as a Complement and Corrective to Existing Approaches." Pages 141–216 in *The Textual History of the Greek New Testament: Changing Views in Contemporary Research*. Edited by Klaus Wachtel and Michael W. Holmes. TCS 8. Atlanta: Society of Biblical Literature.

Mongstad-Kvammen, Ingeborg. 2013. *Toward a Postcolonial Reading of the Epistle of James: James 2:1–13 in Its Roman Imperial Context*. BibInt 119. Leiden: Brill.

Moo, Douglas J. 2000. *The Letter of James*. PilNTC. Grand Rapids: Eerdmans.

Morgan, John. 1588. *A Short Analysis of a Part of the Second Chapter of St. James, from the 14. verse to the End of the Same with a Brief Confutation of the Rhemistes Annotations Thereupon Written*. London: Aggas.

Morgan, Teresa. 1998. *Literate Education in the Hellenistic and Roman Worlds*. CCS. Cambridge: Cambridge University Press.

Mussner, Franz. 1964. *Der Jakobusbrief*. HThKNT. Freiburg im Breisgau: Herder.

Neyrey, Jerome H., and Richard L. Rohrbaugh. 2001. "'He Must Increase, I Must Decrease' (John 3:30): A Cultural and Social Interpretation." *CBQ* 63:464–83.

Nickelsburg, George W. E., and James C. VanderKam. 2012. *1 Enoch: The Hermeneia Translation*. Minneapolis: Fortress.

Niebuhr, Karl-Wilhelm. 1998. "Der Jakobusbrief im licht Frühjüdischer Diasporabriefe." *NTS* 44:420–43.

———. 2004. "'A New Perspective on James?' Neuere Forschungen zum Jakobusbrief." *TLZ* 129:1019–44.

Niebuhr, Karl-Wilhelm, and Robert W. Wall, eds. 2009. *The Catholic Epistles and Apostolic Tradition: A New Perspective on James to Jude*. Waco, TX: Baylor University Press.

Nienhuis, David R. 2007. *Not by Paul Alone: The Formation of the Catholic Epistles Collection and the Christian Canon*. Waco, TX: Baylor University Press.

Nienhuis, David R., and Robert W. Wall. 2013. *Reading the Epistles of James, Peter, John, and Jude as Scripture: The Shaping and Shape of a Canonical Collection*. Grand Rapids: Eerdmans.

Oakes, Peter. 2010. "Urban Structure and Patronage: Christ Followers in Corinth." Page 178–93 in *Understanding the Social World of the New Testament*. Edited by Dietmar Neufeld and Richard E. DeMaris. New York: Routledge.

Osiek, Carolyn, and Jennifer Pouya. 2010. "Constructions of Gender in the Roman Imperial World." Pages 44–56 in *Understanding the Social World of the New Testament*. Edited by Dietmar Neufeld and Richard E. DeMaris. New York: Routledge.

Ott, W. 1973. "Computer Applications in Textual Criticism." Pages 199–223 in *The Computer and Literary Studies*. Edited by A. J. Aitken, Richard W. Bailey, and N. Hamilton-Smith. Edinburgh: Edinburgh University Press.

Overman, J. Andrew. 2008. "Problems with Pluralism in Second Temple Judaism: Matthew, James, and the Didache in Their Jewish-Roman Milieu." Pages 259–70 in *Matthew, James, and Didache: Three Related Documents in Their Jewish and Christian Settings*. Edited by Huub van de Sandt and Jürgen K. Zangeberg. SymS 45. Atlanta: Scholars Press.

Painter, John. 1997. *Mark's Gospel: Worlds in Conflict*. London: Routledge.

———. 1999. "Disciples and Family in Mark 3:13–35." *NTS* 45:498–513.

———. 2001. "Who Was James? Footprints as a Means of Identification." Pages 10–65 in *The Brother of Jesus: James the Just and His Mission*. Edited by Bruce Chilton and Jacob Neusner. Louisville: Westminster John Knox.

———. 2004. *Just James: The Brother of Jesus in History and Tradition*. 2nd ed. Columbia: University of South Carolina Press.

———. 2012. "James." Pages 1–174 in John Painter and David A. deSilva, *James and Jude*. Paideia Commentaries on the New Testament. Grand Rapids: Baker Academic.

———. 2013. "James of Jerusalem." Pages 3566–67 in *The Encyclopedia of Ancient History*. Edited by Roger S. Bagnall, Kai Brodersen, Craige B. Champion, Andrew Erskine, and Sabine R. Huebner. 13 vols. London: Blackwell.

———. 2016. "What James Was, His More Famous Brother Was Also." Pages 218–37 in *Earliest Christianity within the Boundaries of Judaism: Essays in Honor of Bruce Chilton*. Edited by Alan J. Avery-Peck, Craig A. Evans, and Jacob Neusner. BRLJ 49. Leiden: Brill.

Palmer, F. H. 1957. "James i.18 and the Offering of First-Fruits." *TynBul* 3:1–2.

Pardee, Dennis. 1978. "An Overview of Ancient Hebrew Epistolography." *JBL* 97:321–46.

Parker, David C. 2008. *An Introduction to the New Testament Manuscripts and Their Texts*. Cambridge: Cambridge University Press.

Pattison, Bonnie L. 2006. *Poverty in the Theology of John Calvin*. Eugene, OR: Wipf & Stock.

Pearson, Brook W. R., and Stanley E. Porter. 2002. "The Genres of the New Testament." Pages 131–65 in *Handbook to Exegesis of the New Testament*. Edited by Stanley E. Porter. Leiden: Brill.

Penner, Todd C. 1996. *The Epistle of James and Eschatology: Re-reading an Ancient Christian Letter*. JSNTSup 121. Sheffield: Sheffield Academic.

———. 2009. "The Epistle of James in Current Research." *CurBS* 7:257–308.

Perdue, Leo G. 1981. "Paraenesis and the Epistle of James." *ZNW* 72:241–56.

———. 1990. "The Social Character of Paraenesis and Paraenetic Literature." *Semeia* 50:5–39.

Philo. 1929–1953. Translated by F. H. Colson et al. 12 vols. LCL. Cambridge: Harvard University Press.

Plato. 2013. *Republic*. Translated by Christopher Emlyn-Jones and William Preddy. 2 vols. LCL. Cambridge: Harvard University Press.

Polanyi, Karl. 1944. *The Great Transformation*. New York: Rinehart.

———. 1957. "Aristotle Discovers the Economy." Pages 64–94 in *Trade and Market in the Early Empires: Economies in History and Theory*. Edited by Karl Polanyi, Conrad M. Arensberg, and Harry W. Pearson. New York: Free Press.

Popkes, Wiard. 1986. *Adressaten, Situation und Form des Jakobusbriefes.* SBS 125–126. Stuttgart: Katholisches Bibelwerk.

———. 1995. "James and Paraenesis, Reconsidered." Pages 535–61 in *Texts and Contexts: Biblical Texts in Their Textual and Situational Contexts; Essays in Honor of Lars Hartman.* Edited by Tord Fornberg and David Hellholm. Oslo: Scandinavian University Press.

———. 2001. *Der Brief des Jakobus.* THKNT. Leipzig: Evangelische Verlaganstalt.

———. 2004. "Paraenesis in the New Testament: An Exercise in Conceptuality." Pages 13–46 in *Early Christian Paraenesis in Context.* Edited by James Starr and Troels Engberg-Pedersen. BZNW 125. Berlin: de Gruyter.

Porter, Stanley E. 1990. "Is *dipsuchos* (James 1, 8; 4, 8) a 'Christian' Word?" *Bib* 71:469–98.

———. 2004. "When and How Was the Pauline Canon Compiled? An Assessment of Theories." Pages 95–127 in *The Pauline Canon.* Edited by Stanley E. Porter. Pauline Studies 1. Leiden: Brill.

———. 2013. *How We Got the New Testament: Text, Transmission, Translation.* Acadia Studies in Bible and Theology. Grand Rapids: Baker Academic.

Quinn, Jerome D. 1990. "Paraenesis and the Pastoral Epistles: Lexical Observations Bearing on the Nature of the Sub-genre and Soundings on Its Role in Socialization and Liturgies." *Semeia* 50:189–210.

Quintilian. 1921–1922. *The Institutio oratoria.* Translated by H. E. Butler. LCL. London: Heinemann.

Rabe, Hugo, ed. 1913. *Hermogenis Opera.* Rhetores Graeci 6. Leipzig: Teubner.

Rendall, Gerald H. 1927. *The Epistle of St James and Judaic Christianity.* Cambridge: Cambridge University Press.

Rey, Jean-Sébastien. 2009. *4QInstruction: Sagesse et eschatologie.* STDJ 81. Leiden: Brill.

Rhemes New Testament, The. 1582. Rhemes: Fogny.

Richardson, Kurt A. 1997. *James.* NAC. Nashville: Broadman & Holman.

Richlin, Amy. 1988. "Systems of Food Imagery in Catullus." *CW* 81:355–63.

Riesner, Rainer. 2001. "James." Pages 1255–63 in *The Oxford Bible Commentary.* Edited by John Barton and John Muddiman. Oxford: Oxford University Press.

Ripley, Jason J. 2010. "Aqedah." *EDEJ*, 355–57.

Rittgers, Ronald K., ed. 2017. *Hebrews, James*. Reformation Commentary on Scripture, New Testament 13. Downers Grove, IL: InterVarsity Press.

Rohrbaugh, Richard L. 2007. *The New Testament in Cross-Cultural Perspective*. Matrix: The Bible in Mediterranean Perspective. Eugene, OR: Cascade.

———. 2010. "Honor: Core Value in the Mediterranean World." Pages 109–25 in *Understanding the Social World of the New Testament*. Edited by Dietmar Neufeld and Richard E. DeMaris. New York: Routledge.

Ropes, James Hardy. 1916. *A Critical and Exegetical Commentary on the Epistle of St. James*. ICC 13. Edinburgh: T&T Clark.

Rosen-Zvi, Ishay. 2008. "Two Rabbinic Inclinations? Rethinking a Scholarly Dogma." *JSJ* 39:1–27.

———. 2011. *Demonic Desires: "Yetzer Hara" and the Problem of Evil in Late Antiquity*. Divinations. Philadelphia: University of Pennsylvania Press.

Rothschild, Clare. 2017. *New Essays on the Apostolic Fathers*. WUNT 375. Tübingen: Mohr Siebeck.

Rousseau, Adelin. 1965. *Irénée de Lyon: Contre les hérésies livre IV; Édition critique d'après les versions arménienne et latine*. SC 100. 2 vols. Paris: Cerf.

Rummel, Erika. 1986. *Erasmus' Annotations on the New Testament: From Philologist to Theologian*. Erasmus Studies 8. Toronto: University of Toronto Press.

———. 1995. *The Humanist-Scholastic Debate in the Renaissance and Reformation*. Harvard Historical Studies 120. Cambridge: Harvard University Press.

Saller, Richard P. 2002. *Personal Patronage under the Roman Empire*. Cambridge: Cambridge University Press.

Schoedel, William Richard. 1963. "The Appeal to Nature in Graeco-Roman and Early Christian Thought." PhD diss., University of Chicago.

Schrage, Wolfgang. 1973. "Der Jakobusbrief." Pages 1–59 in *Die "Katholischen" Briefe: Die Briefe des Jakobus, Petrus, Johannes und Judas*. NTD 10. Göttingen: Vandenhoeck & Ruprecht.

Schroeder Henry J., trans. 1941. *Canons and Decrees of the Council of Trent: Original Text with English Translation*. Saint Louis: Herder.

Schröter, Jens. 2008. "Jesus Tradition in Matthew, James, and the Didache: Searching for Characteristic Emphases." Pages 233–55 in *Matthew,*

James, and the Didache: Three Related Documents in Their Jewish and Christian Settings. Edited by Huub van de Sandt and Jürgen K. Zangenberg. SymS 45. Atlanta: Society of Biblical Literature.

Scott, James C. 1976. *The Moral Economy of the Peasant: Rebellion and Subsistence in Southern Asia.* New Haven: Yale University Press.

Sevenster, J. N. 1968. *Do You Know Greek? How Much Greek Could the First Jewish Christians Have Known?* NovTSup 19. Leiden: Brill.

Shepherd, Massey H. 1956. "The Epistle of James and the Gospel of Matthew." *JBL* 75:40–51.

Simons, Menno. 1984. "True Christian Faith." Pages 321–406 in *The Complete Writings of Menno Simons c. 1496–1561.* Edited by J. C. Wenger. Translated by Leonard Verduin. With a biography by Harold S. Bender. Scottsdale, PA: Herald Press.

Skehan, Patrick W., and Alexander A. Di Lella. 1987. *The Wisdom of Ben Sira: A New Translation with Notes.* AB 39. New York: Doubleday.

Smith, H. Maynard. 1914. *The Epistle of St. James: Lectures.* Oxford: Blackwell.

Spitta, Friedrich. 1896. *Der Brief des Jakobus.* Göttingen: Vandenhoeck & Ruprecht.

Starr, James. 2004. "Was Paraenesis for Beginners?" Pages 73–112 in *Early Christian Paraenesis in Context.* Edited by James Starr and Troels Engberg-Pedersen. BZNW 125. Berlin: de Gruyter.

Stevenson, T. R. 1996. "Social and Psychological Interpretations of Graeco-Roman Religion: Some Thoughts on the Ideal Benefactor." *Antichthon* 30:1–18.

Stewart, Alistair C. 2014. *The Original Bishops: Office and Order in the First Christian Communities.* Grand Rapids: Baker Academic.

Stokes, Ryan E. 2009. "The Devil Made David Do It … or *Did* He? The Nature, Identity, and Literary Origins of the *Satan* in 1 Chronicles 21." *JBL* 128:91–106.

———. 2014. "Satan, YHWH'S Executioner." *JBL* 133:251–70.

———. 2016. "What Is a Demon, What Is an Evil Spirit, and What Is a Satan?" Pages 259–72 in *Das Böse, der Teufel und Dämonen/Evil, the Devil, and Demons: Dualistic Characteristics in the Religion of Israel, Ancient Judaism, and Christianity.* Edited by Jan Dochhorn, Susanne Rudnig-Zelt, and Benjamin Wold. WUNT 2/412. Tübingen: Mohr Siebeck.

———. 2017. "Airing the High Priest's Dirty Laundry: Understanding the Imagery and Message of Zech 3:1–7." Pages 1247–64 in *Sibyls, Scrip-*

tures, and Scrolls: John Collins at Seventy. Edited by Joel Baden, Hindy Najman, and Eibert Tigchelaar. 2 vols. JSJSup 175. Leiden: Brill.

———. 2019. *The Satan: How God's Executioner Became the Enemy.* Grand Rapids: Eerdmans.

Stowers, Stanley K. 1981. *The Diatribe and Paul's Letter to the Romans.* SBLDS 57. Chico, CA: Scholars Press.

———. 1986. *Letter Writing in Greco-Roman Antiquity.* LEC 5. Philadelphia: Westminster.

———. 1988. "The Diatribe," Pages 71–83 in *Greco-Roman Literature and the New Testament: Selected Forms and Genres.* Edited by David E. Aune. SBLSBS 21. Atlanta: Scholars Press.

Strugnell, John, and Daniel J. Harrington, eds. 1999. *Qumran Cave 4 XXIV: Sapiential Texts, Part 2; 4QInstruction (Mûsār lĕ Mēvîn): 4Q415ff. with a Re-edition of 1Q26.* DJD 34. Oxford: Clarendon.

Tamayo, Juan José. 2017. "Las religiones monoteístas y el mediterraneo: Del mar intercultural a interreligioso a fosa común." Paper presented at the XXIX Congreso de cristianos de base de Asturias. Asturias, Spain, 20 May.

Tamez, Elsa. 1990. *The Scandalous Message of James: Faith without Works Is Dead.* New York: Crossroad.

———. 2007. *Struggles for Power in Early Christianity: A Study of the First Letter to Timothy.* Maryknoll, NY: Orbis Books.

———. 2008. *No discriminen a los pobres: Lectura latinoamericana de la Carta de Santiago.* Estella: Verbo Divino.

Taylor, Mark E. 2004. "Recent Scholarship on the Structure of James." *CurBR* 3:86–115.

Taylor, Mark E., and George H. Guthrie. 2006. "The Structure of James." *CBQ* 68:681–705.

Thompson, Mark D. 2004. *A Sure Ground on Which to Stand: The Relation of Authority and Interpretive Method in Luther's Approach to Scripture.* SCHT. Carlisle: Paternoster.

Thurén, Lauri. 1995. "Risky Rhetoric in James?" *NovT* 37:262–84.

Tischendorf, Constantin von, ed. 1869–1872. *Novum Testamentum Graece … Editio octava critica maior.* Leipzig: Giesecke & Devrient.

Tsuji, Manabu. 1997. *Glaube zwischen Vollkommenheit und Verweltlichung: Eine Untersuchung zur literarischen Gestalt und zur inhaltlichen Kohärenz des Jakobusbriefes.* WUNT 2/93. Tübingen: Mohr Siebeck.

Tuckett, Christopher. 2016. "James and Q." Pages 233–50 in *Scribal Practices and Social Structures among Jesus Adherents: Essays in Honour of*

John S. Kloppenborg. Edited by William Arnal, Richard S. Ascough, Robert A. Derrenbacker, and Philip A. Harland. BETL 285. Leuven: Peeters.

Turner, Victor. 1969. *The Ritual Process: Structure and Anti-Structure.* Lewis Henry Morgan Lectures, 1966. Ithaca, NY: Cornell University Press.

Twelftree, Graham H. 2007. *In the Name of Jesus: Exorcism among Early Christians.* Grand Rapids: Baker Academic.

Van der Westhuizen, J. D. N. 1991. "Stylistic Techniques and Their Functions in James 2:14–26." *Neot* 25:89–107.

Varner, William. 2010. *The Book of James: A New Perspective; A Linguistic Commentary Applying Discourse Analysis.* Woodlands, TX: Kress Biblical Resources.

Verseput, Donald J. 1997. "James 1:17 and the Jewish Morning Prayers." *NovT* 39:177–91.

———. 2000. "Genre and Story: The Community Setting of the Epistle of James." *CBQ* 62:96–110.

Vhymeister, Nancy J. 1995. "The Rich Man in James 2: Does Ancient Patronage Illuminate the Text?" *AUSS* 33:265–83.

Vlachos, Chris A. 2013. *James.* Exegetical Guide to the Greek New Testament. Nashville: B&H Academic.

Vouga, François. 1984. *L' Epître de Saint Jacques.* Commentaire du Nouveau Testament 13a. Geneva: Labor et Fides.

Wachob, Wesley Hiram. 2000. *The Voice of Jesus in the Social Rhetoric of James.* SNTSMS 106. Cambridge: Cambridge University Press.

Wachtel, Klaus. 2015. "The Coherence Method and History." *TC* 20:https://tinyurl.com/sbl0397a1.

Wall, Robert W. 1997. *Community of the Wise: The Letter of James.* New Testament in Context. Valley Forge, PA: Trinity Press International.

Ward, Roy Bowen. 1968. "The Works of Abraham: James 2:14–26." *HTR* 61:283–90.

———. 1969. "Partiality in the Assembly: James 2:2–4." *HTR* 62:87–97.

Wasserman, Tommy. 2006. *The Epistle of Jude: Its Text and Transmission.* ConBNT 43. Stockholm: Almqvist & Wiksell.

———. 2013. "Criteria for Evaluating Readings in New Testament Textual Criticism." Pages 579–612 in *The Text of the New Testament in Contemporary Research: Essays on the Status Quaestionis.* Edited by Bart D. Ehrman and Michael W. Holmes. 2nd ed. NTTSD 42. Leiden: Brill.

———. 2015a. "The Coherence Based Genealogical Method as a Tool for Explaining Textual Changes in the Greek New Testament." *NovT* 57:206–18.

———. 2015b. "Historical and Philological Correlations and the CBGM as Applied to Mark 1:1." *TC* 2020:https://tinyurl.com/sbl0397a2.

Wasserman, Tommy, and Peter J. Gurry. 2017. *A New Approach to Textual Criticism: An Introduction to the Coherence-Based Genealogical Method*. RBS 80. Atlanta: SBL Press.

Watson, Duane F. 1993a. "James 2 in Light of Greco-Roman Schemes of Argumentation." *NTS* 39:94–121.

———. 1993b. "The Rhetoric of James 3:1–12 and a Classical Pattern of Argumentation." *NovT* 35:48–64.

———. 1997. "Rhetorical Criticism of Hebrews and the Catholic Epistles Since 1978." *CurBS* 5:175–207.

———. 2007. "An Assessment of the Rhetoric and Rhetorical Analysis of the Letter of James." Pages 99–120 in *Reading James with New Eyes: Methodological Reassessments of the Letter of James*. Edited by Robert L. Webb and John S. Kloppenborg. LNTS 342. London: T&T Clark.

Watson, Francis. 1994. *Text, Church and World: Biblical Interpretation in Theological Perspective*. Edinburgh: T&T Clark.

Weaver, Joel. 2011. "The Heart of the Law: Love Your Neighbor (Jas 2:8–13)." *RevExp* 108:445–51.

Weima, Jeffrey A. D. 2010. "Sincerely, Paul: The Significance of the Pauline Letter Closings." Pages 307–45 in *Paul and the Ancient Letter Form*. Edited by Stanley E. Porter and Sean A. Adams. Pauline Studies 6. Leiden: Brill.

Weinfeld, Moshe. 1995. *Social Justice in Ancient Israel and in the Ancient New East*. Minneapolis: Fortress.

Wessel, W. W. 1953. "An Inquiry into the Origin, Literary Character, Historical and Religious Significance of the Epistle of James." PhD diss., University of Edinburgh.

Westcott, B. F., and F. J. A. Hort, eds. 1881–1882. *The New Testament in the Original Greek*. 2 vols. London: Macmillan.

Wheeler, Sondra Ely. 1995. *Wealth as Peril and Obligations: The New Testament on Possessions*. Grand Rapids: Eerdmans.

White, John L. 1984. "New Testament Epistolary Literature in the Framework of Ancient Epistolography." *ANRW* 25.2:1730–56.

———. 1986. *Light from Ancient Letters*. FF. Philadelphia: Fortress.

———. 1988. "Ancient Greek Letters." Pages 85–105 in *Greco-Roman Literature and the New Testament: Selected Forms and Genres*. Edited by David E. Aune. SBLSBS 21. Atlanta: Scholars Press.

Whitlark, Jason. 2010. "*Emphytos Logos*: A New Covenant Motif in the Letter of James." *HBT* 32:144–65.

Wilson, Walter T. 1991. *Love without Pretense: Romans 12.9–21 and Hellenistic-Jewish Wisdom Literature*. WUNT 2/46. Tübingen: Mohr Siebeck, 1991.

———. 2002. "Sin as Sex and Sex with Sin: The Anthropology of James 1:12–15." *HTR* 95:147–68.

Windisch, Hans. 1951. *Die katholischen Briefe*. 3rd ed. HNT. Tübingen: Mohr.

Wischmeyer, Oda. 2016. "Zwischen Gut und Böse: Teufel, Dämonen, das Böse und der Kosmos im Jakobusbrief." Pages 153–68 in *Das Böse, der Teufel und Dämonen/Evil, the Devil, and Demons: Dualistic Characteristics in the Religion of Israel, Ancient Judaism, and Christianity*. Edited by Jan Dochhorn, Susanne Rudnig-Zelt, and Benjamin Wold. WUNT 2/412. Tübingen: Mohr Siebeck.

———. 2017. "Luther's Prefaces to the New Testament in Their Hermeneutical and Philological Dimension, Read from an Exegetical Perspective." Paper presented at the Annual Meeting of the Society of Biblical Literature. Boston, MA, 18 November.

Witherington, Ben, III. 2007. *Letters and Homilies for Jewish Christians: A Socio-rhetorical Commentary on Hebrews, James and Jude*. Downers Grove, IL: InterVarsity Press.

Wold, Benjamin. 2018. *4QInstruction: Division and Hierarchies*. STDJ 123. Leiden: Brill.

———. 2019. "Sin and Evil in the Letter of James in Light of Qumran Discoveries." *NTS* 65:78–93.

Wright, N. T. 1992. *The New Testament and the People of God*. Christians Origins and the Question of God 1. Minneapolis: Fortress.

Wuellner, Wilhelm. 1978. "Der Jakobusbrief im Licht der Rhetorik und Textpragmatik." *LB* 43:5–66.

Contributors

Alicia J. Batten is Professor of Religious Studies and Theological Studies at Conrad Grebel University College at the University of Waterloo, in Ontario, Canada. Among her publications are *Friendship and Benefaction in James* (ESEC 15; Deo, 2010; SBL Press, 2017), a commentary on Philemon in the Wisdom Commentary Series (Liturgical Press, 2017), and articles and essays on a variety of topics related to the New Testament, early Christian literature, and the history of biblical interpretation. She is currently coediting a book on dress in Mediterranean antiquity (Bloomsbury T&T Clark) and writing a commentary on the Letter of James (Eerdmans).

Richard Bauckham is emeritus professor of New Testament studies at the University of St Andrews in Scotland. He now lives in Cambridge, England. He is a Fellow of the Royal Society of Edinburgh and a Fellow of the British Academy. He has published widely on the New Testament, Second Temple Judaism, and biblical theology. His books include *Jesus and the Eyewitnesses* (2nd ed., Eerdmans, 2017), *Jesus and the God of Israel* (Eerdmans, 2008), *James: Wisdom of James, Disciple of Jesus the Sage* (Routledge, 1999), and *Gospel of Glory: Major Themes in Johannine Theology* (Baker Academic, 2015).

Stephen J. Chester is the Lord and Lady Coggan Professor of New Testament at Wycliffe College, University of Toronto. His research interests include the history of reception, especially the sixteenth century, and its relevance for contemporary biblical interpretation. He is the author of *Reading Paul with the Reformers: Reconciling Old and New Perspectives* (Eerdmans, 2017).

Luke L. Cheung (Ph.D., University of St Andrews) is Wilson Chow Professor of Biblical Studies at the China Graduate School of Theology, Hong Kong, and an ordained pastor of the Cumberland Presbyterian Church.

He has published numerous books and articles on New Testament studies, usually in Chinese, and is author (Epistle of James, 2008; Epistles of Jude and 2 Peter, 2015; Epistle of Titus, 2019) or coauthor (Epistle of 1 Peter, 1997; Gospel of Mark, 2003; Epistle of James, 2019 [English]) of several Bible commentaries.

Peter H. Davids started writing on James in his 1974 University of Manchester dissertation ("Themes in the Epistle of James That Are Judaistic in Character"), which became the basis for his first commentary (*The Epistle of James*, NIGTC; Eerdmans, 1982). His interest in James has continued through numerous articles, edited works, a second commentary, and most recently *A Biblical Theology of James, 1 and 2 Peter, and Jude* (Zondervan, 2014). He has taught in seminaries and graduate institutions in the United States, Canada, the United Kingdom, the Netherlands, Germany, Austria, and Switzerland. A Roman Catholic priest, he is presently Chaplain to Our Lady of Guadalupe Priory in Georgetown, Texas.

Peter J. Gurry (Ph.D., University of Cambridge) is assistant professor of New Testament at Phoenix Seminary, where he also serves as codirector of the Text & Canon Institute. He is the author of *A Critical Examination of the Coherence-Based Genealogical Method in New Testament Textual Criticism* (Brill, 2017), the coauthor (with Tommy Wasserman) of *A New Approach to Textual Criticism: An Introduction to the Coherence-Based Genealogical Method* (SBL Press, 2017), and the coeditor (with Elijah Hixson) of *Myths and Mistakes in New Testament Textual Criticism* (IVP Academic, 2019).

Matt Jackson-McCabe (Ph.D., University of Chicago) is professor in the Department of Philosophy and Comparative Religion at Cleveland State University. His publications on James include *Logos and Law in the Letter of James* (Brill, 2001; Society of Biblical Literature, 2010). He is also the author of *Jewish Christianity: The Making of the Christianity-Judaism Divide* (Yale University Press, forthcoming in 2020) and editor of *Jewish Christianity Reconsidered* (Fortress, 2007).

Kevin Johnson studied philosophy at Wheaton College and a Master of Divinity at Trinity Evangelical Divinity School. After seminary he served as a missionary in Mexico City for a year and then lived three years in Medellín, Colombia, as a professor at the Biblical Seminary of Colombia. He currently resides in Guatemala, where he continues online teaching with the Biblical Seminary of Colombia and works with Centro Esdras, a Guatemalan ministry focused on holistic mission training. He is married, has one daughter, and serves as a missionary with United World Mission.

Mariam Kamell Kovalishyn (Ph.D., University of St Andrews) is assistant professor of New Testament and biblical studies at Regent College in Vancouver, Canada. Her research interest has consistently returned to the Epistle of James, and her dissertation was specifically on the question of soteriology in James. She is coauthor (with Craig Blomberg) of the volume on James in the Zondervan Exegetical Commentary on the New Testament series (Zondervan, 2008) and has authored numerous articles across the General Epistles, early Jewish literary contexts to the New Testament, and biblical theology.

Darian R. Lockett (Ph.D., University of St Andrews) is associate professor of New Testament at Talbot School of Theology, Biola University. He is author of *Purity and Worldview in the Epistle of James* (T&T Clark, 2008), *An Introduction to the Catholic Epistles* (T&T Clark, 2012), *Understanding Biblical Theology* (Zondervan, 2012), *Letters from the Pillar Apostles: The Formation of the Catholic Epistles as a Canonical Collection* (Pickwick, 2017), and *Reading the Catholic Epistles: An Introduction to a Canonical Collection* (InterVarsity Press, forthcoming). He regularly teaches in the areas of biblical theology, Greek exegesis, and the Catholic Epistles.

Eric F. Mason (Ph.D., University of Notre Dame) is Julius R. Mantey Chair of Biblical Studies at Judson University, Elgin, Illinois. He is the author or editor of numerous books and articles exploring the Epistle to the Hebrews, the Catholic Epistles, and various aspects of Second Temple Judaism, including *'You Are a Priest Forever': Second Temple Jewish Messianism and the Priestly Christology of the Epistle to the Hebrews* (Brill, 2008; SBL Press, 2014) and volumes on Hebrews (edited with Kevin B. McCruden, 2011) and 1–2 Peter and Jude (edited with Troy W. Martin, 2014) in the Resources for Biblical Study series (SBL Press).

Scot McKnight is the Julius R. Mantey Professor of New Testament at Northern Seminary in Lisle, Illinois. He is the author of more than seventy-five books, including *The Letter of James* (NICNT; Eerdmans, 2011), and coeditor (with Joel B. Green and I. Howard Marshall) of the first edition of *Dictionary of Jesus and the Gospels* (InterVarsity Press, 1992) and (with

Joseph Modica) of *Preaching Romans: Four Perspectives* (Eerdmans, 2019). He has been a professor in seminaries and colleges for thirty-eight years.

John Painter (BD, ThSchol, PhD, FAHA) is an Australian Anglican and professor of theology at Charles Sturt University in Canberra, Australia. He is the author of *John: Witness and Theologian* (3rd ed., Beacon Hill, 1986); *Theology as Hermeneutics* (2nd ed., Bloomsbury, 2015); *The Quest for the Messiah* (2nd ed., T&T Clark and Abingdon, 1993); *Mark's Gospel* (Routledge, 1997); *Just James: The Brother of Jesus in History and Tradition* (2nd ed., University of South Carolina Press, 2004); *1, 2, and 3 John* (Liturgical Press, 2002); the commentary on James in the Paideia series (Baker Academic, 2012); and more than one hundred academic articles and chapters.

Ryan E. Stokes (Ph.D., Yale University) is associate professor of religion and director of the Master of Arts in Applied Theology at Carson-Newman University, Jefferson City, Tennessee. He has written extensively on beliefs about demons, evil spirits, and Satan in the Bible and the literature of early Judaism. He is the author of *The Satan: How God's Executioner Became the Enemy* (Eerdmans, 2019).

Elsa Tamez is Mexico-Costa Rican. She is an emeritus professor of the Latin American Biblical University (Costa Rica) and translation consultant for the United Bible Societies. She received her Ph.D. in Theology at the University of Lausanne, Switzerland. She has written several books and countless articles translated into different languages. Among her best-known books in English are *Bible of the Oppressed* (Orbis Books, 1982), *The Scandalous Message of James* (Crossroad, 1990), *The Amnesty of Grace: Justification by Faith from a Latin American Perspective* (Abingdon, 1993), *Struggles for Power in Early Christianity: A Study of the First Letter to Timothy* (Orbis Books, 2007), and *Philippians* (Liturgical Press, 2017).

Tommy Wasserman is professor of biblical studies at Ansgar Teologiske Høgskole, Kristiansand, Norway. He is secretary of the International Greek New Testament Project, has served on the editorial board of *New Testament Studies*, and is currently senior editor of *TC: A Journal of Biblical Textual Criticism*. Wasserman has authored several books, including *The Epistle of Jude: Its Text and Transmission* (Almqvist & Wiksell, 2006), *A New Approach to Textual Criticism: An Introduction to the Coherence-*

Based Genealogical Method (with Peter Gurry; SBL Press, 2017), and *To Cast the First Stone: The Transmission of a Gospel Story* (with Jennifer Knust; Princeton University Press, 2019).

Duane F. Watson (Ph.D., Duke University) is professor of New Testament and Greek at Malone University in Canton, Ohio. He is best known for his work in rhetorical criticism of the New Testament using Greco-Roman rhetoric and has written numerous works on the rhetoric of 1 and 2 Corinthians, Philippians, and the General Epistles. He is coauthor (with Terrance Callan) of *First and Second Peter* (Paideia; Baker Academic, 2012), editor (with C. Clifton Black) of *Words Well Spoken: George Kennedy's Rhetoric of the New Testament* (Baylor University Press, 2008), and author of *Invention, Arrangement, and Style: Rhetorical Criticism of Jude and 2 Peter* (Scholars Press, 1988).

Benjamin Wold is associate professor of New Testament and Ancient Judaism at Trinity College Dublin, the University of Dublin. His research interests include sapiential literature of the Second Temple period, the Jewish context of Christian origins, and especially the Dead Sea Scrolls. His most recent book, *4QInstruction: Divisions and Hierarchies* (Brill, 2018), offers a reassessment of the most significant "wisdom" text discovered at Qumran. He is currently completing a new monograph on 4QInstruction and the Letter of James to be published in 2020.

Kelvin C. L. Yu is assistant professor of biblical studies at the China Graduate School of Theology in Hong Kong. He received a joint Ph.D. degree from the University of Edinburgh and the China Graduate School of Theology in 2017. His doctoral dissertation was published as *Bonds and Boundaries among the Early Churches: Community Maintenance in the Letter of James and the Didache* (Brepols, 2019). His research interest is in New Testament studies and the Second Temple period.

Ancient Sources Index

Modern Authors Index

CPSIA information can be obtained
at www.ICGtesting.com
Printed in the USA
FSHW020548011119
63617FS